Luminos is the Open Access monograph publishing program from UC Press. Luminos provides a framework for preserving and reinvigorating monograph publishing for the future and increases the reach and visibility of important scholarly work. Titles published in the UC Press Luminos model are published with the same high standards for selection, peer review, production, and marketing as those in our traditional program. www.luminosoa.org

Revolutionary Bodies

Revolutionary Bodies

Chinese Dance and the Socialist Legacy

Emily Wilcox

UNIVERSITY OF CALIFORNIA PRESS

University of California Press, one of the most distinguished university presses in the United States, enriches lives around the world by advancing scholarship in the humanities, social sciences, and natural sciences. Its activities are supported by the UC Press Foundation and by philanthropic contributions from individuals and institutions. For more information, visit www.ucpress.edu.

University of California Press
Oakland, California

Suggested citation: Wilcox, E. *Revolutionary Bodies: Chinese Dance and the Socialist Legacy*. Oakland: University of California Press, 2018. DOI: https://doi.org/10.1525/luminos.58

Library of Congress Cataloging-in-Publication Data

Names: Wilcox, Emily, 1981- author.
Title: Revolutionary bodies : Chinese dance and the socialist legacy / Emily Wilcox.
Description: Oakland, California : University of California Press, [2019] | Includes bibliographical references and index. | Wilcox, emily 2019 This work is licensed under a Creative Commons CC-BY-NC-ND license. To view a copy of the license, visit http://creativecommons.org/licenses |
Identifiers: LCCN 2018023689 (print) | LCCN 2018031703 (ebook) | ISBN 9780520971905 (ebook) | ISBN 9780520300576 (pbk. : alk. paper)
Subjects: LCSH: Dance—China—History. | Socialism and dance—China—History. | Choreography—China—History.
Classification: LCC GV1691 (ebook) | LCC GV1691 .W55 2019 (print) | DDC 792.8/0951—dc23
LC record available at https://lccn.loc.gov/2018023689

28   27   26   25   24   23   22   21   20   19
10   9   8   7   6   5   4   3   2   1

For my dance teachers

CONTENTS

LIST OF ILLUSTRATIONS AND AUDIOVISUAL MEDIA

MAP

FIGURES

VIDEO CLIPS

ACKNOWLEDGMENTS

This book has been a long time in the making and would not have been possible without the help of many generous people and institutions.

I first visited China in 2002 as an undergraduate student dancer on a tour with the Harvard University Ballroom Dance Team. I am thankful to James Wang, who organized the tour, and to the U.S.-China Media and Publishing Association, its sponsor, as it was this two-week trip that opened my eyes to the world of dance in China. At Harvard I benefited from the mentorship of several professors, notably anthropologists Arthur Kleinman and Michael Herzfeld and performance scholar Deborah Foster, who guided my initial forays into dance ethnography. In 2003–4 a John Eliot Scholarship from the Harvard-Cambridge Foundation supported my year of study at the University of Cambridge, where historians of science Andrew Cunningham and Simon Schaffer advised me in historical methods. In 2005–8 I benefited from intensive language training at Princeton in Beijing and the Inter-University Program for Chinese Language Study at Tsinghua University. This was made possible by generous grants from the UC Berkeley Center for Chinese Stud-ies, the UC Berkeley Anthropology Department, the US Department of Education Foreign Language and Area Studies Program, and the Blakemore and Freeman Foundations. While living in Beijing, I also had the chance to begin training in Chinese dance, thanks to community outreach programming at the BeijingDance/LDTX Dance Center. My teachers there, Wang Zhuorao and Chen Jie, inspired me to embark on this journey.

In 2008–9 I had the amazing opportunity to spend three semesters as a visit-ing graduate student at the Beijing Dance Academy (BDA), China's premier pro-fessional dance conservatory. This experience provided the basis for my doctoral dissertation and was generously supported by scholarships from the Fulbright Institute of International Education and the University of California Pacific Rim Research Program. I am eternally grateful to the administrators and staff at BDA, who supported my application and granted me this rare chance to study alongside China's most elite dance students. No words can express the deep gratitude I have to my professors at BDA, whose classes in many ways planted the seeds for this book. They include my water sleeve professor, Shao Weiqiu; my sword dance professor, Zhang Jun; my bare-handed *shenyun* professor, Su Ya; my Dunhuang dance professor, He Yanyun; my Uyghur and Han folk dance professor and Chinese national folk dance pedagogy professor, Jia Meina; my Chinese classical dance pedagogy professor, Xiong Jiatai; my Han-Tang Chinese classical dance history and theory professor, Du Le; my Chinese dance basic training professor, Yang Ou; my dance pedagogy theory professor, Lü Yisheng; my *xiqu* theory and history professor, Li Jieming; and my dance criticism professor, Xu Rui. Others who provided me invaluable training in Chinese dance during and after this period include Chen Jie, who taught me Han-Tang Chinese classical dance; Surongna and Wu Dan, who taught me Mongol dance; Liang Yujian, who taught me sword dance; Li Mei, who taught me Korean dance; Wang Jie, who taught me Dai and Tibetan dance; and Jin Ni, who taught me Shangdong Jiaozhou *yangge* and Korean dance.

While I was studying at BDA, I conducted short-term field research in a variety of institutions in Beijing and other places across China, including Chongqing, Fujian, Guangdong, Inner Mongolia, Liaoning, Shaanxi, Shandong, and Sichuan. The aid of countless individuals made these projects possible. A few who went above and beyond, even hosting me in their own homes, were Mandy Xia, Zheng Qu, and Zhao Yuewei. In the course of this research, over one hundred and fifty professional dancers of various ages and backgrounds graciously shared their life stories with me through formal interviews. The stories they shared inspired my interest in Chinese dance history, igniting many of the questions that fueled the research for this book.

The result of my initial field research was a doctoral dissertation submitted in 2011 to the Anthropology Department at the University of California, Berkeley, for a degree in the UC Berkeley/UCSF Joint PhD Program in Medical Anthropology, supported by the faculty research group in Critical Studies in Medicine, Science, and the Body. Although the dissertation bears little resemblance to this book, it was formative in making the research for this book possible. Thus, I am tremendously grateful to my dissertation chair, anthropologist Liu Xin, as well as to my dissertation committee members: anthropologists Vincanne Adams and Alexei Yurchak, performance scholar Shannon Jackson, and historian Michael Nylan. Their impact on my intellectual development was formative, and they continue to be my greatest role models as a scholar and teacher. Other Berkeley faculty whose courses shaped my project in important ways are Judith Butler, Andrew Jones, Aihwa Ong, and Shannon Steen. I continue to treasure the friendships formed through several intellectual communities at UC Berkeley, including the Anthropology Department; the Center for Chinese Studies; the Department of Theater, Dance, and Performance Studies; and the Dance Studies Working Group.

Several caring mentors helped me sort out my multiple intellectual identities and find homes for my work during the early years of my professional career: Xiaomei Chen in the Department of East Asian Languages and Cultures at UC Davis; William Sun in the Schechner Center for Performance Studies at the Shanghai Theater Academy; Yanfang Tang in the Department of Modern Languages and Literatures at the College of William and Mary; Susan Manning, Janice Ross, and Rebecca Schneider, who led the Mellon Dance Studies project; and Kathy Foley, longtime editor of *Asian Theatre Journal*. In the harrowing environment of the postrecession academic job market, early career mentorship and advocacy have become more critical than ever before. These scholars not only offered personal guidance and championed my work but also created vital professional opportunities, in the form of adjunct and visiting positions, postdoctoral fellowships, and publishing platforms. For this largely invisible but indispensable labor, I am extremely thankful.

Between 2011 and 2017, I was fortunate to receive fellowships and grants that allowed me to totally reconceive my project and conduct the new research that resulted in this book. Between 2011 and 2013, while I was a visiting assistant professor at the College of William and Mary, the Shanghai Theater Academy provided me a nonresidential postdoctoral research fellowship that allowed me to conduct archival and ethnographic research in Beijing, Lanzhou, Shanghai, and Hohhot during summer and winter holidays. After I joined the University of Michigan in 2013, the UM Lieberthal-Rogel Center for Chinese Studies became the most important funder of my annual trips to China, during which I revisited previous research sites and developed new projects in Jilin, Xinjiang, and Yunnan. In addition to annual travel grants, the center also generously funded library collection development, grants to support Chinese dance artists in residence, image permission fees, purchasing of rare books and other research supplies, and a major exhibition and conference. Other centers and units at UM that provided financial and administrative support include the University of Michigan Library, the Asia Library, the Institute for Research on Women and Gender, the Rackham Graduate School, the Confucius Institute, the Office of the Senior Vice Provost, the Center for World Performance Studies, the Department of Asian Languages and Cultures, the Dance Department, the Institute for the Humanities, the Undergraduate Research Opportunity Program, and the International Institute. These units sponsored research travel in China, artist residencies at UM, and library collection development, as well as trips to archives in the United States, the United Kingdom, and the Netherlands. Two external fellowships were absolutely critical to the completion of this book, because they provided two much-needed years away from teaching to write and revise the manuscript: an American Council of Learned Societies Fellowship in 2014–15 and a Transregional Research Junior Scholar Fellowship from the Social Science Research Council in 2016–17. In addition to salary replacement funds, these fellowships also supported research travel, purchasing of research supplies, and translation assistance for materials in Uyghur. A manuscript workshop funded by the Dean's Office of the UM College of Literature, Science, and the Arts and hosted by the UM Department of Asian Languages and Cultures was hugely beneficial in allowing me to get feedback on a draft of the book before it went out for external review. The subvention for this book was covered jointly by the Lieberthal-Rogel Center for Chinese Studies Publication Subvention Award and the University of Michigan Open Access Monograph Publication Initiative.

Many librarians, archivists, and dancers helped provide access to historical materials used in this book. For assistance with institutional libraries and archives, I am grateful to staff at the Asia Library at the University of Michigan, the Beijing Dance Academy, China Foto Bank, the China Opera and Dance Drama Theater, the C. V. Starr East Asian Library at Columbia University, the Inner Mongolia Nationalities Song and Dance Ensemble, the International Institute of Social History in Amsterdam, the Jerome Robbins Dance Division of the New York Public Library for the Performing Arts, the Library of Congress in Washington, DC, the Royal Academy of Dance in London, the Shanghai Library, and the *Xinjiang Daily*. For use of personal collections, I am grateful to Chen Ailian, Cui Yuzhu, Fang Bonian, Richard Glasstone, He Yanyun, Jin Ou, Lan Hang, Liang Lun, Lü Yisheng, Gulmira Mamat, Oumijiacan, Sheng Jie, Shu Qiao, Siqintariha, Wan-go H. C. Weng, Hsing Ching Weng Trust, Yang Liping, Ye Jin, Zhang Ke, Zhang Yunfeng, Zhao Qing, Zhao Xiaogang, and the families of Zhang Jun, Zha Lie, and Zhao Dexian. I am especially thankful for the boundless support of the UM Chinese studies librarian, Liangyu Fu. The UM Chinese Dance Collection that she initiated and brought to fruition over the past five years has greatly expanded the possibilities for research on Chinese dance history. Our collaborations on this collection and our related 2017 exhibition, *Chinese Dance: National Movements in a Revolutionary Age, 1945– 1965*, offered a rich intellectual resource for this book. One component of this UM collection, the Pioneers of Chinese Dance Digital Archive (https://quod.lib.umich.edu/d/dance1ic), offers a supplement to this book in that it contains additional photographs of many people and productions discussed here.

A great number of colleagues offered advice and feedback on drafts of this book. For comprehensive feedback on drafts of the full manuscript, I am especially thankful to Miranda Brown, Clare Croft, Nancy Florida, Rebecca Karl, Janet O'Shea, David Rolston, Xiaobing Tang, Wang Zheng, members of the winter 2018 ASIAN 546 graduate seminar, and an anonymous reviewer. For notes on individual chapter drafts and comments offered at conference panels and workshops, I am thankful to Allison Alexy, Cemil Aydin, Erin Brightwell, Rosemary Candelario, Pär Cassel, Tina Mai Chen, Tarryn Chun, Paul Clark, Laurence Coderre, Charlotte

D'Evelyn, Prasenjit Duara, Alissa Elegant, Xing Fan, Mary Gallagher, Ellen Gerdes, Levi Gibbs, Ronald Gilliam, Anita Gonzalez, Engseng Ho, Nicole Huang, Paola Iovene, Reggie Jackson, Imani Kai Johnson, S. E. Kile, Miriam Kingsberg Kadia, Rebekah Kowal, Lanlan Kuang, Petra Kuppers, Siyuan Liu, Xiaozhen Liu, Donald Lopez, Liang Luo, Christopher Lupke, Nan Ma, Jason McGrath, Katherine Mezur, Fangfei Miao, Markus Nornes, Jose Reynoso, Tara Rodman, Youngju Ryu, Aminda Smith, Sue Tuohy, Krista Van Fleit, Judy Van Zile, Ban Wang, Felix Wemheuer, Elizabeth Wichmann-Walczak, and Jongsung Yang. Christina Ezrahi and Akram Hélil provided assistance with sources in Russian and Uyghur, and students Ting Su, Raeann Romel, Yaehyun (Emily) Sohn, and Yucong Hao offered research support. Additionally, this book would not have been possible without the tremendous work and guidance of editors Reed Malcolm and Archna Patel and the entire staff of University of California Press.

Lastly, I would like to thank the communities who have provided camaraderie, care, and mentorship through the final stages of this project. These include members of the Association for Asian Performance, the Association for Asian Studies, the Association for Theater in Higher Education, CHINOPERL, the Dance Studies Association, Performance Studies international, and the Rocky Mountain Modern Language Association. They also include the entire faculty, staff, and students of the Department of Asian Languages and Cultures at the University of Michigan, particularly my extraordinary faculty mentors, David Rolston and Xiaobing Tang. Above all, I would like to thank my wonderful family—especially my mother, Debra Wilcox, and my partner, Chinua Thelwell. Their love and support make everything possible.

Locating Chinese Dance

Bodies in Place, History, and Genre

I stand with twenty other students, mostly women, in a spacious dance studio at the Beijing Dance Academy, facing a wall of mirrors. We are wearing white jackets with "water sleeves" *(shuixiu)*—long panels of silk attached to the ends of our sleeves that stretch about two feet in width and twice the length of our arms. Since we are not moving, the sleeves gather in pearly puddles on the floor. We watch as our teacher, Shao Weiqiu, explains the next movement. "When you are casting out and returning the sleeve, it's important that you allow the sleeve to move at its own speed. Once you give the initial stimulus, let the sleeve do the rest." She turns toward the mirror to demonstrate. The pianist begins to play, and Professor Shao stands with feet together and arms hanging at her sides. Using four counts, she slowly breathes out and sinks into bent knees while lowering her eyes. Then, she rises again for four more counts and gradually lifts her right elbow diagonally forward. When she reaches the highest point, she snaps her arm out straight, palm down, making sure to flick her wrist and spread her thumb and fingers wide. Her movement sends the sleeve unfurling into a flat sheet that hangs temporarily suspended in midair. As the sleeve floats down, Professor Shao follows it, lowering gradually again while keeping her arm out in line with the sleeve. With the fabric now spread on the floor in front of her, she begins the second part of the exercise. Stepping back with her right foot, she flaps the back of her right hand up and then rotates her forearm and tugs sharply back from the elbow, keeping her hand at waist level and parallel to the floor. The sleeve lifts from the ground and paints an airborne parabola in her direction. As if by magic, the sleeve returns to Professor Shao's open palm, gathering in a perfect accordion-shaped pile between her thumb and forefinger. She closes her fist around the wad of fabric and turns to us: "OK, now you try."

Water sleeve is one of several dozen distinct dance styles that make up Chinese dance, a contemporary concert genre that developed during the mid-twentieth century and is widely practiced around the world today. In the People's Republic of China (hereafter PRC or China), Chinese dance is most commonly known as *Zhongguo wudao* (Chinese dance) or *minzu wudao* (national dance). Among Sinophone communities abroad, particularly in Southeast Asia, the term *Huazu wudao* (dance of the Hua people) is also used. In all three the term *wudao*, meaning "dance," can also be shorted to *wu*. Since the 1950s, dance scholars and practitioners in China have generally recognized two subcategories of Chinese dance: Chinese classical dance *(Zhongguo gudian wu)* and Chinese national folk dance *(Zhongguo minzu minjian wu)*.[1] Initially, Chinese classical dance was derived from local theater forms known collectively as *xiqu* (pronounced "hsee-tchü"), such as Peking opera and Kunqu. Now, Chinese classical dance consists of the early xiqu-based style (which includes water sleeve), as well as the more recently developed Dunhuang and Han-Tang styles, among others. Chinese national folk dance has from the beginning combined Han styles (such as Northeast *yangge*, Shandong *yangge*, Anhui *huagudeng*, and Yunnan *huadeng*) with ethnic minority styles (such as Uyghur, Mongol, Korean, Tibetan, and Dai). As in the case of Chinese classical dance, new styles of Chinese national folk dance continuously emerge over time. A key premise of both Chinese classical dance and Chinese national folk dance is that they are modern creations developed through the combination of research and innovation. They are not, nor do their practitioners typically claim them to be, strictly preserved or reconstructed historical or folk forms.

The research that goes into creating Chinese dance encompasses a wide range of performance practices, which may be documented in historical materials or embodied by living communities. The artistic researchers who create Dunhuang-style Chinese classical dance, for example, find inspiration in depictions of dancing humans and deities found at Dunhuang, a Buddhist heritage site in today's Gansu Province that was constructed during the first millennium CE. The artistic researchers who create Han-style national folk dances, by contrast, draw inspiration from popular entertainments and rituals performed in holiday processions and temple festivals among living communities. In many cases, Chinese dance practitioners will combine multiple sources when developing a new dance style. In the case of water sleeve, for example, dancers often study the performances of living xiqu actors, as well as historical sleeve dances documented in ancient and medieval artifacts such as jade pendants, stone relief carvings, tomb statues, historical paintings, and poetry. Engagement with contemporary xiqu performance is evident in Shao Weiqiu's water sleeve dances through the sleeve construction, the techniques used to manipulate the sleeve's movement, and the emphasis on breath and eye expression, all of which are employed in xiqu performance.[2] References to historical sleeve dance are apparent in the scale and shape of Shao's movement and lines, some of which resemble these early images.[3]

Through their emphasis on innovation, Chinese dance practitioners interpret their research to create new forms. The removal of singing or speech in Shao's sleeve dance choreography represents her obvious departure from xiqu, in which song and speech are usually considered essential to a complete performance. The rhythmical mapping of Shao's classroom choreography onto eight-count piano scores and the abstraction of movement sequences independent of narrative context also mark departures from typical xiqu music and stage action. A change from early and medieval sleeve dance is further apparent in the contexts of Shao's choreography. That is, her dances tend to take place in conservatory classrooms, proscenium stages, and film studios, while earlier dances are believed to have taken place in imperial palaces or at ritual sites that facilitated communication with gods and spirits. In her teaching and publications, Shao presents original theorizations of water sleeve movement aesthetics, often drawing on her studies in adjacent fields such as Chinese poetics, ink painting, medicine, and philosophy. Because of the original interpretation involved, Shao's teaching routines and pedagogical methods are considered her own intellectual and artistic creations. Through these contributions, Shao learns from existing forms while also introducing her own ideas and practices, illustrating the basic creative process for making Chinese dance.

Although it is generally less well known among Western dance audiences than China's ballet and modern dance repertoires, Chinese dance is the most widespread concert dance form in contemporary China and also has large transnational followings. According to a report published in 2016 by the Chinese National Academy of Arts in Beijing, Chinese dance represented more than half of all staged dance performances in China in 2015, including those presented by touring international ensembles.[4] These results correspond to what I have observed in my ongoing field research across China during the past ten years, in which I have found Chinese dance to enjoy larger representation in academic teaching programs and performance ensembles, as well as greater financial resources and audiences than other concert dance forms. Dance teachers and choreographers in China create thousands of new classroom and stage repertoires for Chinese dance each year, and local governments and cultural organizations host annual competitions and festivals featuring these performances. Hundreds of degree-granting programs focused on Chinese dance are active across the country, and the genre is also the subject of a large and ever-expanding body of academic research. Chinese dance communities are active not only in China but also in Sinophone and diaspora communities abroad.[5] Thus, while the focus of this book is on the historical development and contemporary practice of Chinese dance in the PRC, this topic covers just one part of a broader transnational phenomenon.

Beyond the concert dance sphere, Chinese dance is connected to a range of other social spaces and activities. Since the 1980s, adapted forms of Chinese dance have been incorporated into commercial performances marketed to tourists in theme parks and popular travel destinations.[6] The amateur performance of Chinese dance is common among schoolchildren and at corporate banquets, and it is also a core component of "square dancing" *(guangchang wu)*, outdoor social dancing typically performed by middle-aged women in parks and other public spaces.⁷ Chinese dance also remains connected to the activities of folk practitioners and other ritual specialists in temple processions, weddings, funerals, exorcisms, and holiday festivals.⁸ Rather than attempt to cover all these arenas, I have limited my attention here to the concert field, focusing on the activities of artists based in professional conservatories and ensembles who create dance mainly for the proscenium stage.⁹ Through this choice, I aim to position Chinese dance in conversation with other recognized concert dance genres around the world, as well as to assert the relevance of dance in modern Chinese cultural studies alongside the more established fields of literature, cinema, drama, visual arts, and music.

This book is arranged chronologically and covers an eighty-year period, beginning in the 1930s and ending in the 2010s. The project is primarily historical: it traces, through a close examination of primary documents, the emergence and transformation of Chinese dance in China during the twentieth and early twenty-first centuries. By weaving together stories about individual dancers, choreographic repertoires, intellectual debates, and institutions, the book also brings an ethnographic sensibility to this historical account. It narrates the development of Chinese dance as a complex cultural phenomenon that transcends simplistic dichotomies between personal and collective, hegemonic and resistive, traditional and contemporary, or embodied and conceptual. Structurally, the book emphasizes process as much as product, to highlight the prolonged labor on- and offstage that sustains dance creation. As such, each chapter traces a period of research and creation that led to an important new development. Chapter 1 follows the wartime dance work that resulted in the dance program presented at the first All-China Literature and Arts Worker Representative Congress in 1949. Chapter 2 builds to the launching of a national dance curriculum and the founding of the Beijing Dance School in 1954. Chapter 3 traces the circulation of Chinese dance on the world stage and the emergence of socialist national dance dramas by the late 1950s and early 1960s. Chapter 4 examines the relationship between Chinese dance and ballet that laid the groundwork for the Cultural Revolution, launched in 1966. Chapter 5 reveals how socialist-era activities formed the foundation for new Chinese dance creation in the post-Mao era of the late 1970s and early 1980s. Finally, chapter 6 presents the accumulation of artistic labor recounted in the book as a whole by treating Chinese dance activities of the twenty-first century as a continuation of trends established over the previous six decades.

Through these historical narratives, a variety of arguments emerge in the course of the book. In chapters 1 and 2, for example, I contend that wartime dance activities carried out in Nationalist-dominated and Japanese-occupied areas and by diverse groups that included individuals of diasporic, non-Han, non-Chinese-speaking, and non-Chinese backgrounds contributed significantly to the early formulation and establishment of Chinese dance. This account complicates the existing assumption that China's early revolutionary socialist culture—of which I argue Chinese dance was an important component—was a product mainly of Chinese Communist Party–led agendas advanced in Yan'an primarily by local-born, Han Chinese individuals. In chapters 3 and 4, I demonstrate that Chinese dance served as the predominant national dance genre of the PRC during the 1950s and early 1960s, where it was part of a broad range of dance styles supported and promoted by the socialist state. While Chinese dance lost its leading status after the Cultural Revolution was launched in 1966 and ushered in a decade dominated by revolutionary ballet, I suggest that the rise of ballet too can be seen as, in part, a product of socialist investment in artistic experimentation and aesthetic pluralism during previous decades. This argument challenges the widespread views that socialist culture was monolithic and that ballet was the main form of China's revolutionary dance creation. In chapters 5 and 6, I argue that Chinese dance in the post-Mao era continues many legacies of the revolutionary wartime and early socialist periods. Although Chinese dance has changed over time, this book dates its emergence to the 1940s and 1950s—the decades of socialist revolution and socialist nation building, respectively—and it argues that the developments of this period have continued to inform dance vocabularies, choreographic methods, theoretical articulations, and institutional structures of Chinese dance since the late 1970s.

Although the book is organized chronologically and traces the historical emergence and transformation of a single genre over time, it does not present this trajectory as a teleological process or Chinese dance as an isolated genre. I do not believe that the Chinese dance of today is, by definition, artistically or ideologically "better" than the Chinese dance of earlier eras. Thus, this book does not support the common assumption that post-1970s economic liberalization produced more artistic innovation than was present in the early socialist decades. Like most art forms born out of revolution, Chinese dance has become less politically challenging over time, and the changing political meanings and uses of Chinese dance, as well as its continuously reinterpreted aesthetic forms, are a core consideration of this account. While Chinese dance today is a socialist legacy, it does not inherit all aspects of this legacy equally. In terms of the nonisolatedness of Chinese dance, I argue that Chinese dance has always been in deep conversations with adjacent dance forms. This book examines, to varying degrees, relationships between Chinese dance and a variety of other dance genres practiced in China during the twentieth and twenty-first centuries. Beyond dance, it also explores links to other artistic spheres, such as theater, music, visual art, and cinema. The close relationship between Chinese dance and xiqu is a recurring theme throughout the book, while cinema also plays an implicit role because the best extant documentation of Chinese dance is in the form of motion picture recordings.

Although Chinese dance has changed significantly over the decades, I suggest that three core commitments have defined the genre throughout its history, giving it continuity amid persistent innovation and redefinition. I call these commitments "kinesthetic nationalism," "ethnic and spatial inclusiveness," and "dynamic inheritance." Beyond guiding the artistic work of dance practitioners, these commitments provide the theoretical and choreographic links that connect Chinese dance of the twenty-first century to its predecessors in earlier eras. These commitments both define Chinese dance as an artistic genre and mark it as a socialist legacy, and they are ultimately what give the genre its revolutionary potential at different times. Since these concepts are important themes throughout the book, it is helpful to briefly introduce them here.

Kinesthetic nationalism is the idea that what distinguishes Chinese dance as a genre is its aesthetic form, not its thematic content or where or by whom it is performed. According to kinesthetic nationalism, what makes Chinese dance "Chinese" is that its movement forms—its movement vocabularies, techniques, and rhythms, for example—are developed through ongoing research and adaptation of performance practices of Chinese cultural communities, broadly defined. In Chinese dance discourse, this idea is most often expressed through the concept of "national form" (minzu xingshi), a term promoted by Chinese Communist Party leader Mao Zedong beginning in the late 1930s that continues to inform the theory and practice of Chinese dance today. When the idea was introduced, "national form" referred to new or yet to be created literary and artistic forms that would express contemporary life and bring about positive social change by being both resolutely modern and rooted in local culture. Thus, kinesthetic nationalism is focused on issues of artistic form and is premised on the idea that the local and the contemporary are mutually reinforcing.

Ethnic and spatial inclusiveness is the idea that Chinese dance should include styles and artists from all ethnic communities and geographic regions across China. As in many places, differences of ethnicity and geography in China often map onto disparities in historical privilege and power. Ethnic and spatial inclusivity, considered radical when it was introduced, proposes that China's national dance forms should not be an expression only of dominant cultural groups—such as the Han ethnicity or the affluent coastal cities—but instead should incorporate the cultures of ethnically and geographically marginalized communities, such as non-Han groups, rural places, and inland regions. While there is no single term like "national form" that expresses this idea in Chinese dance discourse, ethnic and spatial inclusiveness builds on the concepts of the "Chinese nation" (Zhonghua minzu) and "remolding" (gaizao), both of which were important in Chinese socialist culture from the 1940s onward. The concept of the "Chinese nation" theorizes Chinese identity as a historical accumulation of diverse cultures and groups. "Remolding" describes the retuning of artists' sensibilities to shed prejudices, especially those against poor and rural communities.

Dynamic inheritance is a theory of cultural transformation that compels Chinese dance artists to research existing performance forms while also generating original interpretations of these forms. It is guided by the premise that cultural traditions inherently change and that they thus require continual innovation to maintain relevance to the contemporary world. In a basic sense, dynamic inheritance refers to the idea that cultural inheritance and individual innovation are mutually reinforcing processes. In Chinese dance discourse, a common phrase used to describe dynamic inheritance is "inherit and develop" (jicheng yu fazhan). Apart from being an abstract way of defining the artist's goal in a theoretical sense, it also implies a specific set of creative methods.[10] Thus, in both theory and practice, dynamic inheritance is what allows Chinese dance practitioners to take cultural continuity in new directions.

Early in the twentieth century, several prominent artists experimented with new dance choreography that could be considered precursors to Chinese dance. One was Yu Rongling (ca. 1888–1973), the Eurasian daughter of a Qing diplomat who studied dance in Tokyo and Paris between 1895 and 1903 and lived at the court of the Manchu Qing dynasty (1644–1911) during its final years.[11] In 1904 Yu created three "Chinese dances" and performed at least one of them, Ruyi Dance, along with dances in "Spanish" and "Greek" styles, for the Qing empress dowager Cixi at the imperial Summer Palace in Beijing.[12] Another key figure in this preliminary period of experimentation was Mei Lanfang (1894–1961), a male Peking opera star who specialized in female roles and became one of China's most famous celebrities. Between 1915 and 1925, Mei worked with drama theorist and playwright Qi Rushan (1875–1962) to develop a series of new plays that featured long dance sequences.[13] These works not only transformed Peking opera performance conventions but also made dance a more central component of Chinese drama, as well as an emerging symbol of national identity.[14]

Yu Rongling and Mei Lanfang both established important precedents for subsequent Chinese dance developments. One, for example, was their use of existing materials as a foundation for new creation. In Yu's case, her dances were inspired by Yu's study of paintings held in the Qing art collections, as well as her discussions with court musicians.[15] Similarly, Mei and his collaborator Qi took inspiration from Chinese literature and folklore, Buddhist paintings, and visual art from the Tang dynasty (618–907) to create the costumes and movements for Mei's opera dances.[16] Also, like later practitioners of Chinese dance, Yu and Mei both emphasized individual creativity and saw their work as being similar to modernist dance experiments that were taking place at the same time in other parts of the world.[17]

Although they set important precedents, however, Yu's and Mei's approaches each lacked key components of the core commitments of Chinese dance. First, neither explicitly theorized movement form as the central defining feature of what made their dances Chinese. While little is known about Yu's choreographic theory, existing photographs and descriptions of her early Chinese dances do not suggest necessarily a preoccupation with movement form as their defining feature. Mei's collaborator Qi Rushan did leave extensive documentation of his theorization of what made Mei's performances "Chinese," and in these he emphasized modes of theatrical representation (aestheticism over realism), not movement form per se, as the central issue.[18] Second, neither Yu nor Mei explicitly engaged the issue of ethnic and geographic inclusivity in their work. While Yu's *Ruyi Dance* employed a Manchu hairstyle and costuming, this should be interpreted in the historical context as a reflection of the dominant Qing Manchu court culture, rather than an attempt to reflect China's ethnic or geographical diversity. Similarly, while Mei's dances drew characters and plots from Chinese popular stories, the images he depicted on stage were refined figures associated with elite Han culture. The fact that Yu and Mei performed almost exclusively in the coastal urban centers of Beijing, Tianjin, and Shanghai also differentiated them from later Chinese dance practitioners, who hailed from and worked in a much broader range of locations across China.

One reason I date the emergence of Chinese dance to the 1940s is that this was the first time a group of dancers and choreographers set forth repertoires of dance choreography and accompanying theoretical writings that formulated Chinese dance in accordance with the core commitments of kinesthetic nationalism, ethnic and spatial inclusiveness, and dynamic inheritance. There were many individuals involved in this movement. In chapters 1 and 2, I introduce five of the earliest and most influential, who remain key protagonists throughout the remainder of the book. They are Dai Ailian (a.k.a. Eileen Isaac and Tai Ai-lien, 1916–2006), Wu Xiaobang (a.k.a. Wu Zupei, 1906–1995), Qemberxanim (a.k.a. Kangba'erhan, Qambarkhan, and Kemberhan Emet, ca. 1914–1994),[19] Liang Lun (a.k.a. Liu Hanxing and Liu Hanlun, b. 1921), and Choe Seung-hui (a.k.a. Choi Seunghee, Ch'oe Sŭng-hŭi, and Sai Shōki, 1911–1969). Like Yu Rongling and Mei Lanfang before them, all of these dancers had significant international experiences that informed their contributions to Chinese dance. Dai was born and raised in Trinidad and launched her career in London; Qemberxanim was born in Kashgar and launched her career in Tashkent and Moscow; and Choe was born in Seoul and launched her career in Tokyo. Wu, after growing up in China, studied dance in Japan, and Liang, after growing up and beginning his dance career in China, later toured in Hong Kong and Southeast Asia. These dancers' biographies converged in China during the 1940s and 1950s, and, with the exception of Choe, they worked in China for the remainder of their lives. I consider all five to be founding figures of Chinese dance in different ways.

Trinidad-born Dai Ailian receives special attention in this book because she was the first to articulate what would become the three core commitments

FIGURE 1. Dai Ailian in "Jiarong Drinking Party." Published in *Yiwen huabao* 2, no. 5 (1947): 5. Photographer unknown. Reproduction provided by the Chinese Periodical Full-text Database (1911–1949), Quan Guo Bao Kan Suo Yin (CNBKSY), Shanghai Library.

of Chinese dance in her writings and performances (figure 1). As discussed in chapter 1, Dai formulated these ideas and choreographies during the 1940s, shortly after she emigrated to China. Her work achieved national influence in 1946 through the *Frontier Music and Dance Plenary (Bianjiang yinyue wudao dahui)*, a gala-style event that premiered in Chongqing, the wartime National-ist capital. A key document in Dai's early theorization of Chinese dance was the published lecture, "The First Step in Developing Chinese Dance" (Fazhan Zhongguo wudao di yi bu), which was attributed to Dai and delivered at the start of the *Plenary*. Circulated widely at the time in newspapers and magazines, this lecture remains one of the earliest theoretical texts on Chinese dance still extant today. In this lecture, Dai offers early formulations of kinesthetic nationalism, spatial and ethnic inclusiveness, and dynamic inheritance. Regarding kinesthetic nationalism, she writes:

> Over the past three years, the Chinese Dance Art Society [which I led in Chongqing] worked hard to create [new dance works]. The narrative content was Chinese, and the performers were Chinese; yet, we cannot say that these were true Chinese dance dramas. We used foreign technique and footwork to tell the story—much like using a foreign language to tell a Chinese tale—and this was quite obvious to the audience. We can say that the work of the past three years took the first step in establishing dance as an independent art [in China]. But, as for creating "Chinese dance," that was a mistaken direction. It was because of a lack of knowledge about Chinese dance customs that we followed this method. . . . [20]

Dai goes on to explain what she envisions as the correct method for creating Chinese dance, outlining the principles of ethnic and spatial inclusiveness and dynamic inheritance. First, she describes a vast network of people conducting research on existing dance practices, including both Han and non-Han traditions from all areas of the country. Then, she describes them using what they find as the basis to create new dance forms. The *Plenary*, for which Dai's lecture served as an introduction, also modeled this future project in its composition and execution. Absent from the program was all of Dai's earlier choreography that had used either ballet or modern dance as its primary movement form. Instead, the *Plenary* comprised works derived from local performance practices. The works were by artists of diverse ethnic and regional backgrounds and represented what are today recognized as six nationalities and three geographic regions of China. According to Dai, the dances were rooted in local performance forms but reflected new artistic arrangements and ideas. The goal of the project, as Dai described it, was "to establish for the stage a new Chinese modern dance."[21]

Another influential member of this early cohort was Choe Seung-hui, a Korean woman who became the first dancer from East Asia to tour on four continents and gain worldwide fame during the late 1930s (figure 2). As discussed in chapter 2, Choe led the early construction of xiqu-based Chinese classical dance and, together with Qemberxanim and others, established influential precedents for Chinese dance training. In 1945 a journalist in Shanghai recorded a statement by Choe that also foreshadows the core commitments of Chinese dance, especially the idea of dynamic inheritance. Choe was reportedly having a conversation with Mei Lanfang when Mei asked Choe to clarify the role of tradition in her own dance choreography. In response, Choe states, "I do not completely follow inherited dances that previous people have passed down. Some say new creation is

FIGURE 2. Choe Seung-hui in "Hourglass Drum Dance."
Photographer: Studio Iris, Paris. Reproduced with permission from the
private collection of Siqintariha.

destructive to tradition. I rather believe that new creation has always been the
normal development of tradition. In the past, our ancestors' artistic creations were
passed down and became today's art traditions. The new creations of today's artists
will also become the traditions of future generations."[22]

Here, Choe expresses a refreshingly open-ended and self-reflexive notion of
dance creation, its relationship to tradition, and her own role in the production
and reproduction of dance culture. This thoughtful intellectual agenda motivated
the work she and others did to create Chinese dance, as they went on to invent new

choreographic repertoires, perform countless shows around China and the world, and inspire new generations of dancers in their roles as artists, theorists, teachers, administrators, and cultural icons. In this book, I examine the revolutionary bodies that emerged from these dancers' projects and formed the dominant danced expressions of China's socialist culture. In doing so, I seek to do justice to the complexity of their choreographies and the dynamism of their visions, showing how their boldness and imagination gave rise to the richness of China's dance history in the contemporary era.

1

From Trinidad to Beijing

Dai Ailian and the Beginnings of Chinese Dance

Dong d-dong, dong d-dong. A gong sounds as the camera fixes on an empty stage set with an arched footbridge and blossoming tree branch. Dai Ailian emerges dressed in a folkloric costume of red balloon pants and a rose-colored silk jacket, a ring of red flowers in her hair and shoes topped with red pom-poms. Puppetlike, two false legs kick out from under the back of Dai's jacket, while the false torso and head of an old man hunch forward in front of her chest, creating the illusion of two characters: an old man carrying his young wife on his back. This dance is Dai's adaptation of "The Mute Carries the Cripple" (Yazi bei feng), a comic sketch performed in several regional variations of xiqu, or Chinese traditional theater (video 1). This particular version is derived from Gui opera *(Guiju)*, a type of xiqu specific to Guangxi Autonomous Region in south China. Dai demonstrates her dance skill by isolating her upper body and lower body, so that her pelvis and legs convincingly portray the movements of an old man while her torso, arms, and head those of a young woman. As the man, Dai takes wide sweeping steps, kicking, squatting, and balancing with her feet flexed and knees bent between steps, occasionally lurching forward as if struggling to balance under the weight of the female rider. As the woman, Dai grips the old husband's shoulders with one hand while she lets her head bob from side to side, her eyes sparkling as she uses her free hand to twirl a fan, point to things in her environment, and dab the old man's forehead with a handkerchief.

Recorded in New York in 1947 by the China Film Enterprises of America, Inc., Dai Ailian's solo choreography "The Mute Carries the Cripple" is one of the earliest complete works of Chinese dance recorded on film still extant today.[1] Dai, who was born and raised in Trinidad and moved to China in 1941 when

VIDEO 1. Dai Ailian in "The Mute Carries the Cripple." China Film Enterprises of America, Inc., 1947. Video obtained from the C. V. Starr East Asian Library, Columbia University. © Wan-go H. C. Weng, Hsing Ching Weng Trust. Used with permission.

To watch this video, scan the QR code with your mobile device or visit DOI: https://doi.org/10.1525/luminos.58.1

she was twenty-four, developed this work in the early 1940s, during her first years in China.[2] Dai could barely speak Chinese at the time, but she visited Guangxi and learned xiqu movement there from a famous Gui opera actress, Fang Zhaoyuan (a.k.a. Little Flying Swallow, 1918–1949). Dai's study with Fang gave "The Mute Carries the Cripple" a distinctly local movement vocabulary, demonstrated in Dai's circling, bent-legged and flex-footed walks, her manipulation of the fan, and her curving, coordinated articulations of the hands, torso, and eyes. Apart from its xiqu-style movement, the dance also has a local soundscape, employing gong and drum percussion, a libretto sung by a man and a woman using folk-style vocal techniques, and a two-stringed Chinese fiddle, all staples of Chinese village music.[3] Finally, the dance has a narrative structure punctuated with slapstick humor, also a common element of Chinese folk performance. For example, at one point the wife strains to pick flowers from a tree branch just a little too tall. Then, atop the footbridge, she leans forward to view her reflection, nearly causing them to fall in the river.

"The Mute Carries the Cripple" is one of two dances by Dai that appear in the 1947 recording. The other is "Yao Drum" (Yaoren zhi gu), also a solo Dai developed in China during the early 1940s (video 2).[4] Both works reflect the new directions Dai's choreography took after she moved to China, and both became part of the first nationally recognized repertoire of Chinese dance by the late 1940s. Unlike "The Mute Carries the Cripple," which takes Han folk culture as its basis, "Yao Drum" invokes an ethnic minority identity, in this case of the Yao, a historically marginalized people who reside largely in remote, mountainous areas of southwest China.[5]

VIDEO 2. Dai Ailian in "Yao Drum." China Film Enterprises of America, Inc., 1947. Video obtained from the C. V. Starr East Asian Library, Columbia University. © Wan-go H. C. Weng, Hsing Ching Weng Trust. Used with permission.

To watch this video, scan the QR code with your mobile device or visit DOI: https://doi.org/10.1525/luminos.58.2

Based loosely on a ceremonial dance Dai observed while conducting field research in a Yao community in Guizhou, "Yao Drum" has an abstract, form-driven composition organized around the rhythmic progression of the drumbeat. The stage set consists of a painted backdrop depicting a forest landscape and a large circular floor drum. As in the first piece, Dai appears in a folkloric costume, this time featuring the same pom-pom shoes, matching red blouse and calf warmers, a black pleated skirt, and silver head and chest ornaments. Dai dances in circular patterns around the drum, revolving clockwise and counterclockwise in hops, steps, turns, and leg sweeps. There is no musical accompaniment except the sounds Dai makes on the drum with her two drumsticks. These include beats from striking the top of the drum and clacks from hitting the necks of the drumsticks against one another. Dai weaves the beats and clacks evenly between each step at a constant tempo, and as the dance progresses, tension builds through increasingly complex variation in both rhythm and movement. At the climax, Dai is hitting the sticks under one leg as she jumps, striking the drum as she lands, sweeping one foot over the drum while hitting the sticks together above her head, then hooking one foot behind the other for a quick turn before she strikes the drum and the cycle restarts. Dai's visual focus remains on the drum until the end of the dance, when she stops drumming and strikes a pose: standing still behind the drum, she crosses her drumsticks overhead, arches her body back, and looks up in profile.

In their foregrounding of local folk aesthetics and minority themes, "The Mute Carries the Cripple" and "Yao Drum" embody the early values of Chinese dance, a new genre that emerged during the 1940s amid the transformative events of world war, communist revolution, and the intensified global circulation of dancers and dance works. Although many individuals contributed to the founding of Chinese dance during this period, Dai Ailian stands out as particularly influential. Not only was Dai the person who first launched Chinese dance into the realm of China's national discourse, she was also the first person to perform, choreograph, and theorize a repertoire of Chinese dance that is still consistent with the definitions of the genre in use today. Dai's devotion to research on local folk forms and her conceptualization of Chinese dance as essentially modern while also culturally distinct laid the groundwork for the innovative approaches Chinese dance practitioners would advance, often under Dai's leadership, during the period of socialist nation building. As an early leader in the Chinese dance movement, Dai has a historical importance that is unparalleled.

Apart from her historical contributions to Chinese dance, Dai also provides a narrative lens through which to understand major developments in China's dance history during the early twentieth century. Although Dai grew up outside China, her personal experiences mirrored China's own encounters with concert dance during this same period, which were driven largely by intercultural processes. Dai's path from ballet to modern dance to Chinese dance reflects a parallel process that also occurred in China, and it represents the broader shift from a vision of modernity as assimilation into Euro-American culture to one of modernity as the assertion of a distinctly local cultural vision. Dai's encounters with constructed colonial race hierarchies and her efforts to carve out a space for herself within an international dance field that privileged European bodies reflects China's own confrontations with Western cultural hegemony during the early half of the twentieth century. Ultimately, Dai's vision of Chinese dance found audiences and collaborators in China because both were facing a similar conundrum at the time: how to find a form of cultural expression that neither assimilated into Eurocentric norms nor reproduced orientalist and racist conceptions of China, while also recognizing the internal variation and multiplicity that defined China as a modern nation. From the perspective of her biography, Dai's story also reverses the common understanding of cultural relations between the nation and its diaspora. In her case, it shows how a citizen of the diaspora could redefine the nation in cultural terms.

SETTING THE STAGE: DAI AILIAN AND CHINESE DANCE AS A GLOBAL AMBITION

The woman who became known as Dai Ailian was born on May 10, 1916, in Couva, Trinidad. Her grandparents had immigrated there from southern China during the latter half of the nineteenth century, making her a third-generation Chinese Trinidadian. Because Trinidad was at the time a British colony, Dai's citizenship would have been British.[6] Dai attended British-style schooling in Trinidad through the age of fourteen, after which she moved to London with her mother and two sisters. The language Dai spoke growing up was English (she also studied French and Latin in school), and although she learned to speak Mandarin after she moved to China, she never learned Cantonese, her paternal grandparents' native tongue.[7]

Dai's multicultural identity was reflected in her multiple names. When she was born and throughout her childhood, Dai's name was Eileen Isaac. Dai's paternal grandfather, who was Cantonese, was given the surname Isaac upon his arrival in Trinidad, based on the English transliteration of his Cantonese nickname, Ah Sek. Dai never knew for certain her grandfather's Chinese surname, although she later believed it to be Ruan (Yuen).[8] Dai's mother, who was Hakka, had the Chinese surname Liu (Liew) and was known in Trinidad as Francis. When Dai was born, she was given the English name Eileen, from which came her Chinese given name, Ailian. The surname Dai came about when Dai moved to England around 1930. Apparently, when Dai arrived at Anton Dolin's ballet studio, Dolin was surprised to see that his new pupil was Chinese, because the name she had signed in her letters from Trinidad was Eileen Isaac. Dolin asked for her Chinese surname, prompting Dai's mother to produce the surname Tai, from her father's nickname, Ah Dai.[9] Documents of Dai's dance career in England during the 1930s typically use the surname Tai, but with a variety of spellings of her given name. In newspapers and periodicals, she appears as "Eilian Tai," "Ay Lien Tai," "Ai Lien Tai," "Ai Lien-tai," and "Ai-leen Tai."[10] Student records at the Jooss-Leeder School of Dance at Dartington Hall, where Dai studied in the late summer and fall of 1939, include at least three variations.[11] Similarly, during her tours in Hong Kong and the United States in the 1940s, she appeared as either "Tai Ai-lien" or "Tai Ai Lien."[12] This seems to be the English spelling Dai used herself through the early 1950s.[13] The spelling Dai Ailian was a product of the official Pinyin spelling system introduced in the PRC during the late 1950s. It was not until the 1970s, Dai recalls, that her acquaintances in England began to know her by this name.[14]

Early twentieth-century Trinidad, where Dai grew up, was a colonial society governed by legally established racial hierarchies. In the skin tone–based caste system of the time, communities categorized as "white" (mainly British, French creoles, and Venezuelans) possessed a near monopoly on upper-class status, followed by those categorized as "coloured" (including Chinese, South Asians, and light-skinned mixed-race people) and, at the bottom of the social hierarchy, "blacks" (dark-skinned people of largely African descent).[15] For people categorized as coloured or black, upward mobility was often associated with assimilation into white culture, a process Trinidad's small Chinese population was first to carry out.[16] Dai came from a prosperous family that followed this path. When he was eighteen, Dai's father inherited a large fortune that included several orange, coffee, and coco plantations. Eugene Chen (Chen Youren, 1878–1944), a famous diplomat, was the cousin of Dai's mother, and Dai's maternal grandfather at one point apparently owned the famous Pitch Lake.[17] A photograph of Dai's paternal grandparents, father, and aunt taken around the turn of the century shows the entire group dressed in European attire.[18] Dai's family kept black servants and practiced Christianity, and Dai recalls her maternal grandmother dressing at home in Victorian-style skirts and her aunts plucking their eyebrows according to American fashions. When Dai's skin became tanned from playing outdoors, her aunt rubbed her face with Coty powder, a French cosmetic. Dai's childhood bedtime stories included *Alice in Wonderland, Sleeping Beauty,* and *Cinderella,* and piano lessons were required for her and her sisters in hopes of ensuring "good marriages."[19]

Dai's early interest in and access to ballet—a dance form historically associated with European royalty—was a product, in part, of this colonial upbringing. Dai's first ballet teacher was her second cousin Sylvia (Si-lan) Chen (a.k.a. Chen Xuelan and Chen Xilan, 1909–1996), the light-skinned mixed-race daughter of Eugene Chen and his French creole wife, Agatha Ganteaume.[20] Like Dai, Sylvia had been raised in an upper-class Europeanized cultural environment. While living in England, Sylvia was enrolled at the Elms, "a school for the daughters of gentlemen," and she had studied ballet, even partnering in a performance with Dai's later teacher Anton Dolin.[21] Dai was only around five when she learned dance from Sylvia, but the experience left a lasting impression. Sylvia moved to China with her father in the mid-1920s, and later she studied dance in Moscow and became an internationally renowned modern dancer, offering a role model for Dai.[22] When Sylvia left, Dai began studying ballet with Nell Walton, the daughter of an English judge who had a small dance school in Port of Spain, Trinidad's capital city. Because Walton's other students were all white, Dai's mother had to seek special permission for Dai to attend.[23] This would be the first of many dance schools in which Dai was the sole student of Chinese descent.

After Dai moved to England, she continued to gain access to dance styles typically reserved for white students. However, when she began to seek work as a dancer, racial discrimination limited Dai's access to professional roles in these fields. Dai studied with leading figures in the British dance world, including ballet dancers Anton Dolin, Marie Rambert, Margaret Craske, and Lydia Sokolova and modern dancer Lesley Burrows-Goossens. However, while several of Dai's classmates went on to have highly successful dance careers, Dai was unable to find a steady job, and racial bias in casting was likely a factor.[24] Recalling her life in England, Dai describes being stared at constantly and treated as a racial other in everyday interactions.[25] This racial stereotyping also seems to have extended into Dai's professional career, since all of the known roles Dai performed in England were racially designated. Dai recalls her first professional dance role as a Native American group dancer in the 1932 pageant *Hiawatha,* a job she believed she gained because she "had dark skin, and looked a bit like a Native American."[26] In 1937 Dai was cast as a Chinese dancer in the British film *The Wife of General Ling,* and in 1937–38, she performed the role of a Tibetan girl in the dance production *Djroazanmo.*[27] The Mask Theatre, which produced *Djroazanmo,* was the only ensemble that consistently engaged Dai in performances during her time in England.[28]

Although led by two German modern dancers, Ernest and Lotte Berk, the Mask Theatre specialized in works with non-Western themes, ranging from interpretations of Javanese dance to choreographies such as "Voodoo Sacrifice" and "Life of Buddha."[29] In May 1938, a portrait of Dai published on the cover of *The Dancing Times* succinctly expressed the racist assumptions that London's dance environment imposed on her. The caption reads: "Ai Lien Tai . . . She came to England to study ballet . . ., but turned her attention to Oriental dancing as more suitable for her type and style."[30] Bias occurred even at Dartington Hall, an organization known for progressive values.[31] During her four months at Dartington, Dai had trained exclusively in European dance styles, with the stated goal of joining the modern ballet ensemble Ballets Jooss upon completion of her studies.[32] However, when Dartington had to close at the end of 1939 because of the eruption of World War II, Jooss recommended that Dai instead join the ensemble of Ram Gopal, an Indian dance company.[33] "Since you come from the East" was the explanation Dai recalled Jooss offering.[34] Since Dai did not study Indian dance, sending her to Gopal's company clearly had more to do with her race than her dance abilities.

The troubling effects of racism on Dai's early London career are visible in the only surviving recording of Dai's dancing from this period: her brief appearance in the 1937 British film *The Wife of General Ling*.[35] This film is not mentioned in Dai's oral histories and biographies, possibly due to its offensive portrayal of Chinese people. A typical Yellow Peril narrative, the film features a bloodthirsty Chinese villain, white actors performing in yellowface, and a plot that revolves around the efforts of a white male hero to "save" a white woman from her marriage to a Chinese man.[36] Dai's dance embodies China as Yellow Peril by presenting a menacing image that supports racial fears expressed in the film. The scene in which Dai appears takes place during a cocktail party held in the lavish Hong Kong residence of the film's villain, General Ling. Dai plays the role of a dancer performing as entertainment for a group of mainly European guests. Dai's props and costumes set up a stark contrast between her and her audience: as they mingle with drinks and cigarettes, Dai appears flailing a bladed-pole weapon, and while the guests wear waved coiffures, evening gowns, and tuxedos, Dai wears her hair in four hornlike pigtails and is dressed in a short tunic exposing her bare arms, legs, and feet. Dai contorts her face into furrowed brows, a grimacing mouth, and an unfocused gaze, circling the weapon in rings above her head while she rolls her torso and hips in wide circles. Dancing to music conveying fast-paced agitation, Dai grips the pole with both hands, thrusting it rapidly forward and back and side to side. The dance ends with two thrusting lunges, and Dai freezes in a pose in which she appears to stab something. Dai's appearance serves as backdrop to a conversation that confirms the theme of her dance: as he watches her perform, the white male hero of the film learns with horror that all prisoners under Ling's control have just been shot.[37]

It was during Dai's experiences working in London in the 1930s, possibly encouraged by these external forces, that she began to develop a sense of Chinese identity and a desire to create her own Chinese-themed choreography.[38] One development that inspired Dai in this regard was seeing Asian choreographers staging their own works of Asian-themed dance. While "oriental dances" by white performers had been common in London since the early twentieth century, the 1930s saw the rapid increase of dancers and choreographers of Asian descent staging their own concert dance shows in Europe. Among these were Indian dancer Uday Shankar, who toured in London in 1933 and 1937; Japanese dancer Yeichi Nimura, who toured London in 1934; a group of students from Java, Bali, and Sumatra, who appeared in London in 1939; and Korean dancer Choe Seung-hui (also known at the time by her Japanese name, Sai Shōki), whose 1939 New York and Paris shows were covered in London magazines.[39] Dai was clearly aware of some of these dancers, as an interview published upon her arrival in Hong Kong in 1940 lists Uday Shankar and Indonesian dancers among her artistic influences.[40] Dai's biographer Richard Glasstone records her recalling that seeing performances of Japanese, Indian, and Javanese dance in London made her wonder why there were no performances of Chinese dance.[41] These Asian dancers appearing on London's stages were all, like Dai, quite cosmopolitan: Shankar had studied in Europe and collaborated with the famous Russian ballerina Anna Pavlova; Nimura had long been working with modern dancers in the United States; the Indonesian dancers were students based in Holland; and Choe had studied in Japan and toured North America before she arrived in Europe. These artists and their work gave Dai models for envisioning Asian dances as modern art forms. Soon she had developed a desire to travel to China, with the expressed goal of researching and creating what she called modern Chinese dance.[42]

Another dance development that shaped Dai's creative aspirations during her time in London was the emergence of modern ballets dealing with serious social and political themes. The foremost representative of this trend was Ballets Jooss, originally a German company that fled Nazi persecution in 1933 and, from 1935, was based at Dartington Hall in southwest England.[43] The Ballets Jooss toured internationally throughout the 1930s with its hit production, *The Green Table*, which won first prize at the International Dance Congress's choreographic competition in Paris in 1932. *The Green Table* presented what choreographer Kurt Jooss called "a vividly realistic commentary on the destructive forces of war."[44] Centering on the personified figure of Death and satirizing leaders who orchestrate war for personal benefit at the expense of humanity, the dance moved audiences with its haunting imagery, innovative choreographic methods, and incisive social critique.[45] Contrasting Ballets Jooss with the existing Russian-dominated ballet tradition, one London-based critic wrote in 1938, "Ballet Russe is a drug, an escape from reality, while the Ballet Jooss is hard fact, a bringing down to earth, even at times a nasty jolt."[46] When Dai saw *The Green Table* for the first time around early 1939, she recalls, "I was extremely excited, and I felt I had found the perfect form of dance art."[47] Dai approached Jooss after the show backstage and asked to join his ensemble, leading her to enroll as a scholarship student at the Jooss-Leeder Summer School that August at Dartington Hall.[48]

While she was still in England, Dai began staging performances of her own choreography on Chinese themes. The platform that facilitated this breakthrough for Dai was a London-based organization founded in 1937 known as the China Campaign Committee (CCC), whose mission was to generate support and aid for China during the war against Japan, which began in 1937.[49] By 1938 Dai was performing regularly at CCC fund-raising events, where her dancing became a lead attraction.[50] Two dances Dai performed at these events were "The Concubine Beauty Dances before the Emperor" and "March," both solos of Dai's own creation. First devised in 1936, "Concubine" was based on the story of Yang Guifei, a famous imperial consort known for dying in tragic circumstances during a war, which Dai had read about in the British Museum Library.[51] A British reviewer who had seen Dai perform the dance in London described it thus: "To what seemed a plaintive Tartar melody, she danced before her seventh century Emperor, a strange meditative 'inward' dance, humming the tune to herself and making classical and exquisite gestures with her long sleeves and her hands."[52] Dai performed the piece in a xiqu costume given to her by a Malaysian Chinese friend she had met in London. The choreography was Dai's own invention, which she described as "what I imagined to be Chinese dance movements."[53] "March" was developed from a student piece Dai created at the Burrows-Goossens School around 1935.[54] It was set to the third movement of Sergey Prokofiev's "The Love for Three Oranges" and featured powerful, martial arts–like actions performed in a type of Chinese jacket typically worn by men.[55] Describing this dance, a London reviewer covering a CCC benefit event in 1938 called it "ultramodern in military guise, danced by Miss Ai-leen Tai to a thunderous accompaniment of Chinese drums."[56] Through Dai's performances with the CCC, she launched her career as a solo artist through work that blended political activism with innovative interpretations of Chinese themes.

The outbreak of World War II in Europe in 1939 brought Dai the opportunity to travel to Asia. Leveraging her connections in the overseas Chinese community in London, Dai benefited from a funding program designed to repatriate Chinese students to secure a boat passage to Hong Kong. Although a British colony, Hong Kong had a majority Chinese population and was located next to China, making it a good pathway to Dai's ultimate destination.[57] Dai arrived in Hong Kong around March of 1940, just over a month before her twenty-fourth birthday.[58] She stayed there for one year before moving on to China in the spring of 1941.[59] The sea journey from England to Hong Kong was long, taking Dai through Egypt, Sri Lanka, and Malaya (Malaysia), where she reconnected with her older sister, who was married and living in Penang. Dai's sister would provide Dai with living expenses during her year in Hong Kong, allowing Dai to live comfortably and focus on her creative work.[60] Soon after Dai arrived in Hong Kong, she found an invaluable patron in Song Qingling (a.k.a. Soong Ching-ling, 1893–1981), the former first lady of China. Song spoke fluent English and was a close colleague of Dai's relative Eugene Chen.[61] Song took a special interest in Dai, helping her to arrange rehearsal space, providing advice on her dance choreography, and writing her letters of introduction to leading figures in China.[62] Song organized both of Dai's major performances in Hong Kong, held on October 18, 1940, and January 22, 1941, at the Peninsula Hotel and the King's Theatre, respectively.[63] Both events were fund-raisers for the China Defense League, of which Song served as chair. The shows were sold out with audiences of five hundred and one thousand each, and they generated significant positive press for Dai.

While she was in Hong Kong, Dai met and married a famous Chinese cartoonist, Ye Qianyu (1907–1995), whom Song had engaged to draw publicity sketches for Dai's shows.[64] Ye was ten years Dai's senior, had been born and educated in China, and was well-connected in China's art scene.[65] An accomplished visual artist and fluent Mandarin and Cantonese speaker with a basic command of English, Ye translated and interpreted for Dai and helped with set and costume designs during her early years in China.[66]

The dances Dai performed in Hong Kong in 1940–41 illustrated the eclectic style she had developed in England, combining excerpts from ballet repertoire with Dai's original choreography on Chinese and non-Chinese themes.[67] Dai's most popular dances were those dealing with the war, such as "Alarm" and "Guerilla March." "Alarm," which Dai created in London in 1939, was danced in bare feet and used a round drum that Dai held under her left arm and beat with her right hand as she danced.[68] The choreography combined a drumming technique Dai had learned in her modern dance classes with footwork adapted from a Javanese dance Dai saw performed in London.[69] According to Dai, the dance portrayed "the emotional state of a young guerilla fighter on sentry duty for the first time."[70] "Guerilla March" was a development of Dai's earlier work "March," with a new costume featuring the red, blue, and white flag of the Republic of China, at the time a symbol of China's anti-Japanese resistance.[71] A Hong Kong news photograph depicts Dai in the costume: she wears a leotard with the white sun motif emblazoned on her chest, a flag-like swath of fabric draped over one arm, her legs and feet bare. She stands in a wide lunge position and reaches her arms out on a strong diagonal line.[72] Dai performed "Guerilla March," still set to the music of Prokofiev, in both of her Hong Kong shows.[73] Compared to the new choreography Dai would produce in China during the 1940s, her Hong Kong repertoire shows a view of China from outside. The movement vocabularies she used in these works came from her ballet and European modern dance background, dances from other Asian countries she had seen performed abroad, and her own imagination. Additionally, using symbols such as the national flag and the guerilla fighter, works like "Guerilla March" and "Alarm" represented China as an undifferentiated whole, without highlighting variations such as region, ethnicity, or class within the national body. The shift to develop new movement vocabularies based on local performance forms and to express internal differences within China would become the focus of Dai's new work after she left Hong Kong.

DANCE IN WARTIME CHINA: COMPETING VISIONS OF MODERNITY

The world Dai entered when she crossed the border from Hong Kong to China in early 1941 was one in which wartime conditions were generating rapid transformations in culture, including the dance field. To contextualize Dai's early work after her arrival, it is thus necessary to first gain an understanding of the broader dance developments already going on in China at the time. One of the most important factors shaping these developments was the War of Resistance against Japan, begun in 1937. Lasting eight years and fought primarily on Chinese soil, this war impacted almost everyone in China, soldiers and civilians alike. While large swaths of the country were consumed into the rapidly expanding Japanese Empire, an estimated fourteen to thirty million people lost their lives and eighty million became refugees, leading to one of the largest demographic shifts in modern history.[74] Scholarship on China's literary and artistic transformations during the war has been extensive, examining diverse communities from the Japanese-occupied eastern seaboard to the Nationalist-controlled inland areas to the Communist zones.[75] Conventionally, China's wartime cultural developments were seen as a move away from the modernist experiments of the 1920s and early 1930s. Recently, however, scholars have begun to rethink this conception and see wartime culture too as a modernist project. In her study of wartime literature, visual art, and film, Carolyn FitzGerald, for example, argues that a blurring of artistic boundaries and self-consciousness about form characterized wartime art, continuing prewar projects and generating new forms of Chinese modernism.[76] In dance, the war had a similar effect, with debates about genre and form leading to new innovations and competing approaches to the meaning of modernity and modernism in artistic expression.

Before the war, several dance projects were already ongoing in China's major urban areas, all of which were concerned in some way with modern or modernist experiments.[77] As discussed in the introduction, one such project began in the 1900s and 1910s with the modern Chinese-style choreographies of Qing dynasty court lady Yu Rongling (1883–1973) and Peking opera actor Mei Lanfang (1894–1961). Another project began in the late 1910s and 1920s and involved the importation and adaptation of European and American popular dance forms such as ballroom, cabaret, and jazz. The most well-known figures in this field were the composer and songwriter Li Jinhui (1891–1967), who created the first successful Chinese cabaret ensemble, and taxi dancers or dance hostesses, who were essential to early Chinese dance hall and cabaret culture. In Shanghai especially, these dance hall entertainments came to be regarded as symbols of a cosmopolitan modern lifestyle.[78] A third project, which began in the 1920s and 1930s, was the importation and adaptation of Western elite dance forms, such as ballet and European and American modern dance. Key figures in this field were Russian émigrés, responsible for the early transmission of ballet following the Russian Revolution of 1917, and Wu Xiaobang (1906–1995), who imported to China in the 1930s Western modern dance forms and ideas he had studied with Japanese teachers in Tokyo.[79]

The outbreak of the War of Resistance brought new directions to some of these existing dance activities, while also launching completely new dance experiments. By the end of 1937, Japanese armies had occupied the major urban centers on China's east coast, such as Beijing, Harbin, Nanjing, Shanghai, and Tianjin, which had previously been the hubs of the three dance projects launched in the prewar period. While some artists continued their work under Japanese governance, many fled inland, forming new artistic centers in places like Chongqing, Guilin, Kunming, and Yan'an. The operatic experiments of Mei Lanfang were continued in the wartime period through the work of Japanese-trained Korean dancer Choe Seung-hui, the results of which came to fruition after 1949 and are discussed in the next chapter. Cabaret, jazz, and ballroom culture largely continued under the Japanese occupation, as did activities in ballet. Wu's adaptations of Western-style modern dance also continued, although with some new variations as discussed below. The first entirely new dance projects began to emerge in the early 1940s in the inland areas. Among these, the wartime dance movement known as "New Yangge" *(xin yangge)* was the first.

New Yangge symbolized the emerging Chinese socialist culture developed in Yan'an, a remote area located in northwest China that had become the base of the Chinese Communist Party (CCP) in 1935. The establishment of Yan'an coincided with the rise of Mao Zedong as the preeminent leader of the CCP and the driving figure of China's socialist revolution.[80] Mao's principles of socialist cultural production were formulated and promoted in Yan'an during the early years of the war, and New Yangge was the first new artistic genre to be developed out of the direct application of these principles.[81] As its name suggests, New Yangge was a modern performance genre created on the foundation of yangge, an existing folk practice.[82] Before the 1940s, folk yangge was an amateur community performance carried out among predominantly Han communities in rural north China around the New Year holiday. It integrated music, theater, dance, sport, ritual, and popular entertainment, typically featuring processions, group dances performed with lanterns and other props, and skits featuring humorous, often obscene, content.[83] As a localized, amateur, and orally transmitted folk culture, yangge was embedded in the lives of poor peasant communities and thus constituted the type of nonelite local culture that Mao instructed revolutionary artists to study and adopt in their activist work. New Yangge was developed through collaborations between folk performers and communist intellectuals, following cultural directives of CCP policy.[84]

The intellectual underpinnings of the New Yangge movement came from two ideas propagated in the writings of Mao Zedong in Yan'an during the early

1940s: "national forms" *(minzu xingshi)* and "remolding" *(gaizao)*. According to Wang Hui, the "national forms" discussion began with a report Mao gave in 1938 in Yan'an, in which he wrote, "The foreign 'eight-legged essay' must be banned, empty and abstract talk must be stopped and doctrinairism must be laid to rest to make room for the fresh and lively things of Chinese style and Chinese flavor which the common folk of China love to see and hear."[85] Over the next four years, writers across much of China debated the meaning of this position in what became known as the "national forms" debates. The discussion involved not only those in Yan'an but also people working in many of the cities that would later become important sites of the early Chinese dance movement. Wang writes, "The discussion was opened up in Yan'an . . . after which several dozen publications in Chongqing, Chengdu, Kunming, Guilin, the Shanxi-Shaanxi-Henan border region, and Hong Kong got drawn into the conversation; this eventually resulted in the publication of almost two hundred essays and treatises."[86] One central issue in the debate was whether or to what extent national forms could be based on the Westernized cultural practices that had been developed and promoted by many of China's leftist urban intellectuals during the May Fourth New Culture Movement of the 1920s. Another central theme was to what extent local folk and vernacular forms could contribute to the construction of new national forms. Here, the question of form was directly related to the question of audience. In the realm of literature, for example, debaters asked, "What forms should writers use, especially what language, and who were the readers?"[87] In his influential 1940 essay "On New Democracy," Mao clarified his position on the issue of Westernization. He wrote, "To nourish her own culture China needs to assimilate a good deal of foreign progressive culture, not enough of which was done in the past. We should assimilate whatever is useful to us today not only from the present-day socialist and new-democratic cultures but also from the earlier cultures of other nations, for example, from the culture of the various capitalist countries in the Age of Enlightenment. However, we should not gulp any of this foreign material down uncritically. . . . To advocate 'wholesale westernization' is wrong."[88]

The issue of folk and vernacular forms was more controversial and continued to be debated through the 1940s, with strong views on both sides. Within this debate, however, the New Yangge movement was clearly on the side of using folk and vernacular forms as the basis for new national forms. Thus, in the realm of performance, the New Yangge movement offered the first model for how to successfully develop a new revolutionary national form on the basis of local and vernacular culture.

The principle of remolding appeared as a key theme in Mao's 1942 "Talks at the Yan'an Forum on Literature and Art," regarded as his most important treatise on China's revolutionary art and culture. Although related to the issue of national forms, remolding touched on the deeper source of the cultural divide between many communist artists and their rural audiences. Namely, it pinpointed the visceral sense of superiority and disgust that many educated urbanites, even those who were politically progressive, felt toward the majority of China's population at the time: poor illiterate people living in rural areas. "Remolding" in this case referred to the process of psychological and physical self-reform that Mao felt such artists needed to carry out to rid themselves of their elitist attitudes. To illustrate this idea, Mao reflected on his own experience:

> I began life as a student and at school acquired the ways of a student; I then used to feel it undignified to do even a little manual labor, such as carrying my own luggage in the presence of my fellow students, who were incapable of carrying anything, either on their shoulders or in their hands. At that time I felt that intellectuals were the only clean people in the world, while in comparison workers and peasants were dirty. I did not mind wearing the clothes of other intellectuals, believing them clean, but I would not put on clothes belonging to a worker or peasant, believing them dirty. But after I became a revolutionary and lived with workers and peasants and with soldiers of the revolutionary army, I gradually came to know them well, and they gradually came to know me well too. It was then, and only then, that I fundamentally changed the bourgeois and petty-bourgeois feelings implanted in me in the bourgeois schools. I came to feel that compared with the workers and peasants the un-remolded intellectuals were not clean and that, in the last analysis, the workers and peasants were the cleanest people and, even though their hands were soiled and their feet smeared with cow-dung, they were really cleaner than the bourgeois and petty-bourgeois intellectuals. That is what is meant by a change in feelings, a change from one class to another. If our writers and artists who come from the intelligentsia want their works to be well received by the masses, they must change and remold their thinking and their feelings. Without such a change, without such remolding, they can do nothing well and will be misfits.[89]

In this discussion, Mao highlighted the importance of the body in Chinese conceptions of class difference. To carry out revolutionary art, he argued, required not just promoting progressive political messages in one's work but being willing, in a physical way, to be close to the working classes. Remolding meant living with the rural poor, taking part in their physical labor, dressing in their clothes, and reprogramming one's unconscious sensibilities so that even the dirt on their skin would seem clean. Because bodily culture was such an important marker of identity, and so difficult for many to change, it became a central focus in socialist ideas of revolutionary culture and revolutionary transformation. As such, it was the central ideological principle motivating choices about dance form in the New Yangge movement.

The New Yangge performances developed in and around Yan'an during the early and mid-1940s incorporated two types of performance practice, both of which had a dance component. The first type featured dramatic productions known as "yangge theater" (yangge ju), which adapted local musical tunes and performance conventions to perform revolutionary stories, usually centering on poor peasants and their desire for social change. The most well-known examples of this genre were Brother and Sister Open the Wasteland (Xiongmei kaihuang, 1943), The White-Haired Girl (Baimao nü, 1944), and Liu Hulan (1948). The second type featured participatory events such as parades and communal dances, in

FIGURE 3. New Yangge team performing in National Day Parade. Published in *Renmin huabao* 1, no. 1 (July 1950): 1. Photographer unknown. Image provided by China Foto Bank.

which yangge groups entered public spaces performing collective dances accompanied by loud drumming, gongs, and colorful scarves, usually inviting bystanders to join in. Both forms of New Yangge used a specific type of bodily movement known as *niu yangge* (literally, "twist yangge"), referring to a distinctive hip-swiveling walk performed in yangge dance. A common action in *niu yangge* involves the dancer performing a bouncing version of a jazz square (stepping across, back, side, and forward), while the top of the head bobs from side to side, hips twist freely, and wrists spiral in opposite directions with the elbows tucked in and hands spinning, often holding a fan or handkerchief, at waist level. Because of its association with poor peasants and its use in village festivals, this yangge "twist" projected a distinctly lowbrow rural working-class aesthetic that contrasted sharply with the elite, Westernized concert dance forms practiced in China's coastal cities. Over time, the twisting bodies of New Yangge spread across China, becoming a symbol of revolutionary ideals that promoted egalitarianism and placed peasants at the center of a new vision of Chinese modernity (figure 3).

New Yangge was not universally supported, even by artists who considered themselves revolutionary. Because it embodied movement habits of the rural poor, many urban intellectuals were repulsed by the visceral form of yangge choreography. In his study of revolutionary theater in China during the 1940s, Brian DeMare recounts the story of Han Bing, an urban actress who moved to Yan'an during the Japanese invasions but experienced difficulty adjusting to the new performance culture, especially its emphasis on village characters and rural performance styles. According to DeMare, "the real hurdles [for Han Bing] were *yangge* dance and drama. Like the many urbanites that saw *yangge* as ugly, Han Bing looked down on this folk form as low-class and crude."⁹⁰ The crudeness that made urban elites like Han Bing uncomfortable, however, was exactly what gave New Yangge its power as a political statement from the perspective of Mao and his followers. To perform yangge—marching down a village street to the sound of gongs and drums, bouncing up and down and twisting to the beat of the common people—was, for urban elites, to be stripped of the bodily marks of education, cosmopolitanism, and sophistication that separated them from the rural masses. In yangge dramas, traditional hierarchies were reversed, making peasants the heroes. For urban artists like Han Bing, to "twist yangge" meant following the communist dictum to "become one with the masses." Meanwhile, for many peasants and folk performers, it meant learning to see oneself as an agent of revolutionary social change.⁹¹

While New Yangge was taking off in Yan'an, artists who remained in the coastal cities took other approaches to wartime dance culture. Wu Xiaobang, the early importer of Western modern dance from Japan, was one of many Chinese elites who sought alternatives to the local performance aesthetics represented by the New Yangge movement. Wu had grown up under the name Wu Zupei in a wealthy Han family in Suzhou, was educated through the university level in China, and, in 1929, moved to Japan to pursue further study.⁹² During his early trips to Japan between 1929 and 1934, Wu began studying ballet and Western modern dance with Japanese teachers.⁹³ By 1931 Wu had changed his name to Xiaobang, based on the Chinese transliteration of the name of his favorite composer, Frédéric Chopin.⁹⁴ In September 1935, at the age of twenty-nine, Wu gave his first public dance concert in Shanghai, presenting a set of eleven solo works that featured the ballet and Western modern dance forms he had studied in Tokyo.⁹⁵ Photographs in a promotional spread show Wu performing barefoot in a series of poses designed to express different emotions: loss, pain, struggle, disappointment, joy, sadness, and hope (figure 4). According to the description, the dances were set to music by European composers Chopin, Debussy, and Dussek. The headline reads "Gentleman Wu Xiaobang Performs Western Dance Poses."⁹⁶ In one image, of a dance set to Chopin's *Fantaisie-Impromptu*, Wu stands in a belted jacket with legs exposed, standing in what resembles a ballet *passé* with his arms reaching up and forward. In another, of a dance set to Chopin's *Funeral March*, Wu appears in a long black gown with his head thrown back and his spine arched, palms raised as if cupping his heart as an offering to the sky. The accompanying text states that Wu hoped to import Western concert dance to China, as the first step toward developing China's new concert dance.

During the wartime period, Wu continued to envision himself as a conduit for Western dance approaches, which he adapted to China's wartime culture.⁹⁷ In a short interview published in 1937, Wu described the dance style he practiced as "New Dance" *(xinxing wuyong),* using the Japanese neologism *buyō* (in Chinese, *wuyong).*⁹⁸ New Dance, Wu argued, had roots in the United States and Europe: "The

FIGURE 4. Wu Xiaobang in "Funeral March." Published in *Shidai* 8, no. 6 (1935): 12. Photographer: Wan Shi. Reproduction provided by the Chinese Periodical Full-text Database (1911–1949), Quan Guo Bao Kan Suo Yin (CNBKSY), Shanghai Library.

genesis of 'New Dance' was initiated by [the American Isadora] Duncan, then Germany's [Rudolf] Laban originated a new kind of theory, and Germany's Mary Wigman was the one to put 'New Dance' into practice," the interview recounted.[99] Between 1937 and 1941, Wu traveled extensively across southern China, promoting his New Dance in Nanjing, Nanchang, Huizhou (Anhui), Chongqing, Guiyang, Guilin, Changsha, Yangzhou, and Qujiang (Guangdong).[100] During this time, he also periodically returned to Shanghai, and in 1939 he apparently made a brief trip to Hong Kong.[101] Around 1938 Wu spent two months in a village in Huizhou (in Anhui, a relatively poor part of eastern China) and composed a southern drama called "Sending Him to the Front Lines." However, Wu writes that "Although the effect of the performance was positive, many folk artists *(yiren)* did not approve of this method."[102] Thus, after a brief experiment with local form, Wu returned to New Dance. In 1939 Wu returned to Shanghai and began working with a group of students at the China-France Theater School, several of whom had experience with Western-style spoken drama and ballet.[103] Under Wu's direction, they staged a forty-five-minute dance drama called *Poppy Flowers (Yingsu hua)*.[104] While the production had patriotic themes appropriate to the new wartime period and told a leftist story focused on the heroism of Chinese peasants, it does not appear to have employed local dance forms. There is no extant recording of the production, but photographs suggest a European aesthetic, including peasants dressed in white babushkas and flowered aprons and choreography borrowing from ballet and European modern dance. In one image, six dancers playing female peasants stand on the balls of their feet with their torsos erect, arms reaching with palms upward and faces tilted toward the sky. In another, dancers pose with one hand on their hips and the other pointing forward, while others raise their fists in defiance.[105]

In both his prewar and his wartime writings, Wu conceptualized China's local culture as old and backward and Western culture as new and progressive, reproducing the logic of colonial modernity popular among Chinese intellectuals who supported the Westernizing strand of May Fourth–era thought.[106] Before the war, in 1935, Wu's promotional materials had stated, "The dance techniques of Chinese old theater . . . can also be called Chinese dance. However, we all know that the inheritance of these dances does not suit the current society, so we need to create new Chinese dance."[107] This conception of local culture as old reappeared in a 1939 essay, in which Wu derided what he considered the outdated training techniques used in Fuliancheng, a famous school for Peking opera: "The entertainers who grow up in [Fuliancheng]—how could they match the performance techniques needed by modern people!" Wu writes.[108] In 1940, in an essay titled "Chinese dance" *(Zhongguo wuyong)*, Wu conceded that "Chinese dance must have a close connection to its own history."[109] However, when discussing what this would mean, he made it clear that he did not believe such a connection should be predicated on the study of local performance forms. Wu's negative view of local dance culture is expressed clearly when he asserts, "In our own garden, we cannot find even one dance tree. . ... In China people crowd around magicians, streetwalkers, bodyguards, and boxing teachers with open mouths, applauding those who have gone to the *jianghu*."[110] Wu proposed the idea of "national consciousness" (*minzu yishi*), which served implicitly as an alternative to the concept of national form. For Wu, national consciousness "includes all of the citizens' life" and thus has no specific aesthetic form. In this way, Wu called on artists such as himself to lay claim to being "national" without having to perform local movement such as New Yangge, which they regarded as culturally below them.[111] In 1941 Wu directly criticized the widespread interest in folk art that had emerged in recent years. Referring to the period from March 1940 to February 1941, Wu wrote, "During this time, the entire art world was surging with the national forms controversy. Many people believed folk forms are the only source for national forms, driving the car in reverse toward the past."[112] This statement directly opposed the New Yangge movement based on Mao's socialist cultural policies promoted at Yan'an. At this time, Wu also undermined the Maoist idea that intellectuals should learn from peasants, by claiming that it was the peasants who needed him, rather than the other way around.[113] As late as 1944, Wu's published writings on dance training continued to advance concepts he had learned in Japan, such as the coordination of breath and tempo and the use of "natural law" (*ziran faze*), a key component of his theory and practice of New Dance.[114]

During the War of Resistance, the CCP's New Yangge and Wu Xiaobang's New Dance represented competing visions of modernity in China's dance field. For the promoters of New Yangge, local rural movements offered the basis for a new approach to Chinese modernity grounded in the culture of the disenfranchised. Applying the Maoist principles of national forms and remolding, CCP-affiliated activists and their peasant collaborators conceived of yangge folk performance as a powerful and dynamic force that could be mobilized to realize visions for a better future, both in terms of building a stronger, more sovereign nation and of reforming society to be more progressive and egalitarian. In their revolutionary vision of cultural development, the New Yangge promoters redefined local peasant culture, formerly something backward or unenlightened, as the only viable path to the future. As Chang-tai Hung observed, "By putting the common people on center stage, Chinese Communists glorified the power of the masses . . . and argued that . . . the future of China lay not in the coastal cities, but in the interior, in villages."[115] In this new vision of China's future as expressed through dance, local folk performance was recast from something inherently old that holds China back from modernization to the essential foundation for building China's new, modern culture.

In contrast to the proponents of New Yangge, Wu Xiaobang, through his practice of New Dance, argued that China's dance activities, in order to become modern, must depart from local performance forms. Inheriting ideas of the May Fourth era, Wu believed in a strict division between tradition and modernity, in which he associated Chinese culture with the "traditional" and Western culture with the "modern." Applying this logic, Wu insisted that xiqu was old and out of date, even though it was, in fact, a site of constant innovation and immense popularity during the period in which he was writing.[116] In his reflections on the relationship between Western and Chinese performance practices, Wu reproduced Eurocentric and racist views underlying both May Fourth modernization theory and Western modern dance discourse. Thus, although Wu located the origins of New Dance in the United States and Europe, he believed in the universal validity of this dance form, arguing that it was better suited to the expression of Chinese modernity than any performance form that already existed in China. Like many white Euro-American modern dance critics of the time, Wu also clearly distinguished his New Dance from popular dance genres associated with African American culture, such as jazz and tap dance.[117] Whereas Wu described these other genres as morally corrupt and harmful—often citing their perceived excessive sexuality as the reason—the New Dance that he promoted was, in his words, universally "positive" and "healthy."[118] "In any society, dance must go along with the rhythm of contemporary life," Wu wrote, implying that New Dance alone was capable of fully expressing contemporary experience.[119] This view fundamentally clashed with Mao's notion, applied in New Yangge, that Western culture should not be used as a wholesale replacement for local practices and that modern Chinese culture should thus "have its own form." Dai arrived in China in 1941, just as the national forms debates were at their peak. Given her family's cultural preferences for European culture and her professional dance training in Western ballet and modern dance, it seemed likely that she might side with Wu in the ongoing debates. However, she took a different stance.

FROM MARGIN TO CENTER: THE EMERGENCE OF A NATIONAL DANCE MOVEMENT

Between 1941 and 1946, Dai Ailian developed an entirely new choreographic repertoire based on her experiences in China. Exemplified by works such as "The Mute Carries the Cripple" and "Yao Drum," this repertoire set out a third direction for Chinese concert dance that differed from both the New Yangge and the New Dance movements. Ultimately, her approach had more in common with New Yangge, as both were grounded in the study of local aesthetics and sought to develop a new vision of Chinese modernity based on folk and vernacular forms. However, through its incorporation of a much broader range of ethnic and regional culture, Dai's repertoire expanded the New Yangge model to find a path that could represent new and broader understanding of Chinese culture. Due to the unusual conditions of wartime and her personal interests as a dance researcher, Dai spent her early years in China in various locations across the southwest, including Guangxi, Guizhou, Chongqing, and what is today Sichuan. Traditionally, these areas were considered geographically and culturally marginal in the Chinese intellectual imagination.

However, Dai's choreographies reimagined them as the foundation for a new Chinese cultural identity. Because Dai's repertoires highlighted the culture of non-Han groups and places imagined to be located at the geographical margins of China, the name initially given to her early Chinese dance repertoire was "Frontier Dance" (*bianjiang wu*). By the end of the 1940s, however, these dances represented a national dance movement that would replace New Dance and combine with New Yangge as the basis for a new form: Chinese dance.

In the early spring of 1941, Dai and her husband, Ye, left Hong Kong for Macao and from there entered the Chinese mainland. Traveling by a combination of boat, public bus, truck, bicycle, and on foot, they eventually made it to Guilin, a city located in Guangxi about halfway between Hong Kong and Chongqing, where they were headed.[120] Although today Guilin is known largely as a tourist destination with picturesque rock formations, rivers, and rice paddy–filled landscapes, during the war it was a major cultural center due to the influx of artists and intellectuals fleeing the Japan-occupied coastal cities. As Pingchao Zhu has demonstrated, in the early 1940s Guilin was China's biggest hub for experimental theater, where leading dramatists such as Ouyang Yuqian (1889–1962) had taken an interest in Gui opera, a local xiqu form performed in northern Guangxi dialect.[121] In Guilin, Dai saw performances of Gui opera staged by drama reformers but performed by local artists, one of which was "The Mute and the Cripple."[122] Dai sought out the performer of the piece, the famous Gui opera actress Fang Zhaoyuan, and studied with her, laying a foundation for the work Dai would premiere in Chongqing a few years later.

After their stay in Guilin, Dai and Ye went on to Chongqing, at the time the center of the KMT-led Nationalist government and China's wartime capital. They made it to Chongqing around early April 1941, just in time to attend the wedding of Wu Xiaobang and his second wife, Sheng Jie (1917–2017), a former student from the China-France Theater School.[123] That June, Dai gave a joint performance in Chongqing with Wu and Sheng, in which she performed her first new choreography since arriving in China: "Nostalgia" (Si xiang qu), a solo dance set to the eponymous violin solo by Chinese composer Ma Sicong, which was inspired by a Suiyuan folk tune.[124] Dai performed the dance in a Chinese peasant-style costume and expressed the longing for home felt by Chinese war refugees driven out of their homes by invading armies.[125] In addition to "Nostalgia," Dai also performed in a duet with Sheng Jie titled "Joining Forces" (He li) choreographed by Wu.[126] Due to a health complication that required Dai to return to Hong Kong for surgery in the early fall of 1941, she and Ye left Chongqing temporarily and then made a second overland journey from Hong Kong to Chongqing in early 1942.[127] During this second trip, the couple spent about two months visiting Miao (a.k.a. Hmong) and Yao communities in Guizhou Province, where Dai gained her inspiration to create "Yao Drum."[128]

Between 1942 and 1946, Dai spent most of her time in Chongqing, where she focused on building a cohort of students, conducting dance research, learning to speak and read Chinese, and developing her new repertoire. Dai was hired to teach dance at three educational institutions during this period: the National Opera School in 1942–43, the Mount Bi National Social Education Academy in 1943–44, and the Yucai School in 1944–46. During the summer of 1944, she also co-taught a six-week dance summer program.[129] During this time, Dai's spoken and written Chinese improved significantly, and by 1946 she was able to converse in basic everyday Mandarin and read and write some characters.[130] Working with her students, Dai set up two dance research collectives in Chongqing: the Chinese Dance Art Society (Zhongguo wudao yishu she) and the Chinese Folk Music and Dance Research Society Dance Group (Zhongguo minjian yuewu yanjiu she wuyongzu).[131] In 1944 Dai created a series of new works, including "The Mute Carries the Cripple" and "Yao Drum." In June of 1945, she left Chongqing with her husband, Ye, and her student Peng Song (1916–2016), an expert in folk songs who also worked at the Yucai School, to conduct further field research. They initially arrived in Chengdu, where Dai and Ye stayed for a few months with the painter Zhang Daqian, while Peng conducted research in Jiarong and Qiang communities.[132] Later that summer, Peng returned to Chongqing, and Dai and Ye traveled alone to Kangding, located in what is now central Sichuan Province, on the border of what was historically the Kham region of Tibet. Dai stayed in the home of a Tibetan trader from Batang (Ba'an) and studied dance with Tibetans of various backgrounds living in Kangding. Altogether, Dai notated eight Tibetan dances, seven from Batang and one from Garze.[133] In December 1945, Dai and Ye returned to Chongqing.[134]

The culmination of these years of work occurred in the spring of 1946, when a major performance in Chongqing launched Dai and her dancing into the national spotlight. The *Frontier Music and Dance Plenary (Bianjiang yinyue wudao dahui)*, which opened at the Chongqing Youth Hall on March 6, 1946, was a gala-style concert performance featuring fourteen dance, music, and theater works that represented six ethnic groups: Han, Qiang, Tibetan, Uyghur, Yao, and Yi.[135] Dances varied in scale from solos to group works, with themes ranging from religious to romantic. The ethnically mixed cast included Dai and her students at the China Folk Dance Research Group and Yucai School Music Group, most of whom were Han, as well as Tibetan and Uyghur performers from the Frontier School Tibetan Students Group, the Xinjiang Community Association, and the Frontier School Tibetan Students Music and Dance Group. Two female performers from Tibet also participated, as did members of the Central University Frontier Research Group. Of the fourteen pieces presented, seven were new choreographies Dai had created based on her experiences in China. These included her solo "The Mute Carries the Cripple"; a trio version of "Yao Drum"; a Yi-themed group dance, "Luoluo Love Song" (Luoluo qingge); a Buddhism-themed group dance, "Amitābha" (Mituo fu); a Tibetan group dance performed with long sleeves, "Ba'an *xianzi*"; a Uyghur-themed romantic duet, "Kanba'erhan"; and a Uyghur-themed group dance, "Dance Song of Youth" (Qingchun wuqu). Two works were created by Dai's student Peng Song: a duet, "Duan Gong Exorcises Ghosts"

FIGURE 5. Tibetan students performing in Dai Ailian's "Ba'an *xianzi.*" Published in *Jin ri huakan*, no. 2 (1946): 3. Photographer unknown. Reproduction provided by the Chinese Periodical Full-text Database (1911–1949), Quan Guo Bao Kan Suo Yin (CNBKSY), Shanghai Library.

(Duan gong qugui), based on Qiang exorcism rituals, and a Tibetan group dance, "Jiarong Drinking Party" (Jiarong jiuhui), which featured dancers drinking through straws from a large wine vat and ended with a climax of group spins. The remaining five works were contributed by the Tibetan and Uyghur performers: a Tibetan dance, "Spring Outing" (Chun you); a Lhasa-style Tibetan "Tap Dance" (Tita wu); two excerpts of Tibetan opera, "Auspicious Dance" (Jixiang wu) and "Goddess Yi Zhu" (Yi Zhu tiannü); and an improvisational Uyghur dance. A highlight of the evening, according to one critic, was Dai's choreography "Ba'an *xianzi,*" based on her fieldwork in Kangding, which was danced by a group of Tibetan students (figure 5).[136] The work combined six different styles of Tibetan song and dance into a single piece, showing how dances from everyday life could be adapted effectively for the concert stage. The *Plenary* was extremely popular, attracting an audience of over two thousand on its first night. Journalists uniformly described it as "unprecedented," and one asserted that it "has created a new epoch for the future of China's new dance."[137]

There were a number of reasons, political as well as artistic, that the *Plenary* created such a stir in Chongqing and garnered major attention in the national media. The concept of the frontier has a long history in Chinese thought. However, its emergence as a distinctly spatial concept central to national politics was a product of China's early twentieth-century transformation from a premodern empire into a modern nation-state. As James Leibold explains:

> The very concept of Zhongguo[138] presupposes the existence of other, peripheral states or civilizations, and thus it is not surprising that the Chinese term bianjiang can be traced back as far as the fourth century BCE, where the *Zuo zhuan* describes it as an intermediary zone between two sovereign states. But only during the Qing period did the term become common in state discourse with its modern connotation of a linear and exclusionary boundary *(bianjie)* represented on Qing and European maps. Unlike the indistinct waifang (exterior) of old, the bianjiang was in peril under the new global nation-state system unless the state fully exercised its authority over the frontier. In twentieth-century China, the state constructed thousands of miles of roads, telegraph lines, and, most important, railway lines, gradually projecting state power—in the form of its military, political, educational, and economic institutions—into the furthest corners of the nation.[139]

From the 1920s onward, deliberations regarding China's "frontier" and its many non-Han communities were critical components of the political discourses of both China's rival political parties, the CCP and the KMT (a.k.a. Nationalists). Xiaoyuan Liu uses the term "ethnopolitics" to describe these deliberations.[140] During the 1940s, these ethnopolitics surrounding China's frontier dealt typically with territories such as Mongolia, Manchuria, Xinjiang, Tibet, and the southwest—all of which had been part of the Qing Empire (1644–1911) and were claimed by the KMT-led Republic of China (1912–1949) but nevertheless included large communities who spoke and wrote non-Chinese languages and were seen by many as being culturally distinct from China's ethnic majority, now identified as "Han."[141]

A key concept at the center of China's wartime ethnopolitics was the idea of the *Zhonghua minzu* (Chinese nation). Like many terms now fundamentally embedded in contemporary Chinese cultural and political discourse, *Zhonghua minzu* was a modern neologism developed around the turn of the twentieth century through Chinese intellectuals' translingual engagements with emerging discourses about race, ethnicity, and the modern nation-state.[142] The CCP and the KMT each developed their own changing definitions of *Zhonghua minzu,* with the KMT tending to emphasize its unity as a single race or nationality and the CCP tending to recognize the nationality status of non-Han groups. However, during the War of Resistance against Japan of 1937–45, the united front policy between the KMT and the CCP pushed the two parties to find a consensus position that lasted through the war. Xiaoyuan Liu writes:

> By the time of World War II, the two parties' presentation of the "Chinese nation" shared these features: The "Chinese nation," or *zhonghua minzu,* occurred in history long before the modern era; the Han was the magnetic nucleus of the

"Chinese nation"; the formation of the "Chinese nation" involved other ethnic groups, named "clans" by the KMT but "nationalities" by the CCP, that had
either assimilated into or amalgamated with the Han; the official boundaries of
the Republic of China demarcated the territorial domain of the *zhonghua minzu,*
which included all the borderlands inhabited by the non-Han groups; the *zhonghua minzu* was the common political identity for all members of the Republic of
China; equality, not right to secession, should be the ultimate goal pursued by all
ethnic groups in China.[143]

With the end of the War of Resistance against Japan in 1945, the tenuous alliance
between the CCP and the KMT came to an end, leading to the outbreak of full-scale
civil war by the end of 1946, along with the resumption of competitive ethnopolitical
positioning on both sides. Dai's *Plenary* occurred at the moment of this transition
period, when the meaning of *Zhonghua minzu* and the future of China's "frontiers"
were once again coming to the fore as a point of national contestation.

In terms of the dance works she presented on stage and her theorization of
Chinese dance as an amalgamation of Han and non-Han performance practices,
Dai's *Plenary* clearly employed dance as a form of wartime ethnopolitics. At this
moment of transition, however, it was unclear exactly which, if either, side of the
political spectrum the *Plenary* was intended to support. Because it took place in
Chongqing and received support from the local KMT-affiliated government and
frontier schools, some interpreted the *Plenary* as a demonstration of the Nationalists' emphasis on national unity.[144] The use of the term "frontier music and dance"
in the naming of the *Plenary* also linked it to a longer history of performances
employed in the cultural deployment of KMT frontier politics. Events with similar
names had been held in the KMT capital in Nanjing in 1936 and in Nationalist-
controlled Chengdu and Guiyang in 1945.[145] Nationalist use of this model continued in December of 1946, when a "Frontier Song and Dance Appreciation
Performance" was staged in Nanjing in conjunction with meetings of the National
Assembly, to sold-out audiences.[146] As Ya-ping Chen has demonstrated, the KMT-
led government continued to employ Frontier Dance, renamed *minzu wudao* but
still enacted by some of Dai's former students, as a tool for projecting authority
over the Chinese mainland after its move to Taiwan in 1949.[147]

The Nationalists were not alone in using dance in frontier politics, however,
and the *Plenary* also aligned with parallel activities that were emerging in CCP-
occupied territories at the same time. In the spring of 1946, coinciding roughly with
the *Plenary,* a group of cultural activists from Yan'an had moved to Zhangjiakou,
in what is now northwestern Hebei province, where they prepared to establish
the first CCP-sponsored, ethnic minority–focused music and dance ensemble, the
Inner Mongolia Cultural Work Troupe (Neimenggu wengongtuan), which later
became the Inner Mongolia Song and Dance Ensemble. The troupe was formally
established on April 1, 1946, with a membership comprising artists of diverse
ethnic backgrounds and a goal of developing revolutionary performances that

focused on themes and aesthetic forms of non-Han groups in what is now Inner Mongolia.[148] Among those involved in the project was Wu Xiaobang, a new arrival in Yan'an in 1945, who gave dance classes to troupe members and collaborated with local artists to choreograph several Mongol-themed dance works for the troupe's repertoire.[149] By this time, Wu had made the political decision to join forces with the CCP culture activists from Yan'an, despite his artistic protestations over the issue of national form.[150] The establishment of the Inner Mongolia Cultural Work Troupe was important for ethnopolitics, because it illustrated CCP efforts to ally with nationality movements. It preceded the establishment of the Inner Mongolia Autonomous Region in 1947, a symbol of nationality recognition under the CCP.

Dai's personal politics were also complex. Although Dai was based in Chongqing, the seat of the wartime KMT-led Nationalist government, she maintained continued contact with the Communist movement. Given Dai's family background (Eugene Chen was a longtime political opponent of Nationalist leader Chiang Kai-shek), her prior work with the left-leaning CCC in London, and her close ties to Song Qingling in Hong Kong, it seems likely that her political sympathies were with the CCP underground, not with the Nationalist government. In her oral history, Dai recalls that while living in England, she had read Edgar Snow's *Red Star over China*, which inspired her to want to move to the CCP base at Yan'an.[151] While living in Chongqing, Dai and Ye met several times with high-ranking CCP leaders Zhou Enlai and Deng Yingchao, who shared with them knowledge about New Yangge and other Yan'an cultural activities. According to Dai's oral history, Dai and Ye reportedly told Zhou and Deng of their desire to move to Yan'an but were advised that their contributions were more effective in Chongqing.[152] Dai remembers that the Yucai School, where Dai worked from the fall of 1944, was located next door to the Chongqing Eighth Route Army Office, an administrative center for the local CCP. Dai recalls that she often accompanied CCP members who worked there to see performances, including, in 1945, a New Yangge drama presented by an ensemble from Yan'an.[153] Yucai School founder Tao Xingzhi (1891–1946), a key supporter of Dai's Frontier Dance activities, was blacklisted by the Nationalist government and died suddenly in late 1946, possibly because of KMT persecution.[154]

From an artistic perspective, the *Plenary* embodied a new direction for China's dance development whose impact would ultimately outlive the wartime era and make it a foundation for the emergence of Chinese dance under the auspices of the socialist state. Although the label "frontier music and dance" linked the *Plenary* to earlier activities that used this term, Dai's realization was different from its earlier uses. Whereas "frontier dance" had previously been regarded primarily as a medium of education and cultural exchange for Han audiences to learn about non-Han culture, Dai reconceived it as an artistic project aimed at developing shared forms of cultural expression to which Han and non-Han forms and people both contributed. Dai's choreography included both Han choreographies (such as "The Mute Carries the Cripple") and non-Han choreographies (such as

"Ba'an *xianzi*"). Moreover, it featured performances by Han and non-Han dancers together on the same stage. For Dai, new choreographies inspired by Uyghur, Yao, or Tibetan sources were not expressions of cultural difference used to facilitate interethnic understanding; rather, like choreographies based on local Han sources such as Gui opera, these were all essential building blocks for what she envisioned as the same new national modern dance form, what she called Chinese dance.

Dai outlined this new vision in a lecture, presented at the start of the *Plenary*, titled "The First Step in Developing Chinese Dance."[155] In it, Dai called for the creation of a new form of concert dance, what she called in the lecture both "Chinese dance" *(Zhongguo wudao)* and "Chinese modern dance" *(Zhongguo xiandai wu)*, on the basis of existing dance practices from all across China. As discussed in the lecture, Dai argued that Chinese dance should have three defining characteristics, corresponding to the three principles of Chinese dance that I outline in the introduction. First, Dai argued that Chinese dance should use movement vocabularies adapted from local sources, what I call kinesthetic nationalism. Second, she argued that Chinese dance should take inspiration from all existing local performance in China, from Han and non-Han sources in every geographic region, what I call ethnic and spatial inclusivity. And third, she argued that Chinese dance should be new and modern while also learning from the past, or what I call dynamic inheritance.

Dai felt that form, not content, was the key feature that should distinguish Chinese dance from other dance styles. To develop this new form, as Dai envisioned it, would thus require researching all of China's existing performance practices, analyzing them, and using them to inspire new concert choreography. Here, Dai's idea largely followed the understanding of "national form" outlined in Mao's speeches and modeled in the New Yangge movement. However, it had one important difference from New Yangge. That is, rather than simply revolutionizing traditional hierarchies based on ideas of class, education, and urban/rural distinction, Dai's vision also sought to overturn hierarchies based on ideas of ethnicity and geography. New Yangge had treated northern Han culture as the sole foundation for its new national form. Dai envisioned a national dance form that would take inspiration from the existing practices of all China's ethnic groups and regions. Explaining this process as she envisioned it unfolding, Dai wrote, "If we want to develop Chinese dance, as the first step we must collect dance materials from all nationalities around the country, then broadly synthesize them and add development."[156] The dances Dai presented in the *Plenary* program clearly illustrated this idea, since they represented many different ethnic groups and geographic regions, placing special emphasis on southern and non-Han forms. The *Plenary* also highlighted Buddhist culture, which, though integrated into Chinese religious life, was nonnative in origin. Buddhism originated in India and developed local forms in China over the first millennium CE. Although considered one of the "three main religions" of the Han, Buddhism also had deep and culturally distinct historical traditions among non-Han groups in China's border regions, such as Tibetans and

Dai in the southwest and Mongols in the north. It was also a major component of the cosmopolitan culture of China's northwest, where Buddhism interwove historically with the cultural traditions of Islam and religions of Central Asia.

Following Mao's idea of "national forms," Dai regarded Chinese dance as something that did not yet exist but, with effort, could be created. The *Plenary* represented her own initial effort toward its creation, hence the lecture's title, "A First Step. . .." In the lecture, Dai offered a variety of interpretations of the cultural and historical relations among existing dance materials in China, and she explained that she saw Han and non-Han religious practices, theater, and folk dance all as legitimate sources for the new Chinese dance choreography. She also speculated that the modern dances of some non-Han communities, such as Tibetans, retained the sophisticated dance styles of the Tang dynasty, which Dai and others regarded as a historical peak of Chinese dance culture, and which she argued had also been preserved in some modern Japanese dances. While some Chinese critics found Dai's ideas controversial, the debates and responses they sparked launched important conversations that would continue in the Chinese dance field for years to come.[157]

Dai's new Frontier Dance repertoire was not alone in its rethinking of national forms along these lines. Her new choreography, ways of staging non-Han performance, and the ideas she promoted in her lecture resonated with similar activities being carried out by other artists working in parallel in other parts of China. As already mentioned, a group of CCP-affiliated artists from Yan'an were exploring similar approaches with their establishment of the Inner Mongolia Cultural Work Troupe in early 1946. However, similar projects had also been launched earlier in Xinjiang and Yunnan, some led by non-Han artists. In Xinjiang, for example, a Frontier Dance movement was being launched with works that were created, taught, and performed by a Uyghur dancer named Qemberxanim, the person who likely inspired Dai's Uyghur dance "Kanba'erhan" featured in the Chongqing *Plenary* (figure 6).[158] Like Dai, Qemberxanim had a diasporic background and learned dance abroad before she launched her career in China in the early 1940s. Born around 1914 to a Muslim Uyghur family in Kashgar, Qemberxanim had moved as a child with her parents, who were migrant laborers, to the Soviet Union, growing up in parts of what are today Kazakhstan, Kyrgyzstan, and Uzbekistan.[159] Around the time she completed primary school, Qemberxanim was recruited to a professional dance school in Tashkent led by the world-famous Armenian Uzbek dancer Tamara Khanum (a.k.a. Tamara Khonim, 1906–1991).[160] After completing her training, Qemberxanim worked as a professional dancer in the Uzbek Song and Dance Theater, and in the late 1930s, she was recruited to study in Moscow, where she performed at the Kremlin. In early 1942, Qemberxanim relocated back to Xinjiang, where she worked in Dihua (Ürümqi) developing a new dance repertoire based in local dance forms, especially Uyghur dance. After winning several regional dance competitions in Xinjiang, Qemberxanim gained national fame in late 1947 and early 1948, when she starred in a "frontier song and dance" tour by the Xinjiang Youth Ensemble that visited major cities across the Chinese mainland

قمبرخانيم

٥ 罕爾巴康 ↑

FIGURE 6. Qemberxanim on Xinjiang Youth Ensemble China tour. Published in *Yiwen huabao* 2, no. 5 (1947): 2. Photographers: Lang Jingshan et al. Reproduction provided by the Chinese Periodical Full-text Database (1911–1949), Quan Guo Bao Kan Suo Yin (CNBKSY), Shanghai Library.

and Taiwan.[161] Dai and Qemberxanim would meet, most likely for the first time, when this group visited Shanghai in December of 1947.[162] It is unclear how they would have spoken to one another though, since Qemberxanim's primary languages were Uyghur, Uzbek, and Russian, and her knowledge of Chinese was even more limited than Dai's. As discussed in the next chapter, Qemberxanim would, like Dai, become a leading figure in the development of Chinese dance in the early PRC.

Starting in 1945, another parallel project was also happening in Yunnan, led by Liang Lun (b. 1921), another dancer who would go on to play an important role in early PRC dance. Liang was born and raised in Foshan, Guangdong, making his mother tongue, like Dai's paternal grandfather, Cantonese. Like Qemberxanim, Liang had lived abroad when his parents moved to Vietnam as migrant laborers; however, they had moved back to Foshan when Liang was still a toddler.[163] In the mid-1930s, a teenage Liang became involved in amateur drama and singing activities, and after the war with Japan broke out in 1937, he joined an anti-Japanese street theater group. In 1942, while studying theater at the Guangzhou Provincial Art Academy in Qujiang, Liang was exposed to dance for the first time through workshops taught by Wu Xiaobang and Sheng Jie. After moving to Guangxi in 1944, Liang began creating his own dance choreography, collaborating with a woman who would later become his wife, Chen Yunyi (b. 1924). In the spring of 1945, when the Japanese armies reached Guangxi, Liang and Chen fled farther west to Kunming. In Kunming, they founded the Chinese Dance Research Association (Zhonghua wudao yanjiuhui), through which they taught dance courses and staged original dance works, many of which drew on local folk performance such as Guangdong folk dances and Yunnan flower lantern *(huadeng)* theater.[164] In July of 1945, at the time Dai was conducting field research in Sichuan, Liang traveled to Yi communities in the Mount Gui area southeast of Kunming. Based on this research, Liang began to create choreography on Yi themes, and in May 1946, he helped organize a performance in Kunming known as the Yi Compatriots Music and Dance Performance (Yibao yinyue wuyonghui), featuring Yi music and dance performed by Yi artists.[165] Like Dai's *Plenary* in Chongqing one month earlier, the *Yi Compatriots* performance was a major event that attracted the attention of leading intellectuals and artists in Kunming and beyond.[166]

Like Dai and Qemberxanim, Liang took his new dances on tour in the late 1940s. In the summer of 1946, Liang and his friends were facing Nationalist persecution in Kunming and fled for Hong Kong, where they became the first Chinese dance group to perform the new "frontier music and dance" outside China.[167] In December 1946, Liang and Chen would join the China Music, Dance, and Drama Society (Zhongguo gewuju yishe) and begin an influential two-year tour of Thailand, Singapore, and Malaya (Malaysia), during which they helped promote Frontier Dance and New Yangge among overseas Sinophone communities, while also studying local dance styles and created new works inspired by them.[168] In 1947, while on tour, Liang published an essay titled "The Problem of Making Dance Chinese," in which he echoed Dai's vision for a new national style of Chinese concert dance derived from local performance sources. Like Dai, Liang saw non-Han sources as a crucial foundation, together with Han sources, for the creation of this new form. As discussed in the introduction, Liang also located his and Dai's innovations in a longer history of modernist dance experiments in China that also included the earlier works of Liang's teacher, Wu Xiaobang. Within this discussion, Liang clearly identified the Frontier Dance activities of the mid-1940s as the correct path for China's dance development. He saw New Dance and other styles derived from Western modern dance as part of the past, whereas the future was in the creation of new dance forms in a distinctively "Chinese style" that would take inspiration from local theater, religious ritual, and folk performance of Han and non-Han communities.[169]

After their successful performances in Chongqing, Dai and her students took Frontier Dance on the road, first to universities around Chongqing and then to Shanghai, where their art of the margins enthralled a city once considered China's culture center. In a published oral history, Peng Song recalls how, following the *Plenary*, he and other members of Dai's group were invited to teach on university campuses in the Chongqing area, launching a Frontier Dance student movement that soon spread across the country.[170] In August of 1946, Dai traveled to Shanghai and gave a solo tour there just before she and Ye left for the United States.[171] Dai's Shanghai program, though it included some ballet and modern dance, was heavily weighted toward works from the Chongqing *Plenary*. Moreover, the program was arranged to show a developmental progression that started with ballet and Western modern dance and ended in Dai's vision of Chinese dance.[172] In the spring of 1947, while Dai was with her husband in the United States, Peng Song led a group of Dai's former students from the Yucai School to Shanghai, where they gave their own sold-out shows later that fall.[173] Dai and Ye returned to China from the United States in late October of 1947, and Dai begin teaching at the China Music and Dance Academy (Zhongguo yuewu xueyuan), established by Peng and her other students in Shanghai.[174]

By the end of 1946, Dai had become China's most popular dancer (to be upstaged a year later by Qemberxanim), and her name was synonymous with a new path for Chinese concert dance.[175] As seen through the responses of contemporary reviewers, Dai's Frontier Dance had brought to the Shanghai stage something new, namely, concert choreography that reflected the local heritage of China in an ethnically and regionally diverse manner that was linked closely to folk culture. Critics expressed this idea in a number of ways in their 1946 reviews of Dai's Shanghai performances. "This performance gave Shanghai people their first lesson in Chinese dance," one critic wrote.[176] "This is art that comes from the people and touches the root," described another critic.[177] Others echoed: "This is finally China's 'own dance'";[178] "What Dai presents is our own content and form";[179] and "[S]he found Chinese nationality art, our own art, and brought it to Shanghai."[180] Another summed it up: "Frontier Dance makes us proud.... It is ours."[181] Although critics recognized the influence of Western dance on Dai's choreography, they distinguished her approach from the introduction of Western dance approaches associated with New Dance. "She wasn't satisfied with introducing foreign dance to China," one critic wrote.[182] Another elaborated, "[H]er greatest achievement is making Western dance serve China's introduction of national forms."[183] Indicating this difference, none of the critics reviewing Dai's dances called them New Dance *(xinxing wuyong)*. Rather, they came up with new labels that expressed the fact that they saw this style as an entirely new approach, but for which there was yet no standard term. The labels they used included "new Chinese dance" *(xin Zhongguo wudao)*,[184] "Chinese national form dance" *(Zhongguo minzu xingshi wudao)*,[185] "national shared forms" *(minzu gongtong xingshi)*,[186] "national standard art" *(minzu benwei de yishu)*,[187] "China standard dance system" *(Zhongguo benwei de wudao tixi)*,[188] and "Chinese national dance" *(Zhongguo minzu wuyong)*.[189] Soon these diverse labels would converge into the name Dai herself had used: Chinese dance.

CONCLUSION: ASSEMBLING THE NATION

During the War of Resistance, and to a lesser extent the Chinese Civil War, new ways of using dance to explore modern Chinese culture had emerged across China, largely in regional movements that took different directions depending on local conditions and the people involved. In Yan'an and north China, Communist-affiliated artists and intellectuals developed New Yangge, grounded in the adaptation of popular folk performance of rural Han communities in those areas. In Shanghai and other places across the southeast, Wu Xiaobang developed New Dance, premised on introducing and adapting Western dance styles imported to China by way of Japan. In Chongqing and other places across the west and southwest, Dai Ailian, Qemberxanim, Liang Lun, and others developed Frontier Dance, based on the adaptation of regional forms of Han and non-Han performance from remote parts of China. While the circulation of people and print media during the wars generated some communication among these various projects, to a large extent they advanced independently. When the wars ended, and the time came to create unified national dance organizations, it was unclear how the different projects would fit together, or even which would prevail as a guiding direction for dance in the new PRC.

The first time that the many dancers and choreographers involved in these different wartime regional projects assembled in a single place was in the summer of 1949, during a CCP-sponsored event held in Beiping, soon to be renamed Beijing and made the new capital. They met there to attend the All-China Literature and Arts Worker Representative Congress, held July 2–19, 1949, along with hundreds of other delegates. Among the dancers in attendance, Dai was the first to arrive in Beiping. She had moved there from Shanghai in February of 1948, when her husband, Ye, was offered a professorship at the Beiping National Art School, and Dai also soon took up teaching positions at local universities.[190] Peng Song arrived in February of 1949, when he and his wife, Ye Ning (b. 1913), also formerly a student of Dai's at the Yucai School, entered the city on foot, dancing as part of a yangge troupe parading with the People's Liberation Army.[191] Liang Lun arrived next, in late April 1949, by boat from Hong Kong. He had returned to Hong Kong from Southeast Asia just a few months earlier, and he arrived in Beiping early to attend the All-China Youth Federation in May.[192] Wu Xiaobang and Sheng Jie were the last to arrive, reaching Beiping in late June 1949, just a few days before the start of the Congress. They had been teaching at the CCP-affiliated Lu Xun Art School in Shenyang, about four hundred miles northeast of Beiping.[193] With them came two other dance delegates representing the CCP-affiliated northeast: Chen Jinqing (1921–1991), a founding member of the Yan'an New Yangge movement, and Hu Guogang (1921–1983), also from Yan'an, who headed the oldest professional People's Liberation Army dance ensemble.

The Congress was a decisive event for the future of China's arts and culture fields. As Brian DeMare writes, "[The Congress] laid the cultural foundations for the emerging PRC order."[194] Party leaders and cultural representatives gave speeches outlining past and future work, and delegates within each field met to make plans for new organizations and projects in their areas. Apart from meetings, the Congress also hosted performances. From June 28 to July 29, a packed festival featured shows by thirty-four ensembles and more than three thousand performers, including spoken drama, new opera, xiqu, music, film, dance, and storytelling.[195] Two of the festival's evening-length events were dedicated to dance, giving many delegates their first view of wartime choreography from across the country.

Frontier Dance, and to a lesser extent New Yangge, dominated the dance performances at the Congress festival. The first of the two, held on July 19, included dances by the Inner Mongolia Cultural Work Troupe, the 166th Division Propaganda Team (a primarily Korean ensemble), and the Lu Xun Art School Dance Class.[196] Their program featured a number of works based on Inner Mongolian and Korean themes, such as Wu Xiaobang's "Hope" (Xiwang), a Mongol-themed female duet, and "Hand drum dance" (Shougu wu), which used the *nongak*, a type of drum used in Korean peasant dance. The program also included works celebrating labor, such as "Farmer Dance" (Nongzuo wu) and "Blacksmith Dance" (Duangong wu).[197] The second dance event, given the name *Frontier Folk Dance Introduction Plenary (Bianjiang minjian wudao jieshao dahui)*, was held on July 26 and was a joint performance featuring works by Dai Ailian and Liang Lun.[198] The show included Dai's "The Mute Carries the Cripple" and "Yao Drum," along with four other works from the 1946 Chongqing *Plenary*.[199] It also included several items from the Frontier Dance repertoire Liang and Chen had developed in Kunming. These included "Five-Mile Pagoda" (Wu li ting), a small dance drama that used Yunnan *huadeng* folk theater elements; "Dancing the Spring Cow"

(Tiao chun niu), a partner dance that employed rural Han folk dance from Guangdong; and "Axi Moon Dance" (Axi tiao yue), a group dance derived from Liang's work with Yi performers. The program also included Dai's "Sale" (Mai), a short dance drama about a couple of war refugees forced by poverty to sell their child, and several additional dances on minority themes.

Through the 1949 summer activities, it became clear that Dai and her vision would likely lead dance activities in the new PRC. Dai's high position was first indicated in March of 1949, when she was selected as one of twelve individuals to represent China's entire arts and culture sphere at the Paris-Prague World Peace Congress later that April.[200] When the All-China Literature and Arts Worker Representative Congress opened in July, Dai was the only dance delegate serving on the ninety-nine-person Congress Chairs Committee.[201] She also gave the only Congress-wide speech representing the dance field.[202] On July 16, a recording of Dai's speech was broadcast over the Beiping Xinhua Radio Station, making her Trinidadian-accented Chinese the first voice many radio listeners would associate with the new form of art known as "dance work" *(wudao gongzuo)*.[203] That same day, selections were announced for delegates to represent China at the Second World Festival of Youth and Students in Budapest; although the program contained none of Dai's choreography, it nevertheless aligned with her artistic vision. The program included two dances in the style of New Yangge—"Waist Drum Dance" (Yaogu wu) and "Great Yangge" (Da yangge)—and two dances in the style of Frontier Dance—Wu Xiaobang's Mongol-themed work "Hope" (Xiwang), performed by two young women of Mongol ethnicity, and Manchu choreographer Jia Zuoguang's self-performed "Pasture Horse" (Muma wu).[204] On July 21, the All-China Dance Workers Association (Quanguo wudao gongzuozhe xiehui) was formally established, marking the creation of China's first nationwide organization dedicated to dance. The Association's National Standing Committee included representatives from all of the major wartime dance movements.[205] On August 2, it was announced that Dai Ailian had been elected the association's president, with Wu Xiaobang serving as vice president.[206]

As the wartime contestation among regional dance movements came to an end, the 1949 Congress suggested that Dai's Frontier Dance, combined with New Yangge, would be the path forward. Dai's selection over Wu for the presidency of the All-China Dance Workers Association was the clearest indication of this direction. Traditional hierarchies predicted that Wu would have been selected for this position: he was ten years Dai's senior, had been promoting dance in China longer than Dai, was a CCP member and male, and had been born, raised, and educated in China with fluent command of the Chinese language. Dai's selection, however, shows that her vision was the one preferred by the new leadership. Clearly disappointed to be ranked second, Wu complained in his memoir more than thirty years later that the selection committee had been biased.[207] Seeing that his approaches did not have a future in the new capital, Wu left for Wuhan, where he promoted his "natural principle" methods in a new program for training military dance ensembles managed by the People's Liberation Army.[208] Over time, it would be within this genre of Chinese military dance *(junlü wudao)* that Wu's model of New Dance would have its greatest impact.[209] Meanwhile, in the capital, Dai and her colleagues focused on merging New Yangge and Frontier Dance and creating choreography to represent the new nation. Their first challenge in this effort would be *Long Live the People's Victory (Renmin shengli wansui),* a national dance pageant slated for September to celebrate the Chinese People's Political Consultative Congress and the founding of the PRC.[210] Dai would both codirect the production and star in it, working with a group of artists drawn largely from the New Yangge movement and Dai's Chongqing Frontier Dance circle.

Tracing the genealogy of contemporary Chinese dance backward in time, one finds multiple origin points. One possible origin point is Yu Rongling's and Mei Lanfang's early Chinese-themed dances performed in the context of court performance and Peking opera. Another is the launching of the New Yangge movement in Yan'an, based on Mao's principles of national forms and remolding. Still others are Wu's first solo concert of New Dance in Shanghai, Qemberxanim's performances of Uyghur dance in Ürümqi, Liang Lun's stagings of Frontier Dance in Kunming, and Dai's hosting of the Chongqing Frontier Dance *Plenary.* Among these various origin points, I see Dai Ailian's as the most compelling, not just because Dai went on to lead the early national dance movement in the new PRC but because it was Dai who first embodied and theorized the path that Chinese dance would eventually follow. Among the many people who helped create the modern genre of Chinese dance, Dai was the first to insist, categorically, that Chinese dance should pursue a new aesthetic form inspired by local performance practices and that this form should draw on local sources from across the country, including northern and southern, secular and religious, elite and popular, rural and urban, Han and non-Han. Having personally experienced the racist hierarchies embedded in ballet and Western modern dance culture, Dai possessed a critical relationship to these forms that artists like Wu Xiaobang did not. As a result, she was capable of envisioning a future for Chinese dance that did not rely on Western forms as its foundation but instead sought to represent itself, using new movement languages and a new aesthetic vision.

2

Experiments in Form

Creating Dance in the Early People's Republic

As the excitement of 1949 died down, it became clear that China's newly founded dance field was facing serious challenges. Among these, one of the most urgent was a lack of trained performers to populate new dance productions. This problem became exceedingly clear in the two-hundred-person music and dance pageant *Long Live the People's Victory*, staged in the fall of 1949 to celebrate the Chinese People's Political Consultative Congress (Zhongguo renmin zhengzhi xieshang huiyi) and Founding Day (figure 7).[1] Several experienced performers had been strategically cast to raise the show's artistic quality: Wang Yi, a virtuoso folk performer from Hebei, performed a solo in the opening "war drum dance" segment; a group of drummers was brought in from Ansai County in Shaanxi to perform in the "waist drum dance" portion; and Dai Ailian gave a modern dance solo during the climactic final scene showing the leading power of the working classes.[2] Even these highlights, however, could not make up for the almost complete lack of training of most of the performers. Hu Sha (1927–2013), who codirected the production along with Dai Ailian, lamented the situation, writing, "most [of the performers] were students of only a few months, the majority of whom had not studied dance before, and their performance technique was still quite poor."[3] Anyone who has attempted to stage a full-scale dance production, let alone a national pageant, by performers with only a few months of training can certainly sympathize with Hu's distress.

Not surprisingly, the problem of technical quality came up in some reviews of the performance, especially those by respected cultural figures responsible for guiding artistic development in the new society. Tian Han (1898–1968), a leading theater critic, dealt with the issue gently but clearly. While *Long Live the People's Victory* had taken the right approach and had served its immediate purpose, he argued, much

48

FIGURE 7. *Long Live the People's Victory*, 1949. Photographer unknown. Reproduced with permission from the private collection of Zhang Ke.

more work still needed to be done if this type of performance was to have lasting appeal in new China. "We have taken the correct path," Tian wrote, "but we need to keep going and find greater depth. Otherwise, this excitement will not last."[4] The main problem with *Long Live the People's Victory*, Tian argued, was the immaturity of its artistic form, which was especially problematic given the seriousness of the content the production addressed. Hu states that *Long Live the People's Victory* was supposed to embody four themes: "the people's democratic dictatorship, the leadership of the proletariat, taking workers and peasants as the foundation, and national unity."[5] To express these lofty themes using unsophisticated artistic forms, Tian felt, was inappropriate. "The costumes, dancing, and other aspects of the artistic form are still not able to match the conceptual content," he concluded.[6] Reflecting the moment's visionary zeitgeist, Tian was concerned less about the present than about the future. Although *Long Live the People's Victory* satisfied audiences now, he warned that its appeal would not endure. For revolutionary dance to move audiences in the future socialist society, it needed to rise to a higher artistic standard.

This search for a higher standard occupied professional dancers for the remainder of the decade, making the 1950s the most exciting period of growth, experimentation, and innovation in Chinese dance history. For dancers like Dai Ailian, the period presented the special opportunity to build dance institutions from the ground up. However, to do so required not just developing new repertoires and teaching new students but also finding experienced dance artists to help. As Dai had pointed out in her 1946 lecture at the Chongqing *Plenary*, creating Chinese dance could not be done by one person alone; it required a team.[7] Because dance talent was still scarce in the capital, this meant reaching out, beyond Beijing and even outside China. In a letter dated May 2, 1950, Dai wrote to her second cousin Sylvia, then in the United States, inviting her to help with dance work in Beijing:

> My dear Sylvia: . . . For some time I have heard you say that you would like to return to China. . . . If this is still your desire, all I can say is come quickly. We need you very much here, and you will find good working conditions. . . . We need teachers, dancers and choreographers. . . . Please write to me and let me know if you will come, and if you have any difficulties in coming, and in which way we may be able to help you.[8]

Sylvia accepted Dai's invitation, but not until the end of the 1950s, when it was already too late for her to significantly shape the direction of Chinese dance.[9] In the meantime, Dai and her colleagues would find assistance from artists with transnational experience more nearby: Qemberxanim, the Uyghur dancer trained in Tashkent and Moscow, who was by the late 1940s leading a dance movement in Xinjiang, and Choe Seung-hui, the Korean dancer trained in Tokyo who had given a successful solo world tour and was by the late 1940s leading a dance movement in North Korea. As discussed further below, both women would visit Beijing several times in the early 1950s, both concretely impacting new developments in the Chinese dance field.

In many ways, the exuberance of the early 1950s came from the fact that China's dance field—including most of its people, institutions, and dance forms—was extremely young. Wu Xiaobang, the most senior person focused on dance work as of 1949, was just forty-three, while Dai Ailian and Liang Lun were a mere thirty-three and twenty-eight, respectively. China's first national dance company—the Central Academy of Drama (Zhongyang xiju xueyuan, hereafter CAD) Dance Ensemble, led by Dai Ailian—was established in December of 1949 and initially comprised members between the ages of fourteen and twenty-six.[10] In early 1950, a report compared CAD's three cultural work troupes—opera, spoken drama, and dance—concluding that the dance group was "the youngest . . . [and] despite being a performance ensemble in name, is actually training-based."[11] The fact that the majority of the ensemble's 129 members were still in the learning phase reportedly gave the ensemble a sense of newness and exploration. "The new Chinese dance still needs to be created," the report explained, "In the dance troupe, everything is still being explored and tested."[12] As the language of this report makes clear, Chinese dance was still being imagined as something new and in a state of emergence. Much like the dancers who embodied it, Chinese dance was young, hopeful, and forward-looking. Its mature form did not yet exist. It needed to be created.

The relative lack of institutionalized knowledge and technical conventions allowed dancers in the 1950s to engage in a high degree of formal innovation and broad-ranging aesthetic experiments. As in China's other artistic spheres, this was a period rife with debate and disagreement, as well as rushed creation that ended at times in brilliant success and at times in awkward failure. Most often, the truly tantalizing problems clustered around issues of form, not content. After all, as Dai and her followers argued—expressing both Mao's call for national forms and Dai's commitment to developing a new dance language on the basis of local performance practices—it was form that defined Chinese dance. As a result, questions of form motivated the vast majority of dance exploration during this period, when no one could say for certain what Chinese dance was, only that they knew they wanted to create it. Motivated by the call to serve and the need to produce results, sometimes with limited resources, dancers took risks and made do with what they had. It was in these thrilling times that Chinese dance emerged as a coherent artistic form, partly by plan but also by accident.

EARLY ATTEMPTS: *BRAVING WIND AND WAVES* AND *PEACE DOVE*

Two large-scale productions attracted the attention of China's dance field in 1950, one involving Liang Lun in Guangzhou and the other Dai Ailian in Beijing. The Guangzhou production premiered in July 1950 and was a six-act song and dance drama called *Braving Wind and Waves to Liberate Hainan (Chengfengpolang jiefang Hainan)*, based on the military victory of the People's Liberation Army (PLA) on Hainan Island that April.[13] It was created and performed by the South China Cultural Work Troupe (Huanan wengongtuan), with Liang Lun codirecting and serving on the collaborative choreography team with four colleagues.[14] The Beijing production premiered formally in October 1950 and was a seven-act dance drama called *Peace Dove (Heping ge)*, made to celebrate the international peace movement and the Stockholm Appeal, which had been signed earlier that year.[15] It was written by Ouyang Yuqian, then director of CAD, and performed by the CAD Dance Ensemble. Dai starred in the production and also served as a member of the six-person choreography team.[16] *Braving Wind and Waves* and *Peace Dove* had much in common: both were government-assigned projects dealing with current political events; both were created around the same time; and both involved leading choreographers with similar visions for the goals and principles of Chinese dance creation. Nevertheless, the final results of these two works could hardly have been more different, in terms of the dance techniques they employed and their overall aesthetic execution. These divergent productions thus demonstrate the range of possibilities that existed during this first year of the new nation's dance experiments.

Braving Wind and Waves told a triumphant story of the PLA crew that expelled Nationalist forces from Hainan, a tropical island on the southern coast of China, in one of the final military encounters of the Chinese Civil War. The story began with depictions of the suffering of the Hainan people under KMT rule (act 1), followed by the soldiers' training on land and in water (act 2), the soldiers' pact on the eve of battle (act 3), sailing across the sea with the help of local boat rowers (act 4), embarking on land and joining with other PLA forces (act 5), and celebrating with the island's inhabitants, including Li nationality communities (act 6).[17] Audiences described the show as suspenseful and gripping: "The whole drama has so much tension it hardly gave one's nerves a chance to breathe" was one viewer's response.[18] Although the overall tone was heroic and celebratory, it also had variations in mood that lent it a sense of realism. Among the darker issues it explored were the soldiers' fear of death and their lack of experience with fighting on water. The scene in which the soldiers cross the sea on boats depicted them suffering seasickness, and a sense of tragedy accompanied the signing of a blood pact in which soldiers vowed to fight to the death.[19] The production was created specifically to welcome the returning PLA soldiers on their way back from Hainan. Thus, its first audiences were the very people whose story the work narrated.[20]

In terms of performance form, *Braving Wind and Waves* was notable for its blending of diverse mediums and its use of techniques drawn from regional folk performance. In an article published in *Dance News* in 1951, Liang Lun described the formal structure as follows:

> Initially, our plan was to use the dance drama form. However, in our troupe there were only a little over twenty comrades who had dance experience. The majority had experience in theater, music, and stage technology. Under these conditions, it would be difficult to realize the production purely through dance. But, using opera or spoken drama was also difficult to express this content. Also, we wanted to make use of the skills of the performers in each department. So, we decided to use a free form *(ziyou xingshi)* that made dance primary but added song and dialogue. Based on the content, we completely used dance to express the content of the prelude and the first and second scenes of act one. For acts two, three, and four we added speaking, clapper-talk *(kuaiban)*,[21] and singing. Because we aimed to create a sense of power, we also used a method of choral accompaniment. The sixth act then completely used dance.[22]

The dance movements used in the group choreography in *Braving Wind and Waves* were created through experiential research, known as "learning from life." This was an artistic method that Mao Zedong and CCP cultural leaders had widely promoted since the early 1940s in Yan'an, and it informed much dance creation in

FIGURE 8. *Braving Wind and Waves to Liberate Hainan.* Published in *Renmin huabao* 1, no. 6 (December 1950): 37. Photographer unknown. Image provided by China Foto Bank.

China both during and after the socialist period.[23] Describing this choreographic research process as it was carried out for *Braving Wind and Waves*, Liang wrote: "With help from the military, we were able to ride in some of the sailboats they had used. Practicing in the Pearl River, we had boat rowers teach us how to operate the rudder, raise and lower the sails, pull in the anchor, etc. Then, we invited people who had experienced war to tell us stories about training soldiers, crossing the ocean, and embarking on land."[24] Extant stage photographs offer hints of the movements devised from this research: in one, a dancer grasps a rope and thrusts his weight into it, as if maneuvering the sails of a large boat; in another, male and female boat rowers look into the audience and lunge in unison, lifting oars over their heads with one hand and clenching their fists in front of their bodies with the other; in another, soldiers wearing makeshift bamboo life preservers balance on one leg, arms out, with the other leg kicking back and their mouths gulping air as if in midswim (figure 8).[25]

The music and stage design used in *Braving Wind and Waves* also showed formal experimentation and blending of performance styles. Musically, the production had an original score that included twenty-five songs in total. Following a common practice in performance works of the time, some songs drew themes from existing revolutionary music. For example, during the scene in which the soldiers signed their oath, the tune from "Without the CCP There Would Be No New China" was used.[26] Other segments used hybridized compositions that sought to evoke native Hainan music. This occurred in the Li dance segment, which featured a rhythm inspired by Li nationality dance music, played on a Guangdong wooden xylophone accompanied by oboe, flute, clarinet, violin, and cello.[27] The most sonically dominant component of the production's musical score was its percussion ensemble. According to musical directors Shi Mingxin (1929–2002) and Ming Zhi, "percussion accompanied the whole drama from beginning to end, and in the middle sometimes was used on its own."[28] Although the string and wind components of the orchestra used Western instruments and modalities, and the choral music was composed in Western-style four-part harmony, the percussion ensemble was from Chinese opera. Shi and Ming described this component of the score as particularly effective because it used "native-style musical effects," with which audiences were "very familiar."[29] It is unclear whether the specific percussion ensemble used was from Peking opera or Cantonese opera, but in either case it would have included gongs and cymbals, and, depending on the style, either a drum and clappers or woodblocks.[30] One can imagine the rapid "tap, tap, tap" of clappers or woodblocks, punctuated by the "tsah tsah TSANG" and crashing of the cymbals and gongs, all lending rhythm and suspense to the soldiers' dance movements, set against a surging choral and symphonic background. In terms of stage design, simple but realistic sets were used that resembled those of spoken drama or pageants. They included flags, a raised boat deck, boat sails, and a painted backdrop of sky. Costumes were also realistic and simple. They included military uniforms for soldiers, rustic tunics and loose pants for boat rowers, and embroidered jackets, skirts, and loincloths for the Li islanders. All of the dancers performed barefoot, and their makeup was minimal.[31]

The second production, *Peace Dove*, had a more abstract focus on the international peace movement that did not lend itself to the same type of realistic storytelling. Its structure was more symbolic, as demonstrated by the fact that the lead character is an anthropomorphized dove, played by Dai Ailian. The production contained seven acts organized around themes such as opposing US imperialism and financial oligarchy, opposing war and nuclear weapons, and promoting world peace.[32] The story began with a group of doves called to disseminate peace at the beckoning of a red star (act 1), followed by a warmonger dressed as Uncle Sam who injures one of the doves (act 2), a worker who saves the injured dove (act 3), a crowd that is inspired by the doves and angered by the warmonger (act 4), dockworkers who refuse to transport US ammunition slated for Korea (act 5), the warmonger's flouted dream of world domination through financial manipulation and the atom bomb (act 6), and the peace dove's triumphant arrival in Beijing (act 7).[33] As a historic achievement, *Peace Dove* was lauded as the PRC's first "large-scale dance drama."[34]

According to its writer, veteran theater expert and director of CAD Ouyang Yuqian, *Peace Dove* aimed to avoid reportage-like naturalistic mimes and gestures and instead present poetic tableaus that emphasized elemental emotions related to the central theme.[35] In terms of setting, the work was unusual in that every act, with the exception of act 7, took place in unspecified locations outside China.[36] These settings, combined with the foreign symbol of the peace dove and the theme of the global antiwar movement, gave *Peace Dove* a strong aspiration toward internationalism.[37]

In terms of performance form, *Peace Dove* was notable in its adoption of classical and modernist European aesthetics. Structurally, it followed the eighteenth-century European model of the *ballet d'action*, or a story told completely through movement without words. Act 7, set in Tian'anmen Square in Beijing, used Chinese-style dance techniques drawn from New Yangge and Frontier Dance.[38] The remainder of the choreography, however, used the movement conventions and techniques of ballet and Western modern dance. Chen Jinqing, who served as a member of the choreography team, described the choice to use these aesthetic modes as follows:

> The rhythm of the dove is most suitably expressed through ballet technique. Therefore, the first and third acts mainly portray the doves, and these made ample use of ballet technique. In these sections, Dai Ailian's application of foreign technique was very successful. For the workers, masses, warmonger, etc. we used modern dance technique, because modern dance technique is relatively energetic and free. It is suited to expressing contemporary feelings and life. Using both techniques in a single dance drama was in accord with the needs of the script. At the same time, this type of expressive method was also an experiment.[39]

Stage photographs published at the time of the production demonstrate the prominence of ballet vocabulary in *Peace Dove*'s choreography. Dai Ailian, who portrayed the lead dove, danced her role in pointe shoes, a technique specific to ballet, and her duet with the worker in act 2 employed standard ballet lifts such as the "fish dive."[40] The choreography performed by the group of doves was also filled with ballet movement, including balletic port de bras, or arm lines, upward chest carriage, hip turnout, straight legs, and pointed feet (figure 9).[41]

European classical and modernist aesthetics were also evident in the music and costuming designs devised for *Peace Dove*. An original orchestral score was composed that consisted primarily of European string, wind, and brass instruments.[42] At least one segment borrowed a tune from Chopin, and the overall score possessed what one critic called "a strong air of the Mozart era."[43] Costumes combined conventions from Romantic ballets and early twentieth-century European-style Chinese spoken drama. The doves wore white bodices with chiffon butterfly-style sleeves, tutus, and ballet slippers, and on their heads were feathered crowns similar to those worn by the swan characters in *Swan Lake*. The workers were dressed in white collared shirts and overalls typical of proletarian characters in Chinese

FIGURE 9. Dai Ailian and ensemble in *Peace Dove*. Published in *Renmin huabao* 1, no. 6 (December 1950): 38. Photographers: Wu Yinbo and Xia Yuqing. Image provided by China Foto Bank.

wartime political drama, while the warmongers wore tuxedos, top hats, and European-style ball gowns like those used in 1920s- and 1930s-era Chinese spoken drama productions portraying stories set in Europe and the United States.[44]

Stage design was one of the most experimental components of *Peace Dove*. Extant photographs show the use of elaborate sets comprising a combination of industrial landscapes, abstract symbols, and modernist sculpture. In act 1, a red star beacon rises above stage boards cut to resemble ocean waves. In act 2, an empty field is planted with giant swastikas and crosses, and a giant coin stamped with a dollar sign fills one side of the stage. Acts 3 and 4 take place under a towering mechanical construction crane, and the background is lined with smokestacks and cube-like structures resembling a skyline of urban tenements. In act 5 the stage is transformed into a dock with large boats and stacks of shipping crates. Act 6, portraying the warmonger's dream, returns to symbolist abstraction with a towering stack of coins, an atom bomb on wheels with a glamorous woman sitting atop, and a trapezoidal US flag mounted with a model warplane. Finally, act 7 has a painted backdrop of Tian'anmen Square topped with floating images of Mao Zedong and Joseph Stalin shaking hands amid flying doves.

FINDING CONSENSUS: RECEPTION AND DEBATES OVER DANCE FORM

Given the vast differences in approach between *Braving Wind and Waves* and *Peace Dove*, it is not surprising that the critical responses were also quite different.

Overall, *Braving Wind and Waves* received positive reviews and was held up as an example for future dance creation to follow. Meanwhile, the responses to *Peace Dove* were so harsh that by January of 1952, the renowned poet Guang Weiran (1913–2002), who served as head of education at CAD and at first defended *Peace Dove* against critics, published a self-criticism in *People's Daily* in which he accepted culpability and acknowledged the work as a failure.[45] For years, references to *Peace Dove* appeared as examples of what not to do when creating Chinese dance drama, in particular with regard to the question of using ballet movement form.[46] Thus, these two productions not only evince the wide range of variation in early 1950s dance creation but also show how a consensus gradually formed regarding the parameters of Chinese dance as a new artistic medium in the early PRC.

In their responses to *Braving Wind and Waves*, critics were impressed by the extreme ingenuity displayed by members of the creative team, their willingness to draw on diverse performance forms, and their attention to local elements. Initial reviews in national newspapers marveled at how quickly the production was created—under twenty days from conception to premiere—and described it as very effective at devising new mediums to portray its selected themes. One critic wrote, "This drama uses all kinds of new dance forms and its imagery portrays the great struggle of the PLA . . . all very successfully."[47] Photographs of the work received an entire spread in the national magazine *China Pictorial (Renmin huabao)*, significant recognition for a regional production.[48] Additionally, local reception was so positive that the Guangzhou Municipal Committee and the Guangdong Province People's Government Bureau of Education and Culture each awarded subventions of 10 million yuan to help develop the work into a lasting repertory piece.[49] When an international representative team from the World Festival of Youth and Students (Shijie qingnian lianhuanjie) visited Guangzhou, *Braving Wind and Waves* was selected to be performed for the team, and the show had an additional local run of over thirty performances, followed by symposia to discuss its creative process.[50] Finally, a group from the Ministry of Culture was sent to Guangzhou to review the work, and they selected it to be performed in Beijing the following year as part of a national festival.[51]

When *Braving Wind and Waves* was shown in the Beijing festival the following year, it continued to receive positive reviews from Beijing-based dance critics. In his 1951 review of nationwide dance creation over the previous year, China Dancers Association vice president Wu Xiaobang singled out *Braving Wind and Waves* for special praise, calling it "something that dance workers around the country should study."[52] Following the now state-compelled endorsement of local aesthetics, Wu commended the work's creators for adapting elements from Chinese opera and from other styles of local performance—a technique he called "creating as appropriate to the place"—and for boldly pushing the boundaries of existing forms. "Dance workers need to create using a range of forms, not staying limited to the tried methods," he concluded.[53] A review of the national festival argued that the works it featured, including *Braving Wind and Waves*, showed some roughness and lack of polish but concluded that "in terms of the direction of creation and development of new dance art, we can confirm that it is correct."[54] Finally, Hu Sha wrote that while he would like to have seen even more adaptation of native performance styles in the production, he nevertheless still felt that its creative approach was in the right direction.[55]

Whereas critics viewed the blending of artistic mediums and adaptation of local performance in *Braving Wind and Waves* as creative, forward-looking, and appropriate to the tastes of contemporary audiences, they regarded *Peace Dove's* adoption of European classical and modernist aesthetics as morally questionable, unsuited to contemporary audiences, and artistically old-fashioned. Concerns about the work's aesthetic choices apparently began at the level of the ensemble members even before the work went into production. Peng Song, who served on *Peace Dove's* choreography committee and also performed the role of Uncle Sam/warmonger, recalled that when ensemble members were told of the plans, "Some people questioned whether copying the expressive methods of ballet and lacking native dance style was appropriate."[56] Guang Weiran had apparently made a special visit to meet with the ensemble members to subdue their dissent. According to Peng, Guang instructed ensemble members to respect the views of the work's writer and CAD director, Ouyang Yuqian, who was a very respected figure in the cultural community and had great experience with drama creation.[57]

When *Peace Dove* had its initial preview showings, serious concerns were expressed again, this time from audiences. The story is referenced in many contemporary accounts and is widely recognized as a key turning point in the history of both Chinese dance and ballet in China.[58] Peng tells the story as follows:

> *Peace Dove* had two performance periods. The first one was in September, for the opening of the second World Peace Congress, and it took place in Beijing Theater and the Xinhua News Agency Auditorium. The response was good, largely affirming. However, after seeing it, some of the transferred worker-peasant students[59] from CAD cried out in alarm: 'A stage filled with thighs; workers, peasants, and soldiers despise.'[60] Many ridiculed the production for 'corrupting public morals.' In response to this, comrade Guang Weiran defended *Peace Dove* by saying, 'We need to work hard so that in a few decades from now workers, peasants, and soldiers will be able to stomach looking at thighs.' When the critics heard this, they went into an uproar. For this reason, after a few shows *Peace Dove* unfortunately stopped performing. Only act seven 'Peace dove flies to Beijing' was performed at a few galas.[61]

The controversy over *Peace Dove's* aesthetic form revolved primarily around its use of ballet aesthetics, including the technical focus on leg work and the use of short tutus that highlight this component of the movement and the female dancers' bodies. During China's colonial modern period, the exposure of women's thighs had become associated with Westernization and the moral corruption of capitalism. In cities with large foreign populations and semicolonial governance like Shanghai, "thigh dancing" *(datui wu)* was shorthand for dance styles such as cabaret, burlesque, and striptease, all of which were seen as vulgar Western imports.[62] Thus, by calling *Peace Dove* "a stage filled with thighs," the worker-peasant students were locating ballet as part of the cultural legacy of Western concert dance, understood as a form of popular stage dance associated with commercial culture and colonialism in the Chinese historical context. From this perspective, they argued, ballet could not be considered appropriate for a dance form meant to embody revolutionary ideals. In his response, Guang Weiran attempted to reclaim ballet from this interpretation by arguing that it was similar to spoken drama, a Western form that had nevertheless been adapted to Chinese needs. "We just have to think of how the foreign spoken drama form gained practical connection to Chinese people's lives and became accepted by the people, quickly becoming one of our national forms," Guang argued.[63] Many found Guang's claim unconvincing, however, and new criticisms of *Peace Dove* continued to pile up.

The most damning critique came from Zhong Dianfei, a budding film critic who at the time worked in the Ministry of Culture. In late 1950, Zhong published a review of *Peace Dove* in *Literary Gazette (Wenyi bao)*, China's leading literary and arts journal. Like the transferred worker-peasant students, Zhong argued that *Peace Dove* was insufficiently revolutionary. However, rather than taking the perspective that it was morally corrupt and excessively Western, Zhong instead argued that it was simply old-fashioned and artistically uninspired. Zhong hung much of his argument on the fact of Ouyang Yuqian's advanced age—introducing the latter as "an old man already past sixty"—and suggested that the problems with *Peace Dove* resulted largely from Ouyang's being out of touch with the tastes of contemporary audiences.[64] Turning Guang Weiran's claim on its head, Zhang argued that the problem was not that contemporary audiences needed time to rise to the level of art depicted in *Peace Dove*, but, rather, that they were already far beyond it. "The intended audience of today's art is already revolutionary," Zhong argued, "and may have a great deal of experience with revolutionary practice. . . . So, their expectations for art are relatively high."[65] Zhong regarded the plot and expressive modes employed in *Peace Dove* as superficial, ineffective, and tiringly out of date. Although he did not agree with the students, Zhong still condemned the use of European dance technique in *Peace Dove*, on the basis that it was too traditional. "Although ballet is already accepted and has been absorbed in the USSR, it still does not possess a mass quality . . . all traditional artistic forms have limits," Zhong concluded.[66] Thus, rather than making *Peace Dove* revolutionary, the use of ballet, in Zhong's estimation, gave it a retrograde quality.

The idea that using European classical forms made *Peace Dove* seem stuck in the past was a common complaint among contemporary critics. During a symposium held at the Central Music School, the composer Su Xia made a similar argument about *Peace Dove*'s musical composition. Su stated, "The most unharmonious aspect of *Peace Dove*'s score is that on the stage we see typical phenomena of the year 1950, while the music is still in the style of around 1770."[67] Like Zhong, Su found the use of European classicism not just mismatched with the content but also unlikely to appeal to China's new audiences, who Su argued had a strong desire for innovation. The problem, therefore, was not just that the music was of a different time period but that it lacked newness: "Overall, the music is too imitative, and many phrases feel quite familiar," Su chided. From both Zhong's and Su's perspectives, what was needed to attract Chinese audiences and reflect the revolutionary society was innovation, not imitation.

Braving Wind and Waves and *Peace Dove* gave audiences much to think about in terms of what constituted truly revolutionary modes of artistic expression, and they also generated interest in the new creative medium of "dance drama" *(wuju)* among a wider portion of China's cultural and artistic community. By the end of 1950, not just dancers and playwrights but also composers, poets, film critics, and worker-peasant students were all chiming in about the future of Chinese dance form. At the same time, neither *Braving Wind and Waves* nor *Peace Dove* was able to resolve this problem, since neither offered a concrete model for movement conventions for Chinese dance. Although recognized as a positive example, the success of *Braving Wind and Waves* lay in its multimedia composition, realistic storytelling, and adaptation of local music and oral performance, not its innovations in dance form. Thus, when categorizing works in the 1951 dance festival, Hu Sha labeled *Braving Wind and Waves* as a production that contributed to the problem of how to reflect the content of mass struggle but not the problem of how to use local elements and develop national forms in dance movement.[68] At the same time, although *Peace Dove* had attempted to innovate in dance form by using ballet and modern dance, it had not been successful. That is, audiences and critics had not accepted ballet and modern dance as legitimate mediums for expressing Chinese revolutionary culture. This left Chinese dancers once again searching for new formal possibilities.

The uncertainties about dance form manifested in these critical debates over *Braving Wind and Waves* and *Peace Dove* reflect larger questions regarding the relationship between form and content in socialist performance that traced back to the "national forms" debates of the Yan'an period. Specifically, critics and choreographers alike were still trying to determine what role, if any, Western dance forms should play in the making of China's new national forms. At the same time, the issue of how folk and vernacular forms could contribute to these new forms also continued to be a persistent problem. As had happened with Dai's Frontier Dance repertoires during the 1940s, minority forms and xiqu once again appeared as solutions to the problem. At the very same moment that critics were casting their votes on *Braving Wind and Waves* and *Peace Dove,* two new possibilities presented themselves to the Beijing dance community that made possible a shift in this direction. One of these came from Xinjiang and other parts of the former "frontier." The other came from an artist in North Korea who was enthralled with the creative possibilities of xiqu.

NEW VOICES: MINORITY DANCE AND MINORITY DANCERS

The dances of non-Han groups had played an important role in early visions of Chinese dance and in the 1949 All-China Literature and Arts Worker Representative Congress. However, once the early proponents of these forms, most of whom were of Han ethnicity, moved back to Han-dominated urban centers on the east coast, they lost opportunities to conduct fieldwork and collaborate with minority artists, making it difficult to create new works using these dance styles. An attempt to represent minority groups on stage had occurred in the 1949 pageant *Long Live the People's Victory* when, in the final two scenes, dancers dressed as Han, Hui, Miao, Mongol, Taiwanese, Tibetan, and Yi performed together along with dancers dressed as workers, peasants, soldiers, students, and merchants, in an effort to reflect the various social groups thought to form the revolutionary movement.[69] Although the choreographers of this scene had significant experience with minority dance—they included Peng Song, Ge Min, and Ye Ning, all of whom had been involved in pre-1949 Frontier Dance—the fact that the performers were almost all Han students with little dance training and almost no exposure to the culture of the ethnic groups being performed meant that little of the actual formal qualities of minority dance were conveyed. Tian Han's criticism of the formal inadequacy of *Long Live the People's Victory* cited above had noted this scene as particularly problematic. In his words, it appeared to "lack any true sense" of the minority dances that were meant to be portrayed.[70] By the spring of 1950, when this group, now the CAD Dance Ensemble, staged its second major production, *The Great Yangge of Building the Motherland,* portrayals of minorities had dropped out of the choreography.[71]

Just as minority dance seemed to be disappearing from Beijing's dance stages, however, groups of non-Han dancers from border regions—now called "nationality cultural work troupes" *(minzu wengongtuan)*—arrived in Beijing to give their own public performances. In October of 1950, just after *Peace Dove* made its initial appearance in theaters, the first large-scale tour of minority music and dance performed by minority artists was held in Beijing to celebrate China's first National Day.[72] The tour featured 219 performers hailing from four major regions: the Southwest,[73] Xinjiang, Inner Mongolia, and Yanbian.[74] Among the ethnic groups represented were Kazakh, Korean, Manchu, Miao, Tibetan, Uyghur, Uzbek, and

FIGURE 10. Qemberxanim and ensemble on Northwest Nationality Cultural Work Troupe Beijing tour. Published in *Renmin huabao* 1, no. 5 (November 1950): 37. Photographers: Chen Zhengqing et al. Image provided by China Foto Bank.

Yi, among others. The star of the tour was Qemberxanim, the Uyghur dancer from Kashgar who had returned to Xinjiang after studying dance in Uzbekistan and Moscow and gave a national tour in 1947 (figure 10).[75] These dancers and musicians presented a joint four-and-a-half-hour song and dance gala that featured a wide range of artistic styles and genres—from Central Asian Muqam orchestra to Tibetan *xianzi* dance.[76] After premiering at the gala for state leaders and minority representatives at the official minority gift-giving ceremony held on October 3, they gave seventeen additional shows in Beijing and Tianjin, with an estimated total live audience of 150,000. In addition, they participated in numerous banquets and social engagements and took part in artistic exchange and joint performances with local professional performance ensembles.[77]

A documentary film titled *Songs of Tengri Tagh (Tianshan zhi ge)*, directed by He Feiguang (1913–1997), offers a rare glimpse into the dances of Qemberxanim.[78] Shot in Shanghai during the Xinjiang Youth Ensemble tour of 1947–48, the film

VIDEO 3. Qemberxanim and ensemble in "Plate Dance," from *Songs of Tengri Tagh*. Northwest Film Corporation and Central Film Studio, 1948.

To watch this video, scan the QR code with your mobile device or visit DOI: https://doi.org/10.1525/luminos.58.3

recorded music and dance items from the tour, including Qemberxanim performing one of her signature pieces, "Plate Dance" (Panzi wu) (video 3).[79] Taken during an outdoor performance, the yellowed film shows Qemberxanim dancing solo while seven seated musicians offer live accompaniment on an ensemble of Central Asian percussion and string instruments. Bell-like gossamer sleeves hang down from Qemberxanim's arms, and on her head sits a beaded hat topped with feathers, below which waist-length black braids hang down and swing along her back. She holds a plate and a pair of chopsticks in each hand and clinks them like castanets, framing her face with her arms, as she circles the space in floating walks and spins. Eventually, she approaches the audience and lowers to her knees, dipping into a deep backbend. Then, as she is rising back up, she crosses her arms in front of her chest and performs a barely visible side-to-side head shift now iconic of female Uyghur-style dance. A close-up shot shows a confident smile filling her face as she glances sideways toward her audience. It is a dance filled with charisma and subtlety, and the plates and chopsticks make it reminiscent of a banquet performance.

The 1950 minority tour came at a time when members of Beijing's cultural scene were particularly concerned about the future of Chinese dance, and the mature performances of experienced dancers like Qemberxanim offered what many saw as a possible solution to their problems. Conveying the urgency many in the dance field felt at the time, Chen Jinqing, then vice director of the CAD Dance Ensemble, wrote in September, just before the minority tour, that "some are even questioning whether dance is a viable artistic form in China."[80] Part of this concern had to do with a growing malaise toward New Yangge among urban communities, due in part to the disconnect between urban and rural culture and in part to the fact that yangge had been heavily simplified in the New Yangge movement in order to make it more quickly learnable and accessible. As Chang-tai Hung suggests, the boredom urban audiences developed toward New Yangge may explain why the creators of *Peace Dove* turned to ballet and modern dance in an attempt to innovate and find new forms.[81] When this also failed to produce positive results, however, Beijing's dance community fell into a somewhat desperate state; the nationality tour offered the community tremendous new hope. Zhong Dianfei, in his dismal review of *Peace Dove*, offered an aside on the minority tour that implied he saw it as a more viable path for the future of Chinese dance than copying ballet and European aesthetics. "There are still many problems facing the development of Chinese national dance. . . . The recent performances of northwest, southwest, Yanbian, and Mongolian nationality cultural work troupes in Beijing has given us much inspiration in this regard."[82] Zhong compared what he saw as the new, and thus formally exciting, dance styles presented in the minority tour with the familiar, and therefore less interesting, forms used in *Peace Dove:* "if Ouyang had only not chosen such an average expressive medium, [*Peace Dove*] might have [like the tour] also provided inspiration."[83] Other leading critics also responded positively to the tour. In his review of a work by Jia Zuoguang performed by the Mongolian dance ensemble, Wu Xiaobang suggested that it be studied as an alternative to New Yangge dance as, in his words, it was "more suited to the expression of contemporary life."[84] Other critics from outside the dance community claimed to be moved by the performances on the tour and to have thereby gained a new interest in dance art.[85]

Following the minority tour, the central government launched an effort to recruit more minority dance artists into professional positions, and new schools and ensembles were established that were specifically dedicated to training minority dancers and researching and teaching non-Han dance forms. In November of 1950, immediately after the tour, Qemberxanim traveled directly from Beijing to Xi'an, where she was recruited to help oversee plans for the incorporation of minority arts courses into the new Northwest Art Academy (Xibei yishu xueyuan).[86] In 1951 Qemberxanim was appointed founding chair of the academy's Department of Minority Nationality Arts (Shaoshu minzu yishu xi), which became the PRC's first state-sponsored professional program dedicated to training performing artists from minority ethnic backgrounds.[87] Under Qemberxanim's leadership, the program recruited 150 students from eleven different nationalities during its first year, including folk artists, elementary school teachers, students, and government functionaries.[88] The department offered two areas of study: music and dance. Between 1951 and 1953, the dance program focused on what Qemberxanim described as "folk dances and classical works of northwest nationalities, such as Uyghur 'Hand Drum Dance,' 'Dolan Group Dance,' 'Plate Dance,' 'Russian Folk Group Dance,' Kazakh 'Spinning Wool Dance' and 'Moon Moon,' etc."[89] In order to systematize the instruction of basic skills for these dance styles, Qemberxanim developed her own teaching curricula that broke down movements according to seven categories: salutations, head movements, waist movements, steps, arm and hand movements, turns, and squats or pliés.[90] These curricula later served as the foundation for similar courses in minority dance taught at the Beijing Dance School, whose instructors were personally trained by Qemberxanim.[91] In addition to coursework, students in the department participated in frequent performances and also conducted organized field research trips.[92] The graduates of this program went on to become prominent leaders in arts institutions specializing in minority nationality performance across the northwest region.[93]

While Qemberxanim was leading the development of minority dance in the northwest, a national-level institution specializing in minority dance was also established in Beijing. The Central Academy of Nationalities (Zhongyang minzu xueyuan, hereafter CAN) Cultural Work Troupe, established on September 1, 1952, with Wu Xiaobang initially appointed as its director, became the PRC's second national-level dance ensemble, after the ensemble Dai Ailian led at CAD.[94] These two ensembles were China's most important professional dance companies during the early 1950s, with the CAD ensemble ultimately specializing in Han folk dance and the CAN ensemble in dances of minority nationalities.[95] Like Qemberxanim's program, the CAN group focused on recruiting and training performers from minority backgrounds—by the time of its ten-year anniversary, minority artists made up an estimated 60 percent of its total membership.[96] To maintain a connection with minority communities outside the capital, the CAN ensemble made regular trips to border regions to carry out study and exchange. In September of 1952, for example, Wu led over 140 members on a research and study trip to Xi'an, where they performed with Qemberxanim's program at the Northwest Art Academy, before continuing on to Chongqing and other areas across the southwest.[97] Photographs of the ensemble featured in *China Pictorial* in 1952 showed dancers from the troupe performing a wide variety of minority nationality dances, including Yi, Mongol, Yao, Gaoshan, Tibetan, Uyghur, Li, Yanbian (Korean), and Miao.[98] Members of the ensemble also frequently represented China on tours abroad, as discussed in the next chapter. By recruiting and training new dancers and creating new choreography, the CAN ensemble constituted a dedicated center for minority-focused dance activities, ensuring that non-Han dance and dancers retained visibility and influence within China's broader professional dance scene.

LEARNING FROM XIQU: THE BIRTH OF CHINESE CLASSICAL DANCE

The last major experiment of this period in the Chinese dance field also took off at the end of 1950, though because of yet a different set of occurrences. At the same time that *Peace Dove* and the minority tour performances were going on in Beijing, the PRC was entering its first major military engagement with a foreign power—against the United States in the Korean War. Apart from making national unity an increasingly important theme in political and cultural discourse, this also had the effect of encouraging cooperation and exchange between the PRC and North Korea, which included activities in the dance field. It was in this context that Choe Seung-hui, a world-renowned Korean dancer, became intimately involved in shaping the future of Chinese dance. In particular, Choe led the project to create a new Chinese dance vocabulary based on the movement conventions of xiqu, especially those of Peking opera and Kunqu. This work resulted in the dance style that became known as Chinese classical dance.

Xiqu is a synthetic art form that traditionally combines four main elements, known as *chang, nian, zuo, da* (singing, speaking, moving, and acrobatic fighting). Because two of these four main elements deal with bodily movement, dance is considered to be a fundamental part of xiqu performance. Dance in xiqu can range from barely perceptible postural movements, gestures, and hand, head, and facial expressions to complex acrobatic routines that incorporate flips, spins, kicks, and other displays of physical virtuosity. Manipulation of stage properties such as fans, sleeves, swords, and spears is also an essential component of xiqu movement practice. Additionally, movement technique in xiqu typically accords with the social identity of the character being performed, meaning that xiqu movement is encoded with cultural messaging about age, class, gender, ethnicity, morality, and profession.[99] During the early twentieth century, many Chinese artists experimented with the creation of modern dance choreography based on xiqu movement. As discussed in the introduction, Peking opera performer Mei Lanfang and his collaborator Qi Rushan were among those who explored such possibilities, and their work helped lay the foundation upon which Choe built.

Choe Seung-hui is one of the most influential figures in the history of twentieth-century East Asian dance. Because of her move to North Korea in 1946 and subsequent purging by the North Korean regime around 1969, however, research on Choe was banned in both South and North Korea until the late 1980s, and scholarship on her in English was consequently also limited. Since the 1990s, there has been an explosion of new Anglophone scholarship on Choe's career, particularly her 1938–40 world tour and her role as a colonial subject in Japan and Japanese-occupied Korea during the 1930s and early 1940s.[100] One topic that has not received much attention, though, is the latter portion of her career, during which she led the development of new socialist dance pedagogical systems, stage repertoires, and choreographic theories in North Korea and China.[101] Choe's activities in China occurred in two periods that represent two very different political and social contexts: the first was from 1941 to 1946 in the context of Japanese occupation and the War of Resistance against Japan and its aftermath; the second was from 1949 to 1952 in the context of China's socialist nation building, PRC–North Korean socialist cultural exchange, and the Korean War. In the Chinese-language dance scholarship produced in China, the activities in which Choe engaged during both of these periods are now seen as foundational to the history of Chinese dance, particularly to the early development of Chinese classical dance and Chinese Korean dance.[102] Because Choe worked in so many different cultural, geographic, and political contexts throughout her life, her work changed over time and took on new meanings in different places and times.[103]

Choe Seung-hui was born in 1911 into a declining *yangban* family in Seoul during the Japanese colonial rule of Chōsen (Korea), which lasted from 1910 to 1945. In 1926 Choe moved to Tokyo to study with Japanese dancer Ishii Baku (1886–1962), a leading figure in Japan's modern dance movement whose company Choe had seen perform in Seoul earlier that year. Ishii had begun his own dance career in 1912 studying with Italian ballet master Giovanni Vittorio Rossi at the Imperial Theater in Tokyo, and in 1915 he had left the theater to pursue his own dance style.[104] Starting in 1915, Ishii engaged in modernist collaborations with figures such as the composer Yamada Kosaku, who had been exposed to early modern dance while studying abroad in Europe, and around 1922–24 Ishii himself went abroad, visiting Berlin, London, and New York.[105] Choe rose to fame initially as a dancer in Ishii's Tokyo-based company, where she performed an eclectic mix of dance styles and gained a strong foundation in ballet and Western modern dance. In 1929 Choe returned to Seoul to establish her own dance studio, which she ran for about three years before rejoining Ishii in Tokyo. The year 1934 marked a turning point for Choe: she debuted in Tokyo as a solo dancer and presented a large body of new Korean-themed works, which became the basis for her *shinmuyong* repertoire.[106] Over the next few years, Choe rose to become one of the most famous cultural figures in the Japanese Empire, known primarily as a dancer but also as a model, film star, and singer.[107] In late 1937, Choe embarked on a world tour that lasted until 1940. During this time, she performed on three continents, visiting the United States, the Netherlands, France, Italy, Germany, Belgium, Brazil, Argentina, Uruguay, Chile, Peru, Colombia, and Mexico.[108] It was soon after this trip that she began her work in China.

Choe first traveled to China in 1941, the same year that Dai Ailian arrived and just one year prior to Qemberxanim's return. The reason for Choe's visit was different from those of the other two, however, since she was sent as a representative of the Japanese Empire and performed in part for the entertainment of Japanese soldiers.[109] Between 1941 and 1943, Choe performed three tours to Japanese-occupied areas of China and Manchukuo, a Japan-controlled puppet state set up in 1932 in what was previously part of northeast China. Among the cities Choe visited on these tours were Beijing (Beiping), Tianjin, Wushun, Shenyang (Fengtian), Dalian, Jilin, Changchun (Xinjing), Harbin, Qiqihar, Bei'an, Jiamusi, Mudanjiang, Tumen, Nanjing, and Shanghai.[110] By this time, Choe's dances had expanded beyond her earlier Korean-themed *shinmuyong* repertoires to include additional works on Japanese, Chinese, Indian, and Siamese themes.[111] In 1943 Choe sought training from Mei Lanfang in Shanghai and proposed the idea of creating a new dance style by studying and adapting elements of xiqu performance, specifically Peking opera and Kunqu.[112] In 1944, Choe moved to Beiping and set up the Oriental Dance Research Institute (Dongfang wudao yanjiusuo), with support from Mei and other renowned xiqu actors.[113]

Initially, Choe's interest in Chinese dance likely came from a political need to respond to the Japanese imperial regime's cultural policies of pan-Asianism and the ideology of the Greater East Asian Co-Prosperity Sphere. During the early 1940s, when this policy was being implemented, Choe experienced pressure to perform dances reflecting not just Korea but the entire Japanese imperial domain.[114] Choe's relationship to her Chinese colleagues was complex, however. According to Faye Kleeman, Choe "was particularly impressed by Mei [Lanfang]'s resistance to performing for the collaborating regime of Wang Jingwei," and Choe described her own move to Beiping in 1944 as "a form of 'exile.'"[115] Following the end of the Pacific War in 1945, Choe stayed on in Beijing for several months. Facing unwelcoming political climates in both Japan and South Korea, in 1946 she moved to Pyongyang, which would soon be the capital of North Korea.[116] Choe received a warm welcome from the North Korean government, and she performed extensively, in addition to running Pyongyang's first dance school.[117] Following the establishment of the PRC in 1949, Choe's company was invited to Beijing and gave a series of high-profile shows attended by cultural leaders.[118] This marked the beginning of a new period of Choe's engagement in Chinese dance activities, now as part of socialist cultural exchange between the PRC and North Korea.[119]

Choe's major impact on the development of Chinese dance began after China's entry into the Korean War, in November of 1950, when Choe returned to Beijing as a war refugee, her school in Pyongyang reportedly having been destroyed by US bombs and two of her students killed.[120] In Beijing, Choe delivered prominent speeches on Sino-Korean friendship and the urgency of the anti–United States war effort.[121] At the same time, she returned to her earlier project of researching xiqu dance. Between November 1950 and February 1951, Choe worked with Peking opera actor Mei Lanfang and Kunqu actors Han Shichang and Bai Yunsheng to document and analyze the techniques corresponding to various xiqu role types, including the "virtuous female" (qingyi), "coquettish female" (huadan), and "young scholar" (xiaosheng), as well as for stage properties such as the water sleeve.[122] During this time, she also began working with a small group of Chinese students and stated publicly her aim to "help facilitate the Chinese people's development of dance art."[123]

The first member of the PRC dance leadership to forcefully promote Choe's work as a future direction for Chinese dance was Chen Jinqing, then vice director of the CAD Dance Ensemble. As mentioned in the introduction, Chen was originally from Shanghai and had been involved in leftist theater during the 1930s. In 1938 she moved to Yan'an, where she joined the New Yangge movement. Chen helped lead a major CCP-affiliated dance program at the Northeast Lu Xun Arts Academy (Dongbei Lu

Xun yishu xueyuan), and in 1948, she traveled from there to Pyongyang to study at Choe's dance research institute.[124] Chen publicly endorsed Choe in her essay titled "On New Dance Art," which appeared in the same issue of *Literary Gazette* as Zhong Dianfei's critique of *Peace Dove*.[125] After reviewing problems with the post-1949 New Yangge productions, Chen argued that what was needed most to drive China's dance movement forward was higher quality artistic models. Choe, she argued, provided just such a model. Chen identified several of Choe's works as ideal models for Chinese dance creation, including "Breaching Stormy Seas" and "The Woodman and the Maiden." The former, Chen argued, exemplified Choe's masterful approach to dramatic choreography, while the latter offered a useful example of how to adapt folk dance rhythms for the modern stage. In addition to choreography and performance, Chen argued that Choe also had much to offer in the area of dance training. "Choe's set of basic methods and experiences for establishing her native dance basic training program is very worthy of our study," Chen argued, "because we currently need to create our own native dance basic training system."[126] From Chen's account, learning from Choe appeared the most logical next step for China's dance field.

By January 1951, the Chinese Ministry of Culture had recognized the potential value of Choe's work and invited her to move her dance research institute from Pyongyang to Beijing.[127] A special training program called the Choe Seung-hui Dance Research Course (Cui Chengxi wudao yanjiu ban) was established at CAD, scheduled to begin in March 1951.[128] On February 18, the *People's Daily* published a preview of the content of this course, which doubled as an official endorsement of Choe's guidance of China's dance field, in an article by Choe titled "The Future of Chinese Dance Art."[129] The article outlined Choe's plan for "helping China's dance world complete the work of organizing Chinese dance" by designing a new movement system derived from xiqu. Drawing on her twenty years of experience studying and creating new dances based on Korean and other Asian dance traditions, Choe wrote, she would apply the same strategies to document and systematize movements from traditional Chinese sources to create China's "new dance art."

One of the important conceptual contributions of Choe's program was a division of traditional sources into two categories: "folk" *(minjian)* and "classical" *(gudian)*. Rather than indicating the age of a performance practice, these terms indicated differences in social context. In Choe's taxonomy, "folk" referred to dances traditionally performed by peasants. The examples Choe gave in the Korean context were hourglass drum and mask dance, and in the Chinese context yangge, waist drum, and Taiping drum. For Choe, "classical" referred to dances traditionally performed by urban communities or in more formal settings. The examples she gave to illustrate Korean classical dance were sword dance, drum dance, and fan dance, and those for Chinese classical dance were the movements used in Peking opera and Kunqu. While the sources for China's new dance art existed in the movements used in these various folk and classical dance forms, Choe explained, creating new dance art would not mean simply transferring

FIGURE 11. Choe Seung-hui and students at the Central Academy of Drama in Beijing, 1952. Photographer unknown. Reproduced with permission from the private collection of Siqintariha.

these existing movements onto the stage. Rather, as she had learned from her past experience, it would require significant reworking—documenting, analyzing, synthesizing, organizing, systematizing, and creating—to make the movements expressive enough to stand on their own as dance, without the support of lyrics. Echoing Dai's prediction in 1946, Choe warned that this work could not be done by a single person and could not be done quickly—it would require many people's contributions and would take years to accomplish. Its end result would be an independent, artistically complete dance form that both reflected the realities of China's contemporary society and possessed a uniquely Chinese character.[130]

Within a month of the publication of Choe's essay, her plan was already being put into action: a group of young dancers had been recruited from leading ensembles and schools around China and brought to CAD to begin a year of full-time study led by Choe, a course that formally opened on March 17, 1951 (figure 11).[131] The course was given an official quota of 110 students, half from China and half from North Korea.[132] Students included both men and women, and of the fifty-five Chinese participants, at least sixteen were of non-Han ethnicity.[133] Although the students were all college-aged (born between 1929 and 1935), they had a wide range of professional backgrounds. Shu Qiao (b. 1933), from Shanghai, had joined the New Fourth Army's New Peace Traveling Ensemble (Xin'an lüxingtuan) in 1944, at the age of eleven, and by 1951 was working professionally with the ensemble in Shanghai.[134] Siqintariha (b. 1932), from Inner Mongolia, started performing professionally in 1947 and had participated in the 1949 All-China Literature and Arts Worker Representative Congress, the 1949 Budapest World Festival of Youth and Students, and the 1950 minority tour as a leading dancer in the Inner Mongolia Cultural Work Troupe.[135] Meanwhile, Lan Hang (b. 1935), from Beijing, had just been recruited to the CAD Dance Ensemble in 1950, and his first stage experience had been performing in *Peace Dove*.[136] Apart from developing a new basic movement system for Chinese dance and creating new dance works on themes related to the Korean War, the course also aimed to prepare these young dancers to serve as dance cadres who could help lead China's new dance field.[137]

Students in the 1951–52 Choe Seung-hui Dance Research Course received studio training in all of Choe's major areas of expertise, including Korean classical and folk dance, Southern dance *(nanfang wu)*,[138] Soviet ballet and folk dance, New Dance, improvisation, and rhythm, as well as theoretical courses in dance history, political thought, literature, and music.[139] The focus of the course, however, was on studying and organizing basic movements for Chinese dance derived from xiqu.[140] During the course's opening ceremonies, where Mei Lanfang personally endorsed Choe's methods, teachers demonstrated the basic movements that would be taught in each dance style. The description for the xiqu section was as follows:

> Basic movements for Chinese dance organized by Choe Seung-hui. Part one: dance movements of the coquettish female *(huadan)*, young scholar *(xiaosheng)*, virtuous female *(qingyi)*, partnering between virtuous female and young scholar, etc., in Chinese xiqu. These include gait *(taibu)*, horizontal walk *(hengbu)*, diagonal walk *(xiebu)*, brisk steps *(suibu)*, water sleeve *(shuixiu)*, raised sleeve *(yangxiu)*, trembling sleeve *(douxiu)*, spin *(xuanzhuan)*, circling the stage *(pao yuanchang)*, entry and exit *(chu ru chang)*, stalemate *(xiangchi)*, counterpoint *(duiwei)*, eye contact *(duikan)*, falling in love *(xiang'ai)*, expression *(biaoqing)*—looking, happy, timid, anxious, angry, afraid, crying—and everyday movements *(shenghuo dongzuo)*—bowing, putting on make-up, opening and closing the door, going up and downstairs, entering and exiting a bridge, boarding and de-boarding a boat, etc. Part two: basic movements of the martial female *(wudan)*, including short spear *(huaqiang)*—seven kinds of solo spear, nine kinds of dueling spears, and five kinds of double twirling spears— and sword dance—six kinds.[141]

This set of techniques embodied what Choe considered to be the "basic movements" of xiqu dance. By training in these movements, she believed, students

VIDEO 4. "Red Silk Dance," from *Colored Butterflies Fluttering About*. Beijing Film Studio, 1963.

To watch this video, scan the QR code with your mobile device or visit DOI: https://doi.org/10.1525/luminos.58.4

would gain a physical fluency in xiqu movement vocabulary, which they could then use to create their own new Chinese dance choreography. With the advent of xiqu dance, Chinese choreographers would no longer be limited to choosing among the options of yangge, minority dance, vernacular movement, or Western ballet and modern dance to create new works. Rather, they would be able to draw on the local dramatic traditions of Peking opera and Kunqu, using a set of techniques adapted specifically for dancers.[142]

By the spring of 1951, xiqu movement was already appearing in the works of regional ensembles. In the national dance festival held in Beijing that May, South China's *Braving Wind and Waves* had brought the sounds of xiqu to the dance stage with its use of gong and cymbal percussion. However, the work that really caused a stir was the twelve-person "Red Silk Dance" (Hongchou wu) by Changchun City Cultural Work Troupe (Changchun shi wengongtuan).[143] "Red Silk Dance" ingeniously showed how xiqu technique could be blended with yangge folk forms to create new dance styles. A version of "Red Silk Dance" recorded on film in 1963 begins with six women dressed in light blue peasant-style jackets and pants bouncing up and down to a yangge rhythm while waving short red scarves in both hands (video 4). A Chinese folk ensemble accompanies the dancers with a string melody set to gong and cymbal beats and a *suona* (Chinese clarinet), evoking the sounds of a rural festival. Then, six male dancers bound onto the stage in white costumes and head towels, holding sticks with tufts of red fabric on top. With a leap, the men thrust their arms up, and the tufts explode into red silk streamers about four meters long, painting the air in unison looping, swirling red patterns. Finally, the women return with long silks too, and the dancing carries on in a play of melodies, shapes, and stage arrangements.[144]

A major innovation of "Red Silk Dance" was that it melded the silk streamer technique used in xiqu with the bouncing footwork and playfulness of yangge and other folk forms. According to the work's creators, they had spent a year studying and experimenting with the techniques of three different types of traditional performers: yangge dancers, *errenzhuan* (a type of northeastern bawdy song and dance duet, also called *bengbengxi*) performers, and Peking opera actors. The end result was a work that, in their words, "extricated [silk dance] from Peking opera and made it into an independent dance form that, through revision, expresses new content."[145] The silk techniques used in "Red Silk Dance," although commonly perceived today as a fundamental component of Chinese folk dance, were in fact an innovation introduced in 1951 through the popularization of xiqu dance and its experimental blending with New Yangge and other folk forms. After its premiere, ensembles around China clamored to learn the new silk technique. To meet demand, a manual was published in 1953 that provided detailed diagrams and step-by-step instructions.[146] The bulk of the book's technical content was spent explaining how to manipulate the silk streamers. Readers were guided not only on how to construct the streamers but also on how to hold them, how to apply the correct amount of force to provide lift without causing exhaustion to the dancer, and, most importantly, how to achieve the effects of the various shapes and patterns. The book outlined nineteen "basic movements" of silk dance technique, from the simple "small figure eight" to the complex "double figure eight cross circle."[147] Such manuals were one of the ways that xiqu dance, following New Yangge and Frontier Dance, became popularized.

Choe Seung-hui returned to North Korea in October of 1952.[148] However, the nearly two years she spent in the early PRC between 1950 and 1952 left a strong impact on the later development of Chinese dance. As Dai Ailian commented in 1951, "Choe Seung-hui has already sown her dance art seeds, which will continue to grow and blossom on Chinese soil."[149] Between May 25 and June 15, 1952, the Choe Seung-hui Dance Research Course gave its graduation performances in Beijing, which included thirty-two shows seen by over twenty thousand people.[150] One of the most obvious continuities between Choe's work in the CAD program and developments in Chinese dance after her departure was the long-lasting and widespread practice of using xiqu movement as basic training for Chinese dancers. One of China's most important national dance ensembles—the Central Experimental Opera Theater (Zhongyang shiyan gejuyuan), established in Beijing in 1953—would develop xiqu dance by the late 1950s into the basis for a new form of full-length narrative Chinese dance choreography, as discussed in the next chapter. The first arena in which Choe's work would have a significant impact, however, was in China's dance schools.

FIGURE 12. Beijing Dance School graduates and teachers, 1956. Photographer unknown. Reproduced with permission from the private collection of Siqintariha.

CONCLUSION: A NATIONAL CURRICULUM

The formal experiments of the early 1950s occurred in many varieties, from daring stage productions to innovative classroom approaches. They occurred in the capital and in the provinces, driven by artists from the center, the border, and beyond. Events like national festivals and the formation of national ensembles suggested that Chinese dance was coming together as a coherent and recognizable artistic medium. However, the most outstanding expression of this development was the creation of a national training curriculum. Training is fundamental to the production of a dance form, because it is through this process that bodies attain the habits and skills that transform them into dance mediums. By creating a national curriculum, the dance community established a standard that determined what this medium would be—one that extended beyond any single ensemble, choreographer, region, style, or production. It determined what was to become understood as Chinese dance in a strictly formal sense, as defined by a set of fundamental movements and techniques.

The institution in which this curriculum was first worked out and put into practice was the Beijing Dance School (Beijing wudao xuexiao), which opened formally on September 6, 1954 (figure 12).[151] The school was designed to offer a live-in six-year vocational education for students beginning at or under the age of twelve, taking the place of middle and high school.[152] In the 1954 recruitment cycle, in order to fill all levels of the curriculum, the school only recruited new students for the first-year program. It filled the remaining second- through sixth-year slots with individuals already working as professional dancers in ensembles around China.[153] In its first year, the school enrolled a total of 198 students and offered studio training in two major dance styles: Chinese and European. The Chinese dance program offered courses in xiqu-based Chinese classical dance and four styles of Chinese folk dance, including Han, Korean, Tibetan, and Uyghur.[154] The European dance program offered courses in ballet (conceived of as "European classical dance") and European folk dance (also known as "European character dance"), including Russian, Spanish, Hungarian, and Polish.[155] Over the next few years, the student body expanded and diversified, and courses in additional styles were added. By 1956, the school had a total of 328 students, including ten exchange students from the Democratic Republic of Vietnam and twenty-four advanced students from China's regional dance ensembles enrolled in a short-term program in dance drama choreography led by a Soviet instructor, Viktor Ivanovich Tsaplin (1903–1968).[156] In 1957 a new major in South and Southeast Asian dance, known as Oriental Dance (Dongfang wu), was launched, led by four Balinese dance experts from Indonesia.[157] From 1954 to 1966, the breakdown of total graduates in each major was as follows: Chinese dance—390; European dance/ballet—156; choreography—39; Oriental Dance—33.[158] Thus, throughout the pre–Cultural Revolution period, Chinese dance remained the focus of the school's training mission.

The Ministry of Culture, which oversaw the founding of the school, recruited area experts to direct all aspects of the school's operations, including administration, teacher training, management of teaching and research, and student recruitment. Dai Ailian and Chen Jinqing, who were then leading the Central Song and Dance Ensemble, were appointed to serve as the school's first director and vice director, respectively. For teacher training, an intensive program took place between February and July 1954 that prepared over forty teachers.[159] During this program, different experts were recruited to provide training in each dance style: Peking opera and Kunqu specialists Gao Lianjia, Li Chenglian, Hou Yongkui (1911–1981), and Ma Xianglin (1913–1994) led teacher training for Chinese classical dance;[160] Anhui flower drum lantern specialist Feng Guopei (1914–2012) and Hebei yangge specialist Zhou Guobao led teacher training in Han folk dance; Korean dance specialists Zhao Dexian (1913–2002) and Piao Rongyuan (1930–1992), Tibetan *guozhuang* specialist Suona Zhaxi, and Uyghur dance specialist Qemberxanim led teacher training in Korean, Tibetan, and Uyghur folk dance, respectively;[161] and Soviet ballet specialist Ol'ga Il'ina, from the Moscow Choreographic Institute, led teacher training in ballet and European character dance.[162] During the school's first semester, leading members of the Chinese dance field Ye Ning, Peng Song, and Sheng Jie were appointed to manage teaching and research in the Chinese dance program.[163] Yuan Shuihai and Lu Wenjian were appointed to oversee the ballet curriculum.[164] Student recruitment was jointly administered by Chen Jinqing and Ol'ga Il'ina.[165]

The Beijing Dance School's Chinese dance curriculum skillfully united what were now the three established streams of Chinese dance—Han folk dance (inherited from New Yangge), minority dance (inherited from Frontier Dance), and xiqu dance (inherited from Choe's program).[166] The strong impact of all three dance styles within the new curriculum was immediately clear in the school's first year-end performance, held in May of 1955.[167] The production's finale was a work called "Marriage" (Jiehun), composed in the vocabulary of Northeast-style yangge.[168] Its costuming was clearly inspired by New Yangge stage aesthetics, with the groom in overalls, the bride in an embroidered jacket, and the group dancers using handkerchiefs and wearing white head towels.[169] Four works of minority dance were spread throughout the program. They included a Korean-themed dance called "Bright" (Minglang), a Uyghur-themed dance called "Holiday Cheer" (Jieri de huanle), a Tibetan-themed dance called "Friendship" (Youyi), and a Mongol-themed dance called "Ordos" (E'erduosi).[170] Costumes used in these pieces resembled those worn in the 1949 All-China Literature and Arts Worker Representative Congress *Frontier Folk Dance Introduction Plenary* and the 1950 minority tour.[171] Finally, the production contained four Chinese classical dance works inspired by xiqu: "Picking Flowers" (Cai hua), choreographed by Kunqu actor Ma Xianglin; "Young Patriot" (Shaonian aiguozhe) and "Shepard Flute" (Mu di), both choreographed by Peking opera actor Li Chenglian; and "Interrupted Dream" (Jing meng), based on a segment from the famous Kunqu drama *Peony Pavilion*.[172] "Picking Flowers" and "Interrupted Dream" were both performed by students of Choe Seung-hui, and with the exception of "Young Patriot," which followed an aesthetic more akin to spoken drama, costumes for the other Chinese classical dance works resembled designs used in xiqu and regional drama.[173] Of the ten Chinese dance works, eight used musical accompaniment provided by a Chinese-style orchestra, following the norm for Chinese dance practice as developed through *Braving Wind and Waves*, the 1950 minority tour, and successful newer works such as "Red Silk Dance."[174]

As China's only national-level professional conservatory dedicated solely to dance, the Beijing Dance School had an important impact on standardizing and disseminating Chinese dance and its pedagogical methods across the country. The cohort of 1955 graduates were assigned jobs in at least seven locations—including Beijing, Shanghai, Guangdong, Guangxi, Sichuan, Shaanxi, Yunnan, and Jilin—and by 1960, the school's graduates were working in every province and autonomous region across China with the exception of Hebei and Liaoning.[175] Over time, as more students graduated from the school and these students went on to train students of their own in diverse locales across the country, the Beijing Dance School's program gained the status of a national dance curriculum. By 1956 the school had the nickname Cradle of Dancers, indicating that it was China's leading center for dance education.[176] In 1960, when the school published its first edition of *Teaching Method for Chinese Classical Dance*, the print run was 4,500 copies, indicating a plan for widespread use.[177]

Although the school taught multiple dance styles during the 1950s, it was the Chinese dance program that had the greatest impact on China's dance development during this period. Until December 31, 1959, when the Beijing Dance Academy's Attached Experimental Ballet Ensemble was established, all professional music and dance ensembles in China—of which there were dozens across the country by early 1957—specialized in Chinese dance.[178] For this reason, other dance styles had little direct relevance to most dancers' professional work. While ballet was typically seen as a useful form of physical training for dancers during this era, it was not regarded as an important medium for new choreography. After the failure of *Peace Dove*, the next new work based in ballet movement vocabulary did not appear until 1959. Another reason that Chinese dance had the most impact during this period was that the first cohorts of students majoring in non-Chinese styles did not start to matriculate until around 1958, with the first cohort of ballet majors graduating in 1959 and the first cohort of Oriental Dance majors in 1960.[179] Rather than being assigned to other locales, ballet majors were almost all retained either to teach at the school or to join the school's new Experimental Ballet Ensemble (Shiyan baleiwuju tuan), founded in late 1959.[180] Graduates of the school's Oriental Dance program were similarly kept in Beijing first to teach and then to form the new Oriental Song and Dance Ensemble (Dongfang gewutuan), established in early 1962.[181] Thus, while the ballet and Oriental Dance curricula initially trained dancers for a limited set of jobs in institutions found only in Beijing, the Chinese dance curriculum trained dancers for ensembles located all over the country. By the mid-1950s, it was possible to say not only that Chinese dance had been created, but that it had truly become China's national dance form.

3

Performing a Socialist Nation

The Golden Age of Chinese Dance

On the opening pages of the October 1955 issue of *China Pictorial,* a photo spread documents parades held in Beijing to celebrate China's sixth National Day.[1] For the most part, the images depict scenes one might expect for such an event: Mao Zedong and other leaders saluting from atop the rostrum overlooking Tian'anmen Square; schoolchildren walking with bouquets in front of a float displaying the giant slogan "Endorse the Five-Year Plan"; athletes and soldiers marching with flags and guns; military tanks rolling by as warplanes fly overhead; and civilians marching beside a cart displaying a giant tractor. One image, however, seems not to belong. Atop a circular float shaped like a tiered wedding cake stand two rings of dancers in pastel-colored dresses with long hoop skirts and melon-sized lotus blossoms on stalks rising from their skirt edges (figure 13). The dancers' hair is decorated with flowery ornaments, and white flowing scarves sweep down in scallops from their outstretched arms. On the ground, about 150 more dancers wearing nearly identical outfits minus the lotus stalks circle the float on foot in four concentric circles. Dancers in the two outer rings clasp hands, while those on the two inner rings balance lotus blossoms on their outstretched palms. These dancers are part of the National Day parades too. Behind them is the decorated Tian'anmen rostrum and a pillar carrying the phrase "Long Live Chairman Mao!"

The parade dancers described above are performing an adaptation of one of the most widely circulated Chinese dance works of the 1950s and early 1960s: a group piece called "Lotus Dance" (Hehua wu) that was choreographed by Dai Ailian and premiered by the Central Song and Dance Ensemble in 1953.[2] When presented on stage, "Lotus Dance" is typically performed by nine dancers and lasts about six minutes. Here, it has been adapted to a much larger scale for the parade format.

FIGURE 13. "Lotus Dance" in National Day Parade. Published in *Renmin huabao* 6, no. 10 (October 1955): 3. Photographer: Yuan Fen. Image provided by China Foto Bank.

However, the costumes and body postures depicted in the photograph clearly identify it as the same dance.[3] In its composition, "Lotus Dance" is much like the 1951 "Red Silk Dance" discussed in the previous chapter. That is, it presents a new dance form created by merging yangge (northern Han folk dance) with xiqu (traditional Chinese theater). In "Lotus Dance," the yangge component comes from "lotus lamp" *(hehua deng/lianhua deng),* also known as "walking flower lamp" *(zou huadeng),* a type of popular performance practiced in the northwestern Longzhong cultural region in eastern Gansu and northern Shaanxi.[4] Hu Sha had introduced the form to PRC stages through the 1949 pageant *Long Live the People's Victory,* which he codirected with Dai, and from there Dai adapted it again to create "Lotus Dance." While she was choreographing it, Dai also traveled to northern Shaanxi during the 1953 Spring Festival holiday so that she could observe "lotus lamp" performed in a folk setting.[5] The xiqu component in "Lotus Dance" comes from Kunqu, a refined theatrical style developed during the sixteenth century that is associated with the Wu cultural area around what is today Shanghai, Zhejiang, and southern Jiangsu. In early versions of "Lotus Dance," Dai collaborated with Ma Xianglin (1913–1994), a Kunqu actor who participated in the construction of early Chinese classical dance at CAD and the Beijing Dance School.[6] In "Lotus Dance," the dancers sway their upper bodies in slow, graceful lines and circle the stage using rapid, tiny steps that make them appear to be floating, both elements derived from Kunqu movement. With the diaphanous white scarves draped over their light pink upper costumes and long green fringed skirts with adapted lotus "lamps" on their rims, the dance combines disparate performance elements in a new way, producing the new image of whitish-pink blossoms floating serenely on a lake of lily pads.

Despite its clear connection to early PRC dance projects, "Lotus Dance" seems an odd choice for a National Day parade in a socialist country. The dance presents few signs of socialist realism, supposedly the dominant artistic mode of socialism, and it is not clearly linked to themes commonly associated with socialist art, such as class struggle, the military, farming, or factories. Rather, the poetic image of the lotus suggests an underlying religious connotation. As a review published in *Guangming Daily* in 1954 explained, "Lotus Dance" embodies the Buddhist idea of "the lotus that grows in the mud but is not soiled by the mud."[7] Despite such apparent incongruities, however, "Lotus Dance" was a widely celebrated expression of socialist China both at home and abroad during the 1950s and early 1960s. In 1953 China's delegation received an award for the work at the Bucharest World Festival of Youth and Students (WFYS, a.k.a. World Youth Festival), at the time a leading international venue for the presentation of socialist art.[8] A reporter in Romania described the reception of "Lotus Dance" at the festival as follows:

> The fame of the art of Chinese dancers has long since become known in all countries. When the announcer introduced the dance team of the ensemble, her words were drowned by a storm of applause. The orchestra strikes up playing the introduction to the music written by Chian Ku [sic] and Liu Chi for 'The Dance of the Lotus Flowers.' . . . The graceful movements of the young dancers sketch flowers opening up under the warm sun-rays, and then a breeze drives the lotus flowers onto the water's surface. . . . [It shows] the perfection of Chinese dancers.[9]

Many Chinese dance works won awards at WFYS dance competitions, which PRC delegations attended regularly from 1949 to 1962. Due to the prestige associated with these events in China at the time, winning an award at WFYS typically secured a new work inclusion in subsequent domestic events and international tours. This was one reason for the success of "Red Silk Dance," which had won an award at the previous WFYS in East Berlin in 1951.[10] It also contributed to the popularity of the three other new Chinese dance works that won awards at Bucharest in 1953: "Picking Tea and Catching Butterflies" (Caicha pudie), "Running Donkey" (Pao lü), and "Lion Dance" (Shi wu), based on Han folk material from Fujian, Hebei, and Hebei, respectively.[11] After their success at WFYS, both "Picking Tea and Catching Butterflies" and "Running Donkey," along with "Lotus Dance," were popularized in China through a teaching manual like the one published for

"Red Silk Dance."[12] They also became regular items on dance programs designed to represent China to foreign audiences. In 1954, for example, "Lotus Dance" and "Picking Tea and Catching Butterflies" appeared in a Chinese dance tour to India, and in 1955 "Lotus Dance," "Picking Tea and Catching Butterflies," and "Red Silk Dance" all appeared in the program of a Chinese arts delegation to Italy.[13] A souvenir photo album of Chinese dance gifted to the KOLO ensemble of the former Yugoslavia while it was on tour in China is similarly composed.[14] The album likely commemorated a welcome show performed for visiting KOLO members while they were visiting Beijing.[15]

Works like "Lotus Dance" and "Red Silk Dance" continued as symbols of China's socialist culture at home and abroad into the late 1950s and early 1960s. In 1957, when the WFYS in Moscow released a new poster for its folk festival, "Red Silk Dance" was among six dances pictured from around the world.[16] Between 1955 and 1958, *Guangming Daily* reports "Lotus Dance" taking the stage in twelve international locales, including (in order) Indonesia, Burma, Vietnam, Czechoslovakia, England, Switzerland, France, Belgium, Yugoslavia, Hungary, Egypt, and Japan.[17] And both "Red Silk Dance" and "Lotus Dance" appear in extant performance programs from a Chinese tour to Canada, Colombia, Cuba, and Venezuela in 1960 (figure 14).[18] That same year, "Lotus Dance" appeared again in National Day parades in Beijing, now with an updated float design that enveloped the dancers on the central platform in a ring of pink lotus petals.[19] In 1962, when mass performances were held in Beijing to celebrate the twentieth anniversary of Mao's "Talks at the Yan'an Forum of Literature and Arts," "Lotus Dance" was among the featured works.[20] And in 1963, when the Beijing Film Studio released its new color dance film *Colored Butterflies Fluttering About (Caidie fenfei)*, "Red Silk Dance" was among the twelve dances included.[21] In 1964, this film was shown in Norway as part of celebrations for the fifteenth anniversary of the PRC, and the United Arab Republic Embassy in China also showed it to celebrate that country's own national holiday.[22]

Thus, rather than being marginal, Chinese dance was at the center of performances of China as a socialist nation at home and internationally during the late 1950s and early 1960s. In this chapter, I examine this period of Chinese dance choreography, looking first at the circulation of Chinese dance abroad and then at a new form of Chinese dance that emerged during this period, the "national dance drama" *(minzu wuju)*. I argue that the late 1950s and early 1960s marked the golden age of Chinese dance because it witnessed continued innovations in choreographic form, as well as the expansion of the genre to global visibility. The new dances that emerged during this period continued features of Chinese dance that had been established in the wartime period and the early years of the PRC, such as the three principles of kinesthetic nationalism, ethnic and spatial inclusiveness, and dynamic inheritance and the three styles of Han folk dance, ethnic minority dance, and xiqu-based classical dance. They also demonstrated a transformative surge in professionalism, as the first generation

FIGURE 14. "Lotus Dance" on tour in Canada, Colombia, Cuba, and Venezuela. Published in China Art Ensemble performance program, 1960. Photographer unknown. Image obtained from the University of Michigan Asia Library Chinese Dance Collection.

of dancers trained in newly established PRC ensembles and conservatories matured and begin to create and star in their own productions. The new repertoires that emerged in the late 1950s and early 1960s thus also represented the fruition of years of socialist state investment in labor and infrastructure for creating Chinese dance, such as devising curricula, constructing institutions, training dancers, and developing and staging new choreography. As the early pioneers ceded the stage to their younger protégés, this era saw the rise of the first generation of dancers and dance works cultivated entirely in China's socialist dance system. In other words, the dancing bodies representing China on stage were socialist in many ways.

In terms of artistic innovation, the most important and lasting development of the late 1950s and early 1960s, which had a lasting impact on Chinese dance choreography, was the emergence of a new, full-length narrative Chinese dance form. As discussed in the previous chapter, early large-scale dance works like *Long Live the People's Victory*, *Peace Dove*, and *Braving Wind and Waves to Liberate Hainan* were all considered formally insufficient to meet the needs of China's new revolutionary dance culture because none had found an effective way to meld Chinese dance with revolutionary stories. This problem was finally resolved with the premiere of the first full-length national dance drama, *Magic Lotus Lantern (Bao liandeng)*, in August 1957.[23] Dozens of national dance dramas appeared in the following years, coinciding with a mass campaign known as the Great Leap Forward. Like the earlier WFYS competition pieces, they gained wide visibility as symbols of socialist China at home and abroad. However, while both types of choreography embodied socialist ideals, national dance dramas moved beyond the shorter WFYS works in their ability to explore complex political and social issues. In their treatment of themes such as marriage choice, as well as intersections between sex and gender, ethnicity, class, and race, these productions challenged traditional social hierarchies in ways that demonstrated a new critical outlook within the Chinese dance field. In their use of Chinese dance movement to engage these complex issues, the national dance dramas of the Great Leap Forward set a new standard for Chinese dance choreography.

PERFORMING THE NATION ABROAD: CHINESE DANCE IN INTERNATIONAL CONTEXTS

Contrary to common misconceptions, China was not a culturally isolated country during the early decades of the socialist period, nor was it disconnected from the latest trends in global dance creation of the time. The PRC received its first officially recognized international performing arts delegations on the day it was founded, October 1, 1949, and between 1955 and 1968 (after which these activities were stalled temporarily by the Cultural Revolution) an average of sixteen such delegations, the majority of which included dancers, visited China each year.[24] Between 1949 and 1962, China sent dance delegations to all seven WFYS dance competitions, in Budapest (1949), East Berlin (1951), Bucharest (1953), Warsaw (1955), Moscow (1957), Vienna (1959), and Helsinki (1962).[25] At these competitions, China's dancers interacted with dance groups from all over the world. However, these were only 7 of the 166 officially sanctioned performing arts delegations that China sent abroad between 1949 and 1967, which included groups presenting dance, drama, music, and acrobatics. During this period, Chinese delegations that featured Chinese dance performed in over sixty countries (listed with date of first appearance): Hungary (1949), East Germany (1951), Poland (1951), the Soviet Union (1951), Romania (1951), Czechoslovakia (1951), Austria (1951), Bulgaria (1951), Albania (1951), Mongolia (1952), India (1954), Burma (1954), Indonesia (1955), France (1955), Belgium (1955), the Netherlands (1955), Switzerland (1955), Italy (1955), the United Kingdom (1955), Yugoslavia (1955), Vietnam (1955), Egypt (1956), Sudan (1956), Ethiopia (1956), Syria (1956), Lebanon (1956), Chile (1956), Uruguay (1956), Brazil (1956), Argentina (1956), West Germany (1956), Afghanistan (1956), New Zealand (1956), Australia (1956), Cambodia (1957), Pakistan (1957), Sri Lanka (1957), Japan (1958), Luxembourg (1958), Iraq (1959), North Korea (1960), Nepal (1960), Venezuela (1960), Colombia (1960), Cuba (1960), Canada (1960), Norway (1961), Sweden (1961), Finland (1961), Algeria (1964), Morocco (1964), Tunisia (1964), Mali (1965), Guinea (1965), Mauritania (1965), Ghana (1965), North Yemen (1966), Zambia (1966), Palestine (1966), Uganda (1966), Laos (1966), Tanzania (1967), and Somalia (1967).[26] The United States is conspicuously absent from this list, which may explain the persistent incorrect US perception that China was "cut off from the world" during this time. This notion is accurate only if one equates "the world" with the United States.[27]

In this section, I examine the presentation of Chinese dance abroad during the 1950s and early 1960s from two angles: the composition of dance programs and the role of Chinese dance at WFYS dance competitions. I believe these activities are important for understanding the development of Chinese dance for several reasons. First, the presentation of Chinese dance abroad marked a rise in the status of dancers as recognized symbols of China's national culture, as well as an expansion of whose bodies and whose knowledge were generators of cultural prestige on the world stage. Previously, Han men and their artistic products often dominated the representation of Chinese culture abroad. By contrast, in international dance tours of the 1950s and early 1960s, the artistic work of women and ethnic minorities took center stage, allowing them to gain coveted opportunities, elevated social status, and cultural legitimacy. Second, performances of Chinese dance abroad during this period allowed Chinese choreographers to participate in the construction of international dance trends. One stated motivation of early Chinese dance pioneers such as Dai Ailian and Liang Lun was to create novel forms of dance in China that could be performed abroad, so that China would become not only a receiver but also a producer of international dance culture.[28] While Dai and Liang both realized this goal through their own Chinese dance performances in the United States and Southeast Asia during the late 1940s, the tours of the 1950s and early 1960s expanded this project to a much larger scale and reach. Lastly, these performances of Chinese dance abroad also shaped the direction of dance creation in China. As mentioned above, winning awards at WFYS competitions was considered a major honor and often gave new Chinese dance works lasting visibility domestically and internationally. For this reason, Chinese choreographers were incentivized to create works that fit the guidelines and preferences established at WFYS competitions and other international arenas. Performances abroad thus provided an opportunity for Chinese dancers to redefine national culture, gain international influence, and learn about and respond to international dance trends.

On April 29, 1960, a Chinese performance delegation consisting of 101 dancers, Peking opera actors, singers, musicians, and cultural administrators gave a performance in Caracas, the capital of Venezuela, in the first show of what would be a six-and-a-half-month tour to Venezuela, Colombia, Cuba, and Canada.[29] Following a common practice for Chinese state-sponsored international performance delegations both during and after the socialist era, this delegation brought together performers and repertoire from a variety of different ensembles, which were presented abroad under a single group name, China Art Ensemble (Zhongguo yishutuan), only used for international tours.[30] Two extant performance programs from the tour, together with film footage and print sources documenting the dances it included, offer insight into the performances, including which dances were presented and the images of Chinese socialist culture they embodied.[31] From the dances presented on this tour, we can see that ethnic and spatial inclusivity, kinesthetic nationalism, and dynamic inheritance were strong structuring principles that guided the composition of this dance program. Additionally, it is evident that the program highlighted women performers and dance styles that represented minority communities and were initially popularized by ethnic minority artists, although the dancers who actually performed the dances in this particular tour were mainly Han.

An intention to represent ethnic and spatial diversity is clearly reflected in the selection of dance works included in the tour. By 1960 dance tour planners had quite a broad range of options to choose from, because during the 1950s, Chinese choreographers and dancers had created hundreds of new dance works, encouraged by the establishment of state-sponsored professional dance ensembles across the country, as well as frequent dance festivals organized at the local, regional, and national levels. Thirty-three of these new works had received awards at WFYS competitions by 1959, of which nineteen were based on Han sources and thirteen on ethnic minority material.[32] The dance program that the planners ultimately devised for the 1960 tour included twelve items that represented seven ethnic groups. Among the twelve items, five had Han themes: "Parasol Dance" (Huasan wu), "Red Silk Dance," "Harvest Dance" (Fengshou le), "Lotus Dance," and "In the Rain" (Zou yu). The remaining seven were the Dai-themed "Peacock Dance" (Kongque wu), Mongol-themed "Pasture Horse" (most likely Muma wu, a.k.a.

"Tamed Horse"), Yi-themed "Joyful Nuosu" (Kuaile de luosuo), Uyghur-themed "Dance of the Drum" (Gu wu), Mongol-themed "Ordos Dance" (E'erduosi wu), Tibetan-themed "Reba on the Grassland" (Caoyuan shang de Reba, aka "Yipa on the Steppe"), and Korean-themed "Fan Dance" (Shan wu).[33] The importance placed on non-Han groups in this program reflects the continued CCP investment in recognizing ethnic minority "nationalities" as constituent parts of the Chinese nation during this time, a process that occurred in part through ethnic classification projects and the resultant investment of cultural meaning in what were often newly defined ethnic categories.[34] In addition to representing ethnic diversity, the program showed diversity of geographic region. Every major region of the country was represented: "Fan Dance" and "Red Silk Dance" represented the northeast (Jilin and Heilongjiang, respectively); "Tamed Horse" and "Ordos Dance" represented the north (Inner Mongolia); "Dance of the Drum" and "Lotus Dance" represented the northwest (Xinjiang and Gansu/Shaanxi, respectively); "Peacock Dance," "Joyful Nuosu," and "Reba on the Grassland" represented the southwest (Yunnan, Sichuan, and Tibet, respectively); "Parasol Dance" and "Harvest Dance" represented central China (Henan and Jiangxi, respectively); and "In the Rain" represented the southeast (Fujian).[35] Thus, in terms of its selection of material, this dance program projected an image of socialist China as a nation of multiple ethnic groups and diverse regional cultures.

From the perspective of dance form, the program highlighted innovative choreography adapted from local material, showing an ongoing commitment to the creative principles of kinesthetic nationalism and dynamic inheritance developed by early Chinese dance pioneers. One way in which this is demonstrated is through the use of stage props adapted from local performance practice. Such props appear in nearly every item in the dance program, such as paper umbrellas and handkerchiefs in "Parasol Dance" and "In the Rain"; handheld percussion instruments the Central Asian *doyra* and the Tibetan *dhyāngro* in "Drum Dance" and "Reba on the Grassland," respectively; large folding fans in "Fan Dance"; and "big head babies" (*datou wawa*), an oversized doll-like mask used in Han folk performance, in "Harvest Dance." As demonstrated in extant film recordings of these works, the stage properties served not merely as visual ornaments but were integrated into the dance technique, which drew heavily on folk and regional forms. This can be seen in recordings of "In the Rain" and "Harvest Dance" in the 1959 dance film *Hundred Phoenixes Face the Sun (Bai feng chao yang)*, which show a clear debt to movement vocabularies and techniques employed in Fujian and Jiangxi local dialect operas and other Han folk performance styles (video 5). "In the Rain" shows this in the dancers' delicately bouncing footwork, tilting head and torso actions, and circling finger and eye movements. It is also clear in "Harvest Dance" through the dancers' swinging arms, heads, and hips, sideways kicking feet, and exaggerated comic theatricality. Both recordings also feature musical accompaniment provided by an

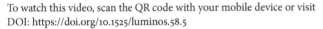

VIDEO 5. "In the Rain," from *Hundred Phoenixes Face the Sun*. Beijing Film
Studio, 1959.

To watch this video, scan the QR code with your mobile device or visit
DOI: https://doi.org/10.1525/luminos.58.5

orchestral score that features folk melodies and instruments.[36] While dance form
clearly takes inspiration from local sources in these works, they also emphasize
artistic innovation. "Reba on the Grassland," for example, followed the pattern of
"Lotus Dance" and "Red Silk Dance" by bringing together disparate performance
elements. As depicted in the 1963 film *Colored Butterflies Fluttering About*, the
dance combines a popular form of Tibetan sleeve dance that would normally be
performed at social gatherings with more acrobatic movements developed by itinerant performers, such as fast turning sequences and varied drumming techniques
(video 6).[37] The recording of "Peacock Dance" in *Hundred Phoenixes Face the Sun*
also shows significant innovations by adapting a dance style previously performed
solo or in pairs into a large group choreography that emphasizes unison movement and geometrical stage formations.[38]

In terms of whose ingenuity and artistic accomplishment this program highlighted, women and ethnic minority artists both appear as important contributors.
Women performers clearly dominated the dance portion of the program. That is,
of the twelve dance items it included, eleven featured female performers, and six
were danced exclusively by women. This marked a clear departure from performing arts tours that represented China abroad in the early decades of the twentieth
century, in which the artists who most often appeared on stage were men, though
often performing in female roles.[39] When it comes to ethnicity, non-Han artists
contributed to this tour too, but as choreographers and models more than as
actual performers. Based on the names and photographs in the printed programs,
it appears that the majority of dancers included in this tour were of Han ethnicity, making it quite different from the composition of delegations to the WFYS

VIDEO 6. Oumijiacan and ensemble in "Reba on the Grassland," from *Colored Butterflies Fluttering About*. Beijing Film Studio, 1963.

To watch this video, scan the QR code with your mobile device or visit DOI: https://doi.org/10.1525/luminos.58.6

competitions, as discussed further below. Thus, for example, the photograph and accompanying caption for the Uyghur item "Dance of the Drum" indicate that the lead role was performed by Zi Huayun (1936–2014), a Han dancer in the Central Song and Dance Ensemble, a group that specialized in Han folk-themed choreography and was made up primarily of Han artists.[40] Nevertheless, many of the non-Han themed items in the program had been created and originally performed by ethnic minority choreographers and dancers who were recognized officially as the creators of these works. "Dance of the Drum," for example, was clearly based on the style of Uyghur dance performed and codified by Uyghur dancer Qemberxanim during the 1940s and 1950s; Qemberxanim herself was a leading teacher and cultural figure promoting the styles at this time. In 1957, two dances in this style—"Plate Dance" (Panzi wu) and "Hand Drum Dance" (Shougu wu)—had won awards for China at the WFYS competition in Moscow. At the competition, these dances had been performed by a woman of Tatar ethnicity, known in Chinese as Zuohala Shahemayiwa (b. 1934), who was originally from Xinjiang but at the time had become a soloist in the PLA General Political Department Song and Dance Ensemble (Zongzheng gewutuan), one of China's top professional dance companies.[41] "Ordos Dance," "Tamed Horse," and "Reba on the Grassland" had also all been choreographed at least in part by minority choreographers, and they had all been originally performed by ethnic minority dancers in events both in and outside China. "Ordos Dance," which was choreographed by Manchu dancer Jia Zuoguang (1923–2017) and starred Mongol dancer Siqintariha (b. 1932), won an award at the 1955 WFYS shortly after it appeared in a graduation performance at the Beijing Dance School, where Siqintariha and Jia were both students at the time.[42] Likewise, "Reba on the Grassland," which was co-choreographed by and starred Tibetan dancer Oumijiacan (b. 1928), won an award at the 1957 WFYS, shortly after it premiered at the Central Nationalities Song and Dance Ensemble, where Oumijiacan was a lead dancer and choreographer.[43] Although the group choreography "Peacock Dance" was created by a Han choreographer, Jin Ming (b. 1926), it was based on a style of dance first developed and performed by a Dai artist originally from Yunnan, Mao Xiang (1923–1986). Mao had won an award for his version of the dance, titled "Peacock Duet" (Shuangren kongque wu) at the 1957 WFYS, the same year that Jin Ming's "Peacock Dance" also won an award, with the lead performed by a dancer of Korean ethnicity, Cui Meishan (b. 1934).[44] By 1960, these dances had all been incorporated into a nationally recognized Chinese dance repertoire that was being performed widely by ensembles across China and also toured abroad. Thus, professional dancers were expected to be able to perform these dances regardless of their ethnic background.

As the above discussion demonstrates, the WFYS dance competitions had a tremendous impact on the constitution of Chinese dance repertoires and tour programs during the late 1950s and early 1960s. Of the forty-one Chinese dance works that won awards at these competitions, a large number went on to become canonical works of Chinese dance, and some are still taught and performed regularly, especially by students, today.[45] This suggests that international performance venues served not only as places to present Chinese dance abroad but also as interactive spaces in which Chinese dance encountered and responded to foreign artists and audiences. Anglophone scholarship on international dance exchange during the Cold War has tended to focus largely on modern dance and ballet, with an emphasis on competition between the two Cold War superpowers: the United States and the Soviet Union.[46] The WFYS competitions present a different view of dance exchange in this period since, as Pia Koivunen has pointed out, they offered an alternative space in which artists could move beyond "Western conceptions and art forms that were developed in the West" and instead foreground artistic projects more of interest in socialist countries and outside the Western cultural sphere.[47] While ballet did play an important role in the WFYS dance competitions, the competitions also placed a large emphasis on national dances—for example, Russian and Eastern European folk dance, Indian classical dances, and Central Asian dance. In the context of WFYS dance exchange, choreography performed in these styles not only generated great prestige and excitement but also served as important vehicles of international connectivity and political activism.[48] Through the structuring of competition rules and the imagery used in promotional materials, WFYS dance competitions encouraged new dance innovation in these styles and presented them as the most important and innovative forms of dance creation happening globally at the time.

The WFYS collection at the International Institute of Social History in Amster-dam offers significant documentation of these dance competitions, helping to recall an important and underresearched piece of dance history that offers essen-tial international context for the development of Chinese dance. As represented in this collection, World Festivals of Youth and Students were major interna-tional gatherings attended by participants from across the world. With the Soviet Union providing the majority of funding and ideological direction, these events placed special emphasis on youth in socialist bloc and formerly colonized coun-tries, as well as left-leaning groups worldwide.[49] For the Chinese youth who par-ticipated, WFYS served as important sites for what Nicolai Volland calls "socialist cosmopolitanism," as well as for what I have described as China's postcolonial, Third Worldist, and inter-Asian internationalist aspirations during the 1950s and early 1960s.[50] It is important to remember that dance competitions were just one of many cultural activities that occurred during these grand events, which had tens of thousands of participants from sometimes more than one hundred coun-tries. In terms of art activities, the 1955 WFYS in Warsaw, for example, included "cultural presentations" of national songs, national dances, ballets, choirs, opera music, symphonic orchestra concerts, theater, pantomime, circus, circus artists, puppet shows, imitators, and amateur concerts, as well as "pre-festival cultural competitions" in literature, journalism, music, fine arts, folklore arts, photogra-phy, and film. Dance competitions fell into a separate program held during the festival, known as "international competitions," which included categories for folk dance, ballet, classic and folk songs, piano, violin, cello, folk music instruments, accordion, harmonica, guitar, and pantomime.[51] In 1957 artists from fifty countries participated in these international competitions, presenting 1,239 performances and winning a total of 945 medals.[52] The performance of national identity was often an explicit framing of these presentations. For example, a program for the 1953 Bucharest festival included a category called "National Cultural Programs," in which the schedule included options such as "Poland," "Romania," "Indonesia," "Brazil," and so on.[53]

Structural aspects of the WFYS dance competitions, such as rules stipulating age of participants and the style, format, and scale of choreographic entries, created opportunities for younger dancers and pushed choreographers to develop dance works within supported styles. Warsaw's 1955 rules, following those established in previous years, specified that all competition participants be no more than thirty years of age by December of the festival year.[54] Since even the youngest among the early Chinese dance pioneers, Liang Lun and Chen Jinqing, were already thirty-four by 1955, this rule effectively restricted participation in the WFYS competitions for the Chinese dance field to that new generation of dancers trained in PRC institu-tions. Another way that the WFYS rules shaped Chinese dance creation was through the categories of dance entry they permitted. As recent studies by Anthony Shay and Christina Ezrahi demonstrate, the Soviet Union mainly promoted two styles of dance during the 1950s: state or national folk dance, as represented by groups such as the State Academic Ensemble of Folk Dances of the Peoples of the USSR, led by Igor Moiseyev, and ballet, as represented by ensembles such as the Mariinsky (later Kirov) and the Bolshoi.[55] This focus in Soviet dance was reflected in the structures of the Soviet-sponsored WFYS dance competitions, at least initially. In 1953 and 1955, for example, dances could win prizes in only two categories: folk dance or ballet.[56] In 1957 the categories of "Oriental classical dances" and "modern ballroom dancing" were added, and in 1962 "modern dance" appeared as a category of competition for the first time.[57] However, folk dance was always the major category for countries like China that did not have professional ballet ensembles. (China's first experimental ballet ensemble was established in late 1959, and it did not become an independent national ensemble until 1964.) Before the addition of "Oriental classical dances" as an option, however, Asian classical dance was apparently sometimes presented in the ballet category under the subcategory of "ballet-character dance." In 1953, for example, Bharatanatyam dancer Indrani Rahman won first prize in the solo portion of this subcategory.[58] The two categories in which Chinese delegations consistently won awards were folk dance and Oriental classical dance, and there is no indication that PRC dancers participated in any of the other dance categories.[59] Apart from performer age and dance style, WFYS competition rules also governed dance length and number of performers. In 1953, for example, all competition dances had to be between three and fifteen minutes.[60] In 1955 folk dance entries were limited to seven minutes and allowed a maximum of eight (or, in some documents, six) performers.[61] By 1957 entries for folk dance and Oriental classical dance could have up to sixteen performers.[62] Sometimes there were separate categories for solo, duet, and group works. While precise regulations fluctuated over time, the general pattern was to encourage the creation of short choreographies in either solo, duet, or group formats.

The official journal of WFYS, *Festival*, frequently published photographs of dance performances, providing a sense of the choreographic sensibilities these events promoted. One of the most common subjects in these images is a group of dancers exhibiting staged versions of Eastern European folk dances. In them, one finds Bulgarian, Polish, Russian, Hungarian, Romanian, and German ensembles of men and women dressed in national costumes, often including long, full skirts, embroidered or striped aprons, puffy blouses, waist-length vests, and boots. The dancers often appear with their hands clasped or arms linked around each other's shoulders and waists, conveying a sense of community bonding through social dance. A strong sense of motion is present in these images, which frequently depict dancers leaping and twirling through space with their skirts and vests lifting into the air. A sense of momentum, speed, and fun pervades these photographs, and dancers are often shown enjoying the thrill of collaborative movement, such as partnered lifts and spins using centripetal force and counterbalance. Apart from these images, Asian and Middle Eastern dances are the next most common. Like their Eastern European counterparts, these Uzbek, Indonesian, Indian, Korean, Mongolian, Egyptian, Syrian, Vietnamese, and Chinese groups also appear in national costumes, which often include flowing robes, sashes, head scarves or hats, and jewelry. Props are especially common among the Korean ensembles, who are pictured dynamically wielding swords, drums, and fans. These images of Asian and Middle Eastern ensembles, like those of the Eastern European ensembles, convey a sense of kinetic dynamism apparent both in groups of dancers moving together in space and in solo actions of individual performers. While ballet is occasionally featured in these photographs, it is not the predominant dance style. Thus, from these publications, one gets a sense that national dances—whether in the form of Eastern European folk dances or Asian and Middle Eastern dances of various forms—were the main dance attraction at WFYS.[63] The implication was that such forms were the most exciting artistic styles of new dance expression among the various international communities in which China saw itself participating.

By examining dance programs China sent abroad and international events in which Chinese dancers participated during the 1950s and early 1960s, one sees that Chinese dance formed an important medium for China's international cultural engagements and national self-projection during the socialist era. In their frequent tours abroad, Chinese dancers represented China as an ethnically and regionally diverse country in which the artistic contributions of women and ethnic minorities became constitutive components of national culture. Likewise, through their participation in WFYS dance competitions, Chinese dancers and choreographers encountered a global dance scene in which national dance emerged as a vibrant space of artistic creation, as well as a dynamic medium for intercultural communication and the expression of left-leaning youth culture worldwide. On the global stage during this period, Chinese dance circulated as a highly visible symbol of the national culture of socialist China.

CREATING NATIONAL DANCE DRAMA: NARRATIVE DANCE ON THE BASIS OF XIQU

While Chinese dance was circulating abroad as an important symbol of socialist China in international dance tours and festivals, it was also continuing to develop in new directions at home. One reason that the late 1950s and early 1960s can be seen as the first golden age of Chinese dance is that this is the era that brought forth the national dance drama, what many Chinese dance choreographers today continue to regard as the most mature form of Chinese dance choreography. Defined as a narrative dance work with a unified set of characters and linear theatrical plot that uses Chinese dance as its core movement vocabulary, national dance drama represented an important departure from existing choreographic experiments of either the wartime period or the early PRC. Up to this point, successful examples of Chinese dance creation had mainly consisted of what are known as "dances" (*wudao*): short, typically nonnarrative works that last fifteen minutes or less, as represented by items in the 1940s Frontier Dance productions and WFYS competition pieces and other new Chinese dance repertoires created during the early and mid-1950s. Works from the 1940s such as "The Mute Carries the Cripple," "Yao Drum," and "Plate Dance" and works from the 1950s such as "Red Silk Dance," "Lotus Dance," "Picking Tea and Catching Butterflies," "Ordos Dance," "Peacock Dance," and "Reba on the Grassland" are all examples of these early short-form Chinese dance choreographies. Because Chinese dance was still an emerging genre when these items were developed, their creators had been concerned primarily with devising new dance vocabularies and stage images by researching and adapting local performance practices and using them to create choreography suited to staged performance, which could then also provide a basis for classroom training. Because the artistic focus at that time had been on new formal movement vocabularies, the creators of these productions had not delved deeply into issues of narrative content, such as the representation of complex characters and theatrical storylines.

Where narrative content had been a concern of wartime and early PRC dance creation by Chinese choreographers was in productions such as Wu Xiaobang's short-form dance drama *Poppy Flowers* in 1939, the historical pageant *Long Live the People's Victory* in 1949, and the experimental long-form dance dramas *Peace Dove* and *Braving Wind and Waves to Liberate Hainan* in 1950.[64] Although these works had some commonalities with the later national dance dramas, they also differed from them in important ways. One commonality between these works and the later national dance dramas was their relatively large scale. As multiact productions involving dozens or even hundreds of performers, these works set a precedent for evening-length "large-scale" (*daxing*) dance productions in later years, of which national dance dramas were the most numerous. Another commonality between these works and later national dance dramas was their aim to tell stories. *Poppy Flowers*, for example, told the story of a group of peasants resisting unfair treatment, while *Long Live the People's Victory* narrated China's modern history and revolution, *Peace Dove* told of a dove who joins with international workers to oppose American warmongering, and *Braving Wind and Waves to Liberate Hainan* recounted PLA soldiers' crossing of the sea to fight one of the final battles of the Chinese Civil War. What differentiated these early works from the later national dance dramas, however, was one of two things: (1) theatrical structure or (2) movement vocabulary. Although *Long Live the People's Victory* used early Chinese dance movement vocabularies derived from Frontier Dance and New Yangge, as a national pageant it covered many different historical periods and did not follow a core set of characters from beginning to end in a single unified narrative. In this sense, *Long Live the People's Victory* exemplified the structure not of a dance drama (*wuju*) but of a pageant, or what would be named in China the "large-scale music and dance historical epic" (*daxing yinyue wudao shishi*), of which the most well-known early example was the 1964 production *East Is Red*.[65] *Poppy Flowers, Peace Dove*, and *Braving Wind and Waves to Liberate Hainan* all had the theatrical structure of a dance drama, in that they had a core set of characters and plot that connected the productions from beginning to end. What makes them different from national dance dramas, however, is that none used the national form—Chinese dance—as their core movement vocabulary. The movement vocabulary for *Peace Dove* was derived from European ballet and Western modern dance, whereas the movement vocabularies for *Poppy Flowers* and *Braving Wind and Waves to Liberate Hainan* were based on Wu Xiaobang's New Dance and its related offshoot, military dance. A major reason that Chinese dance choreographers were so concerned with the development of new Chinese dance vocabularies during the early and mid-1950s was that they saw this as the first step to a large-scale Chinese-style narrative dance.

Institutional investment in the creation of national dance drama began in 1953, the same year that the Ministry of Culture made plans to establish the Beijing Dance School. The nation-level ensemble tasked with this project was the Central Experimental Opera Theater (Zhongyang shiyan gejuyuan, hereafter CEOT), or what is today the China National Opera and Dance Drama Theater (Zhongguo geju wujuyuan), which houses China's leading Chinese dance ensemble.[66] The Ministry of Culture established CEOT as an independent institution in May of 1953 under the directorship of Zhou Weizhi (a.k.a. Zhou Weichi, 1916–2014), a Yan'an veteran and husband of Wang Kun (1925–2014), the singer-actress famous for her lead role in the epoch-making 1945 New Yangge opera *White-Haired Girl*. CEOT initially comprised four performance groups: an opera troupe, a dance team, a Western-style orchestra, and a Chinese music ensemble. Over time these divisions expanded and changed frequently, although the dual focus on opera and dance, both supported by instrumental music, remained consistent.[67] The dance ensemble in CEOT was one of three national-level professional dance groups established by the PRC government in the early 1950s, all three of which were devoted to Chinese dance. Generally speaking, these three ensembles mapped onto the three streams of Chinese dance, with the Central Song and Dance Ensemble focusing on Han folk dance, the CAN Cultural Work Troupe (later the Central Nationalities Song and Dance Ensemble) focusing on ethnic minority dance, and CEOT focusing on xiqu-based Chinese classical dance, although all three groups at times crossed styles. The first two ensembles specialized in short-form repertoires, and many of the new works that won awards in WFYS dance competitions were either created by these two ensembles or later entered their performance repertoires. As mentioned above, members of these ensembles also frequently populated the groups sent to perform abroad on international tours.

Like all of China's early national ensembles, CEOT was initially seeded within an academic institution, from which it then broke off to form an independent performance unit. Like the Central Song and Dance Ensemble, CEOT had been born out of the Central Academy of Drama (CAD) Dance Ensemble established in late 1949 that was led by Dai Ailian. After its failed experiment with *Peace Dove* in 1950, the group was restructured to focus on Chinese dance. In 1951 a group of dance, opera, and music performers was transferred in from Beijing People's Art Theater when that theater was restructured into a spoken drama ensemble, and in December 1951, a newly expanded Central Academy of Drama Attached Song and Dance Theater (Zhongyang xiju xueyuan fushu gewu juyuan) was established, still under Dai's leadership.[68] The first performance after this transition was a gala of ethnic minority dance. However, like *Peace Dove*, this avenue of experimentation was short-lived, since, as discussed in the previous chapter, the CAN group was set up to recruit and train ethnic minority dancers for this purpose. In 1952 the CAD group found its calling when the Ministry of Culture organized a national xiqu festival in Beijing, which involved more than three thousand xiqu artists presenting twenty-one different regional forms from across China.[69] Taking advantage of the influx of folk artists to the capital, the CAD group studied a variety of regional xiqu works, in styles such as Hunan flower drum theater (*huaguxi*), Huangmei opera, Sichuan opera, Min opera, and Huai opera. In the fall of 1952, part of this group broke off to join with the dancers that had just returned from a European tour following the WFYS festival in East Berlin, and together they formed the Central Song and Dance Ensemble. Those who stayed behind at CAD focused on continuing to explore the intersection of dance and xiqu, and it was they who formed the core members of CEOT when it was founded in 1953.[70]

This growing focus on the relationship between dance and xiqu of course coincided with the completion of Choe Seung-hui's course at CAD in 1952, discussed in the previous chapter, which produced an early Chinese classical dance teaching program on the basis of xiqu movement that Choe developed in collaboration with xiqu artists. Following this model, CEOT also used a dance curriculum based on xiqu movement to train its young performers. In July 1953, *China Pictorial* ran a photo spread on dance training in the newly established CEOT, which showed dance students (all young women) in a variety of postures clearly adapted from xiqu movement (figure 15).[71] One mark of xiqu training documented in these photographs is the students' hand gestures. For example, the dancers point with the index figure up and diagonally out at eye level, the other fingers curled in and the pinky slightly raised, as they look in the direction pointed with the head on a slight angle. Or they hold their hands in the "orchid finger" (*lanhua zhi*) position, a technique traditionally used in male xiqu actors' performances of female-role characters, in which the dancer hyperextends her fingers, pressing the first joint of the middle finger forward and pinching the thumb in to meet it, then rotating her

FIGURE 15. China Experimental Opera Theater Dance Team in training. Published in *Renmin huabao* 4, no. 8 (1953): 36. Photographers: Huang Honghui and Hu Songjia. Image provided by China Foto Bank.

wrist so that the palm faces outward. Another mark of xiqu training visible in the photographs is the twisting body positions, in which the dancers' feet, hips, torso, and head act like a corkscrew in space, lending a sense of three-dimensionality and dynamic energy to each position. Of the six photographs included in the spread, only one shows ballet training, as indicated by the dancers' turnout (a practice used in ballet, in which the dancer rotates her legs out from the hip sockets so that the knees and toes point diagonally out or to the side, rather than forward) and straight leg extension ending in a pointed foot. This use of turnout does not appear in the other five photographs, all of which show various kinds of xiqu-based movement. In all five of these photographs, dancers are shown practicing on a floor covered in a thick carpet, also a fixture of xiqu performance that is not used in ballet.

The article accompanying the photographs explains that the dancers are mainly being trained in "Chinese classical dance" (now the standard term for xiqu-based dance), supplemented by courses in Chinese folk and ethnic minority dance and ballet basics. It credits Kunqu actors Han Shichang, Bai Yunsheng, and Ma Xianglin with developing the Chinese classical dance curriculum the dancers are learning. Further invoking Choe's language in her article on Chinese classical dance published in the *People's Daily* in 1951, it describes them as researching dance movements in xiqu and then "adding organization, refinement, and further development to make them into systematic dance."[72] One of the photographs shows Han Shichang personally teaching two students a movement adapted from xiqu, the twisting seated position known as the "crouching fish" (*wo yu*), as other students look on eagerly to learn from Han's guidance.

These early news reports on CEOT clearly linked its mission with the creation of national dance drama, a project that was also associated directly with training performers in the techniques of Chinese dance, especially xiqu-based Chinese classical dance. The article in the *China Pictorial* photo spread described above, when introducing CEOT, explained, "Its task is to cultivate dancers for the Opera Theater and to prepare conditions for the future establishment of national dance drama."[73] The article then went on to explain that the team had nearly one hundred members who had been recruited from across the entire country and that dancers from other ensembles visited CEOT to receive short-term dance training. A few months later the *People's Daily* published another photograph of CEOT dancers practicing xiqu postures on its front cover, with a caption conveying the same message, again focusing on Chinese classical dance training as the means to preparing national dance drama.[74] This emphasis on technical training is not surprising given the ongoing concern with professionalism and new dance vocabularies expressed in writings by dance leaders during the early PRC years. In her endorsement of Choe Seung-hui's dance training curricula in 1950, for example, Chen Jinqing had argued that "studying technique is also to increase capacity for performing characters."[75] However, because this foundation in Chinese classical dance technique was regarded as so essential, it took several years before the first national dance dramas were actually produced.

Training dancers was not the only form of preparation needed to lay the ground for national dance drama. Chinese dance critics, for example, also had to introduce the concept of national dance drama to audiences, while choreographers had to learn how to design and stage these large-scale narrative dance productions, which had few precedents in local performance culture. Unlike in many other parts of the world, China did not have a strong local tradition of staging stories entirely through movement without words, which Chinese choreographers took to be the basic definition of dance drama. Thus, as with the creation of professional dance teaching curricula, they sought to learn existing approaches and structures from other dance traditions, which they intended to adapt to allow for the expression of local forms and content. In the case of national dance drama, Soviet ballet became the most commonly cited foreign model. In part this had to do with timing, since national dance drama emerged at the very moment that Sino-Soviet friendship peaked, which was also a time when narrative dance forms from other Asian countries were also being toured widely in China.[76] In 1954, reviewing a Soviet production of the ballet *La Esmeralda* then on tour in China, choreographer and critic You Huihai (b. 1925) wrote, "Seeing *La Esmeralda* makes us deeply inspired, and we naturally can't help showing excitement for when our Chinese dance artists will be able to learn from the Moscow Music Theater [*sic*] to create a complete Chinese national dance drama."[77] In early 1955, another choreographer and critic, Gao Di'an (b. 1916), published an article proposing a theoretical framework for understanding national dance drama in relation to Soviet ballet. Namely, he argued that national dance drama could grow out of Chinese performing arts traditions (such as xiqu) in the same way that Soviet ballet had grown out of the Russian classical ballet tradition.[78] It was important for Gao that national dance drama borrow theoretical elements from Soviet ballet, such as the principle of socialist realism, but use both local content and local forms. To emphasize the latter, he referred to national dance drama as "national-form dance drama," meaning that it would be composed using Chinese dance vocabularies, not ballet. Possible themes for these new works, according to Gao, included the creation stories of Panggu, Nüwa, and Hou Yi, popular literature such as *Journey to the West* and *A Dream of Red Mansions*, and modern revolutionary history. In terms of form, Gao wrote, national dance drama would incorporate all three styles of Chinese dance, including Han folk dance, ethnic minority dance, and xiqu-based Chinese classical dance, with the goal of updating these styles through constant innovation.

The last step in preparing for the emergence of national dance drama was training choreographers. In the fall of 1955, the Beijing Dance School launched what would be the first of two special two-year courses in dance drama choreography. To benefit from the Sino-Soviet friendship agreements that allowed for Soviet experts to travel to China and work in local institutions, the school set up both of these courses under Soviet instructors. The first course, which lasted from 1955 to 1957, was taught by Soviet character dancer Viktor Ivanovich Tsaplin and cultivated the first cohort of national dance drama choreographers and national dance drama scenarios, including those behind *Magic Lotus Lantern*.[79] The second course, taught from 1957 to 1960 by classical ballet dancer and choreographer Petr Gusev (1904–1987), took a slightly different course, emphasizing the staging of ballet productions by Chinese dancers and the creation of dance dramas that blended Chinese dance and ballet technique. The much-touted first Chinese production of the classic Russian ballet *Swan Lake* was staged under Gusev's guidance, as discussed further in the next chapter.

CEOT premiered its first experimental small-scale national dance drama, *Stealing Immortal Herbs (Dao xiancao)*, in the fall of 1955; two other similar productions followed in the spring of 1957, culminating in its premiere of the first large-scale national dance drama, *Magic Lotus Lantern*, in August of 1957.[80] All of these works showed a close resemblance to xiqu, both in dance form and narrative content, and they were all produced through collaborations between dancers and xiqu practitioners. *Stealing Immortal Herbs*, choreographed by Zheng Baoyun (b. 1927?),[81] was based on a scene from the Chinese story cycle of the *White Snake (Baishe zhuan)* and took direct inspiration from Peking opera and Shaoxing opera (*Yueju*) productions of this popular tale.[82] Two xiqu performers also worked on its choreography: Peking opera actor Zhang Chunhua on the fight scenes, and Kunqu actor Ma Xianglin on the movements and postures of Bai Suzhen, the main character.[83] Three photographs of *Stealing Immortal Herbs* were published in *Dance News* in 1956 and show the use of xiqu-inspired costumes and hair ornamentation, fight scenes using the double sword technique common in xiqu performance, and postures from xiqu movement such as the supplicating kneeling walk and a deep lunge stance known in Chinese classical dance terminology as the "bow step" (*gong bu*).[84] *Magic Lotus Lantern* showed a similar basis in xiqu aesthetics and themes. A direct product of the first Beijing Dance School choreography course led by Tsaplin, it was codirected by two graduates of the course, Huang Boshou (b. 1931) and Li Zhonglin (1933–2018), who had created the work as their final project. Li Shaochun (1919–1975), a renowned Peking opera actor, cosupervised *Magic Lotus Lantern* along with Tsaplin.[85]

Like *Stealing Immortal Herbs*, *Magic Lotus Lantern* was also based on a popular Chinese story cycle widely staged in xiqu performance, *Splitting the Mountain to Save Mother (Pi shan jiu mu)*.[86] In addition to Li Shaochun, another Peking opera artist who contributed to the choreography was Li Jinhong, who helped develop the main character's sword dance scenes.[87] An early review of *Magic Lotus Lantern* published in *Literary Gazette* highlighted its effective adaptation of xiqu material to blend old and new, which audiences apparently found extremely moving. The author wrote, "The content of dance drama *Magic Lotus Lantern* is already familiar to everyone, but its expressive form really is new. During the first dress rehearsal many comrades were moved and some even cried. . . . The choreographers did a good job using the rich dance vocabulary of our country's classical dance and folk dance, and they also daringly absorbed the USSR's advanced methods of dance drama creation. They used [Chinese] classical dance as the foundation to create the *Magic Lotus Lantern* dance drama."[88] Four stage photographs from *Magic Lotus Lantern* published in the inaugural issue of *Dance* in early 1958 further confirm the strong influence of xiqu performance on this work. Costumes and props visibly correspond to xiqu's civil/martial (*wen/wu*) system, as well as to identifiable xiqu role types, such as the virtuous female, the young scholar, and the martial male. As in *Stealing Immortal Herbs*, the dancers' body positions and gestures are also

VIDEO 7. Excerpt of Zhao Qing and ensemble in *Magic Lotus Lantern*.
Shanghai Tianma Film Studio, 1959.

To watch this video, scan the QR code with your mobile device or visit
DOI: https://doi.org/10.1525/luminos.58.7

clearly derived from xiqu movement, as visible in their body carriage, footwork,
positions of the arms and hands in relation to the body and head, and ways of
manipulating traditional stage props such as swords and daggers.[89] Fortunately, a
film was made of this production in 1959, which confirms the centrality of xiqu-
based Chinese classical dance as its primary movement vocabulary (video 7).[90]

Reflecting broader trends in China's xiqu reform movement during the 1950s,
Magic Lotus Lantern adapted a traditional story to highlight a revolutionary theme.[91]
Here, the central theme is freedom of marriage choice, a key concern of revolutionary activists and theater makers in China since the early twentieth century, when
traditional ideas about arranged marriage and gender roles were being targeted for
reform.[92] Comprising three acts and seven scenes, the story focuses on the character
of Third Sacred Mother (San Shengmu), a female immortal who breaks the rules of
the heavenly domain by falling in love with a human, Liu Yanchang. The story begins
in Third's magical mountain temple, where she meets Liu Yanchang, a young scholar,
and the two fall in love. Third leaves the temple to join the human realm, and one
year later she gives birth to a baby boy, Chen Xiang. Knowing that she has broken
immortal law, Third uses a magic lotus lantern imbued with special powers to protect her family from possible retribution. However, Third's elder brother Er Lang
Shen, whose job is to uphold the rules of the immortal realm, is intent on punish-
ing her transgression and ending the unlawful union. During the party celebrating

FIGURE 16. Zhao Qing and ensemble in *Magic Lotus Lantern*. Published in *Renmin huabao* 13, no. 5 (1962): 27. Photographer: Wang Fuzun. Image provided by China Foto Bank.

Chen Xiang's birth, Er sends his servant, a shape-shifting dog, to steal the lantern, leaving Third and her family without protection. Together with his armed guards, Er Lang Shen attacks the family compound, seizes Third, and locks her in a mountain cave. Moved by what has occurred, an old immortal named Master Pili takes Chen Xiang under his care and trains him in martial arts so that he can one day save his mother. Using his newfound skills, together with Pili's magic, Chen eventually defeats Er Lang Shen and frees Third. In the end, the family is reunited, and Third is able to live out her days happily in the company of her loyal lover and her son.[93] In an early review of the production, dance critic Long Yinpei (b. 1932) commended the scriptwriters for their streamlining of the story, writing, "The creators refined and concentrated the plot of the original 'Magic Lotus Lantern' story, taking out Liu's earning of the Number One Scholar title and his marrying of Wang Guiying, Chen Xiang and Qiu'er's beating to death of the Qin official to protect the Second Hall, and other storylines."[94] According to Long, this allowed Third Sacred Mother to emerge as "a typical image of a female within the feudal society raising a flag of resistance against the feudal Confucian ethical code."[95] Another critic echoed this interpretation of Third Sacred Mother as a powerful figure of rebellion, writing "Third Sacred Mother from beginning to end never yields, . . . [and she] who attacks and resists the theocratic order achieves the final victory."[96] In this way, critics imbued Third Sacred Mother with the symbolic power of a revolutionary heroine, like the newly empowered peasant women in New Yangge dramas and the reshaped female leads in works in recently adapted xiqu dramas (figure 16).

As depicted in the 1959 color film, *Magic Lotus Lantern*'s choreography gives full expression to this thematic focus on Third Sacred Mother and her depiction as both a typical character from xiqu performance and an embodiment of modern social rebellion. During the scene of Er Lang Shen's attack at Chen Xiang's birthday celebration, the following choreography unfolds: In the home of Third and Liu, a lively party features group dances with feathered fans, acrobatics, and "big head babies."[97] The couple dances a romantic duet in the courtyard in which Liu performs a typical xiqu-style young scholar character, while Third dances a typical xiqu-style virtuous lady, but with expanded dance movements and a pair of elongated silk streamers with which she paints flowing designs in the air around her body. Suddenly, the festivities halt when disaster strikes: the couple's protective talisman, the magic lotus lantern, has gone missing. Third knows that by uniting with a human she has crossed the "feudal orthodoxy" of the immortal realm.[98] She runs into the bedroom to prepare for a standoff with Er Lang Shen. Discarding her party skirt and silk streamers, Third emerges from the bedroom wearing pantaloons and carrying a pair of swords. She is just in time to find her brother and his armed guards entering the main hall of their home; the guests from the party have disappeared. In a reversal of traditional gender roles, Third jumps forward to fight off the invaders, while Liu hangs behind cradling their infant son in his arms. A battle ensues, in which Third defends her family by spinning, kicking, and clashing swords in typical xiqu-style combat against her brother, his four large male guards, the magic lantern, and the dog assistant. Although outnumbered, magically disadvantaged, and of slighter physical build than her opponents, Third holds her own in the fight. At one point, she shows tremendous strength by pushing off two large guards simultaneously with only the strength of her arms. Finally, Third turns herself over after Er Lang Shen threatens to kill her infant son Chen Xiang. Third is then captured and carted off, her husband and child remaining behind. The fight too much for him, Liu faints, holding a silk scarf by which to remember his valiant lover.

Like other national dance dramas that would come after it, *Magic Lotus Lantern* leveraged years of investment in Chinese dance institutions, choreographic experimentation, and dancer training to produce a new form of large-scale narrative work that could explore socialist themes in a new artistic medium. Zhao Qing (b. 1936), the dancer who played the role of Third Sacred Mother in *Magic Lotus Lantern*, is herself one example of the accumulated investment and how it made such new productions possible. The daughter of one of China's most famous twentieth-century film actors, Zhao Dan (1915–1980), Zhao Qing grew up in Shanghai, where she had initially gained an interest in dance through exposure to foreign ballet films and classes offered by expatriate Russian dance teachers who emigrated to Shanghai after the Russian Revolution of 1917. After the founding of the PRC, Zhao Qing, like most other young dancers in China, turned her attention to Chinese dance. In 1951, at the age of fifteen, Zhao entered the CAD Dance Ensemble, where she was among the first generation of students trained in xiqu-style Chinese classical dance by Kunqu masters Ma Xianglin, Han Shichang, and Hou Yongkui. During this time, Zhao also learned some Anhui-style Han folk dance from a flower drum lamp (*huagudeng*) master who later helped develop the Han folk dance curriculum at the Beijing Dance School, Feng Guopei. In 1953 Zhao joined the Central Song and Dance Ensemble, where she was one of the original performers in Dai Ailian's "Lotus Dance," which she performed abroad that year on a tour to North Korea. In 1954 Zhao tested into the inaugural cohort of students at the Beijing Dance School, where she learned Chinese classical dance, ballet, Chinese folk and ethnic dance, and European character dance. In 1955 Zhao represented China at the 1955 WFYS in Warsaw, performing "Ordos Dance." The following year she was part of the China Art Ensemble that visited Brazil, Argentina, Chile, and Uruguay, where she performed a new Chinese classical dance solo, "Long Silk Dance" (Changchou wu), as well as other WFYS prizewinners like "Picking Tea and Butterflies."[99] During her time at the Beijing Dance School, Zhao had performed a leading role in a Spanish character dance choreography that she adored.[100] Although she had initially been interested in pursuing this style further, conversations she had with a famous Peking opera actor during her trip to Latin America convinced her that it was more important to contribute to Chinese dance.[101]

After Zhao was cast as Third Sacred Mother, she prepared for the role by seeking further training. To deepen her knowledge of xiqu movement, she worked with Peking opera actors Yu Lianquan and Li Jinhong. She also consulted Buddhist art imagery with the assistance of Dunhuang scholar Chang Shuhong.[102] As depicted in the 1959 film, Zhao's main movement vocabulary is characterized by soft, curving torso lines, codified hand gestures, small, rapid stepping actions, and manipulation of silk streamers and double swords, all of which clearly demonstrate her years of training in xiqu-based Chinese classical dance. Her performance of some Han folk dance choreography in scenes such as Chen Xiang's birthday celebration also shows her training in Han folk dance. The emergence of works like *Magic Lotus Lantern* depended on the accumulated effort of many individuals like Zhao Qing, who developed their crafts over time through years of study, practice, and professional experience. To create a national dance drama required the contribution of a large team of people, including choreographers, composers, stage designers, costume designers, scriptwriters, critics, administrators, stagehands, set and costume fabricators, rehearsal directors, and others. All of this labor in turn required resources and support. In the case of China's national dance drama, the resources and support came from a new nationwide infrastructure for Chinese dance that had been carefully constructed and sustained over many years through the work of artists funded by the PRC state. In other words, the new artistic medium of national dance drama was a product of many factors, including, importantly, socialist state investment in Chinese dance.

CHOREOGRAPHING REVOLUTION: NATIONAL DANCE DRAMA IN THE GREAT LEAP FORWARD

The Great Leap Forward was a mass campaign launched in 1958 that impacted every segment of Chinese society, including professional dancers. With the slogan "Go all out, aim high, and build socialism with greater, faster, and more economical results," the campaign called on people in all fields to contribute their utmost to the nation's advancement, with the goal of harnessing the energy of collective labor and continuous revolution to meet or surpass existing production levels, including those of fully industrialized nations such as England and the United States.[103] The campaign is best known in scholarship published outside China for having led to one of the largest famines of the twentieth century and for planting questions about the direction of China's socialist economy and political leadership.[104] The campaign's impact in the cultural fields has only recently begun to receive significant attention within the English-language scholarship, with recent studies of architecture and museums, popular literature, and film all showing important new developments during the Great Leap Forward years.[105] As Krista Van Fleit Hang writes, "While the failures of the Great Leap Forward are severe and must be acknowledged, they should not prevent us from taking the period as a serious object of study, and trying to determine how the tragedies could happen, as well as honestly confronting its successes."[106] In the field of dance, one clear success of the Great Leap Forward was the tremendous output of newly created large-scale dance dramas. China's national dance journal, *Wudao*, founded in 1958, reported on more than twenty such works premiered by various ensembles across the country between 1958 and 1960, which would have been created at least in part during the Great Leap Forward campaign.[107] In terms of dance aesthetics, these productions ranged extensively in style, from xiqu-based Chinese classical dance works similar to *Magic Lotus Lantern*, to works that blended Chinese dance vocabularies with military dance and New Dance aesthetics, to works composed mainly on the basis of Han folk and ethnic minority dance movement. Thematically, these productions also showed great variety, spanning modern historical events and stories drawn from popular legends and folk literature. Thus, whereas scholars in Chinese studies have called on us to see the early and mid-1960s as underexamined periods of creativity in Chinese film and drama, respectively, I contend that the years 1958–1960 mark an especially vibrant era for Chinese dance that deserves further attention.[108]

Rather than attempting a comprehensive account of Great Leap Forward–era dance drama creation, I will briefly examine two important works that provide insight into some broader accomplishments of the period: *Five Red Clouds (Wu duo hongyun)*, by the Guangzhou Military Soldier Song and Dance Ensemble (Guangzhou budui zhanshi gewutuan), and *Dagger Society (Xiaodao hui)*, by the Shanghai Experimental Opera Theater (Shanghai shiyan gejuyuan).[109] Both *Five Red Clouds* and *Dagger Society* premiered in the summer of 1959, the former in

June as part of the Second PLA All-Military Performance Festival in Beijing (after a series of preliminary showings in Guangdong and Hunan earlier that summer) and the latter in August as part of a series of performances staged in Shanghai in honor of the tenth anniversary of the founding of the PRC.[110] Both were large-scale productions that, *like Magic Lotus Lantern*, were made into feature-length color films that closely resemble the stage versions and greatly broadened their circulation and impact.[111] The PLA August First Film Studio released its film of *Five Red Clouds* in January 1960, and Tianma Film Studio released its film of *Dagger Society* around the fall of 1961.[112] Apart from *Magic Lotus Lantern*, these are the only known surviving films of large-scale dance dramas created in China during the late 1950s and early 1960s. Thus, they serve as invaluable artifacts of PRC dance drama creation before the Cultural Revolution.[113]

Both *Five Red Clouds* and *Dagger Society* were direct products of Great Leap Forward cultural policy. In October 1958 a report appeared in the *People's Daily* calling for new artistic creation, using the campaign's language of "launching satellites."[114] In terms of artistic form, it sought new works that were innovative and possessed four specific qualities: national forms, high levels of technical expression, combinations of realism and romanticism, and popular appeal. Thematically, it encouraged artists to explore a range of topics from socialist history to the adaptations of existing stories. Artists were instructed that works should be as collaborative as possible, bridging expertise across fields and between professionals and amateurs. Finally, the report outlined a plan for broad participation and competition. "We call upon the communes, counties, provinces, and each art troupe and art school of every area in the country to actively [contribute]. . . . Selections should be made at each level."[115] According to the report, the best new productions would be selected through this process and would appear in national exhibitions and performance festivals the following year to celebrate the PRC's ten-year anniversary. *Five Red Clouds* and *Dagger Society*, both of which came from ensembles based outside Beijing, were among the many new works created across the country in response to this call for new creation.[116] To illustrate this, a review of the Second PLA All-Military Performance Festival in which *Five Red Clouds* premiered indicated that it was just one of nineteen newly created dance dramas presented at the event, and this was a partial list counting only works dealing with modern themes.[117]

The sheer volume of new works created during this time makes it undoubtedly the most productive era for new Chinese dance choreography in the entire socialist period. Writing in *Wudao* in 1959, Wu Xiaobang called the achievements of national dance drama in just the previous year an "unprecedented major development" that had transformed the artistic scene in China's dance field.[118] What is most interesting about the productions of this period, however, is not their quantity but the new ways they used Chinese dance to create complex characters and stories, which in turn offered new embodiments of Chinese socialist thought and ideology. Like *Magic Lotus Lantern*, *Five Red Clouds* and *Dagger Society* both featured strong female protagonists, following in a pattern of revolutionary drama and film that dates to the early twentieth century and also continued in many works of the later Cultural Revolution era.[119] In their treatment of sex and gender and their ways of addressing these themes in relation to intersectional understandings of class, ethnicity, and race, however, these works presented more radical visions of social critique and transformation than the later works.[120] In this way, these works represent the Great Leap Forward as a time of ideological contestation and experimentation that found expression in the new choreographic form of national dance drama.

Five Red Clouds is a four-act, seven-scene ethnic minority–themed national dance drama set on the island of Hainan in 1943–44, during the latter period of the War of Resistance against Japan.[121] It portrays the struggle of a Li community that is being abused by KMT/Nationalist soldiers stationed on the island, who are abducting Li villagers and forcing them to carry out hard labor against their will. The main character of the story is a Li woman named Ke Ying, whose husband is one of the villagers who has been abducted by the KMT soldiers, leaving her alone to care for their newborn child. After Ke Ying protests the soldiers' actions and is then captured and subsequently set free by her escaped husband and others in her community, the soldiers retaliate by murdering Ke's child and her husband in cold blood. In this melodramatic scene, the Nationalist general seizes the baby from Ke Ying's arms and throws the infant into a burning house, then knocks Ke Ying unconscious. Just as her husband discovers her body and checks to see if she is still alive, he stands up to be immediately shot by a Nationalist soldier. Before her husband dies, Ke Ying wakes up in time to hear him praise the nearby CCP-affiliated battalion who helped him escape from the Nationalists, and he leaves Ke Ying with a symbol of the group, a white piece of fabric printed with a red star. Enraged by the murders of Ke Ying's family, the community bands together to collectively attack the Nationalist camp and free their other abducted friends. Although this raid is initially successful, the soldiers return during the night and again kill many members of the Li community, pushing them to a crisis state. Remembering her husband's story, Ke Ying sets off with the star-printed fabric to seek help from the nearby CCP troops. Meanwhile, the battle continues, until the Nationalist soldiers capture a group of the most resistant Li villagers and chain them together at the center of a large bonfire, suggesting the soldiers are about to burn the Li villagers to death. Just as the Nationalist soldiers are gleefully dancing around the bonfire holding burning stakes, a crash of exploding gunpowder suddenly sounds the arrival of the CCP troops, led by Ke Ying. In the battle that ensues, the Nationalists are defeated, and Ke Ying single-handedly gets revenge on the general who murdered her baby, by chasing him with her upheld dagger and then driving him off the edge of a mountain cliff. The story ends with the Li villagers and the CCP troops celebrating together amidst red flags, as five red clouds rise into the sky, representing a local prophecy of better days to come.

Because this production was created by a military ensemble, rather than an ensemble that specialized in minority performance, the dancers were primarily of Han ethnicity, likely including Wang Shan (b. 1935), who performed the role of Ke Ying.[122] Nevertheless, as in the case of the 1960 touring ensemble discussed earlier in this chapter, the choreography in this work employed movement forms that had initially been developed and promoted by minority artists. As depicted in the 1960 film recording of *Five Red Clouds*, the dance sequence that introduces Wang's character—a slow lilting cross-body step in which the dancer rises and rotates her body in line with the stepping foot as she transfers her weight—is identical to that performed by female dancers in the introductory sequence of "Third Day of the Third Month" (San yue san), a Li-themed small-scale group dance featured in the 1959 film *Hundred Phoenixes Face the Sun* that was originally created by a minority-dominated ensemble. Other elements of the choreography in this piece that appear in *Five Red Clouds* include pendulum-like swinging arm actions, syncopated three-count walks, and perpendicular kicks with hips facing to the side while the arms swing back.[123] "Third Day of the Third Month" was originally premiered in 1956 by the Hainan Nationalities Song and Dance Ensemble *(Hainan minzu gewutuan)*, which included Li dancers.[124] This work achieved national influence in 1957, when the Hainan group presented it at the national music and dance festival in Beijing, where it was singled out for praise by Long Yinpei and Hu Guogang, two influential senior figures in the Chinese dance and military dance fields, respectively.[125] Wang Shan, who began her dance career in 1950 at the Central South Military District Political Department Cultural Work Troupe in Wuhan and then transferred to the Guangzhou Military Soldier Song and Dance Ensemble in 1953, had performed "Third Day of the Third Month" with the Guangzhou ensemble. Although Wang was likely not an ethnic minority, she held a marginal regional status because she had received her training in 1951–53 at the Central South Military Art School (Zhongnan budui yishu xueyuan) in Wuhan, rather than in the capital like Zhao Qing and Shu Qiao, who performed the leads in *Magic Lotus Lantern* and *Dagger Society*.[126] The institutions in which Wang studied and worked had put on two early three-act dance dramas based on the Korean War, *Mother Calls (Muqin zai zhaohuan*, 1951) and *Flag (Qi*, 1954).[127] This meant that she and other members of the *Five Red Clouds* cast had significantly more experience with dance drama performance than the Hainan group, which may explain why they pursued this theme. As later national dance drama productions of the early 1960s show, it was more common for national dance dramas on minority themes to be created and performed by minority-dominated ensembles.[128]

In their creative process for *Five Red Clouds*, the team's scriptwriters and choreographers went to significant lengths to engage the local knowledge of

Li communities in Hainan who were being represented in the production. The imagery of the five red clouds reportedly came from a Li folk story: "Legend says that at dusk, on Five Finger Mountain there often appeared in the emptiness five red clouds. If the clouds fell to the ground, Li people would be able to get out of their bitter fate and achieve happiness."[129] According to the creative team, the story they developed for *Five Red Clouds* combined this folk image with historical accounts of a Li rebellion that circulated in Hainan in the late 1940s, which had previously been organized into a music and dance script under the name "The Story of the Red Flag" (Hongqi de gushi).[130] The creative team interviewed local minority leaders and CCP soldiers and researched historical materials about the Li rebellions, which provided additional details for the story. As with *Magic Lotus Lantern*, they produced a storyline that foregrounded a female protagonist. Additionally, they ensured that the resulting plot struck an ideologically prescribed balance between depicting the Li people as agents of revolution while also insisting that they could not have achieved liberation without the help of the CCP.[131] Apart from reading about Li culture and customs, the group presented early versions of the script to the Hainan Nationalities Song and Dance Ensemble for discussion, and they also visited Li and Miao communities in areas of Hainan depicted in the story, sought assistance from Li and Miao folk artists, and studied at a Li performance festival.[132]

The intersectional outlook of *Five Red Clouds* is expressed narratively and choreographically in a scene that begins about sixteen minutes into the film version, when Ke Ying first visits the Nationalist camp and the audience sees what is going on there. The episode begins when Ke Ying and her community are dancing in celebration of Gong Hu's recent return after having been captured by the Nationalists and then set free by the CCP. When a group of Nationalist soldiers approaches the village in search of Gong, everyone else is able to hide, but Ke Ying gets delayed tending to her baby. After a scuffle between Ke and the Nationalist general, a male relative of Ke's is taken hostage after he tries to protect Ke and her child. Then, as Ke and the others decide what to do, the shot cuts to the Nationalist camp. Although it is now the dead of night, armed soldiers are standing guard vigilantly as Li villagers march in a file, their feet shackled like a chain gang, shuffling along, their heads bent down, lugging heavy rocks and wood beams. When a grey bearded man collapses from exhaustion, he is whipped and forced to continue. Next, the view moves to a group of ten Li women arranged in a circle around a vat filled with rice kernels. In unison, each woman holds a large wooden pole in her hands and thrusts the pole vertically into the vat, crushing the rice to remove its husks. Titled "Rice Husking Dance" (Chong mi wu), this scene references other rice-husking ethnic minority group dances of the period, such as the Wa-themed "Mortar and Pestle" (Chong jiu) dance featured in the 1963 film *Colored Butterflies Fluttering About*. However, whereas the women in "Mortar

VIDEO 8. Excerpt of Wang Shan and ensemble in *Five Red Clouds*.
August First Film Studio, 1960.

To watch this video, scan the QR code with your mobile device or visit
DOI: https://doi.org/10.1525/luminos.58.8

and Pestle" bounce with lightness and appear to be having fun in their work, the women in "Rice Husking Dance" perform their actions laboriously and heavily, as if exhausted and in pain. Between actions, the women in "Rice Husking Dance" hunch over their poles, wipe sweat from their foreheads, and place their hands on their sore lower backs. Sighs of fatigue are audible between strokes, and each step appears a struggle. If their pace slows, guards aim rifles in their direction, forcing them to speed up again (video 8). When Ke's relative is marched in and locked in a nearby cage, the rice-huskers stop their work and try to help him, only to be blocked by the guards. Seconds later, Ke Ying appears and passionately pleads for his release but too is thrown into the cage. After the cage is again locked, the Nationalist general flips over a sign on its door, revealing the words "Exhibition Object: Li." The word "Li" is written with three added strokes meaning "dog," turning it into a derogatory ethnic slur that further compounds the already humiliating message of the sign (Figure 17).[133] As dawn breaks, the rice huskers perform the "Prisoner's Cage Dance" (qiulong wu). Outside the cage, they stretch their arms up toward the sky, as if pleading for help from a higher power. Meanwhile, a chorus in the musical score recites:

Auspicious colored clouds, ya

Which day will you fall down

And glow upon the bitter Li family.[134]

FIGURE 17. Wang Shan and ensemble in *Five Red Clouds*. Published in *Wu duo hong yun: si mu qi chang wuju* (Shanghai: Shanghai wenyi chubanshe, 1963), back matter. Photographer unknown. Image provided by Zha Anbin, from the private collection of Zha Lie.

This scene introduces several important themes that lend broader meaning to the production as a whole. First, the role of motherhood in Ke Ying's characterization is part of a broader engagement with issues of sex and gender that go beyond those in dance works on revolutionary themes created in later periods, such as during the Cultural Revolution. Here, rather than eliminating reproduction and its attendant links to sexuality, family, and romance, the plot and choreography highlight these experiences as factors that contribute to Ke Ying's capacities as a revolutionary heroine.[135] As later scenes show, the plot of *Five Red Clouds* presents Ke Ying's gendered subjectivity as a resource, rather than a liability, to her potential for revolutionary action. For example, they show how her ability to work cooperatively with other women helps her effectiveness in battle, how her presence of mind in the midst of personal tragedy allows her to detect a Nationalist attack in time to warn the village, how her awareness of others during battle allows her to take over the war drum when the male village leader Ah Die is injured, and how trust in her husband allows her to remember his story and go out in search of the CCP troops and ultimately save her community. In each of these later scenes, the choreography emphasizes a union between Ke Ying's sex and gender identity and her revolutionary agency, by employing conventionally gendered movement vocabulary and stage aesthetics to show Ke Ying solving social problems, defeating the enemy in battle, and being a leader. Ke Ying remains clothed in stereotypically feminine, minority-marked costume throughout the production, producing striking images such as the one on the cover of this book, in which a character clearly marked as minority and female is also empowered and celebrated for resisting oppression, even depicted armed with a weapon while backed by an entire community of like-minded supporters. Numerous other clues throughout the narrative hint at a sustained criticism of patriarchy and a promotion of positive female representation. For example, the male village elder Ah Die initially excludes women from war rituals but is forced through the story to acknowledge their contributions, symbolized in the end when he exchanges his tattered old banner for a new red flag. Although Ke Ying initially shows some naiveté when she tries to negotiate with the Nationalist general for her friend's release, and the death of her husband and son make her a definite victim, ultimately, it is she who saves herself by actively seeking out the CCP soldiers, rather than passively being saved by them like heroines in later productions.

Apart from sex and gender, the treatment of ethnicity in the above scene also signals the broader importance of this issue as a key theme dealt with innovatively in *Five Red Clouds*. By pairing the depiction of forced labor with the image of the cage and the derogatory "Exhibition Object: Li" sign, this scene explicitly treats class oppression and the prejudice of Han toward ethnic minorities as intersecting problems faced by ethnic minority communities in Chinese society. Describing this scene in the context of the larger themes of the work, the *Five Red Clouds* creative team wrote, "The Nationalists discriminate against ethnic minorities. This is ethnic contradiction; it is also class contradiction."[136] Within this scene, the "Rice Husking Dance" effectively embodies this intersection between ethnicity and class choreographically, by translating it into kinesthetic expression. Up to this scene, the Li women in *Five Red Clouds* perform mainly dances similar in register to the cheerful, upbeat ethnic minority and Han folk dances typically circulated in China during this time. Through its marked contrast with these standard depictions, "Rice Husking Dance" gives the Li women a multidimensional quality—rather than exotic beauties or idealized rural subjects possessing boundless energy and cheer, they become relatable, realistic women who sweat, get exhausted, feel pain, and worry about their friends. Later in the scene, when these same women perform the "Prisoner's Cage Dance" to a chorus invoking the red cloud imagery, their embodied expressions of yearning for a better life seem to arise from a believable subjectivity that interweaves gender, ethnicity, and class experiences. Ultimately, the overall storyline of *Five Red Clouds* follows a conventional PRC narrative of class struggle and the CCP saving the day. Yet, like other national dance dramas of this period, there is more in the details of the narrative and in the use of Chinese dance choreography that makes it worthy of greater critical attention.[137]

Like *Five Red Clouds*, *Dagger Society* also tells a story inspired by local revolutionary history. Set in Shanghai in the fall of 1853, *Dagger Society* is a seven-scene national dance drama based on a historical uprising led by the Dagger Society against a local Qing official and his Western imperialist supporters.[138] The central protagonist is Zhou Xiuying, a female leader of the Dagger Society rebellion who works alongside two male leaders, the elder Liu Lichuan and the younger Pan Qixiang, the former Zhou's superior and the latter her love interest (figure 18). The story begins on the dock of the Huangpu River in Shanghai, where an altercation takes place between Pan Qixiang and a Qing guard, after the guard has used violence against the local poor while extracting exorbitant land taxes. When Pan is captured, Liu and Zhou launch an armed revolt by the Dagger Society in which they free Pan and seize the local Qing official.[139] Despite the success of this initial venture, however, the Qing official escapes and launches a counterattack supported by Western imperialist troops, aided by a British consul, a French military general, and a foreign priest.[140] A protracted battle ensues that lasts for many months. With help from the local masses, the Dagger Society is able to hold the old city, but their stronghold is severely bombed and food supplies are eventually cut off. As the Dagger Society's situation grows dire, Liu sends Pan on a mission to seek help from the Taiping Heavenly Kingdom, a larger anti-Qing rebel group based in a nearby city.[141] However, Pan dies on route before fulfilling his mission. In the climactic final battle scene, Liu Lichuan is shot in action by the leader of the Western troops right after he has killed the Qing official.[142] Then, Zhou kills the Western troop leader and regroups the remaining members of her militia to plan

FIGURE 18. Shu Qiao and ensemble in *Dagger Society*. Published in *Renmin huabao* 11, no. 16 (1960): 24. Photographer: Wu Yinbo. Image provided by China Foto Bank.

their next steps. The story ends with Zhou raising the flag to lead a diminished but resolute Dagger Society forward into battle, a symbol of the endurance and ultimate victory of the revolutionary fight a century later.

In terms of aesthetic form, *Dagger Society* was, like *Magic Lotus Lantern*, grounded in a movement vocabulary based on xiqu-style Chinese classical dance. Like the CEOT that produced *Magic Lotus Lantern*, the Shanghai Experimental Opera Theater (SEOT) had employed Kunqu actors to train its dancers since the early 1950s.[143] At its year-end performance in 1953, the predecessor to SEOT had presented "Sword Dance" (*Jian wu*), one of the first well-known Chinese dance group works composed entirely in a xiqu-inspired Chinese classical dance style.[144] Shu Qiao, who performed the role of Zhou Xiuying in *Dagger Society*, had both starred in and helped choreograph "Sword Dance," performing it on tour in India, Indonesia, and Burma in 1954 and at the 1957 WFDY Festival in Moscow, where it won a prize.[145] When the national dance publication *Wudao* was established, the cover of its inaugural issue featured a photograph of Shu in a pose from this dance.[146] Apart from xiqu movement vocabulary, *Dagger Society* also used xiqu-inspired costumes, props, and story-telling devices, and, like *Magic Lotus Lantern*, it supplemented this with group dances derived from Han folk performance, in this case also including local traditions of martial arts, mainly from the Jiangnan cultural region near Shanghai.[147] *Dagger Society's* musical score highlighted Chinese instruments, with the *suona* (Chinese clarinet) featured as the main theme for the Dagger Society, the bamboo flute used in a long dream sequence in which Zhou imagines Pan on his journey, and the pipa played in important strategy scenes, such as when Liu sends Pan to seek help from the Taipings. According to one critic, the effect was so good that it convinced some critics who had previously doubted that Chinese music could make for good dance drama scores.[148] As depicted in the 1961 film, the majority of dancing in *Dagger Society* is performed by the Chinese characters (including the Qing guards and officials), who all perform Chinese dance movement styles. The Western characters, by contrast, perform movements and gestures based mainly on Western-style spoken drama (*huaju*), which are supplemented by two short group dances that employ European-style sword fighting and ballroom dance.[149]

Like the creative team for *Five Red Clouds*, the makers of *Dagger Society* conducted extensive research and engaged local knowledge of the people represented, while they also took artistic liberties to develop a story that suited their intended ideological message, here, that the origins of the Chinese communist revolution lie in a longer history of commoner-led rebellions against "the double oppression of imperialism and the feudal court."[150] The historical basis for the production was a collection of primary source documents related to the Shanghai Dagger Society revolt of 1853, which the *Dagger Society* creation team studied in their process of developing the work.[151] According to *Dagger Society's* lead director, Zhang Tuo, the creative team also visited relics and listened to local folk stories about the rebellion, one of which reportedly contained a ballad about a female rebel named Zhou Xiuying.[152] In the final story, the characters Liu Lichuan and Pan Qixiang were loosely based on historical figures documented in the textual sources, while Zhou Xiuying was based on the character from the folk ballad.[153] According to Zhang, the creative team decided to make Zhou the main character because they were inspired by the fact that local people were still singing about her.[154] While the story was set in the past, critics predictably linked it to a longer revolutionary narrative of fighting "imperialist invasion" and "reactionary regimes."[155] One also drew a parallel to the Cold War, comparing the conflict depicted in *Dagger Society* to "the Chinese people's current struggle against American imperialism."[156] Overall, although the *Dagger Society* story ended on a tragic note, making it different from many other stories of the socialist era, it was interpreted as part of a longer revolutionary prehistory of the mass rebellions that gave rise to the PRC.

Whereas the intersectional dimension of *Five Red Clouds* emerges through the treatment of sex and gender, ethnicity, and class, especially as presented in the group dance scenes by minority women characters, in *Dagger Society* it appears

VIDEO 9. Excerpt of Shu Qiao and ensemble in *Dagger Society*. Shanghai Tianma Film Studio, 1961.

To watch this video, scan the QR code with your mobile device or visit DOI: https://doi.org/10.1525/luminos.58.9

in the interweaving of a feminist agenda into a story about racial and economic hierarchies, through the characterization of Zhou Xiuying as an antifeudal, anti-imperialist heroine. Interconnected racial and economic hierarchies are expressed in *Dagger Society* through numerous depictions of imbalanced power relationships between Western and Chinese characters. In one scene, for example, the American, British, and French characters coerce the Qing official into signing an unfavorable customs agreement in exchange for their military aid, while in another, the American character happily reviews an account book showing how much money he is making in China while he is simultaneously overseeing the transportation of opium imports, which are shown being carried on the backs of Chinese laborers.[157] Racial difference is accentuated in these scenes through visual performance effects, which include not only the use of racially designated movement, as discussed above, but also distinctions in costume and the use of elaborate wigs, makeup, and facial prosthetics designed to make the Chinese performers playing the foreign roles appear Caucasian (video 9).[158] Within this racial and economic hierarchy, moreover, is also embedded a gender hierarchy. While male and female characters appear among both the Chinese and Western groups, the Western figures and their local representatives who are shown to exert economic power and threat of violence over the Chinese characters are all men (women are present but play secondary roles), while the Chinese characters subordinated by these actions include both men and women. This distinction is especially apparent during the numerous battle scenes, in which the Dagger Society troops include large numbers of women fighters, while the Western and Qing troops are all male.

Amid this spectrum of interlinked power hierarchies, Zhou Xiuying's character stands out as a striking feminist expression. Heroines in the later revolutionary ballets propagated during the Cultural Revolution were often portrayed either as victims in need of male saviors or as heroes whose revolutionary acts were limited to realms conventionally gendered as feminine. In *Dagger Society*, however, Zhou Xiuying's portrayal follows neither of these later patterns. Rather, from start to finish, she appears consistently as a powerful, competent leader who equals or surpasses her male counterparts in all arenas. In the 1961 film, Zhou supplies weapons to the Dagger Society militia, and she also personally trains the fighters and contributes critical strategic knowledge during meetings with the opposing parties. Moreover, throughout the production, Zhou's levelheaded and steadfast character is contrasted with the hotheaded personality of Pan, who repeatedly causes problems with his uncalculated outbursts. The fact that Zhou is the one who finally defeats the Western military commander and survives the multiple battles to lead the Dagger Society onward at the end of the production also implies that it is revolutionary women like she who ensure the revolutionary movement continues to the next generation. Zhou, whom contemporary critics described using the classical trope of the "woman hero" (*jinguo yingxiong*), performs all these tasks while dressed in stereotypically feminine clothing and dancing in ways coded as feminine within traditional Chinese stage conventions.[159] Her interactions with Pan present her as a sexualized being with a romantic life beyond the revolutionary arena. While certainly conforming to the heteronormative ideas about sexuality and gender difference pervasive in Chinese society at the time, this portrayal is significant within the broader history of Chinese socialist heroines because it means that Zhou does not fall into the mode of "genderless revolutionaries" decried by some later critics of Maoist gender politics.[160] Generated in a historical moment of contested and shifting gender politics during the Great Leap Forward era, Zhou's character represented a vision of female leadership in which femininity was compatible with revolutionary leadership.[161]

Perhaps not surprisingly, *Dagger Society* was one of relatively few leading early national dance dramas that included a well-known female dancer among its top choreographers. In both *Magic Lotus Lantern* and *Five Red Clouds*, Zhao Qing and Wang Shan had performed as leading ladies under teams of male directors. However, in *Dagger Society*, Shu Qiao was recognized officially as both a leading performer and one of the work's head choreographers.[162] Shu was responsible for the group choreography in the "Bow Dance" scene, in which Zhou trains the female and male members of the Dagger Society militia; the scene went on to become a highly popular dance piece independent from *Dagger Society*, winning an award at the last WFYS that Chinese dance delegations attended in Helsinki, Finland, in 1962.[163] From her early choreographic work on "Sword Dance" to the much larger production of *Dagger Society*, Shu helped create a new interpretation of the "martial maiden," a character type once common in Peking opera, where it had been developed and performed primarily by male actors who performed female roles. According to Joshua Goldstein, the martial maiden was defined by "a chivalrous martial spirit and demeanor [,] . . . turning the traditionally gentle and demure *qingyi* [virtuous female] into characters marked by their fortitude, vigor, and martial prowess."[164] Earlier martial maiden characters had often performed in narrative contexts in which they were disguised as men, following the style of heroic female literary characters such as the cross-dressing warrior Hua Mulan.[165] By contrast, Shu Qiao developed a mode of martial maiden performance for Chinese dance in which the female character enters new social spaces and roles while still being recognized as a woman. Because of the popularity of Shu's new choreography, her dances expanded the spectrum of xiqu movement styles taught to women students in Chinese classical dance courses, and this in turn expanded the possibilities for feminine-gendered movement within the new and still developing style of Chinese classical dance.

CONCLUSION: NATIONAL DANCE DRAMA ON STAGE AT HOME AND ABROAD

The latter half of the 1950s and early 1960s was a vibrant period of expansion for Chinese dance in the PRC. Following the establishment of a shared artistic vision for Chinese dance and the founding of national and regional dance ensembles and dance conservatories to carry out this vision during the first half of the 1950s, the latter half of the decade saw the rapid creation and widespread circulation of new Chinese dance choreography around the country and the world. In 1957 reports on a national music and dance festival held that year counted sixty professional ensembles in attendance, suggesting the existence of a nationwide network for Chinese dance performance.[166] In 1958 *Wudao* was established as China's first publicly circulating national dance periodical, creating a venue for dancers across the country to share news and learn about the latest developments in Chinese dance education, choreography, history, and theory.[167] Furthermore, a new type of Chinese dance creation, national dance drama, came into existence during these years, engendering a massive wave of new large-scale choreography quite different from any Chinese dance that had come before. The emergence of this new form made it possible for the movement vocabularies of Chinese dance to be employed to tell complex revolutionary narratives, often with results that were innovative and interesting both artistically and ideologically.

By the late 1950s and early 1960s, it was not only short-form Chinese dance choreography like "Lotus Dance" that was being staged in national celebrations and used to represent China to foreign audiences; the new large-scale national dance dramas such as *Magic Lotus Lantern*, *Five Red Clouds*, and *Dagger Society* were also filling this role, both as live stage productions and as newly created dance drama films. In the fall of 1959, in honor of the tenth anniversary of the founding of the PRC, both *Five Red Clouds* and *Magic Lotus Lantern* were staged in whole or in part as live performances in the capital as part of the official National Day celebrations.[168] Moreover, *Magic Lotus Lantern*, which Shanghai Tianma Film Studio had just released as China's first color dance drama film, was part of the national film exhibition, and it also started to be shown widely in cultural events welcoming foreign delegations visiting China.[169] In 1959 the New Siberia Song and Dance Theater performed *Magic Lotus Lantern*, marking the first time a national dance drama created by Chinese choreographers had been staged by a foreign company.[170] In 1960 both *Five Red Clouds* and *Dagger Society* entered the repertoire of CEOT, indicating their recognition as part of a national repertoire and allowing them to gain increased visibility both at home and abroad.[171] In 1961 CEOT toured *Dagger Society* and *Magic Lotus Lantern*, along with the company's newest xiqu-style national dance drama, *Thunder Peak Pagoda* (*Leifeng ta*, 1960), to the Soviet Union and Poland.[172] And the influence of these Great Leap Forward–era national dance dramas continued into the early 1960s. For example, in 1963 the film version of *Five Red Clouds* was shown abroad to celebrate China's National Day.[173] That same year, the Japanese dance artist Hanayanagi Tokubee (1908–1968), along with his wife and several students, visited CEOT to learn *Magic Lotus Lantern* and then, according to CEOT records, staged the production in Japan later that year.[174] Zhang Tuo reports that in 1964 a Japanese ballet company also performed *Dagger Society* in Japan.[175] While new national dance dramas continued to be created during the early 1960s, however, none of the works of that period achieved the same level of national and international circulation as those of the Great Leap Forward. Like so many other new artistic works of the early 1960s, their lives on stage and screen were to be cut short by a new campaign with a new artistic agenda, the Cultural Revolution.

4

A Revolt from Within

Contextualizing Revolutionary Ballet

One day in the summer of 1966, Shu Qiao, the dancer who played the heroine Zhou Xiuying in *Dagger Society,* was on her way to work. In her memoir, she recalls feeling that something was amiss as she walked along the streets of Shanghai.[1] People in haphazard military uniforms patrolled the sidewalks, and women and shop owners were harassed in public. A sickness in Shu's stomach manifested her impending dread. When she arrived at the ensemble, her fears were confirmed:

> I entered the Theater and saw large-character posters everywhere, on the walls, in the hallways, on the doors. In the rehearsal studio there were rows of large character posters strung up on wires like laundry hung in an alleyway. Suddenly, I saw my own name. It had bright red circles around it and a bright red cross through the middle. It reminded me of the 'execution upon sentencing' in ancient times, and a chill went up my spine. After looking down the rows, I counted at least forty or fifty names with red circles and crosses over them.[2]

The "large character posters" *(dazi bao)* that Shu describes—handwritten signs in large script hung in public places—had been developed in socialist China as a tool for average citizens to participate in political discourse. Although they had been used widely as a medium for personal attacks since at least the late 1950s, their appearance proliferated dramatically in the summer of 1966 with the launch of a new campaign known as the Great Proletariat Cultural Revolution (Wenhua da geming, hereafter Cultural Revolution). During this campaign, not only did a new swath of participants begin to take part actively in public political discourse, but unprecedentedly large segments of society also became targets of political persecution as a result.[3] As a movement that grew out of rifts within the elite ranks of the CCP, the Cultural Revolution is now widely understood as an internal struggle in which Mao sought to purge existing power holders and regain or maintain his central position in China's political leadership. Launched as a mass campaign grounded in the concept of "continuous revolution," the Cultural Revolution empowered average citizens, particularly agitational youth who became known as Red Guards, to stage revolts and attack their authorities. Students turned against teachers, employees turned against administrators, and groups who had felt marginalized within their respective fields found opportunities to seize power from those who had previously been dominant. Since this campaign was carried out more than a decade and a half into China's construction as a socialist nation, however, it called for a revolution within a system that had itself been constructed on revolutionary ideals. In this sense, the Cultural Revolution was also a counterrevolution—a revolt from within that challenged and in many ways redefined already established practices of Chinese socialist life.

In the field of dance, it was artists like Shu—performers, choreographers, teachers, and administrators who had reached high levels of accomplishment and recognition during the first seventeen years of dance creation in the PRC—who found themselves on the receiving end of what developed into quite violent attacks against influential individuals and groups seen to represent the status quo. Even the most revered early pioneers of the Chinese dance movement, most now in their fifties and sixties, were subjected to the attacks. Qemberxanim, for example, a celebrity dancer and highly respected dance educator who directed the PRC's first state-sponsored professional conservatory for ethnic minority performing artists, was labeled a criminal and put on house arrest shortly after the Cultural Revolution began in 1966. At the time, a group of Qemberxanim's colleagues and students used old photographs from her 1947–48 national tour, during which she had performed for Nationalist leaders such as Chiang Kai-shek, to accuse her of harboring antirevolutionary sentiments. Without due process, they confiscated and destroyed her personal belongings and forced her to carry out janitorial work while she lived in abject poverty in a storage room and was subjected to constant surveillance. Qemberxanim's daughter, who had just given birth to a second child, was thrown in jail on grounds of "colluding with a foreign government," because the daughter's father, Qemberxanim's husband, lived in the Soviet Union. Qemberxanim's attackers posted public cartoons caricaturing Qemberxanim's physical appearance and subjected her to large public denunciation sessions in which they shamed and physically abused her in front of large crowds. These sessions often became so violent that Qemberxanim prepared her own funeral shroud and wore it under her clothes, expecting that she would not return alive.[4] Liang Lun, a widely acclaimed choreographer who led important early PRC dance institutions in southern China, recalls being subjected to similar abuses. In one account, he describes being paraded through the city in a truck, wearing a large sign around his neck that read "Liang Lun: Capitalist Roader Cultural Spy."[5]

Dai Ailian, the preeminent national leader of China's dance field in the early PRC era, also became a target. Initially, Dai was pushed out of her administrative roles but managed to avoid the first round of violent attacks in 1966. In late 1967, however, Mao's wife, Jiang Qing, who took on a leadership role in performing arts reforms during the Cultural Revolution, identified Dai by name as someone who should be investigated. Most likely wishing to ingratiate themselves to Jiang and avoid being attacked themselves, Dai's former students and subordinates carried out the instructions, setting a committee to search for "crimes" in Dai's past. Like most targets of the period, Dai was forced to write biographical accounts that could be used as incriminating evidence. Dai's poor written Chinese became additional fodder for her critics, who called her a "foreign/Western devil" *(yang guizi)*. The 1940 photograph in which Dai performed "Guerilla March" dressed in the flag of the Republic of China was used out of historical context to question Dai's fidelity to the CCP. At the same time, Dai's connections with Ye Qianyu and Choe Seung-hui were employed to fabricate accounts of suspected espionage. Finally, the team confiscated Dai's home and subjected her, along with Dai's co-administrator Chen Jinqing, to public denunciations in which they were forced to stand bent over for long periods of time and face other physical abuse. Later, Dai was sent to a farm where she carried out manual labor and tended livestock. After Dai returned from the farm, she was still subjected to various abuses. At one point, she recalls being forced to darn ballet shoes for twenty days and nights without being allowed to sleep.[6] During this time, Wu Xiaobang and other top leaders across the dance field also endured similar treatment.[7]

The impacts of these attacks were not isolated to the lives of a few individuals. Rather, they were part of a systematic restructuring of China's dance field, begun in 1966, that brought major changes to dance work over the next decade. At the heart of these changes was the replacement of Chinese dance with a new dance genre known as "revolutionary modern ballet" *(geming xiandai balei wuju),* which emerged in the years immediately preceding the Cultural Revolution.[8] The work that introduced this new genre was *Red Detachment of Women (Hongse niangzi jun),* a new ballet premiered in early October 1964. It was staged by CEOT's then newly founded Ballet Ensemble, the predecessor to today's National Ballet of China (Zhongyang balei wutuan).[9] The second major work in this style was *White-Haired Girl (Baimao nü),* premiered in May 1965 by the Shanghai Dance School (Shanghai wudao xuexiao).[10] Both of these new productions were adapted from popular Chinese revolutionary-themed works in other media—*Red Detachment* from a 1961 film and *White-Haired Girl* from a 1945 New Yangge drama and a 1950 film. These two productions, along with two subsequent ballets premiered in 1973— *Ode to Yimeng (Yimeng song)* and *Children of the Grassland (Caoyuan ernü)*— dominate public discourse on dance as represented in China's national media from 1966 to 1976. Apart from being performed as live productions, these four ballets were also circulated as films starting in the early and mid-1970s.[11] In contrast to the earlier national dance dramas, which were created on performers specializing in Chinese dance, these new works were created on performers specializing in ballet. The initial cast of *Red Detachment of Women*, for example, had gained their performance experience staging ballets such as *Swan Lake, Le Corsaire, Giselle,* and *La Esmeralda*. Thus, while the new ballets did incorporate some elements of Chinese dance movement into their choreography, such use was limited and did not fundamentally alter the primary movement vocabulary, which was still ballet. When responding to the works at the time they appeared, dance critics categorized them as ballets, not as national dance dramas. This continues to be the way the productions are understood within Chinese-language dance criticism.

The ballets of the Cultural Revolution have already received significant attention in the English-language scholarship, which has examined their aesthetic form and narrative content, as well as their adaptation from earlier film and drama texts and their role within the broader Cultural Revolution performing arts complex, known as the "model works" *(yangban xi)*.[12] My goal here is not to offer a new analysis of these issues. Instead, I aim to shed new light on the ballets of the Cultural Revolution by contextualizing them in a different way—through their relationship to the history of PRC dance in the pre–Cultural Revolution era. With the exception of Paul Clark's book *The Cultural Revolution: A History,* few published writings on the ballets of the Cultural Revolution have considered their position vis-à-vis other genres of concert dance choreography that existed in China at the time the ballets first emerged.[13] As Clark correctly points out, and as this book further demonstrates, the revolutionary ballets were but one in a long line of creative efforts to imagine and embody Chinese socialist culture and modernity through dance. Thus, to understand the significance of revolutionary ballet, it is essential to place it into a longer historical context of PRC dance history. Central to such an examination is the relationship of ballet to Chinese dance.

In this chapter, I examine the longer trajectory of ballet in China as it relates to other dance forms, culminating in an examination of the emergence of the two new ballets *Red Detachment of Women* and *White-Haired Girl* during the mid-1960s, as part of a larger trend of new dance experimentation occurring at the time. In my discussion of ballet's development in China from the 1940s through the 1960s, I argue that ballet served as a constant "Other" against which the Chinese dance "Self" was defined and that this allowed for the erection of firm genre boundaries between Chinese dance and ballet, as well as the subjection of ballet to a subordinate position relative to Chinese dance. At the same time, I show that continued state support for ballet as one of several parallel genres to Chinese dance—along with, for example, military dance and Oriental Dance—demonstrated the fundamentally pluralistic outlook of China's cultural leadership toward dance development during the pre–Cultural Revolution period.

By showing how ballet developed in relation to other dance forms in China before 1966, I challenge the common view that the policies of the Cultural Revolution were a continuation of earlier PRC dance development, in which some argue that ballet had always been the privileged dance form of the PRC due to its association with the Soviet Union. Rather, I suggest that it was the continued subordination of ballet to Chinese dance during the pre–Cultural Revolution era that created a situation in which ballet enthusiasts rose up against Chinese dance practitioners during the early years of the Cultural Revolution. Thus, I argue that the predominance of ballet during the Cultural Revolution years represented a reversal of earlier PRC policies that had supported formal pluralism within a broader structure that privileged Chinese dance over other dance forms.

A SUBORDINATED OTHER: BALLET IN CHINA BEFORE THE CULTURAL REVOLUTION

Decades before the arrival of Soviet teachers, ballet already had a strong presence in several Republican-era Chinese urban centers, where it gained deeply rooted cultural associations and impacted the lives of many who would go on to work later in the PRC dance field. This first wave of ballet activities in China inherited the late nineteenth- and early twentieth-century Russian ballet tradition, which had itself been a development of the earlier ballet traditions developed in French and Italian courts since the European Renaissance.[14] Beginning in the 1920s, Russian ballet gained a presence in China via a group known as the White Russians (bai'e, as opposed to Red Russians), émigrés who fled the Soviet Union in the wake of the Russian Revolution and Civil War of 1917–20 in order to escape the new Bolshevik regime. Chinese cities that received particularly large numbers of these migrants included Shanghai, Tianjin, and Harbin, all of which already had large foreign populations and were located in areas of the country associated with industrialization, urbanization, and histories of imperialism and semicolonial rule. By January of 1933, Russians made up the second largest non-Chinese group in Shanghai after the Japanese, with a population of between fifteen thousand and twenty-five thousand out of a total of just over three million.[15] The majority of these were former merchants, ex-army officials, rich peasants, and university teachers, and many of them were accomplished musicians, artists, writers, and dancers. Local Russian ballet dancers formed their own performance groups that appeared in Shanghai's theaters and nightclubs, giving broader exposure that was complemented by touring performances by international ballet stars.[16]

Many people who would go on to play important roles in the PRC dance field gained their start in dance through training from these White Russian ballet teachers living in China during the 1930s and 1940s, and it was during this time that ballet became associated with the cultural complex of colonial modernity and its related trends of Western-oriented urban bourgeois culture.[17] Zhao Qing, for example, who later played the role of Third Sacred Mother in *Magic Lotus Lantern,* recalls taking expensive ballet classes as a child from a White Russian woman in Shanghai who taught in an upstairs studio next to the Paris Theatre.[18] For Zhao, as for other wealthy urban Chinese at the time, ballet classes were part of a broader class education in European culture that also included learning the piano, participating in spoken drama clubs, and watching British films at the cinema.[19] Wu Xiaobang's wife and artistic collaborator, Sheng Jie, also the child of a wealthy urban Chinese family, had similar exposure to ballet during her youth in Harbin and Shanghai. In the late 1930s, Sheng was an actress in the Western-style spoken drama theater scene in Shanghai, where she met Wu, who had just returned from studying European classical music, ballet, and German modern dance in Tokyo.[20] Some of these early students gained significant expertise in ballet and performed with White Russian ballet ensembles. Korean Chinese dancer Zhao Dexian (1913–2002), for example, had performed with a White Russian ballet ensemble in Harbin during the late 1930s and early 1940s, where he played major roles in full-scale ballet productions. Zhao went on to become a founding member of the China Dancers Association in 1949 and a leader of dance institutions in Yanbian, where he promoted both Chinese dance and ballet in one of the PRC's most active ethnic minority dance communities.[21] Although they focused on other dance styles after 1949, these dancers brought with them significant knowledge of ballet, as well as personal and cultural associations with the form, that would shape the way ballet was interpreted in China in later decades.

Two artists who went on to be important proponents of revolutionary modern ballet in the 1960s gained their early start in the pre-1949 ballet scene led by White Russian teachers in Shanghai. These were Hu Rongrong (1929–2012), who helped found the Shanghai Dance School and led the choreographic team of the 1965 ballet *White-Haired Girl,* and You Huihai (1925–2015), who shaped PRC ballet discourse as a dance critic for the *People's Daily* during the 1950s and early 1960s.[22] Hu Rongrong began her performance career as a child film star around 1935. Throughout the latter half of the 1930s, her career was covered extensively in the Chinese popular press, which nicknamed her "the Shirley Temple of the East."[23] In the early 1940s, Hu began studying vocal and dance performance, and by 1944 journalists reported that she was learning ballet in Shanghai at the school of Russian teacher N. Sokolsky.[24] Sokolsky had trained professionally in classical ballet in Saint Petersburg and, after leaving following the Russian Revolution, toured in Western Europe with the famed Russian ballerina Anna Pavlova.[25] Sokolsky began staging ballet in Shanghai as early as 1929 and was a leading figure in the scene by the mid-1930s, staging annual seasons with works such as *Coppélia, Sleeping Beauty,* and others, performed by dancers from Europe and Russia.[26] When Hu began studying with Sokolsky in the 1940s, the latter was running his Shanghai school together with his

FIGURE 19. Hu Rongrong in *Coppélia*. Published in *Huanqiu*, no. 39 (1949): 25. Photographer: Guang Yi. Reproduction provided by the Chinese Periodical Full-text Database (1911–1949), Quan Guo Bao Kan Suo Yin (CNBKSY), Shanghai Library.

wife, Evgenia Baranova, who had performed in several of the earlier productions.[27] By 1946 photos of Hu performing ballet-style dances in pointe shoes were appearing in Shanghai newspapers and magazines, and in 1948 she performed the lead role of Svanhilda in the Sokolsky school production of *Coppélia*, a nineteenth-century comic ballet (figure 19).[28] An extant English-language program indicates that this production was accompanied by the Shanghai Municipal Symphonic Orchestra and was performed at the Lyceum Theatre on June 19–20, 1948. The program shows a mixed cast of Chinese and Caucasian dancers, as represented in a group photograph and the list of performer names.[29] Along with Hu Rongrong, who is listed in the program as Hu Yung Yung, there also appears a dancer by the name of Hu Hui-Hai, who was almost certainly You Huihai.[30]

This earlier history of urban ballet activity led by White Russian immigrants in pre-1949 China receded into the background after the establishment of the PRC, when such history became a symbol of bourgeois culture and of China's subjection to foreign imperialism, both of which were considered anathema to the new culture of socialist China. As the eclectic group of figures who led China's early dance field came together and consolidated a shared vision for the future of dance in the newly established PRC, ballet became a common foil against which they defined and contrasted their new vision for Chinese dance. All of the early leaders of the PRC dance field had prior familiarity with ballet in some form; during the 1920s and 1930s, Choe Seung-hui, Wu Xiaobang, Dai Ailian, and Qemberxanim had studied various styles of ballet in Tokyo, Trinidad, England, Tashkent, and Moscow, and Liang Lun also studied some ballet in Hong Kong in the 1940s. None of these artists, however, saw ballet as the appropriate style for expressing the new life and cultural sensibilities of contemporary China. Dai Ailian had expressed this view vividly in her 1946 lecture at the Chongqing *Frontier Music and Dance Plenary*, when she compared ballet to "a foreign language" that needed to be overcome to create a new form of Chinese dance.[31] According to Dai's proposal, the very goal of creating Chinese dance was to produce a new "dance language" that could supplant the "foreign language" of ballet. In this way, ballet was encoded as a foreign "Other" against which Chinese dance was constructed as a new Chinese "Self."

Starting with the *Peace Dove* incident of 1950, discussed in chapter 2, debates about ballet among PRC dance critics tended to result in condemnation of Chinese choreographers who used ballet as a medium for new choreographic creation. While critics employed a variety of different arguments to convey this point, the final message was typically that ballet was not an appropriate form in which to express contemporary Chinese ideas through dance, because ballet was regarded as old-fashioned, foreign, bourgeois, and disconnected from Chinese life. Dai's address at the Second National Congress of Literature and Art Workers in September 1953, which served as an expression of official policy following the Rectification Campaign of 1951–52, offers one example of how this relationship was expressed not only by dance critics but also in statements by dance leaders that reflected the state policy. Dai's address repeated Maoist ideals about socialist culture that had emerged during the "national forms" debates of the late 1930s. For example, she started by criticizing China's dancers, including herself, for having held "bourgeois" attitudes and "ignored national traditions" in the past. Then, she outlined a correct future path, which involved pursuing innovation by studying China's own culture.[32] The implied target of such criticisms about being "bourgeois" and "ignoring national traditions" was, at least in part, productions like *Peace Dove*, which had used ballet as a movement language for new choreography performed by Chinese ensembles.

This argument followed a discursive model that would be repeated again and again to subordinate ballet in China's dance field throughout the 1950s and early 1960s.

This complex status of ballet as a foil to Chinese dance that was both ever-present and yet also constantly suppressed can be seen in the institutional development of the Beijing Dance School (BDS). Because BDS was the only institution that hosted Soviet ballet teachers and staged full-length ballet works by Chinese dancers during the 1950s, it had the strongest ballet influence of any dance institution in the PRC and has thus often been regarded as the primary vehicle for introducing ballet to China during the socialist period. Nevertheless, even as BDS was fulfilling a state mandate to "learn from the Soviet Union," it was also continuously criticized for its perceived "excess" of Soviet ballet influence, a cycle of self-adjustment vis-à-vis ballet's symbolic otherness that continues to the present day.[33] Thus, in 1955, just one year after BDS opened, an article in the *People's Daily* criticized the school for ignoring the "antibourgeois struggle" and accepting "nonproletariat values" such as the desire to "only study ballet."[34] In 1956 BDS staged its first complete ballet production, an adaptation of the eighteenth-century French ballet *La Fille Mal Gardée,* under the direction of visiting Soviet instructor Viktor Ivanovich Tsaplin. Although most of the graduation program that year consisted of Chinese dance, critics in *Dance News* still felt that the school was "overly emphasizing the study of ballet" and "creating works that . . . smell of ballet."[35] The following year, in 1957, the school adopted a new educational mission, known as "dividing the disciplines" *(fen ke),* that emphasized a disciplinary separation between Chinese dance and ballet to allay future criticism.[36] This meant that instead of studying all the dance styles offered at the school, which had previously been required for all students, students enrolled in the regular program would now choose one of two tracks: Chinese dance or ballet.[37] To make clear the different cultural associations of the two tracks, the first was called the Department of National Dance Drama (Minzu wuju ke) and the second the Department of European Dance Drama (Ouzhou wuju ke). Hereafter, when the school staged ballet productions, only students in the Department of European Dance Drama would participate, thus leaving the remainder of the students—who constituted the majority, as discussed in chapter 2—to focus on other dance forms.[38]

The intensive development of ballet at BDS that occurred in subsequent years, which culminated in the establishment of the PRC's first ballet ensemble in late 1959, continued in this model of disciplinary separation and thus involved only one portion of the school's students and staff, intentionally isolating ballet activities from other programs at the school. In 1958 the BDS Department of European Dance Drama staged *Swan Lake,* and in 1959 they followed with an adaptation of *Le Corsaire,* both classic works from the nineteenth-century Russian ballet repertoire that were also staged in new versions in the Soviet Union.[39] Both productions were performed by BDS students under the direction of visiting Soviet instructor

Petr Gusev. Stage photographs published in *China Pictorial* show alignment with ballet costuming and stage aesthetics, including tights, tutus, and camisoles, which are traditionally not worn in Chinese dance. They also show clearly the use of ballet movement.[40] While these activities were going on in the ballet program, the Chinese dance program was busy with its own projects. As discussed in the previous chapter, 1958 marked the beginning of a boom in national dance drama creation, in which dance institutions across the country participated. BDS contributed two new national dance dramas to this growing national repertoire: *Rather Die Than Submit (Ning si bu qu)*, based on the revolutionary New Yangge drama *Liu Hulan*, and *Humans Must Overcome Heaven (Ren ding sheng tian)*, about building a water conservancy project.[41] Photographs of the productions published in *Dance (Wudao)* in 1959–60 show the use of costuming consistent with Chinese dance aesthetics and body postures that suggest Chinese dance movement.[42] Within this divided framework, the two dance programs at BDS had separate personnel and different artistic goals, both in terms of training and in the development of repertoire. While the European dance drama program focused on teaching ballet and staging established foreign ballets, the national dance drama program focused on teaching Chinese dance and developing new choreography created by Chinese artists and dealing with local themes.

In 1959 this clear division of labor was disrupted by a third Gusev-directed BDS work, *Lady of the Sea (Yu meiren)*. The work alarmed China's dance critics with its lack of adherence to established genre divisions, leading to another intervention that once again reaffirmed genre boundaries and subordinated ballet to Chinese dance. The story of the production was loosely based on a Chinese folk legend, which was heavily adjusted to suit themes and narrative devices commonly used in ballet choreography.[43] Although no film recordings were made of the original production, Chen Ailian (b. 1939), who performed a lead role, recalled that *Lady of the Sea*'s 1959 choreography combined elements of both Chinese dance and ballet, in a way that had not been done before. According to Chen, this was possible in part because the cast included many students, such as Chen, who had begun studying at BDS before Chinese dance and ballet were made into separate programs. Thus, they were capable of performing both styles well, something that she argued was not replicated in later cohorts.[44] As described by co-choreographer Li Chengxiang (b. 1931), *Lady of the Sea*'s choreography "took [Chinese] national and folk dance as its foundation, and according to the needs of the content and images, broadly and selectively incorporated ballet, Oriental dance, and acrobatic elements from Chinese ethnic minority dance, then blended it all together" (figure 20).[45] Fourteen photos from the 1959 production of *Lady of the Sea* stored in the Beijing Dance Academy Archives indeed show juxtapositions of aesthetic elements that appear

FIGURE 20. Chen Ailian and ensemble in *Lady of the Sea*. Published in *Renmin huabao* 11, no. 1 (January 1960): 26. Photographer: Wu Yinbo. Image provided by China Foto Bank.

jarring when viewed alongside similar documentation of other productions of the period. For example, ballet pointe technique is paired with Chinese dance's bent legs and coiling body positions, and xiquesque accessories and hairstyles are combined with revealing costumes and partnered lifts that challenge xiqu sensibilities.[46]

In the voluminous debates that erupted over *Lady of the Sea* at the time, critics came out both for and against its method.[47] Ultimately, as had happened with *Peace Dove,* the final verdict landed in the opposing camp. Again, the perceived problem was the work's use of ballet as a creative form for communicating with Chinese audiences and expressing themes related to contemporary life in China. As co-choreographer Wang Shiqi reflected in a self-criticism published in *Dance* in 1964, the basic problem with *Lady of the Sea* had been his and the other choreographers' failure to recognize the fundamental differences between Chinese dance and ballet, and, more specifically, ballet's cultural status as a dance practice rooted in European sensibilities and ways of life. Wang wrote:

> On the problem of integrating Chinese classical dance and ballet, we only saw their commonalities, not their differences. In this way, we rigidly and mechanically used pointe technique and other ballet movements. We treated this method as a purely technical problem and did not consider the fundamental issue that any artistic expressive medium bears the marks of its nationality and, thus, necessarily involves the question of national form and national style. We didn't see that ballet's pointe shoes and lifts are a way of expressing emotion specific to European ballets or that their emergence is closely connected to the lifestyles, aesthetic views, and artistic tastes of European people. At the same time, we failed to see that our own national dance art has its own unique form, style, and meter. Therefore, we used the simplified method of mechanical borrowing, which brought some negative consequences for the development of the national dance drama project.[48]

According to Wang, it was the failure to recognize the cultural implications of dance form—the fact that different ways of dancing are connected to place-based cultural values and ways of life—that caused them to make mistakes with *Lady of the Sea.* Furthermore, he argued, by using ballet in what should have been a work of Chinese dance, they had harmed the development of national dance drama. This mistake, Wang went on to explain, went against basic principles of China's socialist cultural policy. Citing Mao Zedong's "Talks at the Yan'an Forum" in 1942, Wang wrote that they had broken Mao's rule that "taking over legacies [here, borrowing ballet] and using them as examples must never replace our own creative work."[49] Thus, the debate over *Lady of the Sea* once again reaffirmed the official policy: while one can learn from foreign artistic genres such as ballet, using these forms cannot replace the new creation of national forms, which in this case meant Chinese dance.

In the years immediately following *Lady of the Sea,* ballet gained a greater footprint in China, while at the same time, its acceptable areas of use remained circumscribed to staging and adapting foreign works, rather than blending Chinese dance and ballet or creating original ballet productions. On December 31, 1959, the Ministry of Culture established the Beijing Dance School Attached Experimental Ballet Ensemble, the PRC's first ballet ensemble, which consisted of recent graduates of BDS and young teachers and students in the school's Department of European Dance Drama.[50] The ensemble's first production, held in early 1960, was *Giselle*, a classic nineteenth-century Romantic ballet.[51] In March 1960, the Shanghai Dance School was established and became the only other institution in China with a dance program designed specifically to train ballet performers. Modeled after BDS and founded with the help of former BDS teachers, the Shanghai Dance School also, like BDS, established separate programs for Chinese dance and ballet.[52] In October of 1960, Tianjin People's Song and Dance Theater, which had previously specialized in Chinese dance, staged a ballet production titled *Spanish Daughter (Xibanya nü'er)*, based on the Soviet ballet *Laurencia* first staged at the Kirov Theater in 1939.[53] This marked both the first full-length ballet work performed in the PRC by Chinese dancers outside the Beijing Dance School or its attached ensemble and the first Chinese production of a modern Soviet *drambalet* (a new type of ballet developed in the Soviet Union), as opposed to Soviet remakes of pre-twentieth-century French or Russian classics.[54] In late 1962 the BDS Attached Experimental Ballet Ensemble followed with its own Soviet drambalet, *Fountain of Tears (Lei quan)*, an adaptation of the Mariinsky production *The Fountain of Bakhchisarai*, which premiered in 1934 and is considered a defining work of the drambalet form.[55] The BDS ensemble's last full-length ballet before *Red Detachment of Women* would be presented in 1964. Returning again to the nineteenth-century Russian repertoire, they staged *Notre-Dame de Paris (Bali shengmuyuan)*, an adaptation of *La Esmeralda*.[56]

In 1961 BDS initiated a second curricular revision, which remained in place until the start of the Cultural Revolution in 1966. What was especially significant about this revision was that, for the first time, it made explicitly clear the intended unequal relationship between Chinese dance and ballet from the point of view of dance training. According to the new plan, which was instituted in April 1961 by a joint committee representing BDS, the Shanghai Dance School, and the China Dance Workers Association, students were still to be recruited into separate programs for Chinese dance and ballet, which were to each have separate administrations, staff, and teaching curricula.[57] However, students in the Chinese dance program would not be required to study any ballet, whereas students in the ballet program would be required to study some Chinese dance. For students in the Chinese dance program, studio course requirements were to include Chinese classical dance (2,216 hours), Chinese national folk dance (676 hours), xiqu tumbling and stage combat (730 hours), and Chinese dance repertoire (1,029 hours).[58] For students in the ballet program, studio course requirements were to include ballet (2,727 hours), European character dance (601 hours), ballet partnering (312 hours), Chinese classical dance (332 hours), and ballet repertoire (1,261 hours).[59] This plan subordinated ballet to Chinese dance by suggesting that Chinese dance was to be incorporated into ballet, but ballet was not to be incorporated into Chinese dance. It also suggested that training in Chinese dance was universally important, while ballet was only necessary for ballet specialists.

Based on the history of how ballet was introduced to and developed in China prior to the mid-1960s, several observations can be made about the status of this dance form in China and its relationship to Chinese dance before the emergence of revolutionary ballet. First, ballet's introduction to China preceded both the development of Chinese dance and the start of the socialist era, meaning that in China, ballet already had deep cultural associations before establishment of the PRC in 1949. According to these earlier cultural associations, ballet was regarded as an elite Western art form that had antirevolutionary connotations because it was introduced to China by White Russians who had been trained in the pre-Soviet system and had fled the revolutionary regime. In semicolonial cities such as Harbin and Shanghai, ballet became a symbol of bourgeois culture and a marker of class status for Westernized, affluent Chinese urbanites. In part due to these earlier associations, after 1949 ballet became the foil against which to construct a new, revolutionary genre of Chinese dance. When local productions occasionally emerged that employed strong ballet aesthetics, such as *Peace Dove* and *Lady of the Sea,* they became lightning rods for critical debate, resulting in poor assessments that further discouraged the use of ballet as a medium for new choreography. The only Chinese institution that promoted ballet as part of its core mission during the 1950s, BDS, was often subject to criticism and as a result made significant efforts to isolate ballet activities and subordinate them to Chinese dance, which was the school's main focus. Throughout the 1950s and early 1960s, China's ballet practitioners engaged mainly in staging foreign productions, including both Soviet versions of pre-twentieth-century French and Russian classics and adaptations of select Soviet drambalets from the 1930s. By the early 1960s, institutions that staged ballet productions in China were limited to three coastal cities, whereas institutions that staged Chinese dance existed all over the country. As Paul Clark writes, "On the eve of the Cultural Revolution, there were about ten major ballets in the repertoire of the two ballet companies based in Beijing and Shanghai . . . . Ballet had no hold anywhere else."[60] Thus, throughout the 1950s and early 1960s, ballet was regarded as a foreign dance form whose ultimate roots were in European culture. While ballet was seen as something from which Chinese dancers should learn and gain experience, the consistent understanding was that ballet should never become a substitute for new creation in Chinese dance.

CONFLICT AND COEXISTENCE: DEBATES ON THE EVE OF THE 1964 RESTRUCTURING

Scholars have often written about revolutionary ballet as if it were a direction in which socialist China's dance field was already moving for many years before the start of the Cultural Revolution. For example, some have argued that the emergence and expansion of a ballet program at BDS in 1954, the founding of a national ballet ensemble in 1959, and the staging of ballets in other cities such as Shanghai and Tianjin by the early 1960s offer historical evidence that revolutionary ballet was always the intended goal of PRC dance creators.[61] Taking this line of reasoning a step further, some have even gone so far as to claim, anachronistically, that ballet had dominated PRC dance creation from 1949 onward. For example, Beijing-based dance scholar Ou Jian-ping, an early proponent of this view in the Anglophone scholarship, writes, "Ballet, which officially came into China via the so-called 'Socialist Camp' headed by the Soviet Union 'Big Brother' in the 1950s, was an instant success. Sino-Soviet friendship was just then at its peak, which naturally led to the enthusiastic, absolute, and essentially blind acceptance of this pure crystallization of Western civilization by both the Chinese State leadership and the professional dance community."[62] Ou also writes, "Ballet has become the preferred national dance genre and has nearly monopolized theatrical dance in mainland China since 1949."[63]

Such claims are quite obviously untrue from a historical perspective. However, they do provoke some important questions about the early history of revolutionary ballet and how it came to emerge as China's dominant dance form during the Cultural Revolution era. As I have suggested here, ballet was long associated with colonial modernity, urban bourgeois culture, and pre-twentieth-century works, making it an unlikely choice for a political campaign that espoused anticolonial values, proletarian culture, and modernization. Moreover, from the 1940s until the mid-1960s, CCP cultural policy had consistently identified the newly created genre of Chinese dance as the officially sanctioned embodiment of China's revolutionary culture in the dance field. Thus, if ballet was, in fact, neither a dominant dance form nor a symbol of revolutionary culture in socialist China prior to the mid-1960s, then how can we explain its emergence and sudden rise to prominence after 1966, during what is now often regarded as one of the most radically revolutionary eras of China's socialist culture?

To answer this question, I argue, requires recognizing controversy and internal divisions, rather than a monolithic authoritarian uniformity, as the historical condition of China's dance field during the socialist era before the Cultural Revolution. That is, even though CCP policy tended to support Chinese dance as the main national project of socialist cultural development in China's dance field from the 1940s to the mid-1960s, competing voices and activities also existed that advocated for alternative possibilities. The BDS ballet program persisted and even gradually expanded during the late 1950s and early 1960s not because of a single dominant vision that marched China's dance development toward the predetermined goal of revolutionary ballet but, instead, because there was no unified vision, and competing agendas persisted in the same space simultaneously. For this reason, in the midst of ongoing controversies surrounding the relevance of ballet to China's dancers and audiences, as well as a nationwide boom of Chinese dance creation that coincided by 1960 with the breakdown in Sino-Soviet relations and departure of all Soviet ballet instructors, ballet practitioners nevertheless remained active as a minority group within China's dance field and were able to advance their agenda despite its often running counter to predominant trends. Instead of demonstrating the homogeneity of China's socialist dance practice during the pre–Cultural Revolution period, the history of ballet in China before 1966 suggests the fundamental heterogeneity of dance activity at this time and the lack of consensus among dance practitioners about the future of dance innovation. Ultimately, revolutionary ballet was able to emerge and gain support because of this broader context of multiplicity. As a product of a time in which divergent paths were possible, revolutionary ballet was one among many options.

Examining dancers' writings in socialist China during the 1950s and early 1960s, one can have no doubt that China's dance field included ballet enthusiasts and that some of these enthusiasts dreamed of a time when ballet would play a larger role in China's dance world than it did then. One such enthusiast was You Huihai, the dancer who had likely performed alongside Hu Rongrong in the Sokolsky ballet school production of *Coppélia* in Shanghai in 1948. In addition to studying with Sokolsky, You had previously been a student of Wu Xiaobang in the early 1940s and had participated in Liang Lun's Frontier Dance group in wartime Kunming. Thus, in contrast to Hu Rongrong, who continued to teach ballet in Shanghai in the 1950s but did not receive national attention again until the mid-1960s, You took up Chinese dance after 1949 and soon rose to national prominence by this route. During the early 1950s, You was a member of important Chinese dance ensembles in Shanghai and Beijing (including both CEOT and the precursor to SEOT), and in 1953, he contributed to the adaptation of "Picking Tea and Catching Butterflies," which won an award at the WFYS that year. You's success in Chinese dance gave him a position of power from which he then began to advocate for ballet. Thus, in 1956, when others were criticizing the BDS graduation performance for what they saw as excessive ballet influences, You published an article in the *People's Daily* in which he reviewed the show positively and called for even more ballet in the future. After praising the students' performance of a waltz scene from the ballet *Sleeping Beauty*, a photograph of which was included in the article, You continued, "This couldn't help but make me think: in our theaters, the staging of a complete exquisite ballet dance drama by Chinese performers is already not so far away."[64] While You was careful to also praise a Chinese dance piece in the show, his enthusiasm for the possibilities of ballet at BDS was clear. You ended the article with what he called "a fantasy for the future," in which he described a snowy evening "in the year 196X," when posters outside the "capital dance drama theater" would advertise the current season of shows. Among the posters he imagined were *White-Haired Girl*, *White Snake*, *Swan Lake*, and *The Nutcracker*.[65]

You would oversee the realization of this goal two years later as a member of the BDS choreography class led by Petr Gusev, who supervised BDS's staging of *Swan*

Lake, followed by *Le Corsaire.* However, by this time You, like many other ballet advocates, was witnessing the exciting developments then happening in national dance drama and was hoping to see China's ballet practitioners also get involved in this wave of new creation. Thus, You was no longer satisfied with simply staging foreign productions; he wanted to see Chinese choreographers create new ballets on Chinese themes. In an article published in *Theatre Gazette* reviewing the state of dance drama in China in early 1959, You began by lavishing praise on the recent boom in national dance drama. He gave special attention to the recently premiered national dance drama *Five Red Clouds,* which he called "an extremely good model for dance dramas dealing with modern themes."[66] You went on to discuss the status of ballet in China. As with the 1956 BDS production, he praised recent developments but also saw them as reason for new aspirations. After commending the performances of *Swan Lake* and *Le Corsaire,* he wrote, "It is without a doubt that upon this tradition of strictly inheriting the ballet dance drama art [by staging foreign ballets], we will in the near future also try out creation that uses the ballet form to reflect the content of our national life."[67] Here, what You likely had in mind was *Lady of the Sea,* which he mentions two paragraphs later is in the midst of being created. This work, he optimistically predicts, will "carry out many new experiments" and promote "mutual study and learning" between national dance drama and ballet. As we saw in the previous section, this production was indeed recognized as a new experiment. However, the method it proposed of "mutual study and learning" between national dance drama and ballet remained an ideal of only a small portion of the dance community.

Early 1964 has often been regarded as the starting point for major political shifts and policy changes that would emerge more fully during the Cultural Revolution.[68] In the dance field, too, early 1964 brought important changes that in some ways served as harbingers for later developments. However, while these changes predicted that ballet would retain and potentially expand its position within China's dance field, they also confirmed the continued importance of other dance styles, chief among them Chinese dance. Early in the year, China's Ministry of Culture implemented two important institutional changes that seemed to suggest a more equal position of ballet to Chinese dance, though still premised on the idea that the two forms should operate as independent, not comingled, art forms. First, on February 27, BDS was divided into two institutions, one called the China Dance School (Zhongguo wudao xuexiao), which would focus on Chinese dance, and the other the Beijing Ballet School (Beijing balei wudao xuexiao), which would focus on ballet.[69] In practice, the two schools still occupied the same physical address and shared a single teaching building. However, this change indicated a renewed commitment to the artistic independence of Chinese dance and ballet as separate artistic forms with their own training missions. In March a similar change was made to the Central Opera and Dance Drama Theater (CODDT, formerly CEOT), dividing it into the China Opera and Dance Drama Theater and the Central Opera and Dance Drama Theater.[70] As with BDS, this division reflected a deepening of what had already been a largely divided system. For example, prior to this change, the CODDT already had separate Chinese- and Western-style ensembles for both opera and music, which had been known as the Number One and Number Two ensembles, respectively. The Number One ensembles had used "national singing style" *(minzu changfa)* and "national orchestra" *(minzu guanxian yuetuan)* and had specialized works by Chinese composers on Chinese themes, whereas the Number Two ensembles had employed "bel canto singing style" *(meisheng changfa)* and a European-style orchestra and had specialized in performed works by foreign composers set in foreign locations.[71] Within the new division, what had previously been the CEOT national dance drama ensemble joined with the Number One groups to form the new "China" ensemble, while what had previously been the BDS Attached Experimental Ballet Ensemble joined with the Number Two groups to form the new "Central" ensemble. In the official CODDT history, published in 2010, this change is described as fulfilling a plan devised originally by Zhou Enlai during the 1950s, according to which divergent artistic paths (in this case, Chinese dance and ballet) could develop simultaneously.[72]

Dance-related writings published around the time of these changes suggest that, beyond simply supporting the parallel development of different art forms, the new institutional divisions were motivated also by a renewed anxiety about the influence of ballet on Chinese dance, as well as a continued lack of consensus about what constituted "correct" revolutionary dance practice. The February 1964 issue of *Dance*, which also included Wang Shiqi's self-criticism about *Lady of the Sea*, was published less than three weeks before the division of BDS and offers great insight into both dancers' concerns and guiding policies during this period. The opening article chronicles the various arguments made during a music and dance symposium recently held in Beijing, in which leaders from the music and dance fields came together with the purpose of "inspecting the status of the implementation of Chairman Mao's arts thought and the Party's arts policies in music and dance work."[73] Many of the recorded conversations from this symposium revolved around questions about how to implement the three guiding principles of the era, known as the "three transformations" *(san hua)*: "nationalization" *(minzuhua),* "revolutionization" *(geminghua),* and "massification" *(qunzhonghua).* According to the report, one of the most serious problems obstructing the implementation of these principles in the dance field was the purportedly excessive psychological attachment many dance workers felt toward ballet. Recounting one dancer's testimony, the report wrote, "One comrade said: I initially opposed those foreign dance theories, but then I became suspicious and vacillated. Finally, I surrendered, groveled, and appreciated them to the point that I was prostrating myself in admiration. What was even worse, not only did I myself get encased in this Western frame, but I used it to encase others. When others opposed it, I spoke in its defense."[74]

Throughout the report, the terms "groveling" *(baidao)* and "foreign/Western dogma" *(yang jiaotiao)* are used pejoratively to condemn a variety of practices related to the uncritical admiration for dance forms classified as *yang*—meaning foreign or Western, here often referring to ballet—that are described as detrimental to China's socialist dance development. Examples of these practices cited in the report include employing too much ballet movement in one's choreography, preferring dance works that incorporate balletic elements such as lifts and jumps, being unwilling to learn from the lives and expressions of the common people because of a preference for ballet themes and aesthetics, and using theoretical principles drawn from ballet choreography to limit new experiments in form or content. While learning from foreign experience was encouraged, the proper way to do this, according to the report, was to "take the self as the subject" *(yi wo wei zhu),* meaning not to lose one's sense of self by copying others.[75] The fundamental problem with *Lady of the Sea,* the report resolved, was that it did not do this. To further clarify this issue, the report confirms that innovation does not mean incorporating foreign or Western things. Using a play on the Maoist slogan "weeding through the old to bring forth the new" *(tuichen chuxin),* which dance workers were supposed to promote, the report states, "innovation absolutely does not mean mechanically copying ballet; that is called 'weeding through the old to bring forth the *yang.*'"[76]

Given that the first revolutionary ballet would appear later that year and that ballet movement would soon become the dictated choreographic mode for portraying Chinese revolutionary heroes in dance, it is interesting to note that in early 1964 a predominant view expressed in China's national dance publications was strong opposition to the use of ballet movement when portraying Chinese revolutionary characters. On this point, the report recounts the following argument made by a symposium participant, which points to the deeper issues involved in attitudes toward ballet at this time: "I don't agree with using ballet to portray themes related to today's China. We should first use ballet to express foreign revolutionary themes. If we [use it to] express China's revolutionary themes, there will be a problem with national feeling. For example, when performing [the revolutionary martyr] Liu Hulan, if [the dancer] goes up on pointe and sticks out her chest, audiences will not be convinced. Using ballet to express Chinese content may happen in the future, but right now I'm afraid it won't do."[77]

Here, the phrase "goes up on pointe and sticks out her chest" provides vivid insight into how dancers at the time imagined ballet bodies and why many saw them as fundamentally incompatible with the presentation of revolutionary Chinese characters. Liu Hulan, a poor peasant girl from rural Shanxi Province who died supporting the revolutionary cause, was originally made famous through a New Yangge drama during the 1940s, in which she was portrayed using movement repertoires derived largely from northern Han folk dances.[78] These movement repertoires, which featured an earthbound, flat-footed stance, swiveling hip and head actions, and a relaxed upper body, were seen as kinetically incompatible with the elongated leg lines, elevated center of gravity, and erect, upward-oriented torso carriage demanded for ballet movement. Indeed, from the perspective of human physiology and movement principles, the two techniques are almost impossible to combine while still maintaining the stylistic integrity of either one. Thus, such a comment pointed to the practical problem that ballet posed for dancers and cho-reographers. That is, when incorporating ballet movement, one was often forced to abandon features of bodily comportment that were not only important from an aesthetic perspective but also carried significant local meanings, such as reflecting age, class, gender, ethnic, and regional identities. For audiences versed in these local meanings, then, a dancer who is performing on pointe and sticking out her chest does not move like the type of person who should be a revolutionary hero in a Chinese socialist story.

This concern about how the incorporation of ballet movement might dilute or distort portrayals of revolutionary Chinese characters was also a concern for dancers and teachers, who were engaged in the processes of performing such roles and teaching students how to move correctly onstage. One article, written by Chen Jianmin, a Shanghai-based dancer then performing the role of Liu Lichuan in *Dagger Society*, explained how he and other dancers in the production took steps to "correctively remove foreign/Western flavor" *(gaidiao yangwei)* from their performances.[79] According to Chen's account, they had worked with leading xiqu practitioners Li Shaochun and Bai Yunsheng (both of whom had participated in the development of Chinese classical dance movement repertoires based on xiqu during the mid-1950s) to clean up their dancing by removing Western elements. First, Chen reported, they removed "ballet turns and leaps," replacing them with xiqu-based alternatives. Next, they made changes to their postural habits. He writes, "The teachers discovered that some of us performers had the habit of stick-ing out our chests, facing our heads up, and looking down, and they pointed out that this was a Western-flavored expression that was often used by performers in ballets. Chinese xiqu performers have to bring their chests in, straighten their necks, and look horizontally."[80] Through this process of correction, Chen and the other dancers became aware of their own habits and were able to bring their per-formances more in line with the images expected for the types of characters they were portraying.

Some worried that the root cause of the problems Chen described stemmed from the stubborn persistence of ballet habits among some Chinese classical dance instructors at BDS. A systematic criticism of such problems appeared in another essay, written by Li Zhengyi (b. 1929), a BDS faculty member who served as longtime head of the BDS Chinese classical dance program and also coauthored the nationally influential Chinese classical dance technique manual published in 1960. In her essay, Li outlined a list of common errors by Chinese classical dance instructors at BDS that arose from introducing ballet elements into Chinese classical dance movement. Describing these problems idiomatically, she categorized them as either "using the Western to change the Chinese" (*yi Xi hua Zhong*) or "using the Western to replace the Chinese" (*yi Xi dai Zhong*), both of which she considered highly problematic.[81] An example of the former was adding turnout—a basic feature of ballet—to Chinese dance movements that did not call for it, while an example of the latter included replacing Chinese classical dance poses, such as *tanhai* (literally, "observing the sea"), with superficially similar ballet positions, such as the arabesque. Avoiding such mistakes, Li argued, was essential to maintain the stylistic integrity of Chinese classical dance technique, which in turn had serious implications for the relationship between art and politics. "The reason for these mistakes, in the final analysis, is being distanced from politics, distanced from the masses, and distanced from tradition," she writes. In other words, introducing ballet elements into Chinese classical dance training, in Li's estimation, equated with not following the principle of "three transformations," of revolutionization, massification, and nationalization.

The Ministry of Culture's decision in February and March of 1964 to restructure BDS and CODDT so that each would henceforth be divided into separate institutions dedicated to Chinese dance and ballet allowed the ballet enthusiasts within China's dance sphere to continue their work in spite of ongoing disapproval and skepticism from the majority of leading figures in the dance field at the time. Thus, as suggested in the CODDT history, it allowed for conflicting agendas to coexist and for divergent artistic visions to be pursued simultaneously. Rather than attributing this decision solely to Zhou Enlai's long-standing artistic vision, however, we can also suggest additional potential motivations for this decision that reflect particular concerns of this historical moment. First, one likely motivation for this decision was a desire to reap the benefits of years of state investment in training specialized ballet dancers that had occurred with the support of Soviet teachers during the latter half of the 1950s and had continued through the early 1960s, led by local dancers with ballet training. By 1964 both BDS and the Shanghai Dance School had cultivated a cohort of students who, after years of training, were now finally fluent in the movement language of ballet, as demonstrated by their ability to stage numerous full-length foreign works, from revised pre-twentieth-century classics to Soviet-era dramballets. Because of the division of disciplines in 1957, these students would not have been able to easily adapt to Chinese dance choreography, so rather than letting their training go to waste, it made sense to give them an opportunity to at least continue the experimental attempts. Moreover, by creating separate institutions, these dancers could continue their work without having what many felt was a distorting effect on the continued development of Chinese dance.

Second, another likely motivation for this decision was the recognition of ballet's usefulness in Cold War diplomacy and, following from this, a desire to assert China's aspiration to superpower status and its self-representational agency vis-à-vis other nations such as the Soviet Union and Japan through ballet. During the early Cold War, ballet emerged as an important artistic medium for international competitions of influence and legitimacy, especially between the United States and the Soviet Union, spurred in part by the defection of Soviet ballet dancers.[82] Initially, PRC cultural planners had focused on Chinese dance as the medium of choice for diplomatic arts missions, as discussed in the previous chapter. However, beginning in the mid-1950s, they also began a strategic effort to have Chinese dancers perform music and dance from Asia, Africa, and Latin America as part of diplomatic activities with nonaligned countries in the Third World.[83] China's Oriental Song and Dance Ensemble, a national-level ensemble established in 1962, was created expressly for this purpose. During the same period, China also received visits by ballet ensembles from countries in Asia and Latin America, suggesting that ballet might be a viable tool of cultural diplomacy for China as well. Especially important in this regard were a tour by Japan's Matsuyama Ballet in 1958 and another by the National Ballet of Cuba in 1961.[84] Chinese ballet dancers made their own first international tour in 1962, visiting Burma, suggesting the beginning of a Chinese strategy to use ballet in diplomatic exchange.[85] China's ambition to rival the United States and the Soviet Union in international influence, which was given force with China's first successful explosion of an atomic bomb in October 1964, provides important historical context for the choice to continue promoting ballet in the era following the Sino-Soviet split of the early 1960s.[86] After 1962 Chinese dance delegations no longer attended the World Festivals of Youth and Students, which had previously offered an important venue for international influence and intercultural exchange through the medium of national dance. Thus, China's cultural leaders may have seen ballet as an important medium through which China could assert its cultural legitimacy in this new era. The fact that dance ensembles in the Soviet Union and Japan had both already performed ballet works on Chinese revolutionary themes—the Soviet Union in 1927 with *Red Poppy* and Japan in 1955 with *White-Haired Girl*—presented a challenge for Chinese choreographers to assert their cultural agency in the international ballet sphere by representing themselves in this medium.[87]

Another important factor to consider in the Ministry of Culture's decision to continue to support the development of ballet, alongside Chinese dance, in its 1964 institutional restructuring of BDS and CODDT was its ongoing commitment to the idea, expressed in Mao's early writings on revolutionary art in the Yan'an era, that some elite Western cultural forms associated with the European Enlightenment had inherent value to China's socialist cultural mission. Like the Western symphonic orchestra, bel canto singing style, and oil painting, ballet was regarded by some members of China's cultural leadership as a universally significant artistic form whose cultural value transcended particular ethnic, racial, or class associations.[88] Building on an earlier tradition of Chinese cosmopolitanism born out of colonial modernity that informed some aspects of socialist internationalism, this view allowed many to see ballet as a symbol of cultural modernity that could serve revolutionary goals.[89] Prior to 1966, this cosmopolitan attitude toward ballet coexisted with the more radically anticolonial cultural agendas embodied in Chinese dance. Although these agendas frequently came into conflict, as in the debates discussed above, they were also considered by many to be mutually compatible, part of an open-minded cultural vision in which different artistic styles could coexist within a pluralistic socialist arts field. At times, as in the case of Dai Ailian, these different agendas were even united in the work of a single person. Thus, while Dai was a leading advocate for the development of Chinese dance, she also contributed to the ballet effort. Through her roles as president of the China Dancers Association in 1949–54, director of the Central Song and Dance Ensemble in 1952–55, principal of BDS in 1954–64, principal of the Beijing Ballet School in 1964–66, and artistic director of the ballet ensembles at BDS and CODDT in 1963–66, Dai oversaw important developments in both Chinese dance and ballet.[90] By treating these fields as complementary, she modeled the diversity of artistic commitments reflected in China's dance field at the time.[91]

A NEW ROUND OF INNOVATION: CHOREOGRAPHIC CREATION IN 1964–1965

From the perspective of choreographic creation, the early 1964 transition did bring important changes to the dance field, particularly in thematic content. As with the banning of historical costume dramas and ghost stories in film and theater, in dance there was a clear shift away from dances based on legends and mythology, as well as works with romantic themes that did not clearly relate to revolution and modern life.[92] Thus, for example, SEOT's successful 1962 production *Hou Yi and Change* (*Houyi yu Change*), a mythology-themed xiqu-style national dance drama that starred *Dagger Society*'s Shu Qiao in the role of Change, was by late 1963 labeled a "poisonous weed"; it could no longer be performed, and some members of the creative team, including Shu Qiao, were criticized.[93] Another highly successful work newly labeled a negative example at this time was BDS's Chinese classical dance solo "Spring, River, and Flowers on a Moonlit Night," which had won an award at the 1962 WFYS competition and was included in the popular 1959 Chinese dance film *Hundred Phoenixes Face the Sun* (video 10).[94] This dance, performed by Chen Ailian from *Lady of the Sea*, was inspired by a Tang dynasty poem and employed the Chinese classical dance movement style developed in the 1950s BDS curriculum and works like *Magic Lotus Lantern*, emphasizing soft, subtle movements, curving

VIDEO 10. Chen Ailian in "Spring, River, and Flowers on a Moonlit Night," from *Hundred Phoenixes Face the Sun.* Beijing Film Studio, 1959.

To watch this video, scan the QR code with your mobile device or visit DOI: https://doi.org/10.1525/luminos.58.10

lines, and a xiqu-style use of breath and eyes to perform sentiment.[95] Clothed in a pastel gown and glittering hair accessories while dancing with two large fans edged in white feathers, Chen performed an otherworldly and romantic feminine image surrounded by flowers and moonlight, similar to the portrayals of female immortals Third Sacred Mother in *Magic Lotus Lantern* and Chang'e in *Hou Yi and Chang'e.* Citing "Spring River and Flowers on a Moonlit Night" by name, the February 1964 symposium report concluded that, though a good example of national form, it did not have sufficient class consciousness and socialist themes to be embraced in the new era.[96] To suit the new policies, in other words, original dance choreography now needed not only to pursue formal innovation, especially through new national forms, but also to deal with characters and themes that had a clear and explicit connection to contemporary life and revolution.

The years 1964–65 witnessed an outpouring of diverse choreography that was designed to meet this new challenge. These works took as their models successful Great Leap Forward–era national dance dramas such as *Five Red Clouds* and *Dagger Society,* which continued to be endorsed as positive examples of socialist dance creation. However, they also built on these earlier works through significant innovations. The first major national event to feature results of these new experiments was the People's Liberation Army (PLA) Third All-Military Arts Festival (Di san jie quanjun wenyi huiyan), which took place in Beijing in the spring of 1964 and featured more than 380 new works of music, dance, folk art, and acrobatics presented by eighteen PLA-affiliated performance ensembles from across

VIDEO 11. Excerpt of "Fires of Fury Are Burning," from *Sun Rises in the East.* August First Film Studio, 1964.

To watch this video, scan the QR code with your mobile device or visit DOI: https://doi.org/10.1525/luminos.58.11

the country.[97] Later that year, the August First Film Studio created two color films documenting twenty-two works from this festival, titled *Sun Rises in the East (Xuri dongsheng)* and *East Wind Forever (Dongfeng wanli).*[98] Of the works documented in these films, three offer especially striking examples of the new ideas being explored in choreography at this time. One of these was "Laundry Song" (Xi yi ge) by the Tibet Military Area Political Department Cultural Work Troupe (Xizang junqu zhengzhi bu wengongtuan), which melded song and dialogue together with military dance and Tibet-style Chinese national folk dance to produce a humorous dance on the theme of soldier-civilian and Han-Tibetan relations in Tibet following the 1959 uprisings.[99] Another of these was "Fires of Fury Are Burning" (Nuhuo zai ranshao) by the PLA General Political Department Song and Dance Ensemble, a small-scale dance drama about racial discrimination in the United States that melded Chinese military dance with Afro-diasporic movement and racial impersonation, offering a message in support of African-American civil rights.[100] Among the many striking images in this dance are an altercation in which a white police officer, who is exposed as a member of the Ku Klux Klan, brutalizes a black boy, which is followed by a battle in which a multiracial group of protestors battles the KKK set against a backdrop of the US Capitol and a giant cross (video 11). Possibly inspired by the Soviet ballet *The Path of Thunder,* which was performed in China in 1959, this dance also built on a longer tradition of using racial impersonation in Chinese theater and dance to address anticolonial and antiracist themes.[101] "Fires

VIDEO 12. "Female Civilian Soldiers," from *East Wind Forever.* August First
Film Studio, 1964.

To watch this video, scan the QR code with your mobile device or visit
DOI: https://doi.org/10.1525/luminos.58.12

of Fury Are Burning" represented a new development for PRC choreography in its
treatment of the then contemporary US civil rights movement and its creation of a
new movement vocabulary blending Chinese military dance with Afro-diasporic
movement elements.

A third work that demonstrated considerable innovation at the 1964 PLA festival was "Female Civilian Soldiers" (Nü minbing) by the Shenyang Army Cultural Work Troupe (Shenyang budui wengongtuan) (video 12).[102] Like "Laundry
Song" and *Five Red Clouds* before it, "Female Civilian Soldiers" followed a long
trajectory of PRC choreography that incorporated choral singing, dating back to
Braving Wind and Waves to Liberate Hainan in 1950. The dance features twelve
women with short braided pigtails dressed in identical light blue peasant-style
pants and jackets with bayoneted rifles over their shoulders and ammunition
packs strapped to their waists. The dance is reminiscent of the group scene "Bow
Dance" in *Dagger Society* in that it employs a Chinese classical dance movement vocabulary adapted almost entirely from xiqu and martial arts movement,
which it arranges in a new way through group sequences in geometrical stage
formations using strict unison choreography. Additionally, as in "Bow Dance,"
the tempo is calm overall and the movements deliberate, conveying a sense of
discipline and focus through the use of slow lowering and rising actions, miming
the balancing and aiming of weapons, and controlled stances on one leg. Also,

like "Bow Dance," the score uses a tune played by a Chinese-style orchestra. Two aspects that differentiate this dance from dances in *Dagger Society*, however, are its use of modern weapons—in this case bayoneted rifles, rather than bows—and the use of simpler and more contemporary-looking costumes that appear more like everyday clothing. At a choreographic level, the dance also departs from earlier works such as "Bow Dance" by depicting women performing flips and other more acrobatic elements from xiqu tumbling sequences that previously were performed more often by male dancers. Finally, by performing stabbing and blocking actions and running and leaping across the stage in groups, the dancers imply readiness for group battle, but without the actual staging of combat scenes against enemy forces that occur in both *Dagger Society* and *Five Red Clouds*. In its images of women soldiers performing in unison with rifles, this dance clearly foreshadows similar dances in the ballet *Red Detachment of Women* that would premiere just a few months later. However, one obvious difference between these works is that while "Female Civilian Soldiers" is composed using Chinese dance movement vocabulary, such scenes in *Red Detachment of Women* are composed almost entirely in ballet movement.

In the fall of 1964, three important works of new choreography premiered in Beijing that demonstrated the new direction of choreography as performed by China's national-level dance ensembles. Like many past dance productions that appeared in the fall season, these works also doubled as celebrations for the October 1 anniversary of the founding of the PRC. The first two of these new works, which premiered in September, were both large-scale dance dramas created by the newly divided dance ensembles of CODDT. The dance ensemble of the China Opera and Dance Drama Theater, which specialized in Chinese dance, presented the national dance drama *Eight Women Ode (Ba nü song)*, and the dance ensemble of the Central Opera and Dance Drama Theater, which specialized in ballet, presented *Red Detachment of Women*. In terms of their subject matter, the two works were similar in that both told stories of women participating in modern Chinese wars. *Eight Women Ode* recounted the story of eight female soldiers who fought in the Northeastern Anti-Japanese United Army during the War of Resistance against Japan and died in 1938 when they threw themselves into the Mudan River to avoid surrendering after they ran out of ammunition. By comparison, *Red Detachment of Women,* which was set on Hainan Island during conflicts between the CCP and the KMT (Nationalists) between 1927 and 1937, portrayed the story of a young woman who, after being abused by a wicked landlord, joins a women's detachment of the Red Army and becomes a revolutionary soldier. When these works first premiered, media reports treated them as a pair and gave them equal attention. For example, *China Pictorial* ran a single-page announcement that contained one identically sized black-and-white photo and one similar-length paragraph of descriptive text for each work.[103] Similarly, *Dance* published back-to-back articles of roughly the same length.[104] In both cases, the works were praised as models of dance creation embodying the "three transformations."

Since *Eight Women Ode* was never documented on film and *Red Detachment of Women* was only filmed seven years later in a revised version, it is difficult to know exactly what the choreography in the original 1964 versions looked like. Zhao Qing, who performed the role of Hu Xiuzhi in the original version of *Eight Women Ode,* recalled its movement vocabulary being grounded mainly in xiqu-style Chinese classical dance.[105] A contemporary review confirmed this, describing *Eight Women Ode* as technically similar to xiqu-style national dance dramas the ensemble had performed previously, such as *Magic Lotus Lantern* (premiered by the ensemble in 1957), *Dagger Society* (imported from SEOT in 1960), and *Lei Feng Pagoda* (premiered by the ensemble in 1960).[106] Another critic noted that *Eight Women Ode* also made use of folk dance material from northeast China, where the story is set, and made important innovations within the Chinese dance vocabularies to suit the work's relatively contemporary setting.[107] Extant performance photographs in the CODDT archive show what appear to be a yangge-style handkerchief dance and a round fan and streamer dance likely also derived from northeastern-style yangge.[108] The photograph published in *China Pictorial* in 1964 shows women in military uniforms holding their hands in fists and striking martial poses that combine Peking opera postures with Chinese military dance.[109] By contrast, all contemporary evidence suggests that the 1964 version of *Red Detachment of Women*, like its 1971 film production, was choreographed primarily using ballet movement. The photograph published in *China Pictorial* in 1964 shows a scene that also appears in the film, in which women dancers balance on pointe in arabesque positions while aiming their rifles.[110] Likewise, contemporary critics described the production as a ballet that incorporated some Chinese dance elements, which is also an accurate description of the choreography in the 1971 film.[111] Bai Shuxiang (b. 1939), who performed the lead role of Wu Qionghua in the 1964 production of *Red Detachment of Women,* was China's prima ballerina at the time, having also performed the lead roles in the Chinese productions of *Swan Lake, Le Corsaire, Giselle,* and *La Esmeralda.* Thus, for both *Eight Women Ode* and *Red Detachment of Women,* the casts were mature dancers with significant achievements in their respective primary movement forms, Chinese classical dance in the case of *Eight Women Ode* and ballet in the case of *Red Detachment of Women.* Both works had innovated by using these respective forms to present stories set in twentieth-century China, something that in the case of Chinese classical dance had been done previously, though not in the same way, by Chinese regional ensembles, and in the case of ballet had been done previously by companies from the Soviet Union and Japan (figure 21).

The last of the three major dance productions premiered in Beijing in the fall of 1964 was *East Is Red (Dongfang hong),* created by a team of artists assembled from sixty-seven different performance ensembles, schools, and other organizations.[112]

FIGURE 21. *Red Detachment of Women.* Published in *Renmin huabao* 16, no. 5 (1965): 22. Photographer: Li Jin. Image provided by China Foto Bank.

Rather than being a dance drama, *East Is Red* was a "large-scale song and dance historical epic" *(daxing yinyue wudao shishi),* meaning that it featured both dance and vocal and instrumental musical performances and that rather than telling a continuous narrative with a set group of characters, it focused on a broader theme, in this case the history of modern China.[113] Although *East Is Red* was not a dance drama, it incorporated a significant amount of dance elements, and many leading choreographers and dancers participated in its original creative team and cast.[114] Thus, it was considered an important event for the dance field, receiving considerable attention from dance critics and extensive coverage in publications such as *Dance.*[115] With a cast of over three thousand, *East Is Red* premiered with grand ceremony on October 1 in the Great Hall of the People in Beijing, for an audience of approximately ten thousand that included top state leaders and foreign dignitaries.[116] A film based on the work, released in 1965, documented the original production almost in its entirely, offering a useful record of its choreography.[117]

The choreography documented in the 1965 film shows that *East Is Red* used a large amount of Chinese dance movement, with the other most commonly used dance style being military dance. Ballet was not a significant part of this production, except in the form of ballet elements, such as individual turns and leaps, that had already long been incorporated into works of Chinese dance and military dance. *East Is Red*'s opening dance, "Sunflowers Face the Sun" (Kuihua xiang taiyang), which was the most commonly reproduced dance in photographs at

VIDEO 13. Excerpt of "Sunflowers Face the Sun," from *East Is Red*. Beijing Film Studio, August First Film Studio, and Central News Documentary Film Studio, 1965.

To watch this video, scan the QR code with your mobile device or visit DOI: https://doi.org/10.1525/luminos.58.13

the time, featured choreography grounded in existing Chinese classical and folk vocabulary (video 13). For example, it features *yuanchang bu* (circling small heel-toe steps), *ping zhuan* (flat turns with arms out to the sides), *woyu* (the spiraling seated position), kneeling backbends, and oppositional hand, head, and hip swaying walks. The dancers also manipulate pairs of large fans, using standard movements used in earlier Chinese dance choreography of Han-style folk dance, Korean-style folk dance, and Chinese classical dance. A later scene, portraying a mother forced out of extreme poverty to sell her daughter, similarly employs standard Chinese dance movements derived from xiqu, such as *tabu* (the T-step position), modified *fanshen* (diagonal upper body rotation), and *guizi bu* (kneeling walks). Throughout *East Is Red*, fight choreography typically features acrobatic tumbling elements adapted from xiqu, sometimes combined with postures borrowed from martial arts and military dance; celebratory scenes typically employ Han and minority folk dances. The most technically elaborate solo dances in the entire production appear in the minority dance segment in scene 6, performed by China's top ethnic minority dance artists of the time. For example, well-known soloists who appeared in this scene in both the 1964 stage version and the 1965 film version included Mongol dancer Modegema, Uyghur dancer Aytilla Qasim, Dai dancer Dao Meilan, Korean dancer Cui Meishan, and Miao dancer Jin Ou.[118] Tibetan dancer Oumijiacan performed in the film version, in addition to serving as a member of the original choreography team.[119] While the choreography in *East Is Red* mainly employed existing dance styles developed in China during the socialist era, it innovated on these styles by expanding them to a much larger scale than had ever been performed in China previously.

The year 1965 brought further experimentation and new innovations in both the form and content of dance choreography, with a special emphasis on dance productions dealing with international themes. After the success of their first project, the *East Is Red* creation team went on in April 1965 to premiere *Fires of Fury in the Coconut Grove (Yelin nuhuo)*, a large-scale song and dance production about the Vietnam War.[120] Meanwhile, many regional song and dance ensembles also premiered their own large-scale music and dance epics about the Vietnam War and anti-imperialist movements in Asia, Africa, and Latin America. Prominent examples of these that appeared in 1965 are the Hunan Provincial Folk Song and Dance Ensemble's *Ode to Wind and Thunder (Feng lei song)*, the Liaoning Opera Theater's *We Walk on the Great Road (Women zou zai dalu shang)*, and Guangxi Folk Song and Dance Ensemble's *Remain in Combat Readiness (Yanzhenyidai)*.[121] In June 1965 the dance drama ensemble of the China Opera and Dance Drama Theater, working with the *East Is Red* choreography group, also premiered its first original full-length dance drama on an international theme. Titled *Congo River Is Roaring (Gangguohe zai nuhou, a.k.a. The Raging Congo River)*, it commemorated the Congolese independence movement and the life of late Congolese leader Patrice Lumumba.[122] Furthering the experiment begun in the 1964 US civil rights–themed work "Fires of Fury Are Burning," the team attempted to employ Afro-diasporic movement vocabularies, here with a focus on West African dance, as the primary movement language in the production. To develop this movement, members of the cast studied with members of China's Oriental Song and Dance Ensemble, who had previously studied in several African countries.[123] Following what was at the time standard practice for Chinese dance works featuring black characters, the dancers in *Congo River Is Roaring* performed with dark body and facial make-up, as well as head wraps and costumes meant to approximate various styles of Congolese urban and tribal dress.[124] However, the goal of this racial impersonation was to celebrate anticolonial themes and the Congolese struggle for national independence.

Another trend that emerged in 1965 was the appearance of new Chinese music and dance productions focused on the revolutionary history of ethnic minority communities within China. In April the Central Academy of Nationalities Art Department, working with the Central Nationalities Song and Dance Ensemble, premiered a new Chinese dance drama, *Great Changes in Liang Mountain (Liangshan jubian)*, which portrayed democratic revolution and socialist construction in an Yi community in Sichuan.[125] Later that year, the Tibet Song and Dance Ensemble, working with other Lhasa-based groups, premiered the new large-scale music and dance historical epic *Reformed Peasant Slaves Face the Sun (Fanshen nongnu xiang taiyang)*, and a multiethnic group of music and dance artists in Xinjiang premiered a "new Muqam" large-scale song and dance work, *People's Communes Are Good (Renmin gongshe hao)*.[126] Although no film recordings remain of these productions, clues about their choreography can be gleaned from published reviews and photographs. According to a review in *Dance*, the Yi-themed production *Great Changes in Liang Mountain* used a primary movement vocabulary derived from a wide range of Yi folk dances documented in Sichuan, Yunnan, and Guizhou, which included the "mouth harp dance," "shawl dance," "drinking song dance," "guozhuang dance," "facing feet dance," and "smoke box dance."[127] Photographs of this work show the dancers performing as Yi villagers wearing long-sleeved jackets and striped skirts or pants, hats with feathers or embroidered head coverings, large earrings, and colorful capes or vests. Their body positions suggest aesthetic continuities with styles of Chinese dance choreography on southwestern ethnic minority themes that had been developing since the 1940s, but with new developments on those themes. Photographs and descriptions of the Tibet and Xinjiang works also provide evidence of continued experimentation in the styles of Tibetan and Xinjiang dance, both forms that had also played a large role in Chinese dance choreography since the 1940s.[128] No pointe shoes or other visual markers of ballet movement appear in any of the extant documentation of these works.

China's two ballet schools each produced new works of ballet in 1965: the Beijing Ballet School's *Red Sister-in-Law (Hong sao)* and the Shanghai Dance School's *White-Haired Girl.*[129] As already mentioned, *White-Haired Girl* went on to be named the second of the two "model ballets" promoted across the country during the early years of the Cultural Revolution and was made into a film in 1971. *Red Sister-in-Law* also enjoyed success during the Cultural Revolution, when it was revised as *Ode to Yimeng (Yimeng song)* in the early 1970s and made into a film in 1975.[130] Based on the evidence of the two films, these works show more variation in vocabulary, more delicacy, and more Chinese dance movement than *Red Detachment of Women*. However, like their predecessor, both are clearly works of ballet that use some Chinese dance elements, not works of Chinese dance.[131] As in *Red Detachment of Women,* pointe technique is used by female dancers throughout both productions, and ballet postures and lines generally dominate the dancers' physical expression, even in scenes of rural celebrations that feature women and men in peasant clothing dancing to folk melodies. At times, a cosmetic folk aesthetic is generated through the use of costuming, music, and material objects such as baskets and handkerchiefs. However, these strategies use extrachoreographic elements to lend a sense of localization to choreography that is grounded firmly in ballet movement. If ballet was a foreign language, as Dai Ailian once suggested, then the style of these works was like a Chinese story told in a foreign language, with occasional Chinese words mixed in but ordered according to a foreign grammar and pronounced with a foreign accent. As in *Red Detachment of Women,* xiqu-style tumbling elements and acrobatic highlights borrowed from Chinese dance appear in the battle sequences in these works. However, the heroic poses of the central protagonists almost always feature ballet body lines, such as arabesques or other poses performed with straight, turned out, and pointed leg lines produced while balancing on a single toe shoe. As with *Red Detachment of Women,* critics described both productions as a ballet works, and they were produced by institutions and casts that specialized in ballet performance.

From the above discussion, it is clear that the years 1964 to 1965 marked a new surge of choreographic creation across multiple fields of Chinese dance, which included xiqu-style national dance dramas on modern Chinese revolutionary history, ballets on modern Chinese revolutionary history, large-scale song and dance epics dealing with both Chinese history and contemporary international events such as the Vietnam War, dance dramas incorporating Afro-diasporic dance elements to address the US civil rights movement and Congolese anticolonial nation building, and both national dance dramas and large-scale music and dance epics dealing with modern revolutionary history in ethnic minority communities within China. While the newly created ballet works were an important part of this broader trend of choreographic innovation, they were by no means the only innovation, nor were they even the ones that received the most attention from critics and the media at the time. One telling example of media attention is the reportage in *Dance,* China's national dance journal. Over the course of 1965, *Dance* dedicated six pages to *White-Haired Girl* and one to *Red Detachment of Women,* while it devoted thirteen pages to *Fires of Fury in the Coconut Grove,* nine pages to *Congo River Is Roaring,* six pages to *We Walk on the Great Road,* and two each to the three large-scale ethnic minority–themed works. Reviews published in *Dance* described the major productions of 1965, like those of 1964, as exemplary models of the "three transformations." Thus, as of late 1965, all of these differing projects appeared to be valid paths for China's future dance development.

CONCLUSION: THE CULTURAL REVOLUTION

On May 16, 1966, the Central Committee of the Chinese Communist Party issued a directive initiating the Cultural Revolution, a new campaign that fundamentally altered the way dance was practiced in the PRC until the mid-1970s. In the weeks following this announcement, the national dance journal *Dance* ceased publication, and dancers employed in professional dance schools and performance ensembles across the country stopped their regular work. As discussed at the beginning of this chapter, a reversal of existing hierarchies soon unfolded, in which longtime leaders in the dance field were denounced and removed from their positions. Recalling the events of the summer of 1966, the institutional history of the Beijing Dance Academy recounts that the two schools then in operation were first occupied by a PLA work team in June, then attacked by outside Red Guards in July, and finally divided into two factions, after which internal attacks began in August and continued until December, when the teachers at both schools were sent to a suburb to carry out manual labor and undergo thought reform.[132] The institutional history of CODDT similarly records that large character posters and denunciations began in May, and from June all artistic creation and performances stopped for the remainder of the year, with the exception of a performance of *Congo River Is Roaring* for the 1966 National Day.[133] Reports in *Guangming Daily* described violent criticisms of cultural leaders continuing in the national performance ensembles through the summer of 1967.[134] In July 1967 *Guangming Daily* reported that remaining students at the Beijing Ballet School had begun to rehearse and perform the ballet *White-Haired Girl*.[135] At the same time, *China Pictorial* ran an article announcing the naming of the eight "model works"—including the two ballets—together with a photograph of Mao's wife, Jiang Qing, dressed in military attire surrounded by a group of Red Guards.[136]

Describing the changes in China's dance field that followed from these events, Wang Kefen and Long Yinpei write:

> In June 1967 the *People's Daily* called for "promoting model works to the entire country." All at once, dance stages across China surged with enthusiasm vying to perform the two ballets. In each province, city, and autonomous region, professional song and dance ensembles and even amateur dance companies, regardless of whether they possessed the conditions to perform ballet dance dramas, and regardless of whether performers had mastered ballet technique, all began to create an unimaginable artistic marvel. Dozens, hundreds of Wu Qinghuas, Hong Changqings, Xi'ers, and Dachuns[137] came to life on stage. The Cultural Revolution brought an abnormal popularization and development of ballet art to China's vast land; the entire country's dance stage turned into a deformed landscape in which ballet was the single blossoming flower.[138]

Recent studies of Cultural Revolution performance culture suggest that actual artistic experiences during this time were often varied and complicated.[139] Indeed, among the dozens of interviews I conducted with dancers who lived through the Cultural Revolution, some revealed creative experiences during this time that went beyond reproductions of the nationally sanctioned revolutionary ballet works.[140] Nevertheless, Wang's and Long's account points to what stands out as the most prominent and dramatic dance trend of the Cultural Revolution period. Namely, in place of a diverse dance field that previously supported active innovation by ensembles across the country in a variety of dance forms, there was now a severely restricted range of creative possibilities, as ballet works produced by two institutions in Beijing and Shanghai became required repertoire for performers across the country. As ballet achieved this new, preferred status, other dance forms, particularly Chinese dance, were actively suppressed.[141]

In a talk she gave in London in 1986, Dai Ailian spoke bitterly of these years and argued, "There was no logic to the cultural policies of the Cultural Revolution."[142] Certainly, from the perspective of dancers of Dai's generation and their immediate students, most of whom saw Chinese dance, not ballet, as the ultimate expression of China's socialist revolutionary culture, the policies of the Cultural Revolution made little sense. They contradicted the CCP vision that had continuously supported these dancers' work and upheld Chinese dance as the country's national dance form. At the same time, however, there were also many who disagreed with the previous system and stood to benefit from a change of direction. Insofar as the Cultural Revolution was about the disruption of existing power hierarchies, promoting ballet allowed those who had been disenfranchised previously to rise up against those who had enjoyed a monopoly of influence. As Paul Clark points out, divisions in the dance world broke down along lines of the dominant and the nondominant, where the dominant referred to "the mainstream efforts from the 1950s and early 1960s at melding an indigenous and modern form of dance."[143] Thus, it was in part due to the unwavering support the socialist state had given to Chinese dance during more than two decades of socialist cultural development during the pre–Cultural Revolution period that the nondominant group that gained power during the Cultural Revolution ended up being, ironically, the group that supported ballet. The lead choreographer of *Red Detachment of Women*, Li Chengxiang, who had also been one of the choreographers of *Lady of the Sea*, expressed in 1965 his excitement at having finally proven wrong those who doubted whether ballet could be used to perform Chinese proletarian heroes.[144] For artists like Li and others who had long been supporters of ballet but had worked during a period when ballet was constantly criticized and subordinated to Chinese dance, the Cultural Revolution offered an opportunity to finally gain long desired recognition and opportunities.

Accounts suggest that not only choreographers but also dancers played a role in advocating for the rise of revolutionary ballet during the early years of the Cultural Revolution. Liu Qingtang (1932–2010), who played the hero Hong Changqing in *Red Detachment of Women*, was one of the most energetic supporters of Cultural Revolution policy in the dance community, and he took advantage of the campaign to advance his own career. Liu was famous for having organized and personally overseen the largest number of public denunciations of artists in the Beijing dance scene during the early years of the Cultural Revolution, including those of his initial dance partner, Bai Shuxiang. In his denunciation sessions, Liu used cruel tactics that drove several of his victims to suicide. He also had a reputation for abusing his power to take sexual advantage of younger women. Although Liu had begun training in ballet late in life, he gained lead roles because he was physically strong enough to perform lifts, a skill considered necessary for ballets.[145] Liu reportedly portrayed the role of Hong Changqing over five hundred times between 1964 and 1972, and he also appeared in the 1971 film, gaining significant personal fame. By 1975 Liu had ascended to the position of deputy minister of culture, the highest post ever held by a dancer at the time. After the end of the Cultural Revolution, in 1982, Liu was sentenced to prison on counts of conspiracy supporting activities of the Gang of Four, as well as public defamation of innocent persons and personal misconduct.[146]

From an artistic perspective, some argued that revolutionary ballet was consistent with artistic and ideological agendas of earlier socialist dance creation, especially when viewed within the limited sphere of ballet. In one of the first reviews of *Red Detachment of Women,* which served as a model for later interpretations, choreographer Huang Boshou wrote:

> In the past, ballet was a tool used to display the nobility and aristocracy, to propagate feudal and bourgeois morality, and to beautify the rule of the bourgeoisie. Meanwhile, the working people did not have the right to enter the ballet stage, and even when they did occasionally appear it was only to be portrayed as foolish clowns, to be disrespected and made fun of. The choreographers and performers of *Red Detachment of Women,* in order to express our country's life of seething revolutionary struggle and revolutionary worker, peasant and soldier images, whether through themes, medium, plot, character, or language, have broken down the previous conventions of ballet, bravely innovated, causing ballet to undergo a revolutionary change.[147]

Here, Huang interprets the use of ballet form in the revolutionary ballets not as a copying of Western forms, as it was often described by Chinese dance critics in the past, but rather as an intervention that fundamentally revolutionized the Western form itself. Through their adaptation of ballet to contemporary local narratives, as well as their introduction, even superficially, of Chinese dance elements, Huang argued that the creators of the revolutionary ballets did enact innovation and localization within the art of ballet. In this way, he argued, Chinese choreographers and dancers gained artistic agency even though they were enacting this agency by way of an imported movement vocabulary. From this perspective, the emergence of revolutionary ballet allowed Chinese dancers to position themselves as equal participants in a global conversation of ballet exchange, joining the growing number of countries that were promoting their own stylistic visions of ballet internationally during this period.

Through its promotion of ballet as the new national dance form, together with the suppression of Chinese dance practitioners, institutions, and repertoires, the Cultural Revolution left a deep mark on China's dance field. No new choreographic works were reported on in the national media from 1966 until the early 1970s; this absence represented a significant departure from the previous years, when new dance creation had emerged continuously across the country at a breakneck speed. As professional ensembles were closed down or consolidated, dance conservatories stopped admitting students, and leading artists were put on house arrest, jailed, and sent to labor camps, the institutional structures that previously supported Chinese dance creation stopped functioning as they had before. Under these circumstances, one development that emerged was that ballet reached a much wider audience in China than it ever had previously. Moreover, through its new promotion as a symbol of the Cultural Revolution, ballet became culturally recoded in the eyes and bodies of a new generation of Chinese dancers and audiences. That is, instead of seeing ballet as traditional, foreign, and bourgeois, as it had previously been understood, many now saw it as modern, familiar, and revolutionary. By 1967 a new name had been introduced for the ballet works that even erased their identity as ballet. The new term, "revolutionary modern dance drama" *(geming xiandai wuju)*, eroded the previous distinction between national dance drama and ballet, further undermining the status of Chinese dance.[148] As time passed, the younger generation invested ballet with their own meanings, and many either forgot that Chinese dance ever existed or began to see it fundamentally as a thing of the past. By the end of the Cultural Revolution, however, Chinese dance would return, with new meanings in a new historical context.

The Return of Chinese Dance

Socialist Continuity Post-Mao

With its suppression of early socialist dance projects in favor of the newer form of revolutionary ballet, the Cultural Revolution decade of 1966–76 nearly brought an end to Chinese dance, as both an artistic project and a historical memory. Prior to the Cultural Revolution, Chinese dance had been the dominant concert dance form in the PRC. Most new dance choreography created between 1949 and 1965 had been in the genre of Chinese dance, and Chinese dance was the dance style officially promoted domestically and abroad as an expression of China's socialist ideals and values. However, with the introduction of new cultural policies beginning in 1966, a decade of support for ballet and suppression of Chinese dance nearly wiped out memories of pre–Cultural Revolution activities in China's dance field. Although many Chinese dance institutions that had been forced to shut down in 1966 reopened in the early 1970s, by the beginning of 1976 they were still banned from performing most pre–Cultural Revolution Chinese dance repertoires, and ballet was still dominating the curriculum used to train new dancers. Dance films created before the Cultural Revolution were still censored from public view, meaning that most audiences had not seen pre–Cultural Revolution repertoires, either live or on screen, for at least a decade. For children and adolescents too young to remember the pre–Cultural Revolution period, revolutionary ballet had become the only kind of socialist dance they knew. For them, revolutionary ballet was socialist dance.

In the years immediately following the Cultural Revolution, a revival of Chinese dance occurred across the country: dancers who had spent years in rural labor camps or banned from work returned to their professional jobs; dance institutions that had been shut down or forced to focus on ballet during the Cultural

Revolution were restored and allowed to return to their pre–Cultural Revolution projects; and dance repertoires that had been banned during the previous decade started to be once again staged and shown. All of a sudden, stages that had been dominated for years by dancers on pointe performing pirouettes and arabesques were now being filled with a new cast of dancing bodies, performing regional folk and minority rhythms and historical images from China's past. For those who knew little about China's dance history in the pre–Cultural Revolution period, these changes looked like something new that departed from the Maoist tradition. In other words, they seemed to be part of what Geremie Barmé called "de-Maoification," or a general move away from socialist traditions begun in the late 1970s that resulted in the development of a new, post-Mao culture.[1] While the argument of de-Maoification certainly makes sense in some respects, it also leaves out a very important part of the picture. This is because, in the dance field, many of the developments that appeared "new" or "non-Maoist" to audiences of the late 1970s and early 1980s were in fact returns to pre–Cultural Revolution Maoist dance culture. As I argue in this chapter, the resurgence of local dance styles and historical themes that occurred in China during the late 1970s and early 1980s represented not a departure from, but a return to, core dance projects of the socialist period.

In the decade immediately following the Cultural Revolution, two phenomena emerged in China's dance field that constituted continuities with, rather than departures from, early socialist dance traditions. First, from the end of 1976 to the end of 1978, there was a general reassertion of pre–Cultural Revolution socialist dance culture, as dance repertoires developed in the years from 1949 to 1966 were revived, dancers who had been leaders in Chinese dance before the Cultural Revolution were returned to positions of influence, and institutional structures were returned to the conditions in which they had operated under socialist state leadership prior to 1966. Once these changes were in place, starting in 1978, a series of new large-scale creations in the genre of Chinese dance began to emerge, and several of these gained national attention in 1979 during a national theater festival held in honor of the thirtieth anniversary of the founding of the PRC. While these dance dramas initiated a new period of dance creation in terms of their movement vocabularies and star performers, on the whole, they represented continuations of activities begun in the pre–Cultural Revolution period. A close look at the historical development of these works, including the artistic and institutional supports that made them possible, shows that they grew in important ways out of projects that had begun under Maoist state support. In this sense, while these new dance dramas indeed represented important departures from the dance activities of the Cultural Revolution, they were still very much connected to socialist dance and Maoist culture.

Two dance dramas featured in the 1979 festival would go on to have an especially lasting impact on post-Mao Chinese dance culture, with continuing relevance through the 1980s and 1990s and into the twenty-first century. One was Yunnan Province Xishuangbanna Dai Nationality Autonomous Region Song and Dance Ensemble's *Zhao Shutun and Nanmunuonuo* (Zhao shutun yu nanmunuonuo), also known as *The Peacock Princess* (Kongque gongzhu). The other was Gansu Provincial Song and Dance Ensemble's *Flowers and Rain on the Silk Road (Silu hua yu)*. By bringing to fruition the results of long-term regional research projects, these works introduced new diversity to the Chinese dance stage, including, in the case of *Zhao Shutun and Nanmunuonuo*, new stories derived from local literary traditions and, in the case of *Flowers and Rain on the Silk Road*, new movement vocabularies developed from Tang dynasty Buddhist historical artifacts. *Zhao Shutun and Nanmunuonuo* was responsible for launching the career of Yunnanese Bai dancer Yang Liping (b. 1958), who went on to become one of the most famous and influential dancers in Chinese history. Yang's subsequent works "Spirit of the Peacock" (Que zhi ling, 1986), *Dynamic Yunnan* (*Yunnan yingxiang*, 2003), and *The Peacock* (*Kongque*, 2013) were all further developments upon Yang's breakout role as the Peacock Princess in *Zhao Shutun and Nanmunuonuo*. Similarly, *Flowers and Rain on the Silk Road* launched the popularity of a new dance style known as "Dunhuang dance" *(Dunhuang wu)*, which is now one of the most popular styles of Chinese classical dance in practice today. Through subsequent works introduced in the 1980s, Dunhuang dance in particular, and the image of the Silk Road and Tang dynasty court dance more broadly, would, like Yang Liping's peacock dances, go on to be enduring themes in Chinese dance through the twenty-first century.

While the revival of Chinese dance that occurred in the first post-Mao decade brought back some aspects of Maoist dance culture, it did not place equal emphasis on all aspects of the socialist legacy. On the one hand, the new Chinese dance repertoires of the post-Mao era placed great importance on the Maoist principle of national form by continuing research into local dance heritage and by developing dance works that emphasized local imagery, sound, and movement vocabularies. In this sense, these works returned to the aesthetic practice of "self as subject" that had guided China's socialist dance field before the Cultural Revolution. On the other hand, however, Maoist principles such as remolding and socialist intersectionality did not receive the same emphasis in this new era. Whereas heroic characters were once portrayed as peasants and working people, in the new post-Mao works these characters were just as often portrayed as princesses, kings, and merchants. The critical treatment once given to social justice issues relating to gender, ethnicity, race, and class now largely faded away, while conservative treatments of women, in particular, were resurgent in post-Mao dance narratives. By the end of the twentieth century, Chinese dance faced new challenges as dance styles imported from the United States and other Westernized, capitalist countries found increasing welcome among Chinese dancers and dance audiences. At the same time, emphasis on the market and privatization led to a widespread commercialization of dance, through new industries from nightclub culture to tourism. Without the post-Mao return of Chinese dance, however, these developments would all have taken a different course.

REVIVING THE SOCIALIST SYSTEM: PEOPLE, INSTITUTIONS, AND REPERTOIRES

Mao Zedong, who had led the Chinese Communist Party since 1935, died on September 9, 1976, at the age of eighty-two. Approximately one month later, four leading figures in the Cultural Revolution, known as the Gang of Four, were arrested, and the process of evaluating the Cultural Revolution began. Over the next year and a half, the dance field would come to a consensus that the policies of the Cultural Revolution had distorted Maoist culture and that, in particular, it had been wrong to attack and suppress the dance activities of the pre–Cultural Revolution period.[2] Dancers condemned the Gang of Four, calling them "the chief criminals who strangled the arts revolution."[3] In their criticisms of the Cultural Revolution, dancers singled out Mao's wife, Jiang Qing, for especially harsh critique. Jiang had been a member of the Gang of Four; she took credit for the creation of revolutionary ballet and led the effort to suppress Chinese dance during the Cultural Revolution. Many dancers saw Jiang as personally responsible for their own negative treatment during the previous decade, as well as for the dismantling of dance forms, institutions, and repertoires they had spent decades creating. Thus, in late 1976, an article published in *Dance* magazine concluded that "Jiang Qing really knew nothing about the arts and got in the way of positive work," and regarding her preference for ballet, it went on: "Jiang Qing spoke loudly about 'worn-out western conventions' but in fact worshipped foreign things. . . . She was a slave to the West who felt that even the moon would be better if it were foreign."[4] By the end of 1977, China's dance leaders had reached the consensus that to correct the mistakes of the Cultural Revolution and move forward with China's dance development, first there needed to be a revival of pre-1966 socialist dance work.

The first step in this revival was the return of experienced performers, choreographers, teachers, and researchers who had been sent to labor camps or otherwise barred from professional activities during the Cultural Revolution. This was a gradual process that occurred at different times for different people. After they were denounced and punished, some established dancers and choreographers were brought back selectively in the early 1970s to assist with the revision and creation of revolutionary ballets or to perform the roles of villains in revolutionary ballet productions. Others remained in labor camps, or in some cases jail, until several years after the Cultural Revolution ended. As a whole, however, 1976 did mark an important turning point. Most dance institutions that existed before 1966 were officially "rehabilitated" *(huifu)* during the years between 1976 and 1978, making this the peak period for reinstatements of dancers to professional positions. By 1979 almost everyone who had been working professionally in the dance field prior to 1966 and who was still alive and still wished to be involved in dance activities had returned to their pre–Cultural Revolution place of residence and was working again in dance-related jobs. Typically, they returned to the same institutions they had worked in before, meaning that they now had to live and labor alongside some of the same people who had denounced and attacked them a decade earlier.

The reconstitution of China's pre-1966 dance field that took place between 1976 and 1978 was grounded in the reestablishment of early Mao-era professional dance institutions. One of the first to be restored was *Wudao*, China's national dance journal. The journal had stopped publication in May 1966 and was restored in early 1976, with its first new issue appearing in March.[5] Another major institution, the Beijing Dance School, was restored in December 1977, after having been divided into two schools in 1964, closed down in June 1966, and then replaced during the early 1970s by ballet-focused programs within special Cultural Revolution–era art schools.[6] China's five national-level dance ensembles—the Central Song and Dance Ensemble, the Central Nationalities Song and Dance Ensemble, the China Opera and Dance Drama Theater, the Oriental Song and Dance Ensemble, and the Central Opera and Dance Drama Theater—were also restored to their pre–Cultural Revolution organizational status and names by 1978.[7] Like BDS, these ensembles had suspended operation in 1966 and had been replaced by ballet-focused institutions.[8] Once the pre–Cultural Revolution institutions were restored, the temporary ones that had been set up during the Cultural Revolution were all formally disbanded.[9] In addition to institutions based in Beijing, revivals took place all over China. For example, in 1976 military-affiliated performing arts ensembles in Nanjing, Jinan, Chengdu, Lanzhou, Guangzhou, Lhasa, and Kunming were restored to their pre–Cultural Revolution organizational status and names.[10] At the end of 1977, the Guangdong branch of the China Dance Workers Association was officially revived and resumed operations.[11] In June 1978, the Shanghai Cultural Bureau announced that the Shanghai Dance School would be reopened.[12] By the end of 1978, local branches of the China Dance Workers Association in Shanxi, Yunnan, Liaoning, Xinjiang, Shandong, and Sichuan had also been restored.[13]

This gradual return to pre–Cultural Revolution conditions also applied to the top echelon of leaders in the dance field. These individuals, like other dance professionals, had been forced out of their jobs and disappeared from the public eye during the Cultural Revolution. Gradually, by the end of the 1970s, their names began to reemerge in the news, as they regained leadership status. The first major figure to reappear was Dai Ailian, whose last mention in a mainstream national newspaper had been in April 1966. Dai's name resurfaced in October 1975, when she was among the arts representatives in attendance at an official National Day reception.[14]

Wu Xiaobang, whose last mention had been in October 1962, reappeared two years after Dai, in the roster of the 1977 National Day festivities.[15] Qemberxanim, last mentioned in March 1963, reappeared in 1978, when she, Dai, and Wu all gave talks at a meeting to mark the revival of the China Dancers Association.[16] By the time of the Fourth Literature and Arts Congress in October 1979, the dance chairpersons roster was filled with leading dance figures from the pre–Cultural Revolution era.[17] New leadership appointments made during the 1979 congress were all leaders from the early socialist period. Qemberxanim earned the highest appointment as a vice chairperson of the China Literary Federation.[18] The next highest position, as chairperson of the China Dancers Association, went to Wu Xiaobang, while the positions of vice chairs went to Dai Ailian, Chen Jinqing, Qemberxanim, Jia Zuoguang, Hu Guogang, Liang Lun, and Sheng Jie.[19] Of these eight, six had been on the original standing committee of the China Dancers Association formed in the summer of 1949, while all held high positions in the dance leadership in the early 1950s.[20]

The restoration of early socialist leadership teams also occurred at the level of individual dance institutions. A clear example of this is the case of BDS. The person appointed in August of 1977 to oversee the revival of the school was Chen Jinqing, the veteran of the New Yangge movement who had served as the school's vice principal from 1954 to 1964 and then served as principal of the China Dance School until 1966. Chen's first job when she returned was to clear wrongful accusations made during the Cultural Revolution. Then, Chen was tasked with returning all personnel, administration, and teaching activities to their pre–Cultural Revolution arrangements.[21] By October of 1977, the school had terminated the ballet-focused curriculum instituted in the early 1970s and resumed the dual-track system practiced in 1957–66, in which students majored in either Chinese dance or ballet. The faculty was also restructured into two corresponding units, as it had been prior to the Cultural Revolution. Li Zhengyi (b. 1929), who had held leadership positions in the school's Chinese dance program throughout the pre–Cultural Revolution period, was appointed head of the Chinese dance unit. Zhang Xu (1932–1990), who had been codirector of the ballet program from 1957 to 1962, was appointed head of ballet.[22]

Apart from the return of institutions and people, the period from 1976 to 1978 also saw a large-scale return of pre-1966 dance repertoires. The return of these repertoires served several purposes: first, they allowed younger audiences, many of whom had never seen these works because of their suppression during the Cultural Revolution, to become acquainted with Chinese dance; second, it allowed the older generation of dancers who had just returned from years away to refresh their old skills; and third, it allowed the younger generation of performers who had been recruited during the Cultural Revolution to see and learn the canonical works of the Chinese dance repertoire. The first socialist dance classic to greet new audiences was the 1965 film based on the 1964 production *East Is Red*. On January 1, 1977, the film was rereleased and shown in movie theaters around China.[23] Although *East Is Red* had been one of the most widely acclaimed works of the Maoist period, the ten-year gap in its circulation led journals such as *Dance* to treat it like a new production, publishing lengthy introductions, scene summaries, and promotional photographs.[24] The penultimate scene of the film would have been especially striking to viewers in 1977. The performers in this scene include pre-1966 minority dance celebrities, such as Uyghur dancer Aytilla Qasim (Ayitula, b. 1940), Korean dancer Cui Meishan (b. 1934), Dai dancer Dao Meilan (b. 1944), Miao dancer Jin Ou (b. 1934), Mongol dancer Modegema (b. 1942), and Tibetan dancer Oumijiacan (b. 1928). The dancers perform in front of a painted backdrop modeled after the Tian'anmen Gate. Using a variety of rhythms, movement vocabularies, and props developed for the representation of minority groups in the early socialist period, they perform short group dance segments representing seven different ethnicities: a Mongol portion using drink cups like castanets; a Uyghur portion using round hand drums; a Tibetan portion featuring long sleeves; a Dai portion using flower arches and elephant leg drums; a Li portion featuring straw hats; a Korean portion with hourglass drums; and a Miao reed pipe dance.[25] Many of these techniques and props had been banned in the Cultural Revolution years.[26] Thus, such a scene, despite being twelve years old, would have felt fresh to young viewers.

Live revivals were the most common method of restoring the Chinese dance repertoire. During the years 1977–78, many companies revived their best productions from the first golden age of Chinese dance drama in the late 1950s, most of which had not been performed for about fifteen years. The first of these revivals took place in Shanghai in mid-January 1977, when the Shanghai Opera Theater restaged its 1959 hit *Dagger Society*.[27] The second major work, performed in Beijing in August 1977, was Shenyang Military Political Department Song and Dance Ensemble's *Butterfly Loves Flower (Die lian hua)*, also based on a work originally premiered in 1959.[28] By 1978 live revivals of *Five Red Clouds* (1959) and *Magic Lotus Lantern* (1957) were also being performed in Guangzhou and Beijing, respectively.[29] Many of these productions were performed by members of their original casts. For example, Zhao Qing, now age forty-two, once again performed the heroine Third Sacred Mother in *Magic Lotus Lantern* when it was staged for the 1978 National Day celebrations.[30] As with the *East Is Red* film, the revivals of these works generated opportunities for leading dancers from the pre–Cultural Revolution era to reenter the public eye. The staging of these performances also provided opportunities to reeducate audiences and the younger generation about the history of Chinese dance and its role in China's revolutionary arts tradition. Thus, articles appeared explaining the provenance of each production, its historical accolades, and how it came to be attacked during the Cultural Revolution.[31]

An important dance tour to the United States during this period demonstrates the extent to which the pre-1966 repertoire and its stars had been revived and made the focus of new performance in the immediate post-Mao years. In the summer of 1978, a group of thirty-five dancers, along with fifty-five Peking opera performers and at least forty musicians and singers, toured the United States under the name Performing Arts Company of the People's Republic of China.[32] As the first major PRC performance group to tour the United States, this was an event of historic significance. Thus, it is interesting that most of the dancers and works chosen for the tour were from the pre–Cultural Revolution period. The star dancers featured in the tour included specialists in Chinese minority dance Aytilla Qasim, Cui Meishan, and Modegema and specialists in Chinese classical dance Chen Ailian (b. 1939), Sun Daizhang (b. 1937), and Zhao Qing (b. 1936). Apart from a few excerpts from *Red Detachment of Women* and *White-Haired Girl*, the dance works performed on the tour were mainly Chinese dance choreographies from the 1950s and early 1960s.[33] The average age of female soloists on the tour was thirty-nine, sixteen years beyond what was considered prime performance age for female dancers in China at the time.[34] This and the fact that the most recent work presented was excerpts from *White-Haired Girl*, already thirteen years old, suggests that the revival of pre-1966 artists and repertoires, rather than the foregrounding of new works, was the priority for this tour.[35]

The first new dance films created in the post-Mao era clearly demonstrated the return of pre–Cultural Revolution dance forms. The first, released in 1978 by Changchun Film Studio, was *Butterfly Loves Flower*, based on the 1977 revival of the 1959 dance drama of the same name.[36] The second, released in 1979 by the Inner Mongolia Film Studio, was *Rainbow (Caihong)*, based on a collection of old and new works by the Inner Mongolia Song and Dance Ensemble (Neimenggu gewutuan).[37] Thematically, both films levied attacks on aspects of the Cultural Revolution. *Butterfly Loves Flower* undermined Jiang Qing by celebrating Yang Kaihui, Mao Zedong's first wife.[38] Meanwhile, *Rainbow* emphasized the independence of Inner Mongolian nationality art, which had been suppressed during the height of the Cultural Revolution.[39] What is most striking about the two films, however, is their revival of the local movement conventions and vocabularies developed in the pre–Cultural Revolution era. Pointe work, the dominant feature of revolutionary ballet, is eliminated completely in both films. In *Butterfly Loves Flower*, group choreography returns almost completely to vocabularies based on folk and xiqu movement. While Yang Kaihui's character still uses a considerable amount of ballet leg work, such as arabesques, jumps, and kicks, her hand and arm movements incorporate more local elements than typical heroines in revolutionary ballets. The final scene of *Butterfly Loves Flower*, in which dancers perform in long gowns, with Tang-style hair ornaments and silk streamers, is reminiscent of 1950s-era Chinese classical dance repertoires such as Zhao Qing's dances in the 1957 production *Magic Lotus Lantern.*⁴⁰ *Rainbow* is even more pronounced in its rejection of ballet vocabulary and return to pre–Cultural Revolution forms based on local-style movement. Several of the dances it features are direct revivals of Inner Mongolia–themed repertoires popular in the early socialist era, such as "Oroqen dance" (Elunchun wu), "Goose Dance" (Yan wu), and "Ordos Dance."⁴¹ Solo dances are performed by artists who achieved peak popularity in the 1950s and early 1960s, such as Jia Zuoguang and Siqintariha. Meanwhile, new dances presented in the film, such as "Rainbow" (Caihong), advance earlier methods of adapting folk and minority movement.⁴²

By 1979 China's dance field had basically been restored to its early 1960s conditions, in terms of people, institutions, and dance repertoires. The final step in the revival was to once again start the process of creating new large-scale Chinese dance productions. Following the same method used in the pre–Cultural Revolution period, the Ministry of Culture encouraged new creation by hosting a national festival. Following the model established for the ten-year anniversary festival in 1959, the ministry invited entries from ensembles across the country, which went through rounds of selection at the local and provincial levels. Works chosen for national presentation showed in Beijing starting on January 5, 1979, and continued until February 9, 1980. Seven full-length dance dramas appeared in this festival, two of which would have an especially lasting impact on the new era of Chinese dance creation: *Zhao Shutun and Nanmunuonuo*, which launched the career of Yang Liping, famous for her "Dai peacock dance"; and *Flowers and Rain on the Silk Road*, which introduced Dunhuang dance and started a trend of dances set in the Tang dynasty.⁴³

YANG LIPING'S PEACOCK DANCE: REWORKING A MAO-ERA IMAGE

To comprehend the significance of the 1979 Beijing showing of Dai dance drama *Zhao Shutun and Nanmunuonuo*, it is necessary to first move ahead in time to 1986, when Yunnanese Bai dancer Yang Liping would captivate China with her solo "Spirit of the Peacock" (figure 22). Yang premiered "Spirit of the Peacock" at the 1986 Second All-China Dance Competition, where it won first-place awards in both performance and choreography and quickly became one of the most popular Chinese dance works of all time.⁴⁴ The dance begins with Yang twirling counterclockwise at center stage while holding the fringe of her floor-length white gown out at shoulder level, so that she appears enveloped in a swirling corkscrew (video 14). She crouches to the ground and then slowly stands up again, this time in the silhouette of a peacock. Her right hand holds the skirt behind in a crescent shape like the bird's tail, while her left arm stretches up vertically to form its long, slender neck. She bends at the wrist, presses her thumb and index finger tightly

FIGURE 22. Yang Liping in "Spirit of the Peacock," 1997. Photographer: Ye Jin. Reproduced with permission from the private collection of Ye Jin.

together, and splays out her middle, ring, and pinky fingers like a fan. Twitching up, down, forward, and back, Yang's hand mimics the movements of a bird's head through precise, staccato actions. The peacock's beak opens and closes, its crown feathers contract and release one by one, and its neck bends and straightens in

VIDEO 14. Yang Liping in "Spirit of the Peacock," October 2007. Used with permission from Yunnan Yang Liping Arts & Culture Co., Ltd.

To watch this video, scan the QR code with your mobile device or visit DOI: https://doi.org/10.1525/luminos.58.14

fluid waves. Yang bends her elbow, making the peacock's beak preen the top of her head. As the dance develops, Yang's choreography shifts from direct imitation to more abstract representations. Seated on the ground with her back to the audience and upper body tipped forward, she lifts her arms into a horizontal position, undulating them in a waving line that invokes the surface of rippling water, or a bird's flight. The dance reaches a climax when, between a series of spins, Yang grabs the ends of her skirt with both hands, stretches her head upward, and moves up and down in place while flapping both arms, creating semicircles of fabric on either side of her body. Then she circles back to the beginning, repeating the twirling sequence and ending in the peacock silhouette.[45]

Today Yang Liping is one of China's only dancers who has become a household name. She is a popular media celebrity and also a distinct voice in the dance world, with her own performance brand and aesthetic theory.[46] Yang's fame has been built largely on the domestic and international success of her peacock dance renditions, which she further developed in two commercially successful large-scale productions: the 2003 *Dynamic Yunnan* and the 2013 *The Peacock*.[47] Yang's "Spirit of the Peacock" has many layers of signification: it has become an emblem of Dai culture, a regional brand of Yunnan Province, and a symbol of Chinese culture among overseas Sinophone communities.[48] Although Yang has often positioned herself and her artistic approaches in opposition to established conventions of Chinese dance, her rise to fame and the peacock choreography at its core are both products of early Mao-era dance activities that first appeared in the 1950s and then experienced a revival in the late 1970s. Rather than being a new development attributable to the de-Maoification of Chinese culture, Yang's "Spirit of the Peacock" and her career as a nationally and even internationally recognized dance artist since the 1980s are both direct outgrowths of China's socialist dance developments.

"Spirit of the Peacock" is a revision of choreography first created in Yunnan thirty years earlier by the Xishuangbanna Nationality Cultural Work Team (Xishuangbanna minzu gewutuan), as part of a dance-based dramatization of sections from the Dai epic *Zhao Shutun*. Titled *Zhao Shutun and Nanwuluola* and starring Dai dancer Dao Meilan as the Peacock Princess, it was documented first in 1956 in Yunnan and then in 1957 in Beijing, when it appeared in a national music and dance festival.[49] Between 1961 and 1963, the Xishuangbanna ensemble further developed this work into a five-act dance drama titled *Zhao Shutun*, initially starring Yu Wanjiao as the Peacock Princess, which was suppressed from the mid-1960s under Cultural Revolution policies.[50] During the Chinese dance revival of the late 1970s, the Xishuangbanna ensemble began to recover the production, this time in seven acts with the title *Zhao Shutun and Nanmunuonuo* and with a nineteen-year-old Yang Liping performing the role of the Peacock Princess.[51] Yang performed the work first in 1978 at a provincial-level festival in Yunnan, then in Beijing during the 1979 national festival, and finally in 1980–81 on international tours to Hong Kong, Singapore, Burma, and Thailand.[52] By 1982 Yang had been transferred to the Central Nationalities Song and Dance Ensemble in Beijing, where she launched her career as a soloist.[53]

The Xishuangbanna dance drama productions were not the only precursors to "Spirit of the Peacock." In her 2008 dissertation on the evolution of the modern Dai peacock dance, Ting-Ting Chang shows how the work can be traced to three other nonnarrative predecessors: Mao Xiang's 1953 male-female "Peacock Duet" (Shuangren kongque); Jin Ming's 1956 female group dance "Peacock Dance" (Kongque wu); and Dao Meilan's 1978 female solo dance "Golden Peacock" (Jinse de kongque). Chang demonstrates how the modern peacock dance became a nationally recognized symbol of Dai culture in China during the mid-1950s, which was then suppressed during the Cultural Revolution and subsequently revived and further developed in the late 1970s and 1980s. According to Chang, the most crucial innovation in the peacock dance form occurred in 1953, when male Dai dancer Mao Xiang dispensed with the dance's traditional bamboo-frame tail and wing props and incorporated a woman dancer into a style previously performed only by men (figure 23).[54] Mao had introduced his version of the dance to choreographers in Beijing by 1954.[55] One of them, male Han choreographer Jin Ming (b. 1926), adapted it into his own version of the peacock dance at the same time that the Xishuangbanna ensemble was creating its first version of the Dai *Zhao Shutun* epic in Yunnan.

While the modern Dai peacock dance as a genre clearly has roots in the early nonnarrative socialist-era dance experiments Chang outlines, the specific image

FIGURE 23. Peacock dance performed with traditional bamboo-frame tail and wing props. Published in *Renmin huabao* 5, no. 3 (1954): 15. Photographer unknown. Image provided by China Foto Bank.

Yang portrays in her "Spirit of the Peacock" solo can also be seen as a reworking of a dance image developed in a different set of narrative dance works also from the early socialist period. Thus, Yang's "Spirit of the Peacock" is a continuation not only of innovations by Mao Xiang and Jin Ming in 1953 and 1956, as Chang shows, but also of the "Peacock Princess" motif performed in the Xishuangbanna ensemble's narrative dance dramas, as well as other new expressive forms adapted from the *Zhao Shutun* epic between 1956 and 1963. In other words, both the Dai peacock dance as a form of modern stage choreography and the character of the Peacock Princess that Yang portrays are continuations of Mao-era projects of Chinese dance creation.

The image of the Peacock Princess comes from the *Zhao Shutun* epic, the local Dai variant of an old story found in many Asian literary traditions, including Burmese, Chinese, Hmong, Indian, Laotian, Thai, Tibetan, and Yi.[56] In Thai literature, a tradition closely related to Dai, the story is known as "Suthon Chadok" or "Prince Suthon and Princess Manora" and is part of the *Pannasa Jataka* (fifty Jatak tales or *Panyasa Chadok*), a Pali text dating to around the fifteenth to seventeenth centuries.[57] Describing the story as performed in Thai dance dramas, ethnomusicologist Terry Miller writes, "The term *manora*, usually shortened to *nora*, refers to a famous story of Indian origin. Manora, a heavenly bird-maiden, comes to the earthly plane and marries a human prince, Suthon (in Sanskrit, Sudhana). They become separated, and Suthon seeks to travel to her realm to regain her. *Nora* is often described as dance-drama, but the emphasis is on dance rather than on drama. The main characters are dancers, considered to be heavenly bird-like creatures *(kinnara)*, and the costume includes wings and a tail. . . . "[58]

In Xishuangbanna Dai communities during the mid-twentieth century, the *Zhao Shutun* story was performed orally in the form of long poems by singing experts known as *zhangha* (in Mandarin, *zanha*) or *moha*, who performed these works on important occasions such as new house ceremonies, weddings, and monk promotions.[59] In Maoist China, interest in the Dai *Zhao Shutun* epic blossomed in 1956–57, when Chinese-language print versions started to appear in major publications, both in new forms composed by Han writers such as Bai Hua (b. 1929) and in edited translations from handwritten Dai scripts and oral transmission.[60] Between 1956 and 1963, Chinese artists adapted the story not only into dance drama productions but also into a watercolor graphic storybook *(lianhuanhua)* in 1957; a Peking opera based on a script by Guo Moruo in 1957; an illustrated children's book published in English, French, and German in 1961; a Yunnan flower lantern drama *(huadengxi)* in 1963; and a color stop-motion puppet animation film in 1963.[61]

Two scenes from the *Zhao Shutun* stories of the 1950s and early 1960s represent possible sources of inspiration for the image presented in Yang Liping's 1986 "Spirit of the Peacock" solo: both begin with an immortal peacock lady who entrances a human audience, and both end with her flying off to her mystical homeland in the sky, where she escapes the dangers of the human realm. While the general structure of the two scenes is similar, their narrative contexts, tones, and meanings are different, providing a complex set of intertexts for Yang's 1986 solo dance. Thus, the literary, aesthetic, and religious content of the *Zhao Shutun* epic imbues Yang's dance with a complexity and depth it would not have had without the foundation of these early Mao-era adaptations.

The first scene from the *Zhao Shutun* stories echoed in "Spirit of the Peacock" is the one in which Prince Zhao first sees and becomes enchanted by the Peacock Princess. While there are many versions of this scene, the most common in the adaptations of the 1950s and early 1960s depicts the human prince Zhao Shutun hunting in the forest and suddenly seeing a lake where the seven daughters of the Peacock King are bathing, playing, or dancing. When the young women become aware of the prince's presence, they fly away. A Chinese translation published in 1956 recounts:

> A hunter runs out from the bamboo forest
> Riding a horse and carrying a bow and arrow

He is following a golden deer
From the forest he chases it to the lakeside
The young hunter ah
His eyes like two bright pearls
. . . .
Sink into the center of the lake
The setting sun casts his shadow on the lake
Alarming the seven ladies
Like sparrows seeing a hawk
They drape on their feathers and fly into the distance
The lake returns to stillness
The birds also return to the forest
Only the hunter ah
Continues to gaze at the clear sky.[62]

The story is then told again from the prince's view, when he describes his experience to a monk in a nearby temple:

I do not know whether I am in a dream
Or really living in the human world
I saw in the lake seven ladies
Like lotus flowers giving off a delicate fragrance
They wore golden belts on their bodies
On their necks pearls glistened luminously
But they have already flown to the heavens
I do not know whether they came from the sky or . . .
Like rainbows they made my eyes dizzy
Like eagles [they] snatched away my heart.[63]

Unfortunately, none of the Xishuangbanna ensemble's early dance adaptations of the *Zhao Shutun* story are recorded on film. However, we know that the 1956 version included an extended scene much like this one: it depicted the prince hunting, seven princesses dancing next to a lake, the princesses flying away using peacock-feather gowns, and the princesses bathing in the lake while being watched by the prince.[64] According to a review, the partner dance between Prince Zhao and Nanmunuonuo (here Nanwuluola) used the existing "peacock dance" familiar in Dai areas, and in the scene by the lake, Nanmunuonuo looked in the reflection to fix her hair.[65] Still photographs from 1957 show Nanmunuonuo wearing a long, flared white skirt with peacock feather designs at the bottom and a gauze cape and collar decorated with large spots (figure 24).[66]

Puppet choreographies in the 1963 stop-motion animation film adaptation offer the best documentation of early Mao-era dance interpretations of this scene (video 15).[67] Just before the lakeside scene in the film, we see Zhao with his bow and

FIGURE 24. Dao Meilan and ensemble in *Zhao Shutun and Nanwuluola*. Published in *Wudao congkan*, no. 1 (May 1957): front matter. Photographer unknown. Image obtained from the University of Michigan Asia Library Chinese Dance Collection.

arrow on horseback chasing a deer through the forest. Then the deer disappears, and Zhao peeks through some foliage to find a lake radiating with beams of colored light in the shape of a peacock tail. Suddenly, a single female figure appears twirling and floating atop the surface of the lake. She is dressed in a strapless white gown like the one Yang wears in "Spirit of the Peacock," but she also carries a long white sash from which she sprinkles flower petals that turn into water lilies.[68] Stepping on land, she puts on her white peacock gown, which has a similar design to the costume shown in the 1957 photographs of the Xishuangbanna ensemble's dance production.[69] Her sisters refer to her as Nan Muluna. Dressed in her white peacock gown, she spins in place with her arms spread out at shoulder level, as special effects make her appear to transform from a human to a peacock and back to a human. After observing herself and fixing her hair in the lake's reflection, she continues dancing at the water's edge, turning and lifting her hands above her head, and finally strikes a pose much like Yang's famous peacock silhouette: her left hand is poised above her head, right hand down, with one leg kicking back and lifting her skirt. At this point, Nan is joined by her six sisters, although she continues to perform solo movements while they execute a synchronized routine, much like Jin Ming's 1956 *Peacock Dance*.[70] The Peacock Princess choreography here is similar to "Spirit of the Peacock": it includes spinning continuously with one hand raised, transforming into a peacock while jumping in the air, and flapping the arms out at the sides like wings.

Apart from the lakeside dance, the second segment of the *Zhao Shutun* stories that finds resonance in Yang's "Spirit of the Peacock" is the scene in which

VIDEO 15. Excerpt of *Peacock Princess*. Shanghai Animation Film Studio, 1963.

To watch this video, scan the QR code with your mobile device or visit
DOI: https://doi.org/10.1525/luminos.58.15

Nanmunuonuo is about to be executed and performs one final dance in the human realm before flying back to the peacock kingdom. In most versions of the story, this scene is a moment of tragic tension, because viewers, like the humans in the story, do not know Nanmunuonuo will be able to escape. A commenter on the 1978 dance drama suggested that this scene is a "small climax" within the overall story.[71] In Mao-era adaptations, this part of the plot had special ideological significance because it illustrated how religion can be manipulated by those in power for political gain. In the 1956 *Frontier Literature* translation, after Zhao has gone off to war, Zhao's father has a strange dream. Worried that this dream may be a bad omen, the king invites the help of ritual specialists, known as Mogula, to interpret it. They declare it a terrible omen with only one solution:

> Only by killing Nanchuona [Nanmunuonuo]
> Using her blood as a sacrifice to the common people's gods
> Is it possible to eliminate the people's calamity
> And cause you to be reborn.[72]

At dawn, the designated hour of the Peacock Princess's execution, she pleads to be given her peacock gown so that she can "dance one last time":[73]

> The queen timidly brings out the peacock gown
> Nanchuona takes it and puts it on
> She thanks the queen
> And softly begins to dance
> Lifting her head, she looks out in all directions

The common people are gathered all around
She looks at every face
But cannot find Zhao Shutun
She says farewell to the people
Then flies toward the housetops
As her feet leave the ground
Her tears sprinkle like rain.[74]

This scene did not appear in the Xishuangbanna ensemble's 1956 dance production, which enacted only the part of the *Zhao Shutun* story in which the prince and princess meet and fall in love. However, the scene most likely did appear in the longer five-act version the ensemble developed between 1961 and 1963,[75] and it played a prominent role in the 1978 version. A critic reviewing *Zhao Shutun and Nanmunuonuo* when it was performed in Beijing in 1979 described the scene as follows: "Before the peacock princess is executed, she tearfully requests her peacock gown so that she can dance her last peacock dance for the people of Mengbanjia. Just as the crowds are being entranced by her beautiful and moving dance, the peacock princess opens her two wings and flies toward Mengdongban—the land of the peacocks."[76]

As with the dancing in the lakeside meeting scene, the best indication of what early Maoist dance interpretations of the dancing in the execution scene may have looked like comes from the 1963 stop-motion animation film. It is also in these scenes that we find connections to Yang's "Spirit of the Peacock."

In the film, Nan Muluna performs her final dance on a raised wooden pyre that doubles as a stage. Dressed in the same white dress she wore by the lakeside, she performs a long solo dance that includes several movements found in Yang's later dance: a pose standing on one foot with one arm raised and the other lowered and her foot kicking up behind, a standing spin with her arms out to the sides at shoulder height, a crouched position with upper body bent forward and arms raised to horizontal, and a twirl holding the fringe of her skirt. Although the dance also shares some arm movements and body positions with Jin Ming's 1956 *Peacock Dance*, the footwork and hip and torso actions are different. Notably, the film choreography lacks the up and down bouncing rhythm and S curve hip and torso opposition of Jin Ming's choreography, movement that is widely considered defining of Dai dance. Like Yang's "Spirit of the Peacock," the film replaces the percussive musicality with a melodic one and changes the focus of movement from leg and hip articulations to arm actions, static poses, and twirling spins.

The Xishuangbanna ensemble's 1978 dance drama *Zhao Shutun and Nanmunuonuo* provided the link between embodied Mao-era imaginings of the Peacock Princess and its continued reinterpretation in Yang's repertoires of the 1980s and beyond. In his review of *Zhao Shutun and Nanmunuonuo* when it appeared at the national theater festival in Beijing in 1979, Jia Zuoguang offered the following description of the movements Yang performed: "The bending and extension of her arms and the contrast between stillness and movement all give people a very refreshing and new feeling. In terms of artistic method, the choreographers employed a virtual approach in their characterization of Nanmunuonuo. They used several typical peacock movements and poses—such as raising up the right hand while grabbing the skirt with the left hand, keeping the upper body still while tip-toeing across the stage in dainty steps—showing the audience that she is a peacock."[77]

This performance clearly built on Mao-era choreographic conventions documented in the 1963 film, such as the focus on hand and arm movement, the use of rhythmic variation and departure from downward-focused foot and hip actions, and the pose with one arm raised and the other lifting the hem of the skirt. The costuming in the 1978 production also inherited conventions from Mao-era imagery. A portrait of Yang in her Nanmunuonuo costume published in May of 1979 showed her draped in a light-colored gauze cape with a collar decorated with spots, much like those worn by Dao Meilan in 1956 and 1957.[78] While building on the past, Yang's 1978 performance also provided a basis for future work. Participants in a 1979 symposium on *Zhao Shutun and Nanmunuonuo* lauded Yang's beautiful body lines and her unusually expressive hands and arms, two features that would go on to form the foundation of Yang's peacock dance style.[79] In Yang's 1979 portrait, we also see the germination of her distinctive "peacock head" hand movements in "Spirit of the Peacock": Yang's left hand is raised over her head, with the wrist bent, index finger and thumb pinched together, and other three fingers extended.

Watching Yang Liping perform "Spirit of the Peacock" is like seeing a master magician at work; with each flick of her wrist or elbow, she conjures up a new landscape of images. While they seem spontaneous, these images in fact rely on careful choreographic strategies, which Yang has in part cultivated herself and in part inherited from previous artists. With her choreographic interplay between performing woman and performing peacock, Yang evokes the essential magic of the Peacock Princess in the *Zhao Shutun* story: her ability to shape-shift from human to bird while retaining the best characteristics of both. Yang performs large portions of her choreography in "Spirit of the Peacock" with her back to the audience, allowing viewers to indulge in sights of her exposed upper back, shoulders, and arms. With her arms spread out horizontally and fluttering in rippling actions, her torso remaining at a constant level, and her lower body concealed from view by her shimmering gown, viewers familiar with the *Zhao Shutun* story might project themselves into the role of Prince Zhao Shutun gazing enchanted at the immortal peacock ladies bathing in the forest lake. Later in the dance, when Yang spins and simulates a bird leaping into flight, the viewer may project themselves into Nanmunuonuo's character, imagining her escape from the execution pyre. Similarly, one might imagine the onlookers in the story, struck by the miraculous sight of a woman in flight. While Yang's performances are stunning without these added layers of interpretation, they help to explain the lasting appeal of her peacock dances, not just in China but across Asia. Early Mao-era experiments and their revivals were essential in making Yang's performances and their layered intertextuality possible. At the same time, Yang's reinterpretation of them gave the *Zhao Shutun* story a new range of embodiments aesthetically attuned to the tastes of a new generation.

STAGING DUNHUANG: *FLOWERS AND RAIN ON THE SILK ROAD*

Apart from Xishuangbanna's *Zhao Shutun and Nanmunuonuo*, the other new choreography that stunned audiences in the 1979 festival was Gansu's *Flowers and Rain on the Silk Road. Flowers* was a six-act large-scale dance drama that premiered in Lanzhou in the early summer of 1979.[80] It was then staged at the Great Hall of the People in Beijing on October 1 (National Day), 1979, where it became one of the most popular items in the entire national festival program, winning "first place" in all categories.[81] Between 1979 and 1982, the Gansu ensemble performed *Flowers* live more than five hundred times, in cities across China as well as in Hong Kong, North Korea, France, and Italy.[82] During this time, another ensemble also toured *Flowers* to the United States and Canada.[83] In 1982 Xi'an Film Studio adapted *Flowers* into a color film, which began showing in theaters in early 1983.[84] In 2008 the Gansu Provincial Song and Dance Theater (Gansu sheng gewu juyuan) developed an updated version of *Flowers*, which was performed at the National Center for the Performing Arts (Guojia dajuyuan) in Beijing in August of 2009 for the sixtieth anniversary of the PRC.[85] By that time, *Flowers* had been performed live over sixteen hundred times for more than three million people in twenty countries and territories across the world.[86]

As one of the most innovative dance productions in Chinese dance history, *Flowers* represented a major development for both the content and form of national dance drama. In his 1979 review, Wu Xiaobang pronounced that "The performance of *Flowers* . . . has opened a new path for Chinese dance drama themes and has carried out brave experiments with dance drama art, producing innovation and breakthroughs."[87] The work's most important contribution was its bringing together of three thematic and visual elements that would all become extremely common features of Chinese dance choreography from this point onward: the visual imagery of Dunhuang art, the theme of intercultural interaction on the Silk Road, and the historical setting of the Tang dynasty.[88] Dunhuang art refers to the Buddhist paintings and statues found in a cave-temple complex called the Mogao caves, located in the desert near the modern city of Dunhuang in northwest China (figure 25). As Ning Qiang summarizes: "The Dunhuang caves consist

FIGURE 25. A reconstruction of Mogao Cave 45 at the Dunhuang Museum in Dunhuang, China, 2016. Photographer: Dan Lundberg.

of 492 grottoes carved in a gravel conglomerate cliff that are full of wall paintings and painted sculptures and an additional 230 caves at the northern end of the same cliff. The 45,000 square meters of paintings and 2,400 sculptures remaining in the caves span a period of a thousand years, from the fifth to the fourteenth century C.E., and visually represent with vivid detail the culture and society of medieval China."[89] The complex imagery in Dunhuang art includes extensive representations of anthropomorphic figures in motion, including numerous scenes of staged performance.[90] As Lanlan Kuang has observed, music and dance performance based on this imagery—what is now known as *Dunhuang bihua yuewu*—is one of the most common mediums through which Chinese national identity is projected in spaces of global cultural exchange in the twenty-first century.[91] *Flowers* was the first widely successful large-scale example of *Dunhuang bihua yuewu*, making it an important starting point for this influential genre of contemporary Chinese performance art. As discussed further below, Dunhuang art shapes all aspects of the thematic content and aesthetic execution of *Flowers*, from its plot and characters to its set and costume design to its movement vocabularies.

The Silk Road and the Tang dynasty are in some ways extensions of the Dunhuang theme. The Silk Road refers to a vast network of trade routes, which were also pathways of intense cultural and political exchange that from before the first millennium connected various Chinese dynasties to historical civilizations in what are today known as Central Asia, South Asia, and the Middle East. Dunhuang was historically one of the most important sites along these routes, and its collections reflect the diverse cultural influences that flowed along them, making Dunhuang what Valerie Hansen calls "a time capsule of the Silk Road."[92] Because Dunhuang was for the most part under Chinese rule from 111 BCE onward, it can be regarded as a specifically Chinese part of both Silk Road history and Chinese history.[93] Also, because Dunhuang faded as a major site of Silk Road exchange after the year 1000, its collections peak during the period known as the Tang dynasty (618–907 CE), which is widely regarded as a high point in the development of Chinese arts and literature—especially in poetry, music, and Buddhist visual arts—and in China's embrace of foreign culture.[94] Chang'an (Xi'an), the Tang capital, grew into the largest city in the world at the time and attracted diverse people from across Asia.[95] By setting its story on the Tang dynasty Silk Road, *Flowers* both maximized the multicultural imagery of Dunhuang art and expressed a period in Chinese history that, for many, was associated both with cultural pride and a spirit of openness to the world.

Flowers presented a fictional story that allowed for the incorporation of key people and places associated with Dunhuang, the Silk Road, and the Tang dynasty. The prelude takes place in the desert, identified in the program notes as "During the Tang Dynasty, on the Silk Road."[96] Against a backdrop of camel caravans and windstorms, Chinese painter Shen Bizhang and his daughter, Ying Niang, save the life of a Persian trader, Inus, who has fainted in the desert. After Inus departs, a gang of bandits abducts Ying Niang. Act 1 takes place many years later in the bustling Dunhuang market, where Shen sees Ying working as an indentured performer with a troupe of traveling entertainers. Inus, who happens to be conducting business in the market, frees Ying from the troupe by paying the troupe head. Scene 2 is set inside the Mogao caves, where Shen is employed as a painter. Ying dances for her father, inspiring him to paint the "reverse-played *pipa*" *(fantan pipa)*, a famous scene from the Dunhuang paintings in which a dancer plays the pipa (a lute-like musical instrument) behind her head while standing on one leg. The corrupt market head schemes to employ Ying as a court entertainer, so Shen sends her with Inus to Persia. When the market head finds out, he chains Shen inside the cave as punishment. Scene 3 takes place in Inus's palace-like residence in Persia, where Ying learns Persian dances and teaches Chinese crafts to the women in Inus's home. Then Inus is called to appear at the Tang court, and Ying goes with him. Meanwhile, scene 4 moves back to the Mogao caves, showing the captive Shen dreaming of his daughter. A Tang governor comes to the cave to burn incense, sees the beautiful paintings, and frees Shen. Scene 5 takes place on the Silk Road, where Inus's caravan is robbed by a strongman sent by the market head.

VIDEO 16. Excerpt of He Yanyun and ensemble in *Flowers and Rain on the Silk Road*, 1980. Unofficial stage recording. Used with permission from He Yanyun.

To watch this video, scan the QR code with your mobile device or visit DOI: https://doi.org/10.1525/luminos.58.16

Shen lights a warning beacon but is killed. Scene 6 takes place at the international diplomatic council where Inus serves as a delegate. Ying performs at the council and exposes the market head, avenging her father and bringing peace to the Silk Road. The epilogue shows the ten-mile roadside pavilion, where guests and hosts say goodbye to one another and vow long-lasting friendship.

Imagery derived from Dunhuang art features prominently in *Flowers*. The opening scene is a darkened stage on which spotlights follow two women suspended from the ceiling, appearing to be flying while dancing with long silk scarves. Contemporary critics recognized these figures as *apsaras (feitian)*, a type of celestial being commonly depicted in Buddhist and Hindu art.[97] They are ubiquitous in Dunhuang; experts sight *apsaras* in 270 of the 492 Mogao caves, with a total of 4,500 individual depictions.[98] Dunhuang imagery also appears in Ying Niang's choreography. As Zhao Xian argued, Ying's ten solo dances together present an entirely new movement system: "Dunhuang dance."[99] In scene 1, when Ying performs with the band of itinerant entertainers, the body lines used in her choreography match the postures of dancing figures in Dunhuang. Like the Dunhuang figures, she maintains Indic *tribhanga (san dao wan)*, or tri-bent pose, throughout, characterized by flexed ankles and feet, bent knees, and angled hip and elbow lines (video 16). Her iconic "reverse-played pipa" stance appears first in this scene and then is repeated in scenes 2, 3, and 4, forming the production's most recognizable dance motif.[100] In scene 6, Ying dances solo atop a circular podium, also a common feature of Dunhuang dance imagery, and in scene 4 she is accompanied by groups of dancers playing musical instruments such as vertical flutes, long-necked lutes, pan pipes, and *konghou* (ancient harp), echoing similar scenes in Dunhuang paintings.[101] Apart from the dancers' movement vocabularies and props, the stage sets and dancers' interactions with them also bring Dunhuang imagery on stage. In scenes 2 and 4, the stage is made up to look like a realistic replica of a Dunhuang grotto, with life-sized statues and a four-sided backdrop covered in enlarged, full-color replicas of Dunhuang wall paintings. In scene 2, Shen's act of painting recalls the process by which the caves were constructed. In scene 4, the Tang governor's visit to pray and give offerings reenacts the religious functions these spaces would have had. A common refrain by critics was that *Flowers* had "brought the Dunhuang murals to life."

Significant research went into the creation of *Flowers*. As described by Liu Shaoxiong (1933–2015), who headed the choreography team, the process began by making a site visit to the Dunhuang grottoes, where they viewed the paintings, listened to researchers explain the imagery, and learned about the site's history.[102] Next, they created some exploratory works and tested various plot structures until they created a story that was both well-suited to dance drama and consistent with historical evidence.[103] To create the Dunhuang dance vocabularies, Liu and two young performers copied over one hundred sketches of Dunhuang dance poses, which were provided to them by researchers at the Dunhuang Cultural Relics Research Institute. Then they spent time studying the images and developing dance movements from them. Beyond learning to perform each static posture, they also analyzed the images to determine whether they represented fast or slow actions, what the implied directions of movement were, and possible links between poses. Many of the portraits in the Dunhuang paintings were meant to represent heavenly, rather than earthly, beings. However, Liu and the others reasoned that all of the movements were likely modeled on dances performed by human performers, so it would be acceptable to use them interchangeably in the choreography.[104]

Because their goal was artistic creation, not exact historical revival, the choreographers then went to work innovating on the movements they had derived from the Dunhuang images. For example, they incorporated familiar actions from Chinese classical dance, such as *yuanchang* (circling the stage in brisk heel-toe walks) and *fanshen* (barrel turns), and they introduced acrobatic elements from ballet, such as lifts and adapted *fouetté* turns. Finally, they sought outside experts to help with the foreign dance choreography, such as the dance sequences for Inus and the other Persian characters and other styles for the twenty-seven-country gathering in scene 6.[105] Ye Ning, an expert in Chinese classical dance and veteran in the Chinese dance field, commended the balance Liu and his team had struck between research and innovation. She wrote, "The creation of *Flowers* is both difficult and precious: difficult in its bringing to life of the still postures from the paintings and using them to portray characters; precious in its breaking the old conventions of dance language and composition to innovate."[106]

As the first large-scale dance drama to be set in the Tang dynasty, to take up the Silk Road as its theme, and to realize a complete dance vocabulary based on movements derived from Dunhuang art, *Flowers* brought many important innovations to the Chinese dance stage. However, these innovations, like those of Yang Liping's peacock dances, had pre–Cultural Revolution precedents. The link between Dunhuang and the modern Chinese dance movement began as early as 1945, when early Chinese dance pioneer Dai Ailian traveled to Chengdu on her way to conduct field research on Tibetan dance and ended up staying for several months with Zhang Daqian, at the time one of China's foremost experts on Dunhuang painting. Zhang's relationship to Dunhuang is legendary in the history of Chinese art. As Michael Sullivan and Franklin D. Murphy write, "no artist did more to put this treasure-house of ancient Buddhist wall painting 'on the map' than Zhang Daqian."[107] Between 1941 and 1943, Zhang had spent two and a half years working in the Mogao caves, "listing, cataloguing describing, and making exact copies of the most important frescoes . . . [and] produced 276 full-size copies on silk and paper."[108] These works were exhibited and had such a significant impact that China's minister of education set up the National Dunhuang Art Research Institute in 1943. The first director of this new institute, Chang Shuhong (1904–1994) would later serve as an official advisor on *Flowers and Rain on the Silk Road.*[109] Around 1942 in Chongqing, Dai Ailian's husband, Ye Qianyu, was one of the artists inspired by seeing Zhang's paintings exhibited. In 1943 Ye worked briefly as a war correspondent in India, where he saw performances by Indian dancers that furthered his interest in Zhang's Dunhuang-based paintings.[110] In 1944 Ye wrote to Zhang and asked if he could visit and study with him in his home in Chengdu. Zhang agreed, and Ye ended up working with him from late 1944 through the summer of 1945.[111] When Dai arrived in Chengdu in June of 1945, she also stayed with Zhang for about three months, during which time she recalls "appreciating many of his paintings."[112]

Dai's early theorization of Chinese dance as essentially inclusive of non-Han dance styles may have been shaped by her experiences interacting with Zhang and seeing his copies of Dunhuang wall murals. In 1946, when Dai presented her *Frontier Music and Dance Plenary* in Chongqing, she presented an argument in her accompanying lecture that suggested many of the dance styles practiced in China's Tibetan areas and in countries near China, such as Japan, retained cultural legacies from the influences of the Tang dynasty. "At around the end of the Tang," Dai wrote, "dance went from a period of greatness to one of gradual decline."[113] She went on to argue that the reason similarities could be found between some

FIGURE 26. "Apsaras." Published in *Zhongguo minjian wudao tupian xuanji* (Shanghai: Renmin yishu chubanshe, 1957), n.p. Photographer unknown. Image obtained from the University of Michigan Asia Library Chinese Dance Collection.

dances practiced among Tibetan communities in western China and among some dancers in Japan is that both communities had preserved dance styles that were once practiced in the Tang dynasty. Dai's suggestion that these be considered legacies of "Han influence" is problematic in historical perspective. Nevertheless, her theorization of Chinese dance history shows that she saw the dances of the Tang dynasty—likely represented in part by those depicted in Zhang's Dunhuang paintings—as an imagined source for the dance practices she was collecting and using to devise a new form of modern Chinese dance. In 1954 Dai created a duet called "Apsaras" *(Feitian)*, the first work of modern Chinese dance choreography based on imagery from the Dunhuang paintings (figure 26).[114] A repertoire piece of the Central Song and Dance ensemble, the dance featured two women performing with long silk streamers, with dance movements designed to imitate flight.[115] Photographs of "Apsaras" continued to appear in Chinese mainstream media until 1963, suggesting that the work enjoyed a long period of popularity during the pre–Cultural Revolution period.[116]

Exhibitions and research on Dunhuang art and Tang dynasty dance were common in early socialist China and also impacted the field of dance research, laying a foundation for the creation of *Flowers* decades later. In 1951 the Central Ministry of Culture and the Dunhuang Cultural Relics Research Institute hosted a major exhibition of Dunhuang art in Beijing, with nine hundred facsimiles of Dunhuang murals, models of the Mogao caves, and replicas of Dunhuang statues.[117] After the show, there were plans to publish a book and to create a film based on the content that would be shown all over China.[118] Two other exhibitions were held in Beijing in 1954 and 1955, the latter including a replica of an entire grotto, based on Mogao cave number 285, known for its depictions of *apsaras* playing musical instruments.[119] Around the time of these exhibitions, China's dance researchers also began to show interest in Dunhuang art and Tang dynasty dance history. In 1951, an image of *apsaras* from the Dunhuang paintings appeared on the cover of *Dance News*.[120] In 1954 *Dance Research Materials* republished a long and substantive article by Yin Falu (1915–2002), a professor in the Chinese Department at Peking University, that explained what Dunhuang art reveals about Tang dynasty music and dance.[121] Two of Yin's key points would later be emphasized in *Flowers and Rain on the Silk Road*, namely, that Dunhuang art is a product of the labor of working people and that Dunhuang art reflects intercultural exchange between Central Plains Chinese culture and the cultures of Central, West, and South Asia. In 1956 all three of China's major dance publications—*Dance News, Dance Study Materials*, and *Dance Series*—included content dealing with Dunhuang and Tang dynasty dance.[122] One of the images printed in these publications was of the Dunhuang "reverse-played pipa" dance pose.[123] In 1958 *Dance* published a review of a small museum of Chinese dance history that had been set up by the China Dance Research Association, which displayed replicas of Tang dynasty dance statues, dance scenes from Dunhuang paintings, and a section of dance notation found in the Dunhuang manuscript collection.[124] In 1959–60, articles on Tang dynasty dance continued to appear in *Dance*, highlighting intercultural interaction, citing Dunhuang dance documents, and arguing for the importance of historical research for new creation.[125]

The idea that Chinese dance choreography should take inspiration from historical sources such as the Dunhuang murals and other Tang Dynasty artifacts was a topic of discussion for China's dance researchers in the early socialist era. Wu Xiaobang and Ye Ning, who both praised *Flowers* in 1979, had each published essays calling for greater attention to historical dance materials back in the mid-1950s. As head of the Dance Art Research Association, Wu Xiaobang wrote in 1956 that two international dance ensembles that had toured China in 1955—one a Japanese kabuki troupe and the other a performance ensemble from India—convinced him and others at the association that the Chinese dance field should focus more attention on historical materials.[126] Similarly, Ye Ning, who had served as founding head of BDS's Classical Dance Research Group, wrote in 1956 arguing that the sources for Chinese classical dance movement vocabulary should go beyond xiqu and include dance styles from all of China's historical periods.[127] Because xiqu emerged only around the twelfth century, Ye was referring specifically to the need to study earlier dance traditions, such as those of the Tang. "From the perspective of the development of China's dance art tradition, dance in xiqu is only one period of dance's overall history. So, we should study both xiqu dance and the dance tradition from before xiqu," Ye wrote.[128] The impact of these views can be seen in the choreography of *Magic Lotus Lantern*, the large-scale Chinese classical dance drama that premiered in 1957 (see chapter 3). *Magic Lotus Lantern* opens with a scene inside a temple on Mount Hua in northwest China, in which dancers imitate statues of heavenly beings that come to life.[129] The lead character, Third Sacred Mother, performed several solo dances in which she danced with long silk streamers, much like the dancing figures depicted in Dunhuang paintings. Moreover, she used *mudras*, or hand gestures derived from Buddhist art, in some of her choreography. In an interview published in 1958 about her creative process for this role, the dancer Zhao Qing stated that because *Magic Lotus Lantern* is a Tang dynasty legend, she had studied historical materials mainly from the Tang dynasty, including Dunhuang paintings, to conduct research and develop the movements used in her choreography.[130]

Links between *Flowers* and early Chinese dance activities can also be traced through the lives of key artists who participated in the production. Liu Shaoxiong, one of *Flowers'* lead choreographers, began performing with the Gansu Cultural Work Troupe in 1949, when he was just sixteen. During the 1950s, Liu performed many well-known works of Chinese dance, and in 1954, he was sent to study at the Central Song and Dance Ensemble, where Dai Ailian was at the time creating "Apsaras." After working for several more years as a performer of Chinese dance in Gansu, Liu returned to Beijing in 1958 to participate in the choreography course led by Soviet instructor Petr Gusev at BDS. As a student in this course, Liu participated in the creation of *Lady of the Sea* (*Yu meiren*, 1959), an experimental dance drama that blended multiple dance forms. After graduating in 1960, Liu returned to Gansu and began working professionally as a choreographer.[131] Another dancer involved in *Flowers* who personally links the earlier and later periods of Chinese dance history is Chai Huaimin, the dancer who played the role of Chinese painter Shen Bizhang. Chai had entered the Gansu ensemble in 1956 and had been one of the company's leading male performers in the early 1960s.[132] He Yanyun (b. 1956), the much younger female dancer who played the role of Ying Niang, entered the Gansu ensemble in 1970, during the Cultural Revolution, and thus had limited experience with Chinese dance works of the early period. However, the first major role that He performed was Sister Ying from *Ode to Yimeng*, the revolutionary ballet containing the largest amount of Chinese classical dance movement.[133] To perform this role, He would have had to master not just ballet movement vocabularies but also many Chinese dance movements and performance conventions developed in the pre–Cultural Revolution period.

CONCLUSION: CHINESE DANCE IN A NEW ERA

The revival of Chinese dance that occurred during the immediate post-Mao years brought with it a new surge in Chinese dance creation that continued into the 1980s. After the success of the two 1979 hit dance dramas *Zhao Shutun and Nanmunuonuo* and *Flowers and Rain on the Silk Road*, a flood of new national dance dramas appeared that similarly highlighted ethnic minority literature, Buddhist imagery, and stories set in the Tang dynasty or similar historical settings.[134] The first of these, which was also part of the national festival and premiered in early 1980, was *Princess Wencheng (Wencheng gongzhu)*, a joint production of China Opera and Dance Drama Theater and the Beijing Dance Academy, which chronicled a seventh-century marriage between a Tang princess and a Tibetan king.[135] Like its predecessors, *Wencheng* featured new dance languages developed from research on Tang dynasty artifacts, as well as new variations on existing dance styles developed in the pre–Cultural Revolution period.[136] Another example of this trend was the Chengdu Song and Dance Ensemble's Tibetan-themed *Woman of Benevolent Actions (Zhuowa sangmu, 1980)*, which was made into a film released by Emei Film Studio in 1984.[137] Like its predecessors, the 1982 films based on *Zhao Shutun* and *Flowers*, *Woman of Benevolent Actions* blends imagery from local religion and folk performance into Chinese dance choreography set in ornate architectural settings and magical outdoor spaces.[138] Sun Ying's national dance drama *Dancers of the Tongque Stage*, premiered in 1985 by the China Opera and Dance Drama Theater, moved further back in time, with a fictional story of court dancers set in the beginning of the Wei-Jin period (220–440 CE).[139] Like *Flowers*, this work introduced a new Chinese classical dance vocabulary inspired by historical artifacts, what became known as "Han-Tang Chinese classical dance" *(Han-Tang Zhongguo gudianwu)*.[140]

While the revival of Chinese dance represented important continuities between this period and the pre–Cultural Revolution socialist era, there were also important divergences. With some exceptions, a shift occurred in the thematic focus of national dance drama, especially the class backgrounds of the leading characters. Whereas the socialist-era art system encouraged stories focused on the struggles and achievements of the disenfranchised, in the post-Mao period, more and more works tended to focus on leading characters who came from royal or otherwise privileged backgrounds. The Persian merchant Inus in *Flowers* is one example of a hero who would have been implausible during the socialist era, when foreign merchants were almost universally depicted as villains.[141] The stories and settings had also changed. In place of communities fighting for collective social transformation, plots now focused more on individuals seeking love or personal happiness. In place of villages and rebellions, audiences were more likely to see palaces and weddings. The range of possibilities for female characters that had opened up during the early period of national dance drama also narrowed. Reflecting a retrenchment of conservative gender norms across many fields in China at the time, dance drama heroines now often lost their status as subjects with agency and were turned back into objects to be desired, protected, or exchanged by men.

During the 1980s, Chinese dance increasingly came into competition with other dance styles, especially those newly imported from the United States that emphasized individual expression, such as modern dance, disco, and street dance. The post-Mao introduction of American modern dance began with visits by Asian American dancers Ruby Shang and Wang Xiaolan, which took place in 1980 and 1983.[142] These activities were followed by the experimental modern dance program launched by Guangdong-based dance educator Yang Meiqi in the late 1980s, which had support of the American Dance Festival and the US-based Asian Cultural Council. This led in 1992 to the founding of the Guangzhou Modern Dance Company.[143] Also in the 1980s, China experienced a national wave of disco dancing, followed soon after by *piliwu*, an early form of Chinese hip-hop that gained nationwide popularity by the late 1980s.[144]

Because of their association with a new, individual-focused experience of post-Mao modernity, these dance movements forced Chinese dance practitioners to reassess their mission and identity. When Chinese dance was first developed in the late 1940s and early 1950s, it was conceived of as something essentially new, which could give expression to China's modern national identity and embody the contemporary experiences and values of a constantly changing, revolutionary society. In the postrevolutionary period, how would Chinese dance maintain this sense of contemporaneity while choreographic trends seemed to be moving it toward increasingly more distant historical content? How would Chinese dance continue its socialist foundation while adapting to new social values and forms of artistic expression? These are some of the questions that motivated the legacies and innovations of Chinese dance at the start of the new millennium.

6

Inheriting the Socialist Legacy

Chinese Dance in the Twenty-First Century

In 2014 Xinjiang-born Uyghur dancer Gulmira Mamat (a.k.a. Gulimina, b. 1986) won first place on Zhejiang Satellite TV's popular Chinese television dance show *So You Think You Can Dance—China,* season 2 *(Zhongguo hao wudao).*[1] In the season finale, she secured her title by performing a Tajik-style choreography, traditionally one of the less commonly taught minority dance forms in professional dance schools in contemporary Xinjiang (figure 27). As the lights come on, a bird's call sounds, and Gulmira sits kneeling, still, with her eyes closed. She holds her elbows out to either side, parallel to the floor, with her hands palm-down, fingertip-to-fingertip in front of her chest.[2] She wears a round beaded hat with a red veil down the back, her hair in two long braids. Her dress is bright red with geometrical patterns embroidered along the chest, cuffs, and belt. As a flute plays, her hands begin to shudder, and she raises them slowly above her head, then opens her eyes, smiling. Still kneeling, she performs a series of staccato hand gestures that frame her head and chest, then dips into a deep backbend. A male dancer joins her on stage in a matching costume and circles around her, appearing to play a flute. Flirtatiously, they slide from side to side, looking sideways at one another and bobbing their shoulders in unison. Gulmira pretends to play a drumbeat on the male dancer's back, and they shift around one another to form complementary poses.

There is much in Gulmira's dancing that recalls the style of her predecessor, Uyghur dancer Qemberxanim, who began performing modern nationality dances in Xinjiang more than seventy years earlier. The emphasis on face-framing hand and arm movements, the backbends from a kneeling position, the rhythmic use of the upper body, the combination of running footwork and turns, and the charismatic smile and use of the eyes all recall the documentary footage taken during

FIGURE 27. Gulmira Mamat in Tajik-style dance from *So You Think You Can Dance—China,* season 2, 2013. Photographer unknown. Reproduced with permission from the private collection of Gulmira Mamat.

Qemberxanim's 1947–48 tour. Indeed, Gulmira directly inherits Qemberxanim's dance legacy. Gulmira graduated from and now teaches at the Xinjiang Art Academy Dance Department (Xinjiang yishu xueyuan wudao xi), a program founded by Qemberxanim in the 1950s, when she also served as the school's dean.[3] Today, two busts of Qemberxanim sit on the academy's campus, and a dedicated Qemberxanim Image Showroom displays a photographic exhibit about her life, including pictures of her with her early cohort of students, many of whom went on to teach at the academy.[4] According to Dilaram Mahamatimin (b. 1961), whose mother was an early student of Qemberxanim's and who is now a retired dance teacher at the academy herself, the dance program still teaches many routines originally choreographed by Qemberxanim, and they treat Qemberxanim's style as a model for correct technique.[5] Since Gulmira studied at the academy from age twelve onward, her entire professional dance education comes from this institution and, with it, the foundation of movement practices that Qemberxanim developed and transmitted through her students and their students.[6]

For Gulmira, inheriting the socialist dance legacy of Qemberxanim is not only a matter of preserving and passing on the dance vocabularies and performance styles that Qemberxanim developed but also of continuing to advance Xinjiang dance through individual innovation, in the way that Qemberxanim herself did.

As a young dancer in the early 1940s, one of the ways that Qemberxanim earned her fame was by introducing new interpretations to the existing Xinjiang dance styles she performed. At the time, simply performing in public as a woman was a major innovation, since it challenged Central Asian Muslim mores about the appropriate display of women's bodies in public, bringing women into a professional sphere previously dominated by men.[7] "Plate Dance" (Panzi wu), a solo that used plates and chopsticks for props as discussed in chapter 2, was generated through a combination of what Qemberxanim learned from studying with folk artists and what she added based on her own artistic sensibilities. According to Qemberxanim's biographer Amina, after Qemberxanim learned the technique from a local folk performer, she added creative innovations that "increased the dance's rhythmic feeling and its technical dexterity."[8] Qemberxanim also adapted dance styles from contemporary Uzbekistan to recreate dances documented in the historical records but no longer practiced in Xinjiang.[9]

In 2015 Gulmira, also an active choreographer, staged her own evening-length production of Xinjiang dances that similarly introduced her own stylistic adaptations and innovations. The performance, self-titled *Gulmira*, was held at the National Center for the Performing Arts in Beijing, as part of an event called "Twelve Days of Dance" that presents the work of young choreographers from across China.[10] As stated in the program, the event comprised three parts: the first devoted to "presenting traditional national dances"; the second to "blending traditional nationality dance elements with modern choreographic methods . . . to reflect Gulmira's own growth and transmutations"; and the third showing "the forward development of all of Xinjiang's nationality dances according to the footsteps of the times."[11] Performed by Gulmira, her students, and colleagues from Xinjiang and other parts of China, the evening showcased Gulmira's high-energy, percussive style of Xinjiang dance, which emphasizes fast pacing, driving rhythms, extreme back flexibility and fluidity, and staccato isolations of the chest, head, and hands.[12] In her self-choreographed Uzbek-style solo "Dance Is Life" (Xin dong wu dong), Gulmira bounds across the stage in a purple and yellow pant costume, yellow feathers blowing in her hat as she performs lightning-fast chain turns, shakes and snaps her hands in the air above her head, and slides across the floor on her knees. In her Uyghur-style solo "Girl in Bells," by the influential Ürümqi-based Uyghur choreographer Jasur Tursun, she performs a deconstructed rendition of Uyghur dance integrated with LED graphics (video 17). On the whole, Gulmira's movement is larger, faster, crisper, and more bombastic than Qemberxanim's, adapted to the pacing of contemporary television performance and live viewing audiences. At the same time, it retains many of the performance conventions and movement vocabularies established through the works of Qemberxanim and other leading Xinjiang-based dancers during the socialist period. Although her execution and choreography are new, Gulmira builds on an established modern tradition of movement techniques, styles, and vocabularies passed down through the

VIDEO 17. Gulmira Mamat in "Girl in Bells," 2015. Performed at the Xinjiang Television Studio in Ürümqi. Used with permission from Gulmira Mamat.

To watch this video, scan the QR code with your mobile device or visit DOI: https://doi.org/10.1525/luminos.58.17

decades from dancers who came before her. Going forward, Gulmira's innovations now also become part of this modern regional dance form.

The methods by which dancers inherit China's socialist dance legacies in the twenty-first century are as diverse as the institutions, ensembles, and individuals engaged in the work of teaching, creating, and performing Chinese dance. Rather than attempt a comprehensive account of Chinese dance in contemporary China— a project that itself could fill several books—in this chapter, I examine three case studies, each of which illuminates a different aspect of the diverse processes of inheriting socialist dance in China today. First, I consider the pedagogical dimension of socialist dance inheritance, taking as an example the Chinese dance programs at the Beijing Dance Academy. Analyzing BDA's 2004 production *Dances of the Great Land (Dadi zhi wu)* and my own experiences studying at BDA in 2008–9, I consider the school's ongoing commitment to research as both a socialist legacy and a way of fostering innovation in Chinese dance in the twenty-first century. Next, I consider two types of contemporary Chinese dance choreography that reflect current directions in Chinese dance. First, I examine the 2008 dance drama *Maritime Silk Road (Bihai silu)*, directed by celebrity choreographer Chen Weiya (b. 1956) and produced by Guangxi-based Beihai Song and Dance Drama Theater, as an example of the large entertainment-driven productions that present Chinese dance for nonspecialist audiences. Second, I examine a series of works premiered between 2002 and 2014 by Beijing-based choreographer Zhang Yunfeng (b. 1972), as an example of more experimental choreography aimed largely at others in the professional dance community. In all three cases, I argue that the inheritance of socialist dance is a dynamic and self-conscious process in twenty-first-century China, in which practitioners continue to renew and redefine Chinese dance as an ongoing, always unfinished, work in progress.

THE BEIJING DANCE ACADEMY: LINKING RESEARCH AND THE CLASSROOM

In 2004 the Beijing Dance Academy (BDA, formerly the Beijing Dance School) celebrated its fiftieth anniversary. Taking this opportunity to reflect on its past and future, BDA hosted a series of international and domestic symposia on dance education, and it staged a total of eleven evening-length productions, all designed to take stock of and expand upon the current work of its various departments and programs.[13] *Dances of the Great Land*, an evening-length gala put on by BDA's Department of Chinese National Folk Dance (Minzu minjian wudao xi), was one of these productions.[14] *Dances* opened with a surging sea of red, as over a hundred BDA students took the stage performing the iconic "twisting yangge" now associated with the early decades of China's communist revolution, as discussed in chapter 1.[15] Parading in interlocking patterns of rows and circles, the dancers step across the stage bobbing their heads and shaking their hips, while drawing circles in the air with long red scarves tied around their waists. Adapted from the 1991 award-winning competition choreography "A Twisting Yangge Performer" (Yi ge niu yangge de ren), this piece honors the lives of folk artists such as traditional yangge experts while also being a tribute to the communist New Yangge movement of the 1940s, which marks the beginning of the dance tradition carried on in the department (figure 28).[16] This introduction is followed by fifteen works representing six different nationalities—five Han, four Korean, two Tibetan, two Dai, one Mongol, and one Uyghur. The dances are extremely diverse in tone, scale, content, and movement vocabularies. This diversity reflects the department's historical and contemporary mission, which is to study, research, and innovate with the wide-ranging dance forms of China's different geographic regions and ethnic communities.

As suggested by its opening yangge dance sequence, *Dances of the Great Land* traces its roots to China's wartime and early socialist-era dance projects. The program notes, for example, specifically cite Dai Ailian's 1946 lecture "The First Step in Creating Chinese Dance," Dai's "Ba'an *xianzi*" Tibetan-style early Frontier Dance choreography, and the Han folk dance Anhui Huagudeng Curriculum developed in 1953 by Sheng Jie and Peng Song, declaring them as predecessors to the choreography presented in *Dances of the Great Land* and the other research and teaching projects put forward as part of BDA's 2004 half-centenary celebrations.[17] The structure and composition of *Dances* also furthers this comparison.

FIGURE 28. Opening scene of *Dances of the Great Land*, 2004. Photographer: Ye Jin. Reproduced with permission from the private collection of Ye Jin.

With its compilation of short dances in diverse Han and minority styles, *Dances* recalls the programs of early Frontier Dance productions such as the 1946 *Frontier Music and Dance Plenary* and the shows at the 1949 All-China Literature and Arts Worker Representative Congress, as well as student graduation performances held at BDS in the 1950s. The selection of specific dance styles featured in the production also indicates connections to these early projects: of the six nationalities represented in *Dances*, five (Han, Korean, Tibetan, Mongol, and Uyghur) also played important roles in early Frontier Dance and the BDS curriculum.[18] This connection to early Chinese dance history was brought to life during the show in 2004, when Dai Ailian herself attended as a guest of honor. Eighty-eight years old at the time, Dai stood, beaming, at the center of the postshow photograph, where she was surrounded by several generations of teachers and students carrying on her artistic vision.[19] This was the realization of the proposal Dai had made back in 1946, for a team of dancers dedicated to researching and adapting folk dances from every corner of China for the modern stage. Her vision had not only come to fruition but was still vibrant nearly six decades later.

Reflecting the principles of China's early socialist dance movement, national forms and remolding remain central commitments evident in the choreography in *Dances of the Great Land* and the conservatory program of which it is a product. All fifteen works derive their basic movement vocabularies and dance rhythms from research and innovation into local performance. The work that follows the opening yangge sequence is a Tibetan-themed group dance, "The People Closest to the Sun" (Li taiyang zui jin de ren), cochoreographed by Tsering Tashi (Cairang Zhaxi) and Guo Lei (b. 1962). Performed by fourteen male dancers, it adapts a type of large round drum strapped to the dancers' backs and played with curved drumsticks described in Tibetan scripture.[20] The drum is used in religious performances at Gongkar Chö Monastery, near Lhasa.[21] To the deep vibrations of Tibetan horns, the dancers bend forward in wide stances and extend their arms and drumsticks out to the side. Then, in unison, they cross their arms over their chests and hit both sides of the drums behind them, creating a loud crash. The dancers rise up to step, lifting their knees high and jumping in place, and then throw their arms up and crouch down, crossing their arms again to beat the drums. As they turn and walk to the back of the stage, their stance is wide and their bodies sway from side to side, as their arms swing out in alternation with each step.[22] While this drumming technique is relatively new to the concert stage, the choreographers apply movement principles and vocabularies from established forms of Tibetan drum dance to create a new style inspired by local sources. This dance is followed by a Han-style female solo titled "Phoenix Picking Peonies" (Feng cai mudan), choreographed and performed by Yang Ying using the movement vocabulary of Shandong Jiaozhou yangge. Maneuvering a large pink fan with a spinning tassel on one end, Yang takes rapid fluttering steps and twists and compresses her torso to create curving lines, while she pulls the fan through the air, painting silky arcs around her body. A high-pitched *suona* (Chinese clarinet) and gong and drum percussion carry the tune, contributing to what the choreographer calls the work's "earthy flavor."[23] Although the movement vocabularies are familiar, Yang finds new expressive potential by transforming key movements and breaking down conventional connections between steps, yet maintaining the overall movement style.[24]

By definition, Chinese national folk dance focuses on dance forms associated with communities considered nonelite by traditional Chinese standards. The Han portion of the subgenre is dominated by dances originally derived from peasant performance or sources otherwise considered vulgar or low class, while the ethnic minority portion is associated with ethnic and religious groups that have often been marginalized or disenfranchised due to their minority status. Thus, although the works presented in *Dances* are performed by professional dance students at an elite educational institution, the dance styles they perform have popular, rather than refined, aesthetic associations.[25] In terms of thematic content, many of the works in *Dances* also portray nonelite characters. A good example of this is the duet "Spouses" (Laoban), a comic dance sketch by Xin Miaomiao that portrays an elderly couple. The humble background of the characters is conveyed through their costuming and the use of slapstick humor, a common feature of low-status characters in Chinese folk theater. The old wife, whose hearty smile is made up to appear as if she were missing a few teeth, chases her husband around their home with a fan; then, when she is not looking, the husband grabs it and taps her on the buttocks, laughing. The choreography employs recognizable actions from Shandong-style yangge dance, including arm swings, clapping, bouncing walks, kicks, and head wobbles. Pop culture references are also thrown in for comedic effect, such as the wife's "air guitar" on her fan and the husband's "batusi," a V-shaped finger gesture over the eyes originally from the 1960s *Batman* television show.[26] A very different approach to nonelite characters appears in "Fan Bone" (Shan gu), a Korean-themed female solo choreographed by Zhang Xiaomei. In crisp, sweeping actions set to a rapid drum beat, the dancer opens and closes a large paper fan, then jumps, twirls, and runs, while staring at the audience with a wayward smile. According to Zhang, this work takes inspiration from the Korean folk dance "Dance of the Prodigal Nobleman" (Korean *Hallyangmu*, Chinese *Xianlang wu*) but uses it to portray an old folk performer who is slightly drunk and lamenting the hypocrisy of the world.[27] Like the opening yangge sequence, this dance foregrounds the folk artist, considered the authentic subject of many of the dance styles taught and studied in the department.

Dances of the Great Land, like BDA as a whole, inherits from early socialist choreographers the idea that Chinese dance, although derived from research into folkloric, traditional, or historical performance forms, is a modern concert dance genre that exists independently from these forms. During the late 1990s, Chinese dance scholars began to articulate this distinction in the field of Chinese national folk dance by using the opposing terms "academic-style folk dance" (*xueyuan pai minjian wu*) and "original-environment folk dance" (*yuanshengtai minjian wu*). The former refers to Chinese concert dance choreography such as that presented in *Dances of the Great Land*, while the latter indicates folk dances performed by non-conservatory-trained individuals in other contexts such as public squares, temples, harvest celebrations, and weddings.[28] In the years leading up to 2004, the three BDA faculty members who conceptualized and directed *Dances*—Pan Zhitao (b. 1944), Ming Wenjun (b. 1963), and Zhao Tiechun (b. 1963)—all contributed to theorizing the relationship between conservatory-style folk dance and original-environment folk dance in twenty-first-century China.[29] In an essay published in 2003, Zhao described the work he and his colleagues were doing as "distilling the 'folk' onto the 'stage.'"[30] Zhao also portrayed the conservatory classroom as a "bridge" that connects the "source," or folk dance in its authentic environment, to the "flow," or folk dance as staged performance.[31] In order for the classroom to serve this purpose meaningfully, Zhao argued, it must be like a person reaching simultaneously in two directions: "stretching one hand toward tradition to seek the soul (respecting historical traditions) and one hand toward modernity to seek ideas (developing and innovating)."[32] *Dances of the Great Land* presents the results of this approach.[33]

In my experiences studying at BDA in 2008–9, I observed faculty and students alike putting Zhao's metaphor into action. Research was emphasized in all areas of Chinese dance taught at BDA, not only in Chinese national folk dance but also in Chinese classical dance. This research took place in many ways. Some focused on moving outside the classroom to seek out and study performance practices beyond the sphere of concert dance. Others focused on bringing outside forms into the classroom, where the forms became the basis for new choreographic creation. In both cases, faculty and students ultimately used the classroom as a space to devise new movement possibilities through which forms from outside the concert dance sphere could inspire new vocabularies or techniques for stage performance.

One way that faculty at BDA conduct research is by bringing techniques used in traditional and folk performance into conservatory spaces. This occurred, for example, in my Han nationality folk dance *(Hanzu minjian wu)* course in the spring of 2009, when my professor, Jia Meina (b. 1942), introduced stilts *(gaoqiao)* into our class. The style of yangge we were learning in this course was a form popular in the Northeast, around Harbin and Heilongjiang, in which folk performers twirl handkerchiefs or fans in their hands while dancing on stilts. Typically, in conservatory dance settings, students learn to use the fans and handkerchiefs and to imitate the types of movements performed by folk artists while walking on stilts, but the stilts themselves are omitted. Because this course was at the graduate level, Jia decided that it was important for students to experience actual stilt-walking, which she framed as a form of embodied research into folk practice. The stilts were about one and a half feet tall, made of wood, with small platforms on the top for placing the feet and long red ribbons that tied around one's ankles to secure the stilts in place. It was telling to see how the introduction of this simple folk element turned a class of highly skilled dancers into bumbling novices. We soon realized that dancing on stilts was out of the question; if we could manage to get into a standing position, let go of the barre, and take a few hesitant steps, this would be a major accomplishment for the ninety-minute class. I remember everyone lined against the walls of the studio, groping at the walls and barres for support as we struggled just to get from the ground into a standing position. Although the stilts were by no means tall by folk standards, it was a frightening experience to stand on them, much more so than I would have anticipated without having tried it myself. While this was only a short exercise, walking on the stilts helped the other students and me to better grasp the movement dynamics of the dance we were learning— the circling hands, the swaying hips, the wobbling head actions. We could see how many of these actions derived from the physicality demanded by walking on stilts. Of those among my classmates who would go on to become national folk dance instructors and choreographers in conservatory settings, many would pursue this research further by going to study with folk artists, observing stilt performances in the field, and studying historical films, photographs, and other documentation.[34]

Several of my professors at BDA were engaged in research projects that brought them into regular contact with performers in other disciplines, and they used this research to develop new movement vocabularies that they then introduced into the conservatory dance classroom. Shao Weiqiu (b. 1967), the professor who taught my Chinese classical dance studio courses in water sleeve discussed in the introduction, began conducting research on water sleeve movement and pedagogy in the early 1990s.[35] When I took her courses in 2008–9, she was conducting a long-term research project on the use of sleeves in different regional xiqu forms, supported by funding from BDA and the Beijing municipal government. As part of her research, Shao visited xiqu ensembles in different parts of China, learning and documenting the different ways sleeves were used by xiqu performers.[36] In 2004 Shao had authored the authoritative print-format conservatory curriculum that informed the teaching of sleeve dance movement in professional dance classrooms across China, and when I studied with her, she was beginning to write a new one.[37] In 2011 Shao received a national grant from the Ministry of Culture that allowed her to develop this research into an updated curriculum, which she published in DVD format two years later.[38] Another professor I had who was involved in similar long-term research was Zhang Jun (b. 1963), who taught my Chinese classical dance studio courses in sword dance. Like Shao, Zhang had been researching Chinese classical dance pedagogy since the 1990s.[39] Zhang's research dealt with the sword sequences used in Chinese martial arts and *taijiquan* (tai chi), for which he spent his mornings regularly in parks studying with local master practitioners. Between 2007 and 2011, Zhang held the first place title in the middle-age bracket of "Chen-style Taijiquan" and "Chen-style Taiji Sword" in the Beijing Martial Arts Taijiquan, Sword, and Pushing Hands Competition, a demonstration of his intensive investment of time and serious study.[40] In 2004 and 2012, Zhang published two conservatory curricula on Chinese classical dance sword dance, which resulted from the accumulation of this research and his classroom teaching experience.[41] Both Shao and Zhang regularly incorporated xiqu and martial arts knowledge into their classroom teaching, from their theorization of the aesthetic principles of sleeve and sword movement to their use of traditional terminology and explanation of movement sources and their compositional design and physical execution of dance movements. Following Zhao's metaphor of the bridge, Shao and Zhang served as conduits between the conservatory classroom and the xiqu and martial arts arenas. They made their classrooms into artistic laboratories for embodied research that transcended, but at the same time informed, their work in Chinese dance.

The type of research I experienced and observed at BDA is typical of many other dance institutions in China. Through site visits across the country, I have observed similar faculty-led dance research projects going on in most major professional dance conservatories. Chinese dance professors are constantly developing new dance vocabularies, whether based on newly discovered archeological artifacts, ethnographic studies, or inspiration from films, literature, and other cultural courses. A program is ongoing to support the creation of new basic training curricula in areas with large minority populations, so that these schools can replace ballet or Chinese classical dance basic training with new technique courses more grounded in local aesthetics. Many of these research projects also extend through transnational artistic networks. In Inner Mongolia, for example, I observed conservatory dance professors introducing new Mongol dance classes developed after studying abroad or conducting research in the country of Mongolia. Similarly, in the Yanbian Korean Autonomous Prefecture, I interviewed conservatory dance professors who had developed new courses based on research in North and South Korea. While I was studying at BDA, a teacher from Japan taught the ceremonial dance "Prince of Lanling" (Lanling wang) to a group of faculty and graduate students, as part of their research into Chinese court dance traditions. The Chinese dance professionals I have observed and worked with in China describe research, teaching, and choreography as interrelated. From the classroom level, they all fuel new innovation.

MARITIME SILK ROAD: DANCE DRAMA IN THE ERA OF "ONE BELT, ONE ROAD"

For students who graduate from professional dance conservatories such as BDA, one of the most common career trajectories, apart from teaching and research, is becoming a professional performer in a national, regional, or local song and dance ensemble. In these ensembles, a type of dance they are almost certain to perform in is the large-scale dance drama. As was the case in the late 1950s, narrative dance drama continues to be the most prevalent form of large-scale new choreography produced in the Chinese dance field today. One reason for the high status of dance dramas is the amount of funding they command in China's contemporary performing arts economy: in 2017, the China National Arts Fund (Guojia yishu jijin) set a maximum budget of 4 million RMB (approximately $635,000) for a single new large-scale dance drama production, the same amount allocated for large-scale operas and musicals.[42] Thus, the creation of a new dance drama is a major undertaking for a Chinese dance ensemble, which occupies large teams of artists and can in some cases become the signature work of a company that continues to be performed for years or even decades. As a type of choreography first developed during the Mao era, as discussed in chapter 3, the large-scale Chinese dance drama is a socialist legacy. In this section, I examine how this choreographic form has evolved and lives on in the twenty-first century.

The curtain rises to reveal a brightly lit stage buzzing with the activity of about thirty dancers, all of whom seem to be very busy. Dressed in vibrant hues of red, yellow, blue, and purple, they run, prance, and tiptoe across the stage, rolling wine barrels, suspending lanterns, and shaking out pieces of red fabric. It is act 1, the wedding scene, in *Maritime Silk Road*, a dance drama premiered in 2008 by the Beihai Song and Dance Drama Theater (Beihai gewu juyuan) in Guangxi, in southern China. At the back of the stage stands a wooden ship the size of a small house. Its masts rise up through the ceiling like pillars, and ropes stretch down on diagonals, like a circus tent. Suddenly, a spotlight lands on a woman dressed in red at the center of the stage. Peering out beneath her red bridal veil, she greets the audience with a short solo. Tipping her head from side to side, she sweeps both hands with her hips twice to the side in unison, then steps with a heel and corkscrews around, one hand draped over her shoulder. Just as she finishes her turn, a man comes leaping toward her across the stage. Dressed in all white, with a large red flower tied across his chest, he takes a short bow. The bride is rushed away by her friends, while the groom is at center stage, commencing a series of turns on one leg—one, two, three, four, five, six, seven, eight . . . he ends with a confident stance and holds up one fist triumphantly. The audience bursts into applause. Even more people join the stage, and a long celebration ensues. Finally, the couple is left alone. Under a full moon rising behind the ship's silhouette, they perform a duet of sensuous embraces that slide, seemingly without effort, into stunning lines and acrobatic lifts. In one move, the wife hugs the man's waist, after which he squats back onto his heels, and she lifts her feet off the ground, balancing her body in a horizontal hover. Then she tips her legs up into a vertical inversion, her hips poised on his knees. A swirl of cascading turns ensues. The wife lands on a rope swing and pendulums high above the stage while the groom flips and turns below. The couple ends gazing into the distance together from atop the ship's mast.

I saw *Maritime Silk Road* in August of 2013 when it was performed in Beijing, its second tour of the capital in two years.[43] Like *Gulmira* in 2015, this show took place at the National Center for the Performing Arts (NCPA), China's most prestigious performance venue, which opened in 2007. The building has a distinctive architectural design—a glass and titanium ellipsoid surrounded by an artificial lake—making it a modern cultural landmark of the capital. Chinese dance features prominently in NCPA's programming, alongside other forms of concert dance, as well as theater, singing, and orchestra. On the same night as *Maritime*, another local dance company was also performing there: TAO Dance Theater (Tao shenti juchang), at the time China's most internationally acclaimed modern/contemporary dance ensemble.[44] While TAO performed in the 500-seat downstairs Multi-functional Theater, *Maritime* was staged in the 2,400-seat upstairs Opera Hall, the same space used for operas and ballets. Several other large-scale domestic dance productions were scheduled there over the coming weeks: a Miao-themed music and dance drama, *Niangx Eb Sangb;* a ballet production featuring *Le Sacre du Printemps* and *The Firebird;* and *Confucius*, a Chinese classical dance national dance drama employing large amounts of Han-Tang vocabulary.[45] While TAO's show drew many obviously non-Chinese audience members and had a bilingual (Chinese and English) program, *Maritime* had a Chinese-only program and an audience that appeared almost entirely Chinese.

The story told in *Maritime Silk Road* is based on an actual historical sea voyage launched in the year 111 BCE that began in Hepu, part of Beihai, where the ensemble that produced the show is based. According to archaeological and textual records, the Chinese emperor Han Wudi deployed a fleet of ships to transport gold and silk from the ancient harbor of Dalang (in modern-day Hepu) to a kingdom on the Indian Ocean island now known as Sri Lanka.[46] This trip is significant because it is the first known government-orchestrated long-distance ship voyage in Chinese history, making it widely believed to be the starting point for China's formal participation in the international sea trade now known as the maritime Silk Road.[47] The fictional narrative unfolds around the story of a boatman, Dapu, who gets sent on the voyage and has to leave his wife, Ahban, on the day after their wedding, hence the scene described above. While Dapu is on his journey, a storm strikes, and he ends up saving the life of Meilisha, a princess from the kingdom on Sri Lanka. Although the princess expresses a romantic interest in Dapu, he remains faithful to Ahban. The princess is moved by Dapu's loyalty, and she asks her father to provide a ship so that Dapu can return home. In a tragic twist, Dapu returns home to find that Ahban has been waiting steadfastly for him, but because she insisted on standing lookout on the seashore, her body turned to stone. With great effort, Dapu is able to bring her back to life, and the story ends with the couple's happy reunion. A coda of red ship sails and boat workers suggests an explosion of trade on the maritime Silk Road.

Like most large-scale dance dramas staged by government-affiliated song and dance ensembles in twenty-first century China, *Maritime* is a high-budget production with a large and star-studded creative team and ample use of stage technology and special effects. A team of twenty-two creatives, including ten choreographers, worked on various aspects of the design and story, and a cast of sixty-seven dancers performed in the production. The director, Chen Weiya, and writer, Feng Shuangbai (b. 1954), are both highly influential figures in China's dance field: Chen was codirector of choreography for Beijing's Olympic Opening Ceremonies, and Feng was director of the Dance Research Institute at the Chinese National Academy of Arts. The guest soloists, Liu Fuyang (b. 1985) and Sun Xiaojuan, who danced the roles of Dapu and Ahban, are also highly sought after: both are graduates of top Chinese dance conservatory programs, and both previously worked in national-level dance ensembles and often get hired as guest soloists in dance dramas by regional ensembles.[48] In 2011 Liu also gained mainstream popularity when he appeared on *So You Think You Can Dance—China*, season 1 (Wulin zhengba) and became a top contestant.[49] Stage technology and special effects appear in the use of digitally animated projections, which appear on a translucent screen that allows them to interact with onstage action. One such projection is used to simulate an ocean map and show the trajectory of the ship's voyage along Southeast Asia and into the Indian Ocean. Another is used during the thunderstorm scene, when Meilisha falls off her ship deck and Dapu dives down to rescue her. Creating a film-like effect, the projection makes the stage appear to be temporarily submerged underwater. Using a rope suspension system, Meilisha and Dapu appear to swim in the ocean and then make their way back to the surface. According to Chen, the scene invariably earns applause from audiences.[50]

Following China's socialist national dance drama tradition, *Maritime* boasts a creative process that emphasizes research and focuses on the exploration of local and regional themes. One way this commitment appears in *Maritime* is through the production's plot. The story weaves together three types of material: textual documentation of Han Wudi's sea mission; archaeological evidence of the building of ships in Dalang harbor; and a local folk story. The story describes a rock formation called "seeking husband cliff" *(wang fu yan)*, in which a fisherman's wife, named Ahban, turns to stone from standing on the cliff edge after her husband is lost at sea.[51] The production's stage properties and soundscape also emphasize research and local sources. Hepu County contains approximately ten thousand underground tombs, most of which date to the Han dynasty (206 BCE–220 CE); it is one of the largest and best preserved collections of early tombs in China, and about one thousand of them have been excavated since the 1950s.[52] To reflect the local material culture of Dalang harbor and the maritime Silk Road of 111 BCE, *Maritime*'s designers based the props used in the production on items discovered in these tombs that are stored in the Hepu Museum. To introduce a local aesthetic to the musical score, the composer used the single-stringed zither *duxian qin*, a folk instrument specific to the Guangxi region. Apart from their value as research, these aspects of the creative process also had a commercial incentive: they helped make *Maritime* a successful regional branding tool for the Beihai area. Fixed local performances were incorporated into the Beihai tourism scheme, helping to brand "maritime silk road history" as a selling point for the city, and a Guangxi-based real estate company became a corporate sponsor for the production.[53]

The political implications of *Maritime*'s story also give it important continuities with China's socialist dance drama tradition. From its emergence in the late 1950s, national dance drama has consistently been used as an educational medium to disseminate government supported political ideals. Taking leading early works discussed in chapter 3 as examples, *Magic Lotus Lantern* promoted the idea of marriage choice and equality of the sexes, *Five Red Clouds* advocated the historical view that minority groups contributed to China's communist revolution, and *Dagger Society* advanced the idea that China's peasant revolution was an anti-imperialist cause. Similarly, in the post-Mao works discussed in chapter 5, *Flowers and Rain on the Silk Road* promoted the introduction of a market economy and international trade. In *Maritime*, the story helps promote China's expanded maritime presence in Asia, explored specifically here through China's relationship with Sri Lanka. When *Maritime* was created in 2008, the Chinese government had just launched a major infrastructure development project in Sri Lanka for the Hambantota container port shipping facility, which was set to increase China's trade capacity in the Indian Ocean.[54] In 2009 the CCP Publicity Department endorsed *Maritime* by making it one of six song and dance drama productions awarded a Best Works Award (Wu ge yi gongcheng) for the period of 2007–9.[55] In 2011 *Maritime* went on tour abroad to Malaysia and Sri Lanka, coinciding with the launching of another Sri Lankan–based, Chinese-funded port project in Colombo.[56] The content of *Maritime* very clearly supports a positive view of these Sri Lankan infrastructure projects. Two of the five acts in *Maritime* are set in the kingdom on Sri Lanka, focusing first on the warm welcome Dapu and his team receive from the local king and then on the friendship that develops between Dapu and Meilisha. The theme of mutual aid comes out clearly when Dapu rescues Meilisha and then is repaid by the king's provision of boats for Dapu to return home. Thus, the narrative presents the message that China's expanded sea presence promotes mutual benefit and political alliances.

Beyond the specific relationship between China and Sri Lanka, *Maritime* also supported the ideas behind Chinese head of state Xi Jinping's foreign policy and economic initiative, One Belt, One Road (Yi dai yi lu), introduced formally in 2013 as a main project of the Xi administration. Through its focus on the origins of China's participation in the maritime Silk Road, *Maritime* historicizes, through cultural and artistic expression, the "Road" portion of Xi's initiative, which proposes to revive the ancient sea routes by building a "21st-Century Maritime Silk Road" of economic integration linking Southeast, South, and North Asia.[57] *Maritime* enjoyed continued success during the years 2012–13, when this new initiative was first entering Chinese official discourse, with tours in Beijing and South Korea.[58] By 2013 it had been performed more than two hundred times.[59] *Maritime* was the first in a series of large-scale dance dramas to take up the theme of the maritime Silk Road, a topic that became prominent in China's government discourse starting around the CCP's Eighteenth National Congress in 2012.[60] *Maritime*'s first trip to Beijing in 2012 was part of the official festival activities held in honor of the Congress, and its second trip to Beijing, in 2013, coincided with the launch of One Belt, One Road.[61] The success of *Maritime* has led to new projects that continue its model, such as the Fujian Province Song and Dance Theater's 2014 dance drama *Dream of the Maritime Silk Road (Sihai meng xun)*. In 2015 *Dream* toured UN and EU headquarters in New York, Paris, and Brussels, and in 2016, it launched a tour of Association of Southeast Asian Nations members Malaysia, Singapore, and

Indonesia.[62] Chinese media reports explicitly called the tours cultural promotion for One Belt, One Road.

Maritime's use of dance form to express intercultural interaction and friendship also builds upon established legacies in China's socialist dance tradition. One way it does this is by using movement form as an expression of cultural identity. In the scene when Dapu and his crew arrive in the kingdom in Sri Lanka, cultural identity is expressed through the movement vocabularies performed by the local characters, which clearly differ from those danced by Chinese characters in the earlier wedding and sailing scenes. With their lower bodies, the Chinese characters perform more positions with their legs straight or somewhat bent and their knees and toes pointing forward, whereas the Sri Lankan characters have more positions with their knees deeply bent and their knees and toes turned out. With their upper bodies, the Chinese characters perform corkscrew turns and arm movements across the body with palms facing down, diagonally out, or in toward the body. The Sri Lankan characters, by contrast, use planar turns and arm movements on either side of the body with their palms facing upward. By having the characters perform these contrasting movement vocabularies, the choreographers follow a socialist tradition in which dance movement is linked to cultural identity and marks differences between ethnic, racial, or cultural groups. This practice is used, for example, in *Dagger Society* to distinguish between the Chinese and Western characters. Such differentiation is also practiced between the Chinese and Persian characters in *Flowers and Rain on the Silk Road*. Building on another socialist tradition, *Maritime* also stages dance exchange as a metaphor for intercultural friendship. In the duet between Dapu and Meilisha, the dancers teach one another their respective dance movements. For example, Dapu stands behind Meilisha, placing his hands out to the side, turning his palms up, and lifting one foot with his knees turned out, legs bent, and ankles flexed. In this scene, Meilisha is clearly the teacher and Dapu the student, and at the end Dapu thanks her for teaching him her dance. This act of learning the dances of other countries as a sign of friendship was the core principle of China's dance-as-diplomacy efforts during the 1950s and early 1960s. This practice was institutionalized in the Oriental Song and Dance Ensemble, a national troupe the Chinese government established in 1962 specifically to carry out this type of artistic exchange.[63]

The technical term used most frequently to describe *Maritime*'s choreographic mode is "historical dance drama" *(lishi wuju)*, a category first widely used to describe the 1959 national dance drama *Dagger Society*. Although the movement vocabulary used in *Maritime* is more eclectic than that in *Dagger Society*, it nevertheless inherits many aspects of the socialist legacy of national dance drama that *Dagger Society* represents in terms of its choreographic practices, intended audience, and social positioning. Like national dance dramas before it, *Maritime* exhibits a theatrical approach to dance choreography, which emphasizes qualities that appeal to popular audiences, such as linear storytelling, complex and realistic sets, high energy and virtuosic dancing, and sentimental characters. Chinese dance critic Mu Yu categorizes *Maritime* and works like it as "mainstream dance drama" *(zhuliu wuju)*—works that follow performance conventions familiar to Chinese audiences and that have attained a hegemonic status in China's dance field.[64] There is no clear equivalent to the Chinese mainstream dance drama in the United States or Western Europe, since it constitutes a category of popular large-scale art dance that has yet to emerge, for the most part, in those places. In its overall tone and target audience, the Chinese mainstream dance drama is less like ballet, contemporary dance, or the opera and more like a Broadway musical. While certainly only accessible to those in middle-class or higher income brackets, mainstream dance drama appeals to a broader target audience in China than most other dance genres. It is designed to be accessible, entertaining, and, in some cases, educational. It is perhaps in this sense that *Maritime* most closely resembles its early socialist predecessors. It is a form of mass-oriented art, aimed at being innovative and creative while moving the common viewer.

CHINESE AVANT-GARDE: ZHANG YUNFENG'S EXPERIMENTAL CLASSICISM

If *Maritime Silk Road* is created for the mainstream viewer and designed to entertain and persuade, then the choreography of Zhang Yunfeng is created for the specialist viewer and designed to tantalize and question. Zhang, who teaches Chinese dance choreography at BDA and also works as an independent choreographer with his own jointly operated Beijing-based independent studio, is one of the leading voices in twenty-first-century Chinese classical dance. As discussed in chapter 2, Chinese classical dance is a subgenre of Chinese dance that was first formulated during the early 1950s through collaborations between leading xiqu actors such as Mei Lanfang and Bai Yunsheng and a world-renowned Korean dancer, Choe Seung-hui. During the latter half of the 1950s and early 1960s, Chinese classical dance was instituted as a basic training system for students learning Chinese dance (modeled after ballet in the Soviet system), and it was also the first widely used movement vocabulary for national dance drama, modeled in works such as *Magic Lotus Lantern* (1957) and *Dagger Society* (1959). Although suppressed during the Cultural Revolution (1966–76), Chinese classical dance was revived in the post-Mao period and expanded with the introduction of new non-xiqu-based movement vocabularies, such as Dunhuang and Han-Tang. In the twenty-first century, Chinese classical dance remains a central focus of Chinese dance pedagogy and choreography. The China National Opera and Dance Drama Theater (Zhongguo geju wujuyuan), China's top professional dance ensemble for national dance drama, primarily creates work using Chinese classical dance vocabulary.

Lead roles in national dance dramas also typically go to dancers trained in Chinese classical dance. When national dance dramas are selected to tour abroad, they are often also classical-style national dance dramas.

Zhang belongs to a cohort of young choreographers who are reimagining the content and form of Chinese classical dance for the twenty-first century. Zhang first began to influence the Chinese classical dance scene in the early 2000s, when he was still an undergraduate student. Originally from Fujian Province in southeast China, Zhang was "discovered" in 1996 by a well-known dance critic, Yu Ping (b. 1954), when two of Zhang's works won second place awards in Fujian's provincial-level dance competition. In 1997 Zhang moved to Beijing to pursue a BA in choreography at BDA, and in 1999, when he was just a sophomore, his self-choreographed, self-performed solo "Wind's Chant" (Feng yin) won second place at the Beijing dance competition.[65] Zhang's career took off in the early 2000s, when he earned a series of wins at national competitions for solo choreography set on fellow BDA students: first, in 2000 and 2001, "Begonia" (Qiuhaitang, 2000) and "Wind's Chant" (Feng yin), both performed by Wu Weifeng (b. 1980), took first place in the Peach and Plum Cup and the All-China Dance Competition, respectively; then, in 2002, "Chess King" (Qi wang), performed by Hu Yan (b. 1980), and "Rouge" (Yanzhi kou), performed by Liu Yan (b. 1982), were awarded outstanding creation awards in the Lotus Cup.[66] Competition solos are by definition small in scale: they feature only one dancer and last around six to eight minutes each. Moreover, as works created for competitions typically attended only by other professional dancers, they often are not well-known to mainstream audiences. Nevertheless, these works have a profound impact on the Chinese dance field, often becoming the subject of intense debates and inspiring new choreographic directions.

In his early award-winning competition solos, Zhang established a distinctive approach to Chinese classical dance choreography that would constitute a signature personal style and a new direction for the field as whole. Zhang's approach was defined by two types of experimentation: formal experimentation by exploring new possibilities for Chinese classical dance movement and thematic experimentation by replacing representations of historical figures with representations of historical self-reflexivity as a modern condition. The second contribution was especially important, because it widened the scope of potential content for Chinese classical dance choreography. Specifically, it made the modern and contemporary Chinese literary canon a legitimate source of intertexts for Chinese classical dance creation, especially when such works contained self-conscious reflection on the relationship between the modern world and China's premodern past. Since the post–Cultural Revolution revival of Chinese dance in the late 1970s, new Chinese classical dance dramas had mainly taken up three themes: adaptations of classical literature, portrayals of premodern historical figures, or modern revolutionary narratives.[67]

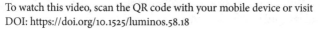

VIDEO 18. Liu Yan in "Rouge," 2002. Used with permission from Zhang Yunfeng.

To watch this video, scan the QR code with your mobile device or visit DOI: https://doi.org/10.1525/luminos.58.18

While adaptations of modern Chinese literature, such as writings by Lu Xun, Ba Jin, and Cao Yu, entered the repertoires of some Chinese ballet companies in the early 1980s, they were rare in Chinese classical dance productions through the end of the 1990s.[68] In 2002 Chinese dance critic Jin Hao reported that many of his colleagues felt that when creating Chinese classical dance choreography, "themes should be limited to ancient history and poetry of the Tang and Song Dynasties."[69] Zhang's competition works clearly challenged this perspective: "Begonia," "Chess King," and "Rouge" were all based on works of Chinese literature written in the twentieth century.[70] Through his interpretations of modern and contemporary literature in the format of Chinese classical dance, Zhang moved beyond representing the past and instead took up self-conscious reflection on modern relationships to the past as his central theme. I first look at how Zhang develops this theme in "Rouge." Then I examine two recent larger-scale productions.

"Rouge" opens with a dark stage filled with red smoke and the theme music from Wong Kar-wai's 2000 film *In the Mood for Love*, set in 1960s Hong Kong (video 18).[71] Before the dance has begun, the music sets in motion a web of associations: melancholia, romance, unfulfilled desire, nostalgia. Suddenly, a woman dashes onto the stage. She is dressed in a wine-red body-hugging *qipao* with high slits on both sides, her hair in a 1930s wave, and she is carrying a small handbag. She runs in zigzags, looking from side to side expectantly and flapping her free hand, as if searching for something through the smoke. Then she pauses and begins to walk backward, seemingly arrested by a memory. She reaches her hand out slowly behind her, and her eyes fix on a point beyond the audience. Then her tone shifts, and she is suddenly an elegant lady, head held high, aware of her own beauty. She reaches her hand up behind her head and into the air and glances upward,

FIGURE 29. Liu Yan in "Rouge," 2002. Photographer: Ye Jin.
Reproduced with permission from the private collection of Ye Jin.

miming a flirtatious laugh. Beginning with a playful sequence of spins and tiptoe-
ing steps, she then moves into a series of passionate and ecstatic poses, arms reaching out from her chest, head thrown back, legs stretching out into space. Two and
a half minutes into the work, a spotlight lands on the dancer, and her movement
stops. The sensuous string melodies are replaced with a jarring single piano chord.
Standing in place, she executes a controlled leg lift—front, to side, to vertical, and
then back. With a kick, she reaches both hands up and nearly touches her foot
behind her head, in a "reverse kick golden crown" *(daoti zijinguan)*, an acrobatic
movement from Chinese classical dance (figure 29). Another piano chord sends
a jolt through her body. She bends forward suddenly, then tries to run, but seems

to have no energy. Blue light casts an ominous glow on the stage. After a few more piano jolts, melody returns to the music, but it now has an eerie tone, like a tape player with low batteries. Matching the sound of the music, Liu moves into a series of grotesque positions. She lowers into a deep backbend, her head inverted toward the audience, her torso bobbing up and down while her arms grasp, tentacle-like, at her neck. In a floor sequence, she hyperextends her legs, bends back, and again strokes her throat. Finally, the tension breaks with the introduction of a third and final musical transition, to a crackling old-timey version of "Deep Sigh/Burying the Heart" (Changtan/Zang xin), a song used in the 1991 Stanley Kwan film *Center Stage (Ruan Lingyu)*, about the tragic life of 1930s Shanghai film actress Ruan Lingyu.[72] Liu runs toward the audience and slowly moves one hand to her mouth, eyes bright, as if she has finally found what she is looking for. She reaches downward, her brow twisted with longing, emotion seeming to pour from her chest. But then she turns and unceremoniously walks upstage, her shoulders slightly hunched, deflated. She makes a final turn and runs again to the front of the stage, as if soaking in one last bit of the glow that remains there. She snatches an imaginary something from the air and pulls it into her chest, a smile of pleasure briefly returning to her face. Then, standing in place facing the audience, she tilts her head back until it disappears from view. Still standing, one hand still on her chest, the other outstretched with the handbag dangling on her elbow, she resembles a decapitated mannequin. She reaches her right hand up to where her head would be and flutters it momentarily in space. Then, the arm falls and bounces in the air, appearing lifeless. Still frozen in her headless pose, the music and lights fade, and the dance is over.[73]

The character in this dance is based on Ruhua (sometimes translated "Fleur"), the protagonist of the 1986 novella *Rouge* by Hong Kong writer Li Bihua (a.k.a. Lillian Lee, b. 1959), made into a film in 1987 by Stanley Kwan.[74] As depicted in the film, the story has two timelines: one is set in 1934, when Ruhua is a prostitute who commits double suicide with her lover, Shi'er Shao, after the two find out they cannot be together; and one in 1987, when Ruhua's ghost returns in search of her lover, whom she believes did not die. As Rey Chow has demonstrated, the story is essentially nostalgic, on two levels: Ruhua's nostalgia for her own past romance, and her 1987 observers' nostalgia for a past in which love like Ruhua's was real. Chow writes, "*Rouge* is, in this regard, not only the story of a ghost talking nostalgically about a past romance, but is itself a romance with Ruhua, a romance that is nostalgic for superhuman lovers like her."[75] In the end, Ruhua does locate her lover, who turns out to be a disappointment: having squandered his family's fortune long ago, he is an irresponsible father and an opium addict, who works as an extra on a Hong Kong film set. In the film, Ruhua approaches Shi'er Shao on set, where actors dressed in historical costumes are flying around performing a martial arts romance. A pitiful sight, Shi'er Shao crouches in a dark corner amidst trash while taking a hit of opium. The scene highlights contrasts: his elderly appearance with the youthful image of Ruhua; his drug dependence with the magical flight of the martial arts actors.[76] Reading Kwan's film *Rouge* in the context of Hong Kong's 1997 handover from the United Kingdom to the PRC, David Eng has argued that this ending conveys a disappointment not only with Ruhua/Fleur's personal search but also with the larger idea of an imagined Chinese cultural past that her love with Shi'er Shao represents. Eng writes, "If the initial images of *Rouge* originally work by impelling our nostalgic desire for a colorful, passionate, and 'traditional' past, Fleur's final reunion with Chen [Shi'er Shao]—with the image of an inadequate, senile, and decrepit old man—challenges not only our desire for this lost past, but the very purity of these Chinese cultural 'roots' and 'origins.'"[77] The story ends with Ruhua giving her locket of rouge—a souvenir of their past love—back to Shi'er Shao and telling him she will no longer wait for him. The locket, after which the story is named, thus represents the past love that no longer exists, what Chow calls "a corpse of love."[78] Finally, Ruhua walks through a mist-filled doorway, turns back with a faint smile, and disappears.

There are clearly several layers of meaning operating in Zhang's seven-minute dance work "Rouge." The multiply intertextual soundscape, the use of a Hong Kong theme on the five-year anniversary of the handover, and the portrayal of a 1930s prostitute as a potential embodiment of Chinese tradition are among many elements that beg to be considered. Here, I will focus on how Zhang interprets the character of Ruhua through interventions in Chinese classical dance movement to articulate a self-conscious and fraught relationship to the past. From the moment Ruhua appears on stage, it is obvious that the character being portrayed is not like the premodern, mythical, or revolutionary women typically portrayed in Chinese classical dance works. Her sleeveless red *qipao*, the slits that expose her bare legs, and her handbag all mark her as part of China's early twentieth-century urban commercial culture. As Chinese dance critic Jin Qiu has noted, her way of walking is intentionally inelegant within the context of Chinese classical dance conventions.[79] She runs on her tiptoes and bounces up and down, rather than using the standard level, heel-toe walk, and her arms wave wildly without following any established form. Rather than portraying a character who embodies tradition—such as earlier female classical dance competition solos "Zhao Jun Crosses the Frontier" (Zhao Jun chusai, 1985) and "Mulan Returns" (Mulan gui, 1987), both of which are based on heroines from Chinese classical literature—"Rouge" presents a modern character tormented by romanticized attachments to the past. This relationship is in part expressed through the selective use of conventional classical dance movements. Rather than providing a coherent vocabulary, such movements enter the choreography like sudden flashes and then disappear again—a turn here, a spiral there, a kick there. The overall emotional state being portrayed, as Jin Hao points out, is one of "eagerly hoping, with anxious expectancy" and "mournful feelings of a tragic love affinity."[80] But what is she hoping for, what is the object of her love, and why is it tragic? The most concentrated use of Chinese classical dance vocabulary appears during the middle portion of the choreography, when the lighting grows dark and the menacing piano chords bring convulsive thrusts to her body. These movements are often made grotesque, such as in the dangling backbend, the hyperextended leg lines, and the balance poses that last just a bit too long for comfort. In the abstracted context of the dance setting, the object of Ruhua's romantic longing becomes muted, and what appears to torment her is not a specific love affair or a person but, rather, a generalized sense of a memory that cannot be retrieved. Throughout the dance, she repeats a movement of reaching out expectantly into space, as if trying to grab something that is not there. The last time she does this, she seems to actually have grasped whatever it is and brought it to her body. Just as she does this, however, her eyes roll back and she moves into the mannequin pose, as if the moment of retrieving the longed-after memory is also the moment of death. If Ruhua represents the past, nostalgia for the past, or an anxious longing to recover the past, then the final image gives a dark assessment of such a quest. It ends with the character presented as a headless corpse—a body still standing but without a spirit and without life.

Zhang's later works continue to develop this theme of self-conscious reflection on the role of the past in the present. In 2013 Zhang staged a major full-length production titled *Fat Tang Thin Song* (*Fei Tang shou Song*), which he co-created with another leading Chinese classical dance choreographer, Zhao Xiaogang. *Fat Tang Thin Song* was staged publicly on May 18–19 at Tianqiao Theater, an important dance venue in Beijing.[81] The work was an independent production by Beijing Idle Dancers Studio (Beijing xian wuren gongzuoshi), the Beijing-based choreography platform established jointly by Zhao and Zhang in 2009.[82] The cast of the production included many of the most famous Chinese classical dance performers in the country, the majority of whom Zhang and Zhao had collaborated with previously in competition choreography and other projects.[83] Influential senior figures in the dance field also served as artistic advisors.[84] The work attracted significant attention from Chinese dance professionals, students, and critics, and, afterward, a symposium on it was held at the PLA Art Academy in Beijing that included many of China's leading choreographers and dance scholars.[85] While both praise and critique emerged in the symposium, overall Chinese dance experts celebrated *Fat Tang Thin Song* for its serious and thoughtful approach to art and its willingness to experiment.

Fat Tang Thin Song is a ninety-minute work divided into twelve segments performed by a total of over fifty dancers.[86] While it is large in scale, however, it does not follow the model of conventional Chinese dance drama. For example, it has no unifying plot, and stage sets are minimal and impressionistic, rather than elaborate and realistic (figure 30).[87] In promotional materials, *Fat Tang Thin Song*'s format was designated not as "dance drama" (*wuju*) but as "dance theater"

FIGURE 30. Zhang Yunfeng and ensemble in *Fat Tang Thin Song*, 2013. Photographer: Ye Jin. Reproduced with permission from the private collection of Ye Jin.

(wudao juchang), after the German *Tanztheater*, a form associated with late twentieth-century choreographer Pina Bausch (1940–2009).[88] Thematically, the work is designed as a reflection on two periods in Chinese history: the Tang (618–907) and the Song (960–1279). Specifically, it takes the poetry of these periods as a point of departure. The program notes, themselves written in a poetic fashion, begin as follows: "Pacing between the lines of Tang *shi* and Song *ci*/now thinking, now dancing unrestrained . . . "[89] The terms "fat" and "thin" in the work's title suggest two opposing sensibilities, which the choreographers associate with these two historical periods and their poetry—the Tang as bold and exuberant and the Song as restrained and meticulous. Embodiments of historical figures appear throughout: imperial consort Yang Guifei and her lover, the emperor Tang Xuanzong; the poets Li Bai, Du Fu, and Su Dongpo; the monk Xuanzang; the poets Li Qingzhao and Bai Juyi; and the empress Wu Zetian. Additional figures come from Dunhuang art, a particular interest of Zhao, who is from Lanzhou and trained with Gao Jinrong (b. 1935), a leading exponent of Dunhuang dance. While these figures are all common in Chinese classical dance choreography, Zhang and Zhao intentionally portray them in unconventional ways. A duet between Li Bai and Du Fu, for example, imagines their contrasting personalities in a teacher-student relationship, rather than a more conventional depiction of them composing poetry over wine; a solo portraying Wu Zetian explores her human qualities, rather than making her grand and elusive.[90] Wu Weifeng, a leading Chinese classical dancer who portrayed the character of Li Bai, said that the choreography was unlike any dance he had performed before.[91] Tian Yi, a Fudan University graduate and dance enthusiast who

VIDEO 19. Excerpt of Zhang Yunfeng and ensemble in *Fat Tang Thin Song*, 2013. Performed at Tianqiao Theater in Beijing. Used with permission from Zhang Yunfeng and Zhao Xiaogang.

To watch this video, scan the QR code with your mobile device or visit DOI: https://doi.org/10.1525/luminos.58.19

saw *Fat Tang Thin Song*, said the portrayals differed from conceptions of these historical figures she had learned in school.[92] When explaining Zhao and Zhang's approach to the representation of historical characters, Zhao emphasizes their desire not to represent the past directly but to make it relatable as a contemporary experience. He uses the phrase *"jie shi huan hun,"* meaning "to reincarnate in another's body," to describe this approach: "We might find that the historical figure resembles our neighbor, or she possesses a type of anxiety that a contemporary person also feels."[93] The choreographers' goal, therefore, is to shorten, rather than lengthen, the distance between contemporary audiences and the past by allowing viewers to project themselves into historical scenes and empathize with grand personages, seeing them as everyday people.

To help produce this sense of closeness, Zhang and Zhao insert a modern figure into the choreography, who mediates between the audience and the historical images. The character is an older man, with graying hair and mustache, dressed in a type of floor-length black robe associated with early twentieth-century scholars. Zhang, who dances the role of this character, says he is inspired by the artist Zhang Daqian (1899–1983), who, as discussed in chapter 5, spent about two years working inside the Dunhuang caves and created the first widely influential copies of their images.[94] Zhang's character is woven through *Fat Tang Thin Song*, at times interacting with the historical figures, at times watching or being watched by them, and at times seeming to conjure them as dreams in his mind. The opening scene begins with Zhang standing under a spotlight with his back to the audience, seemingly alone (video 19). As he crouches, however, his movement reveals another dancer standing immediately upstage: a woman dressed in a rose-colored gown and tall hair ornament, like a palace dancer in a Tang painting. At first, his movements seem to bring her to life. When he moves an arm, she mirrors him in her own vocabulary. Then he stands behind her, operating her arm like a marionette. However, the relationship between them soon unravels. He reaches a hand toward her, and at the moment his fingers touch her back, she launches into a rapid spin around the stage, the layers of her gown flowing out like a top. Was it his push that started her motion, or was she eluding him? He remains on stage as she dances but does not look at her. Are they even aware of the other's presence? As Zhang walks slowly from left to right, other figures appear on stage, all moving in the opposite direction, at different speeds: a many-handed bodhisattva with red and white haloes, a buxom (drag) queen in voluminous trailing robes and glistening jewels in her hair, a thin pilgrim hunched over in rags. When the queen steps on stage, Zhang falls backward to the floor, as if blown over by a strong wind. Reclining on the ground, he continues to stare out in a dreamlike state. Is he in the Dunhuang caves, seeing the painted images swirl around him? The other figures seem oblivious to Zhang and he to them. Just as he is about to walk offstage, though, the queen glances back in his direction, then continues her procession. The title of this segment is "The High Tang Is a State of Mind." Whose state of mind? This is the scene's—perhaps the entire work's—query.

On July 7, 2014, Zhang premiered another group work that dealt with the self-conscious framing of modern relationships to the past. Titled *Rite of Spring (Chun zhi ji)* and premiered by the Beijing Dance Academy Youth Ensemble (Beijing wudao xueyuan qingnian wutuan), it engages one of the most frequently adapted pieces in European modern dance history: Vaslav Nijinsky's *Le Sacre du Printemps (Rite of Spring)*, first staged by Sergei Diaghilev's Ballets Russes in Paris in 1913. The story in *Le Sacre du Printemps* is based on an imagined "pagan" ritual, in which a virgin female is forced to dance herself to death as a sacrifice to the gods. The work drew on an aesthetic of primitivism popular in European modernist circles in the early twentieth century, and in place of the turned-out, elevated, and ethereal ballet vocabularies, it used a turned-in, stomping, and earthbound aesthetic.[95] The work's shocking rejection of ballet movement led it to be celebrated as a freeing act that helped initiate modern dance in the West.[96] According to one account, "*Sacre* was nothing less than a watershed: by pushing his vocabulary beyond the limitations imposed by four centuries of academic tradition and by enlarging the possibilities of what could be shown onstage, Nijinsky paved the way for virtually all the modern-dance developments of the twentieth century."[97] In his *Rite*, Zhang maintains both the sacrifice and the rejection of movement convention that defined Nijinsky's version. However, in Zhang's reinterpretation, the choreographer challenges the way they are typically understood. Rather than seeing them as liberating, he uses them to reflect on the destructive impulse of the modernist drive, especially what it does to modern relationships with cultural heritage.

Of all of Zhang's works to date, *Rite of Spring* is the furthest from Chinese dance in terms of its performance aesthetics and movement vocabulary. Qualities typically highlighted in Chinese dance—such as circling and spiraling trajectories, wringing and curving of the torso and limbs, and an emphasis on restraint and nuance—are absent in the work. Instead, the dancers move in straight lines and planes, their bodies remaining erect and their limbs outstretched, with an incessant explosiveness that offers little subtlety. As with Nijinsky's *Sacre*, this choice is jarring given that the company on which Zhang's *Rite* was first staged—the Beijing Dance Academy Youth Ensemble—comprises almost entirely award-winning performers of Chinese dance. In Zhang's version, the sacrificial virgin is replaced by a vase of blue and white porcelain *(qinghua ci)*—once a coveted good from China in the global economy and now a common symbol of cultural heritage in China. In the dance, the vase is carried by a whiskered old man, who tosses it to the other dancers, none of whom wants to hold onto it. Like a hot potato, the vase bounces from one hand to another, until, at the end of the piece, it smashes to the floor, breaking into an explosion of blue and white shards.[98]

Zhang's use of a movement vocabulary that rejects the conventions of Chinese dance, combined with his depiction of the blue and white vase as the sacrifice, all suggest that this is a piece reflecting on the destruction of China's cultural heritage. But who is portrayed as the agent of this destruction, and what is Zhang's message about it? Apart from the man holding the vase, the other dancers are all wearing a uniform costume—a form-fitting turtleneck leotard with long fringe on the bottom and exposed legs. The costumes are black for the male dancers and red for the women. The women wear short black wigs that resemble a bob, while the men's heads are covered in tight black fabric. The tight costumes, short hair, and exposed legs all give the dancers in black and red a modernist look within the context of Chinese dance aesthetics, especially in contrast to the old man, who is dressed in a Qing-style *tangzhuang* and knobbed skullcap. A number of scenes suggest that the people in black and red not only neglect the man and his vase but also actively attack them: in one sequence, they trample the man as he lies on the floor hugging the vase; in another, they crowd in around him until he has to hold the vase up in the air to avoid its being pushed out of his hands. In this scene, the dancers enhance their menacing appearance by pulling their turtlenecks up over their mouths and noses and flapping both hands with fingers splayed out next to their cheeks, looking like fangs. When asked about his inspiration for the work, Zhang pointed to the social movements of twentieth-century Chinese history: "Really, starting with the May Fourth era, every social movement has been one of destruction and then rebuilding, destruction and then rebuilding . . . We have always been in this kind of social environment, experiencing a kind of crisis. I think this kind of crisis is very terrifying."[99] If we take Zhang at his word, the piece is not necessarily about the destruction of cultural heritage itself but about the social environment that precipitates a sense of crisis linked to reflection on the past. Once again, Zhang turns the audience's attention away from the past itself and toward a self-conscious concern with the past and with what this concern produces in the modern era.

Zhang's concern with the role of the past in modern experience harks back to a long history of artistic creation in China that deals with these themes. Since at least the beginning of the twentieth century, Chinese artists and intellectuals have grappled with the dual problem of how to overcome the limitations of traditional culture to create a modern society while inheriting cultural foundations that support collective identities and build meaningful links to the past. This challenge has been at the heart of Chinese dance, an art form whose fundamental concern has been making local performance culture span the divide between past and present to speak meaningfully to the future. In Zhang's work, as in the work of many contemporary choreographers of Chinese dance, engagement with local material comes through in multiple ways. We find it in modern literary and film references, engagement with historical knowledge and the classical literary tradition, and uses of material culture such as costumes and props, in addition, of course, to diverse movement forms. What makes these works, and Chinese dance as a whole, cohere as a genre today is this use of local culture as a starting point for generating new art and new ideas. Chinese dance is not defined by how much it preserves traditional performance practices in some imagined original or protected form. Rather, it is defined by its engagement with a dynamic constellation of sources and references that, while constantly shifting, is believed to be centered in China. As this constellation changes, Chinese dance changes as well.

CONCLUSION: RED LEGACIES

In their edited collection *Red Legacies in China*, Jie Li and Enhua Zhang consider the cultural dimensions of what Li calls "remainders and reminders of the Communist Revolution in the post-Mao era."[100] In postsocialist China, it has become increasingly important to understand and evaluate the legacies of socialism, especially as direct knowledge of those periods fades with the generations who lived through and remember them. As Li points out, the continued impact of red legacies in China today needs to be understood not only through examination of experiences and memories rooted in direct experience but also through constructed histories and "what is transmittable across generations."[101] One potential loss in this process of transmission is the knowledge of what cultural practices are red legacies. Chinese dance is one such cultural practice whose identity as a red legacy is easily forgotten because so much about it does not seem to fit with stereotypical ideas about Maoist culture dominant today. Its decentralized historical origins; its focus on local aesthetics and historical and folk forms; its concern with the expression of local, regional, and ethnic diversity; and its intersectional approach to political representation all make Chinese dance seem inconsistent with the family resemblances typically assumed to obtain for China's socialist culture. Perhaps the most significant factor that generates this feeling is the suppression of Chinese dance during the Cultural Revolution, a time that for many has become equivalent to the Maoist era. Due to this imagined equivalence, assigning the label "red" to anything not consistent with Cultural Revolution culture produces cognitive and affective dissonance. Such dissonance, I believe, is nevertheless necessary to gain a deeper understanding of China's socialist-era culture. Recognizing the redness of Chinese dance is not only about setting right the historical record; it also means dismantling monolithic conceptions of Chinese socialist culture and admitting the aesthetic and political multiplicities that coexist within this legacy.

The fact that Chinese dance is a red legacy that continues to thrive in China today makes it all the more important for considering the nature and ongoing impacts of the socialist era in contemporary China. What has allowed Chinese dance to transcend its historical moment of origin and remain embedded in the fabric of artistic practice in the postsocialist era, when so many other aspects of the Maoist world have either gone out of popularity or reemerged but only within the explicit frame of "red culture"? Chinese dance is a red legacy that has made a successful transition into the post-Mao period and has managed to retain some of its socialist values while still being accepted by artists and audiences alike as a meaningful and enjoyable medium for aesthetic expression. What can this status tell us about other red legacies that remain active in Chinese culture but are not typically recognized as such? Why have some legacies been resilient and adaptive, while others remain fixed as symbols of a past time?

In the case of Chinese dance, one feature that has contributed to the resilience of this form is its emphasis on constant renewal and change. From the genre's beginnings, practitioners of Chinese dance have insisted that research and innovation are essential processes in the construction of a national dance form, and they have treated this project as always ongoing and unfinished. During the socialist era, these values became regular components of dance work, consolidated through the institutional habits of Chinese dance schools, research institutes, and performance ensembles. With the revival of these bodies in the immediate post-Mao period, these practices were carried forward into postsocialist dance work, where they provided a framework for the continuous infusion of new form and content, giving the genre the flexibility to transform and remain relevant with the times. As long as there is funding for these programs and dancers continue to learn the values and skills necessary to research and innovate, Chinese dance will go on transforming and will maintain its dynamism for decades to come.

GLOSSARY OF CHINESE TERMS

PEOPLE

Aytilla Qasim	阿依吐拉
Bai Hua	白桦
Bai Shuxiang	白淑湘
Bai Yunsheng	白云生
Baoyinbatu	宝音巴图
Chai Huaimin	柴怀民
Chang Shuhong	常书鸿
Chen Ailian	陈爱莲
Chen, Eugene	陈友仁
Chen, Jack	陈伊范
Chen Jinqing	陈锦清
Chen, Sylvia	陈雪兰/陈锡兰
Chen Weiya	陈维亚
Chen Yunyi	陈韫仪
Choe Seung-hui	崔承喜
Cui Meishan	崔美善
Dai Ailian	戴爱莲
Dao Meilan	刀美兰
Dilaram Mahamatimin	地拉热·买买提依明
Fang Zhaoyuan	方昭媛

Feng Guopei	冯国佩
Feng Shuangbai	冯双白
Gao Di'an	高地安
Gao Jinrong	高金荣
Guang Weiran	光未然
Gulmira Mamat	古丽米娜·麦麦提
Guo Lei	郭磊
Han Shichang	韩世昌
Hanayanagi Tokubee	花柳德兵卫
He Feiguang	何非光
He Yanyun	贺燕云
Hou Yongkui	侯永奎
Hu Guogang	胡果刚
Hu Rongrong	胡蓉蓉
Hu Sha	胡沙
Hu Yan	胡岩
Huang Boshou	黄伯寿
Ishii Baku	石井漠
Jasur Tursun	加苏尔·吐尔逊
Jia Meina	贾美娜
Jia Zuoguang	贾作光
Jiang Zuhui	蒋祖慧
Jin Ming	金明
Jin Ou	金欧
Lan Hang	蓝珩
Li Bihua	李碧华
Li Chengxiang	李承祥
Li Jinhui	黎锦晖
Li Shaochun	李少春
Li Zhengyi	李正一
Li Zhonglin	李仲林
Liang Lun	梁伦
Liu Fuyang	刘福洋
Liu Min	刘敏
Liu Qingtang	刘庆棠
Liu Shaoxiong	刘少雄

Liu Yan	刘岩
Long Yinpei	隆荫培
Ma Sicong	马思聪
Ma Xianglin	马祥麟
Mao Xiang	毛相
Mei Lanfang	梅兰芳
Ming Wenjun	明文军
Ming Zhi	明之
Modegema	莫德格玛
Oumijiacan	欧米加参
Ouyang Yuqian	欧阳予倩
Pan Zhitao	潘志涛
Peng Song	彭松
Piao Rongyuan	朴容媛
Qemberxanim	康巴尔汗·艾买提
Shao Weiqiu	邵未秋
Sheng Jie	盛婕
Shi Mingxin	施明新
Shu Qiao	舒巧
Siqintariha	斯琴塔日哈
Song Qingling	宋庆龄
Sun Daizhang	孙玳璋
Sun Xiaojuan	孙晓娟
Tao Xingzhi	陶行知
Tian Han	田汉
Tsering Tashi	才让扎西
Wang Kun	王昆
Wang Shan	王珊
Wang Shiqi	王世琦
Wu Weifeng	武巍峰
Wu Xiaobang	吴晓邦
Xin Miaomiao	新苗苗
Yang Guifei	杨贵妃
Yang Liping	杨丽萍
Yang Ying	杨颖
Yang Zongguang	杨宗光

Ye Ning	叶宁
Ye Qianyu	叶浅予
Yin Falu	阴法鲁
You Huihai	游惠海
Yu Ping	于平
Yu Rongling	裕容龄
Yu Wanjiao	玉婉娇
Zha Lie	查烈
Zhang Jun	张均
Zhang Jun	张军
Zhang Ke	张苛
Zhang Minxin	章民新
Zhang Xiaomei	张晓梅
Zhang Xu	张旭
Zhang Yunfeng	张云峰
Zhao Dan	赵丹
Zhao Dexian	赵得贤
Zhao Qing	赵青
Zhao Tiechun	赵铁春
Zhao Xiaogang	赵小刚
Zheng Baoyun	郑宝云
Zhong Dianfei	钟惦棐
Zhou Guobao	周国宝
Zhou Weizhi	周巍峙
Zi Huayun	资华筠
Zuo Qing	左青
Zuohala Shahemayiwa	左哈拉·莎赫玛依娃

INSTITUTIONS

All-China Dance Workers Association *Quanguo wudao gongzuozhe xiehui* 全国舞蹈工作者协会

Beihai Song and Dance Drama Theater *Beihai gewu juyuan* 北海歌舞剧院

Beijing Ballet School *Beijing balei wudao xuexiao* 北京芭蕾舞蹈学校

Beijing Dance Academy *Beijing wudao xueyuan* 北京舞蹈学院

Beijing Dance Academy Youth Ensemble *Beijing wudao xueyuan qingnian wutuan* 北京舞蹈学院青年舞团

Beijing Dance School   *Beijing wudao xuexiao*   北京舞蹈学校

Beijing Idle Dancers Studio   *Beijing xian wuren gongzuoshi*   北京闲舞人工作室

Central Academy of Drama   *Zhongyang xiju xueyuan*   中央戏剧学院

Central Academy of Drama Attached Song and Dance Theater   *Zhongyang xiju xueyuan fushu gewu juyuan*   中央戏剧学院附属歌舞剧院

Central Academy of Nationalities   *Zhongyang minzu xueyuan*   中央民族学院

Central Experimental Opera Theater   *Zhongyang shiyan gejuyuan*   中央实验歌剧院

Central Nationalities Song and Dance Ensemble   *Zhongyang minzu gewutuan* 中央民族歌舞团

Central South Military Art School   *Zhongnan budui yishu xueyuan*   中南部队艺术学院

Changchun City Cultural Work Troupe   *Changchun shi wengongtuan*   长春市文工团

China Art Ensemble   *Zhongguo yishutuan*   中国艺术团

China Dance Drama Ensemble   *Zhongguo wujutuan*   中国舞剧团

China Dance School   *Zhongguo wudao xuexiao*   中国舞蹈学校

China Music and Dance Academy   *Zhongguo yuewu xueyuan*   中国乐舞学院

China Music, Dance, and Drama Society   *Zhongguo gewuju yishe*   中国歌舞剧艺社

China National Arts Fund   *Guojia yishu jijin*   国家艺术基金

China National Opera and Dance Drama Theater   *Zhongguo geju wujuyuan*   中国歌剧舞剧院

Chinese Dance Art Society   *Zhongguo wudao yishu she*   中国舞蹈艺术社

Chinese Dance Research Association   *Zhonghua wudao yanjiuhui*   中华舞蹈研究会

Chinese Folk Music and Dance Research Society Dance Group   *Zhongguo minjian yuewu yanjiu she wuyongzu*   中国民间乐舞研究社舞踊组

Chinese People's Political Consultative Congress   *Zhongguo renmin zhengzhi xieshang huiyi*   中国人民政治协商会议

Choe Seung-hui Dance Research Course   *Cui Chengxi wudao yanjiu ban*   崔承喜舞蹈研究班

Dance Drama Research Group   *Wuju yanjiu xiaozu*   舞剧研究小组

Department of European Dance Drama   *Ouzhou wuju ke*   欧洲舞剧科

Department of Minority Nationality Arts   *Shaoshu minzu yishu xi*   少数民族艺术系

Department of National Dance Drama   *Minzu wuju ke*   民族舞剧科

Department of National Folk Dance   *Zhongguo minzu minjian wu xi*   中国民族民间舞系

Folk Xiqu Ensemble   *Minjian xiqutuan*   民间戏曲团

Gansu Provincial Song and Dance Theater   *Gansu sheng gewu juyuan*   甘肃省歌舞剧院

General Political Department Song and Dance Ensemble   *Zongzheng gewutuan*   总政歌舞团

Guangzhou Military Soldier Song and Dance Ensemble *Guangzhou budui zhanshi gewutuan* 广州部队战士歌舞团

Hainan Nationalities Song and Dance Ensemble *Hainan minzu gewutuan* 海南民族歌舞团

Inner Mongolia Cultural Work Troupe *Neimenggu wengongtuan* 内蒙古文工团

Inner Mongolia Song and Dance Ensemble *Neimenggu gewutuan* 内蒙古歌舞团

National Ballet of China *Zhongyang balei wutuan* 中央芭蕾舞团

National Centre for the Performing Arts *Guojia dajuyuan* 国家大剧院

New Peace Traveling Ensemble *Xin'an lüxingtuan* 新安旅行团

Northeast Lu Xun Arts Academy *Dongbei Lu Xun yishu xueyuan* 东北鲁迅艺术学院

Northwest Art Academy *Xibei yishu xueyuan* 西北艺术学院

Oriental Dance Research Institute *Dongfang wudao yanjiusuo* 东方舞蹈研究所

Oriental Music and Dance Course *Dongfang yinyue wudao ban* 东方音乐舞蹈班

Oriental Song and Dance Ensemble *Dongfang gewutuan* 东方歌舞团

Shanghai Dance School *Shanghai wudao xuexiao* 上海舞蹈学校

Shanghai Experimental Opera Theater *Shanghai shiyan gejuyuan* 上海实验歌剧院

Shenyang Army Cultural Work Troupe *Shenyang budui wengongtuan* 沈阳部队文工团

South China Cultural Work Troupe *Huanan wengongtuan* 华南文工团

TAO Dance Theater *Tao shenti juchang* 陶身体剧场

Tibet Military Area Political Department Cultural Work Troupe *Xizang junqu zhengzhi bu wengongtuan* 西藏军区政治部文工团

Worker Peasant Soldier Ballet Ensemble *Gongnongbing balei wujutuan* 工农兵芭蕾舞剧团

World Festival of Youth and Students *Shijie qingnian lianhuanjie* 世界青年联欢节

Xinjiang Art Academy Dance Department *Xinjiang yishu xueyuan wudao xi* 新疆艺术学院舞蹈系

Xishuangbanna Nationality Cultural Work Team *Xishuangbanna minzu gewutuan* 西双版纳民族歌舞团

DANCES, FILMS, AND OTHER ARTISTIC WORKS

"Amitābha" *Mituo fu* 弥托福

"Apsaras" *Feitian* 飞天

"Auspicious Dance" *Jixiang wu* 吉祥舞

"Axi Moon Dance" *Axi tiao yue* 阿细跳月

"Ba'an xianzi" *Ba'an xianzi* 巴安弦子

"Begonia" *Qiuhaitang* 秋海棠

Bindweed Flower Manluo hua   蔓萝花

"Blacksmith Dance"   *Duangong wu*   锻工舞

"Bow Dance"   *Gong wu*   弓舞

Braving Wind and Waves to Liberate Hainan   *Chengfengpolang jiefang Hainan*   乘风破浪解放海南

"Bright"   *Minglang*   明朗

Brother and Sister Open the Wasteland   *Xiongmei kaihuang*   兄妹开荒

Butterfly Loves Flower   *Die lian hua*   蝶恋花

Center Stage   *Ruan lingyu*   阮玲玉

"Chess King"   *Qi wang*   棋王

Children of the Grassland   *Caoyuan ernü*   草原儿女

Colored Butterflies Fluttering About   *Caidie fenfei*   彩蝶纷飞

Congo River Is Roaring   *Gangguohe zai nuhou*   刚果河在怒吼

"Cup and Bowl Dance"   *Zhong wan wu*   盅碗舞

Dagger Society   *Xiaodao hui*   小刀会

"Dance Is Life"   *Xin dong wu dong*   心动舞动

"Dance of the Prodigal Nobleman"   *Xianlang wu*   闲良舞

"Dance Song of Youth"   *Qingchun wuqu*   青春舞曲

Dances of the Great Land   *Dadi zhi wu*   大地之舞

"Dancing the Spring Cow"   *Tiao chun niu*   跳春牛

"Deep Sigh/Burying the Heart"   *Changtan/Zang xin*   长叹/葬心

Dream of the Maritime Silk Road   *Sihai meng xun*   丝海梦寻

"Duan Gong Exorcises Ghosts"   *Duan gong qugui*   端公驱鬼

Dynamic Yunnan   *Yunnan yingxiang*   云南映象

East Is Red   *Dongfang hong*   东方红

East Wind Forever   *Dongfeng wanli*   东风万里

Eight Women Ode   *Ba nü song*   八女颂

"Fan Bone"   *Shan gu*   扇骨

"Farmer Dance"   *Nongzuo wu*   农作舞

Fat Tang Thin Song   *Fei Tang shou Song*   肥唐瘦宋

"Female Civilian Soldiers"   *Nü minbing*   女民兵

"Fires of Fury Are Burning"   *Nuhuo zai ranshao*   怒火在燃烧

Fires of Fury in the Coconut Grove   *Yelin nuhuo*   椰林怒火

"Five-Mile Pagoda"   *Wu li ting*   五里亭

Five Red Clouds   *Wu duo hongyun*   五朵红云

Flag   *Qi*   旗

Flowers and Rain on the Silk Road   *Silu hua yu*   丝路花雨

Fountain of Tears   *Lei quan*   泪泉

"Friendship"   *Youyi*   友谊

Frontier Folk Dance Introduction Plenary   *Bianjiang minjian wudao jieshao dahui*   边疆民间舞蹈介绍大会

Frontier Music and Dance Plenary   *Bianjiang yinyue wudao dahui*   边疆音乐舞蹈大会

"Girl in Bells"   *Lingdang shaonü*   铃铛少女

Goddess Scatters Flowers   *Tiannü sanhua*   天女散花

"Goddess Yi Zhu"   *Yi Zhu tiannü*   意珠天女

"Golden Peacock"   *Jinse de kongque*   金色的孔雀

"Goose Dance"   *Yan wu*   雁舞

Great Changes in Liang Mountain   *Liangshan jubian*   凉山巨变

"Great Yangge"   *Da yangge*   大秧歌

"Hand drum dance"   *Shougu wu*   手鼓舞

"Holiday Cheer"   *Jieri de huanle*   节日的欢乐

"Hope"   *Xiwang*   希望

Hou Yi and Chang'e   *Houyi yu Chang'e*   后羿与嫦娥

"Hourglass Drum Dance"   *Changgu wu*   长鼓舞

Humans Must Overcome Heaven   *Ren ding sheng tian*   人定胜天

Hundred Phoenixes Face the Sun   *Bai feng chaoyang*   百凤朝阳

In the Mood for Love   *Faa yeung nin wa/Hua yang nian hua*   花样年华

"Interrupted Dream"   *Jing meng*   惊梦

"Jiarong Drinking Party"   *Jiarong jiuhui*   嘉戎酒会

"Kanba'erhan"   *Kanba'erhan*   坎巴尔韩

Lady of the Sea   *Yu meiren*   鱼美人

"Laundry Song"   *Xi yi ge*   洗衣歌

"Lion Dance"   *Shi wu*   狮舞

Liu Hulan   *Liu Hulan*   刘胡兰

Long Live the People's Victory   *Renmin shengli wansui*   人民胜利万岁

"Long Silk Dance"   *Changchou wu*   长绸舞

"Lotus Dance"   *Hehua wu*   荷花舞

"Luoluo Love Song"   *Luoluo qingge*   倮倮情歌

Magic Lotus Lantern   *Bao liandeng*   宝莲灯

Maritime Silk Road   *Bihai silu*   碧海丝路

"Marriage"   *Jiehun*   结婚

"Militiawomen of the Grassland"   *Caoyuan nüminbing*   草原女民兵

"Mortar and Pestle"   *Chong jiu*   舂臼

Mother Calls   *Muqin zai zhaohuan*   母亲在召唤

"Mulan Returns"   *Mulan gui*   木兰归

"The Mute Carries the Cripple"   *Yazi bei feng*   哑子背疯

"Nostalgia"   *Si xiang qu*   思乡曲

Notre-Dame de Paris   *Bali shengmuyuan*   巴黎圣母院

Ode to Wind and Thunder   *Feng lei song*   风雷颂

Ode to Yimeng   *Yimeng song*   沂蒙颂

"Ordos"   *E'erduosi*   鄂尔多斯

"Ordos Dance"   *E'erduosi wu*   鄂尔多斯舞

"Oroqen dance"   *Elunchun wu*   鄂伦春舞

"Pasture Horse"   *Muma wu*   牧马舞

Peace Dove   *Heping ge*   和平鸽

"Peacock Dance"   *Kongque wu*   孔雀舞

"Peacock Duet"   *Shuangren kongque wu*   双人孔雀舞

The Peacock Princess   *Kongque gongzhu*   孔雀公主

"The People Closest to the Sun"   *Li taiyang zui jin de ren*   离太阳最近的人

People's Communes Are Good   *Renmin gongshe hao*   人民公社好

"Phoenix Picking Peonies"   *Feng cai mudan*   凤采牡丹

"Picking Flowers"   *Cai hua*   采花

"Picking Grapes"   *Zhai putao*   摘葡萄

"Picking Tea and Catching Butterflies"   *Caicha pudie*   采茶扑蝶

PLA Third All-Military Arts Festival   *Di san jie quanjun wenyi huiyan*   第三届全军文
艺会演

"Plate Dance"   *Panzi wu*   盘子舞

Poppy Flowers   *Yingsu hua*   罂粟花

"Prince of Lanling"   *Lanling wang*   蘭陵王

Princess Wencheng   *Wencheng gongzhu*   文成公主

"Prisoner's Cage Dance"   *Qiulong wu*   囚笼舞

Rainbow Caihong   彩虹

"Rainbow"   *Caihong*   彩虹

Rather Die Than Submit   *Ning si bu qu*   宁死不屈

"Reba on the Grassland"   *Caoyuan shang de Reba*   草原上的热巴

Red Detachment of Women   *Hongse niangzi jun*   红色娘子军

"Red Silk Dance"   *Hongchou wu*   红绸舞

Red Sister-in-Law   *Hong sao*   红嫂

Reformed Peasant Slaves Face the Sun   *Fanshen nongnu xiang taiyang*   翻身农奴向太阳

Remain in Combat Readiness   *Yanzhenyidai*   严阵以待

Rice Husking Dance   *Chong mi wu*   舂米舞

Rite of Spring   *Chun zhi ji*   春之祭

"Rouge"   *Yanzhi kou*   胭脂扣

"Running Donkey"   *Pao lü*   跑驴

"Sale"   *Mai*   卖

"Shepherd Flute"   *Mu di*   牧笛

So You Think You Can Dance—China, season 1   *Wulin zhengba*   舞林争霸

So You Think You Can Dance—China, season 2   *Zhongguo hao wudao*   中国好舞蹈

Songs of Tengri Tagh   *Tianshan zhi ge*   天山之歌

Spanish Daughter   *Xibanya nü'er*   西班牙女儿

"Spirit of the Peacock"   *Que zhi ling*   雀之灵

Splitting the Mountain to Save Mother   *Pi shan jiu mu*   劈山救母

"Spouses"   *Laoban*   老伴

"Spring Outing"   *Chun you*   春游

"Spring, River, and Flowers on a Moonlit Night"   *Chun jiang hua yueye*   春江花月夜

Stealing Immortal Herbs   *Dao xiancao*   盗仙草

"The Story of the Red Flag"   *Hongqi de gushi*   红旗的故事

Sun Rises in the East   *Xuri dongsheng*   旭日东升

"Sunflowers Face the Sun"   *Kuihua xiang taiyang*   葵花向太阳

"Sword Dance"   *Jian wu*   剑舞

"Tap Dance"   *Tita wu*   踢踏舞

"Third Day of the Third Month"   *San yue san*   三月三

Thunder Peak Pagoda Leifeng ta   雷峰塔

"A Twisting Yangge Performer"   *Yi ge niu yangge de ren*   一个扭秧歌的人

"Waist Drum Dance"   *Yaogu wu*   腰鼓舞

We Walk on the Great Road   *Women zou zai dalu shang*   我们走在大路上

White Haired Girl   *Baimao nü*   白毛女

White Snake   *Baishe zhuan*   白蛇传

"Wind's Chant"   *Feng yin*   风吟

Woman of Benevolent Actions   *Zhuowa sangmu*   卓瓦桑姆

Wulan Bao   *Wulan bao*   乌兰保

"Yao Drum"   *Yaoren zhi gu*   瑶人之鼓

Yi Compatriots Music and Dance Performance   *Yibao yinyue wuyonghui*   夷胞音乐舞踊会

"Young Patriot"   *Shaonian aiguozhe*   少年爱国者

Zhao Jun Crosses the Frontier"   *Zhao Jun chusai*   昭君出塞

Zhao Shutun and Nanmunuonuo   *Zhao Shutun yu Nanmunuonuo*   召树屯与婻木诺（婻）娜

PERIODICALS

Beijing wudao xueyuan xuebao	北京舞蹈学院学报
Bianjiang wenyi	边疆文艺
Caodi	草地
Changjiang daxue xuebao	长江大学学报
Daguanyuan zhoubao	大观园周报
Dazhong dianying	大众电影
Dazhong yingxun	大众影讯
Diansheng zhoukan	电声周刊
Dianying	电影
Dianying xinwen	电影新闻
Dianying zhi you	电影之友
Dongnan feng	东南风
Duhui	都会
Funü wenhua	妇女文化
Gengyun	耕耘
Guangming ribao	光明日报
Haichao zhoukan	海潮周刊
Haifeng	海风
Haijing	海晶
Haiyan	海燕
Han haichao	瀚海潮
Hong meigui	红玫瑰
Huanqiu	寰球
Jia	家
Jianguo	建国
Jiefangjun yishu xueyuan xuebao	解放军艺术学院学报
Jin ri huakan	今日画刊
Jin ri Zhongguo	今日中国
Keguan	客观
Kexue zixun	科学咨询
Kuaihuo lin	快活林

Lianhe zhoubao	联合周报
Meigui huabao	玫瑰画报
Meishu zazhi	美术杂志
Minjian	民间
Minzu yishu yanjiu	民族艺术研究
Nanfang ribao	南方日报
Nanjing zhongyang ribao zhoukan	南京中央日报周刊
Piao	飘
Qi ri tan	七日谈
Qiaoyuan	侨园
Qingming	清明
Qingqing dianying	青青电影
Renmin huabao	人民画报
Renmin ribao	人民日报
Renmin xiju	人民戏剧
Renmin yinyue	人民音乐
Renmin zhoukan	人民周刊
Ri yue tan	日月谭
San liu jiu huabao	三六九画报
Shaanxi xiju	陕西戏剧
Shandong Jiaozhou yangge	山东胶州秧歌
Shanghai tan	上海滩
Shanghai texie	上海特写
Shenbao	申报
Sixiang zhanxian	思想战线
Taipingyang zhoubao	太平洋周报
Tongzhou gongjin	同舟共进
Wanhuatong	万花筒
Wencui	文萃
Wenhua jiaoliu	文化交流
Wenhui bao	文汇报
Wenxian	文献
Wenyi bao	文艺报
Wenyi yanjiu	文艺研究
Wudao	舞蹈

Wudao congkan	舞蹈丛刊
Wudao pinglun	舞蹈评论
Wudao tongxun	舞蹈通讯
Wudao xuexi ziliao	舞蹈学习资料
Wudao yanjiu	舞蹈研究
Xi shijie	戏世界
Xiang-Hai huabao	香海画报
Xiao Shanghairen	小上海人
Xibei tongxun	西北通讯
Xiju bao	戏剧报
Xiju zazhi	戏剧杂志
Xin guancha	新观察
Xin yiyuan	新艺苑
Xingye youcheng	兴业邮乘
Xinjiang yishu	新疆艺术
Xinmin bao	新民报
Xinxing	新星
Xuesheng bao	学生报
Yan-Huang chunqiu	炎黄春秋
Yanjing xinwen	燕京新闻
Yi si qi huabao	一四七画报
Yishu bai jia	艺术百家
Yishu pinglun	艺术评论
Yiwen huabao	艺文画报
Yiyou	益友
Yucai jianjie tongxun	育才简介通讯
Zazhi	杂志
Zhong-Mei zhoubao	中美周报
Zhong-Su wenhua zazhi	中苏文化杂志
Zhong yi	中艺
Zhongguo dianying	中国电影
Zhongguo yitan huabao	中国艺坛画报
Zhongguo yitan ribao	中国艺坛日报
Zhonghua quanguo tiyu xiejinhui tiyu tongxun	中华全国体育协进会体育通讯
Zhongyang ribao	中央日报

OTHER TERMS

academic-style folk dance   *xueyuan pai minjian wu*   学院派民间舞

Anhui flower drum lamp   *Anhui huagudeng*   安徽花鼓灯

apsara   *feitian*   飞天

bel canto singing style   *meisheng changfa*   美声唱法

bengbengxi   *bengbengxi*   蹦蹦戏

Best Works Award   *Wu ge yi gongcheng jiang*   五个一工程奖

big head babies   *datou wawa*   大头娃娃

blue and white porcelain   *qinghua ci*   青花瓷

bow step   *gong bu*   弓步

brisk steps   *suibu*   碎步

Chinese classical dance   *Zhongguo gudian wu*   中国古典舞

Chinese dance   *Zhongguo wudao*   中国舞蹈

Chinese modern dance   *Zhongguo xiandai wu*   中国现代舞

Chinese nation   *Zhonghua minzu*   中华民族

Chinese national folk dance   *Zhongguo minzu minjian wu*   中国民族民间舞

Chinese opera   *xiqu*   戏曲

ci   *ci*   词

circling the stage   *pao yuanchang*   跑圆场

clapper-talk   *kuaiban*   快板

classical   *gudian*   古典

coquettish female   *huadan*   花旦

correctively remove foreign/Western flavor   *gaidiao yangwei*   改掉洋味

counterpoint   *duiwei*   对位

crouching fish   *wo yu*   卧鱼

Dai dance   *Daizu wu*   傣族舞

dance   *wudao/wu*   舞蹈/舞

dance drama   *wuju*   舞剧

dance-theater   *wudao juchang*   舞蹈剧场

dance work   *wudao gongzuo*   舞蹈工作

diagonal walk   *xiebu*   斜步

Dunhuang   *Dunhuang*   敦煌

Dunhuang bihua yuewu   *Dunhuang bihua yuewu*   敦煌壁画乐舞

Dunhuang dance   *Dunhuang wu*   敦煌舞

entry and exit   *chu ru chang*   出入场

errenzhuan   errenzhuan   二人转

everyday movements   shenghuo dongzuo   生活动作

expressions   biaoqing   表情

eye contact   duikan   对看

falling in love   xiang'ai   相爱

fanshen   fanshen   翻身

flower drum theater   huaguxi   花鼓戏

flower lantern   huadeng   花灯

flower lantern drama   huadengxi   花灯戏

folk   minjian   民间

folk artists   yiren   艺人

foreign/Western   yang   洋

foreign/Western dogma   yang jiaotiao   洋教条

free form   ziyou xingshi   自由形式

Frontier Dance   bianjiang wu   边疆舞

gait   taibu   台步

graphic storybook   lianhuanhua   连环画

groveling   baidao   拜倒

Gui opera   Guiju   桂剧

guozhuang   guozhuang   锅庄

Han nationality folk dance   Hanzu minjian wu   汉族民间舞

Han-Tang   Han-Tang   汉唐

Han-Tang Chinese classical dance   Han-Tang Zhongguo gudianwu
汉唐中国古典舞

historical dance drama   lishi wuju   历史舞剧

horizontal walk   hengbu   横步

Hua nationality dance   Huazu wudao   华族舞

jianghu   jianghu   江湖

inherit and develop   jicheng yu fazhan   继承与发展

Korean dance   Chaoxian wu   朝鲜舞

Kun opera   Kunqu   昆曲

large character posters   dazi bao   大字报

large-scale   daxing   大型

large-scale music and dance historical epic   daxing yinyue wudao shishi
大型音乐舞蹈史诗

lotus lamp   hehua deng/lianhua deng   荷花灯/莲花灯

mainstream dance drama   *zhuliu wuju*   主流舞剧

martial female   *wudan*   武旦

massification   *qunzhonghua*   群众化

military dance   *junlü wudao*   军旅舞蹈

model works   *yangban xi*   样板戏

Mongol dance   *Menggu wu*   蒙古舞

national consciousness   *minzu yishi*   民族意识

national dance   *minzu wudao*   民族舞蹈

national dance drama   *minzu wuju*   民族舞剧

national forms   *minzu xingshi*   民族形式

national orchestra   *minzu guanxian yuetuan*   民族管弦乐团

national singing style   *minzu changfa*   民族唱法

nationality cultural work troupes   *minzu wengongtuan*   民族文工团

nationalization   *minzuhua*   民族化

natural law   *ziran faze*   自然法则

New Dance   *xinxing wuyong*   新兴舞踊

Northeastern Han folk dance   *Dongbei yangge*   东北秧歌

"One Belt, One Road"   *Yi dai yi lu*   一带一路

orchid finger   *lanhua zhi*   兰花指

Oriental Dance   *Dongfang wu*   东方舞

original-environment folk dance   *yuanshengtai minjian wu*   原生态民间舞

Peking opera   *Jingju*   京剧

piliwu   *piliwu*   霹雳舞

raised sleeve   *yangxiu*   扬袖

reincarnate in another's body   *jie shi huan hun*   借尸还魂

remolding   *gaizao*   改造

reverse kick golden crown   *daoti zijinguan*   倒踢紫金冠

reverse-played pipa   *fantan pipa*   反弹琵琶

revolutionary ballet   *geming xiandai balei wuju*   革命现代芭蕾舞剧

revolutionary modern dance drama   *geming xiandai wuju*   革命现代舞剧

revolutionization   *geminghua*   革命化

seeking husband cliff   *wang fu yan*   望夫岩

Shandong Han folk dance   *Shandong yangge*   山东秧歌

Shaoxing opera   *Yueju*   越剧

shi   *shi*   诗

short spear   *huaqiang*   花枪

singing, speaking, moving, and fighting   *chang nian zuo da*   唱念做打

single-stringed zither   *duxian qin*   独弦琴

Southern dance   *Nanfang wu*   南方舞

spin   *xuanzhuan*   旋转

square dancing   *guangchang wu*   广场舞

stalemate   *xiangchi*   相持

stilts   *gaoqiao*   高跷

suona   *suona*   唢呐

sword dance   *jian wu*   剑舞

taijiquan   *taijiquan*   太极拳

take the self as the subject   *yi wo wei zhu*   以我为主

tanhai   *tanhai*   探海

thigh dancing   *datui wu*   大腿舞

three transformations   *san hua*   三化

Tibetan dance   *Zangzu wu*   藏族舞

trembling sleeve   *douxiu*   抖袖

tribhanga   *san dao wan*   三道弯

twist yangge   *niu yangge*   扭秧歌

using the Western to change the Chinese   *yi Xi hua Zhong*   以西化中

using the Western to replace the Chinese   *yi Xi dai Zhong*   以西代中

Uyghur dance   *Weiwu'erzu wu*   维吾尔族舞

virtuous female   *qingyi*   青衣

walking flower lamp   *zou huadeng*   走花灯

water sleeve   *shuixiu*   水袖

weeding through the old to bring forth the new   *tuichen chuxin*   推陈出新

White Russians   *bai'e*   白俄

woman hero   *jinguo yingxiong*   巾帼英雄

xianzi   *xianzi*   弦子

xiqu   *xiqu*   戏曲

yangge theater   *yangge ju*   秧歌剧

young scholar   *xiaosheng*   小生

yuanchang   *yuanchang*   圆场

Yunnan flower drum   *Yunnan huadeng*   云南花灯

zanha   *zanha*   赞哈

NOTES AND REFERENCES

INTRODUCTION

Chinese characters for the titles of all periodicals cited in these notes, along with the names of people and institutions, titles of dance works or films, and other Chinese terms mentioned in the text and notes, can be found in the corresponding sections of the glossary of Chinese terms. Full citations are provided in the notes when a source is first referenced. Citations for items published in Chinese by authors with Chinese names list the author's surname first, following the format used for most Chinese names throughout this book. For periodical citations in which no volume number appears, year of publication indicates the volume. When inclusive page numbers of a journal article or a book chapter are followed by numbers within that range, the second number indicates the page on which the quoted material appears. All translations are my own unless otherwise attributed.

1. *Zhongguo minzu minjian wu* is also translated "Chinese ethnic and folk dance." On the etymology of this term, see Xu Rui, "Dangdai Zhongguo minzu minjian wudao de renshi yanbian yu gainian chanshi," *Beijing wudao xueyuan xuebao*, no. 1 (2010): 4–10.

2. On sleeves in contemporary xiqu performance, see Emily Wilcox, "Meaning in Movement: Adaptation and the Xiqu Body in Intercultural Chinese Theatre," *TDR: The Drama Review* 58, no. 1 (Spring 2014): 42–63.

3. On sleeve dance in early and medieval China, see Susan N. Erickson, "'Twirling Their Long Sleeves, They Dance Again and Again . . .': Jade Plaque Sleeve Dancers of the Western Han Dynasty," *Ars Orientalis* 24 (1994): 39–63; Wang Kefen, *Zhonghua wudao tushi* (Taipei: Wenjin chubanshe, 2001).

4. Ou Jianping, ed., "2015 niandu Zhongguo wudao fazhan yanjiu baogao," *Wudao yanjiu* 148 (January 2016): 1–48. Chinese dance accounted for 54 percent of all shows, while ballet and modern/contemporary dance, the two other genres discussed, accounted for 28 and 16 percent, respectively.

5. For studies of diverse dance practices in Sinophone and Chinese heritage communities outside the People's Republic of China (PRC), see Soo Pong Chua, "Chinese Dance as Theatre Dance in Singapore: Change and Factors of Change," in *Dance as Cultural Heritage*, vol. 2, ed. Betty True Jones (New York: Congress on Research in Dance, 1985), 131–43; William Lau, "The Chinese Dance Experience in Canadian Society: An Investigation of Four Chinese Dance Groups in Toronto" (MFA thesis, York University, 1991); Hsiang-Hsiu Lin, "Cultural Identity in Taiwanese Modern Dance" (PhD diss., San José State University, 1999); Ya-ping Chen, "Dancing Chinese Nationalism and Anticommunism: The *Minzu Wudao* Movement in 1950s Taiwan," in *Dance, Human Rights, and Social Justice: Dignity in Motion*, ed. Naomi M. Jackson and Toni Samantha Phim (Lanham, MD: Scarecrow Press, 2008), 34–50; Sau-ling Wong, "Dancing in the Diaspora: Cultural Long-Distance Nationalism and the Staging of Chineseness by San Francisco's Chinese Folk Dance Association," *Journal of Transnational American Studies* 2, no. 1 (2010), https://escholarship.org/uc/item/50k6k78p; Szu-Ching Chang, "Dancing with Nostalgia in Taiwanese Contemporary 'Traditional' Dance" (PhD diss., University of California, Riverside, 2011); Hui Wilcox, "Movement in Spaces of Liminality: Chinese Dance and Immigrant Identities," *Ethnic and Racial Studies* 34 (2011): 314–32; SanSan Kwan, *Kinesthetic City: Dance and Movement in Chinese Urban Spaces* (Oxford: Oxford University Press, 2013); Soo Pong Chua, "Chinese Dance: Cultural Resources and Creative Potentials," in *Evolving Synergies: Celebrating Dance in Singapore*, ed. Stephanie Burridge and Caren Cariño (New York and London: Routledge, 2015), 17–30; Yatin Lin, *Sino-Corporealities: Contemporary Choreographies from Taipei, Hong Kong, and New York* (Taipei: Taipei National University of the Arts, 2015); Shih-Ming Li Chang and Lynn Frederiksen, *Chinese Dance: In the Vast Land and Beyond* (Middletown, CT: Wesleyan University Press, 2016); Ya-ping Chen, "Putting Minzu into Perspective: Dance and Its Relation to the Concept of 'Nation,'" *Choreographic Practices* 7, no. 2 (2016): 219–28; Loo Fung Ying and Loo Fung Chiat, "Dramatizing Malaysia in Contemporary Chinese Lion Dance," *Asian Theater Journal* 33, no. 1 (2016): 130–50; Yutian Wong, ed., *Contemporary Directions in Asian American Dance* (Madison: University of Wisconsin Press, 2016).

6. Geoffrey Wall and Philip Feifan Xie, "Authenticating Ethnic Tourism: Li Dancers' Perspectives," *Asia Pacific Journal of Tourism Research* 10, no. 1 (2005): 1–21; Pál Nyíri, *Scenic Spots: Chinese Tourism, the State, and Cultural Authority* (Seattle: University of Washington Press, 2006); Xiaobo Su and Peggy Teo, "Tourism Politics in Lijiang, China: An Analysis of State and Local Interactions in Tourism Development," *Tourism Geographies* 10, no. 2 (2008): 150–68; Jing Li, "The Folkloric, the Spectacular, and the Institutionalized: Touristifying Ethnic Minority Dances on China's Southwest Frontiers," *Journal of Tourism and Cultural Change* 10, no. 1 (2012): 65–83.

7. Florence Graezer, "The *Yangge* in Contemporary China: Popular Daily Activity and Neighborhood Community Life," trans. Dianna Martin, *China Perspectives* 24 (1999): 31–43; Jonathan Scott Noble, "Cultural Performance in China: Beyond Resistance in the 1990s" (PhD diss., Ohio State University, 2003); Ellen Gerdes, "Contemporary *Yangge*: The Moving History of a Chinese Folk Dance Form," *Asian Theatre Journal* 25, no. 1 (2008): 138–47; Chiayi Seetoo and Haoping Zou, "China's Guangchang wu: The Emergence, Choreography, and Management of Dancing in Public Squares," *TDR: The Drama Review* 60, no. 4 (2016): 22–49.

8. Heping Song, "The Dance of Manchu Shamans," *Shaman* 5, no. 2 (1997): 144–54; Erik Mueggler, "Dancing Fools: Politics of Culture and Place in a Traditional Nationality Festival," *Modern China* 28, no. 1 (2002): 3–38; Ellen Pearlman, *Tibetan Sacred Dance: A Journey into the Religious and Folk Traditions* (Rochester, VT: Inner Traditions, 2002); Feigrui Li, "Altogether Dances with God: Recording China's Exorcism Dance Culture," *Asian Social Science* 5, no. 1 (2009): 101–4; David Johnson, *Spectacle and Sacrifice: The Ritual Foundations of Village Life in North China* (Cambridge, MA: Harvard University Asia Center, 2010).

9. For more on the interactions between concert dance and these other spheres of activity, see Emily Wilcox, "The Dialectics of Virtuosity: Dance in the People's Republic of China, 1949–2009" (PhD diss., University of California, Berkeley, 2011); Emily Wilcox, "Dancers Doing Fieldwork: Socialist Aesthetics and Bodily Experience in the People's Republic of China," *Journal for the Anthropological Study of Human Movement* 17, no. 2 (2012), http://jashm.press.uillinois.edu/17.2/wilcox.html; Emily Wilcox, "Selling Out Post-Mao: Dance Work and Ethics of Fulfillment in Reform Era China," in *Chinese Modernity and the Individual Psyche,* ed. Andrew Kipnis (New York: Palgrave Macmillan, 2012), 43–65; Emily Wilcox, "Moonwalking in Beijing: Michael Jackson, *Piliwu,* and the Origins of Chinese Hip-Hop" (lecture, University of Michigan Lieberthal-Rogel Center for Chinese Studies Noon Lecture Series, Ann Arbor, MI, February 20, 2018).

10. Emily Wilcox, "Dynamic Inheritance: Representative Works and the Authoring of Tradition in Chinese Dance," *Journal of Folklore Research* 55, no. 1 (2018): 77–111.

11. Nan Ma, "Dancing into Modernity: Kinesthesia, Narrative, and Revolutions in Modern China, 1900–1978" (PhD diss., University of Wisconsin, Madison, 2015), 29–87, 46–47.

12. Ma, "Dancing into Modernity," 73–79.

13. Catherine Yeh, "Experimenting with Dance Drama: Peking Opera Modernity, Kabuki Theater Reform and the Denishawn's Tour of the Far East," *Journal of Global Theatre History* 1, no. 2 (2016): 28–37.

14. Joshua Goldstein, "Mei Lanfang and the Nationalization of Peking Opera, 1912–1930," *positions* 7, no. 2 (1999): 377–420.

15. Ma, "Dancing into Modernity," 73.

16. Goldstein, "Mei Lanfang," 391–94.

17. Ma, "Dancing into Modernity"; Yeh, "Experimenting with Dance Drama"; Catherine Yeh, "Mei Lanfang, the Denishawn Dancers, and World Theater," in *A New Literary History of Modern China,* ed. David Wang (Cambridge, MA: Harvard University Press, 2017).

18. Ma, "Dancing into Modernity"; Joshua Goldstein, "Mei Lanfang," 384–86.

19. The birth year on Qemberxanim's PRC documents is 1922, but some dance historians in Xinjiang now believe she was born in 1914.

20. Dai Ailian, "Fazhan Zhongguo wudao di yi bu," *Zhongyang ribao,* April 10, 1946.

21. Ibid.

22. Luo Chuan, "Cui Chengxi er ci lai Hu ji," *Zazhi* 15, no. 2 (1945): 84–88, 86.

CHAPTER 1. FROM TRINIDAD TO BEIJING

1. Dai Ailian et al., *Zhongguo minjianwu liang zhong: Dai Ailian biao yan* (New York: Zhongguo dianying qiye guoji gongsi, n.d.); John Martin, "The Dance: Notes: Plans and Programs in the Summer Scene," *New York Times,* August 10, 1947; "Two Chinese Dances,"

Popular Photography 25, no. 3 (September 1949): 130. The recording was shot in color on 16 mm Kodachrome film while Dai and her husband were visiting the United States in 1946–47. Dai also performed during her visit. Jane Watson Crane, "China War Cartoonist Visits US," *Washington Post*, November 3, 1946; "The Week's Events: Original Ballet Russe at Metropolitan," *New York Times*, March 16, 1947; "Chinese Evening—Tai Ai-lien," New York performance program, Sophia Delza Papers, (S)*MGZMD 155, Box 50, Folder 9, Jerome Robbins Dance Division, New York Public Library for the Performing Arts.

2. Dai Ailian (dictated), Luo Bin and Wu Jingmei (recorded and organized), *Wo de yishu yu shenghuo* (Beijing: Renmin yinyue chubanshe, 2003), 87–88; Richard Glasstone, *The Story of Dai Ailian: Icon of Chinese Folk Dance, Pioneer of Chinese Ballet* (Hampshire, UK: Dance Books, 2007), 29–32, 97.

3. Frederick Lau, *Music in China: Experiencing Music, Expressing Culture* (New York: Oxford University Press, 2008).

4. This work also went by the titles *Yao wu* (Yao dance) and "Yao Ceremonial Prelude." Dai Ailian, *Wo de yishu*, 134.

5. Ralph A. Litzinger, *Other Chinas: The Yao and the Politics of National Belonging* (Durham, NC: Duke University Press, 2000).

6. The following evidence suggests that Dai held a British passport: Dai's second cousin Sylvia Chen, who was born in Trinidad in 1909, had a British passport; in the Dartington Hall records from 1939, Dai's name is listed in the Student Roster, but she does not appear on the Aliens' Register; Dai recalls in her published oral history that she had no Chinese passport when she traveled from the United Kingdom to Hong Kong in 1940. Jay and Si-lan Chen Leyda Papers, Box 28, Folder 3, Passports, Tamiment Institute Library, New York University; Student Roster dated September 25, 1939, in Students: T Arts Dance 1, Folder D, Jooss-Leeder School of Dance, Dartington Hall Trust Archives; Aliens' Register: T Arts Dance 1, Folder E, Jooss-Leeder School of Dance, Dartington Hall Trust Archives. Dai Ailian, *Wo de yishu*, 77.

7. In her Chinese-language recorded oral history, Dai makes clear that she spoke no Chinese (Mandarin or Cantonese) before arriving in China in 1941. In one anecdote, Dai recounts that her husband, Ye Qianyu, spoke to her father in Cantonese when they visited Trinidad in 1947 and that she could not understand what her husband and her father were saying. According to Dai, the only person in her family who regularly spoke Cantonese was her paternal grandmother, always with many English words mixed in. Dai's mother and her aunts and uncles on her mother's side only spoke English, while Dai's formal education was, in Dai's words, "completely in Western culture." Dai Ailian, *Wo de yishu*, 2, 12, 74. Chinese scholars who knew Dai personally say that even after she had lived and worked in China for many decades, the language in which she was most comfortable was always English.

8. Dai Ailian, *Wo de yishu*, 1–3.

9. Ibid., 2.

10. These names appear in the *Dancing Times*, the *Times*, the *China Press*, the *Sunday Times*, the *South China Morning Post*, and the *Daily Telegraph* from September 1937 to November 1938.

11. Her name is typed in the student register as "Eileen Tay," with a handwritten note in the margin reading "= Ailien Tai." Then, her name appears in the list of student addresses and a student performance program as "Ai Lien Tai." Student roster, Dartington Hall Trust

Archives; End of Term Dances, December 15, 1939, in Students: T Arts Dance 1, Folder D, Jooss-Leeder School of Dance, Dartington Hall Trust Archives; student address list in Ballets Jooss, T Arts Dance 1A, Folder E, Jooss-Leeder School of Dance, Summer Schools, Dartington Hall Trust Archives.

12. "Chinese Evening—Tai Ai-lien," Sophia Delza Papers; John Martin, "The Dance: Notes." See also numerous reports in the *South China Morning Post* in 1940–41.

13. In a letter from Dai dated May 2, 1950, sent from Beijing, she signs "Ai-lien," with "Tai Ai-Lien" typed below. Dai Ailian to Sylvia (Si-Lan) Chen, Jay and Si-Lan Chen Leyda Papers and Photographs, 1913–1987, TAM.083, Box 28, Folder 7, Tamiment Library and Robert F. Wagner Labor Archive, New York.

14. Dai Ailian, *Wo de yishu*, 4.

15. Lloyd Braithwaite, "Social Stratification in Trinidad: A Preliminary Analysis," *Social and Economic Studies* 2 (November 2–3, 1953): 5–175.

16. According to Braithwaite, this had to do with the fact that Chinese were lighter skinned and had "good hair," as well as their historical occupations as traders, retailers, restaurateurs, and cleaners, rather than as indentured servants or "coolies" (a category dominated in Trinidad by South Asians). As of 1944, only 1 percent of the Trinidad population was Chinese, whereas 2.75 percent was white, 14 percent was mixed race or "coloured," 35 percent was south Indian, and 46.88 percent was of African descent. Braithwaite, "Social Stratification in Trinidad," 10–11, 50–52.

17. Eugene Chen's mother was the elder sister of Dai Ailian's maternal grandmother. Dai Ailian, *Wo de yishu*, 6–7.

18. Glasstone, *The Story of Dai Ailian*, xi.

19. Dai Ailian, *Wo de yishu*, 8–13.

20. Ibid., 14–15. On Agatha Ganteaume, see Harvey R. Neptune, *Caliban and the Yankees: Trinidad and the United States Occupation* (Chapel Hill: University of North Carolina Press, 2007), 47.

21. Yuan-tsung Chen, *Return to the Middle Kingdom: One Family, Three Revolutionaries, and the Birth of Modern China* (New York: Union Square Press, 2008), 65; Si-lan Chen Leyda, *Footnote to History* (New York: Dance Horizons, 1984), 17.

22. On Sylvia Chen, see Mark Franko, *The Work of Dance: Labor, Movement, and Identity in the 1930s* (Middletown, CT: Wesleyan University Press, 2002), 85–90; S. Ani Mukherji, "'Like Another Planet to the Darker Americans': Black Cultural Work in 1930s Moscow," in *Africa in Europe: Studies in Transnational Practice in the Long Twentieth Century*, ed. Eve Rosenhaft and Robbie John Macvicar Aitken, 120–41 (Liverpool: Liverpool University Press, 2013); Julia L. Mickenberg, *American Girls in Red Russia: Chasing the Soviet Dream* (Chicago: University of Chicago Press, 2017).

23. Dai Ailian, *Wo de yishu*, 17.

24. Glasstone, *The Story of Dai Ailian*, 7–10.

25. Dai Ailian, *Wo de yishu*, 76.

26. Ibid., 35–36. This production was apparently put on annually at Albert Hall by the Royal Choral Society. For a description, see "The Royal Choral Society: Hiawatha," *Times*, June 11, 1935.

27. "Eilian Tai," *Dancing Times*, September 1937, 699; "Arts Theater: A Tibetan Fairy Tale," *Times*, October 13, 1937; "From Tibet to Troy," *Sunday Times*, Sunday, August 7, 1938.

28. This work was apparently unpaid. Richard Glasstone, *Story of Dai Ailian*, 12.

29. "Mask Theatre Re-Opens," *Daily Telegraph*, October 26, 1936; S. Cates, "The Mask Theatre," *Dancing Times*, August 1937, 549–51; "The Use of Masks," *Times*, March 8, 1938; "Ai Lien Tai," *Dancing Times*, May 1938, cover; W. A. D., "Poet Laureate's Ballet," *Daily Telegraph*, April 1, 1939; "Rudolf Steiner Hall," *Times*, April 1, 1939.

30. "Ai Lien Tai," *Dancing Times*, May 1938, cover.

31. Larraine Nicholas, *Dancing in Utopia: Dartington Hall and Its Dancers* (Alton, UK: Dance Books, 2007).

32. The curriculum included ten parts: Dance Technique (including classical ballet), Eukinetics, Choreutics, Improvisation, Dance Styles (including period and national folk dances), Dance Script (Labanotation), Musical Education, Dance Composition/Dance Practice, Practice for the Stage/Experience of Production, and Teaching Method with Amateurs. "The Jooss Leeder School of Dance," publicity brochure, T Arts Dance 1A, Folder G, Jooss Leeder School/Dance Performance Programmes, Dartington Hall Trust Archives. On Dai's stated intention of joining Ballets Jooss, see Dai Ailian, *Wo de yishu*, 46.

33. On Ram Gopal, see Ketu Katrak, *Contemporary Indian Dance: New Creative Choreography in India and the Diaspora* (New York: Palgrave Macmillan, 2011), 39–40.

34. Dai Ailian, *Wo de yishu*, 56.

35. *The Wife of General Ling*, directed by Ladislao Vajda (Shepperton, UK: Shepperton Studios and Premier-Stafford Productions, 1937; rereleased on DVD by Televista, 2008). On Dai's participation in the film, see *Dancing Times*, September 1937, 699.

36. Jeffrey Richards, *Visions of Yesterday* (London and New York: Routledge, 1973); Gina Marchetti, *Romance and the "Yellow Peril": Race, Sex, and Discursive Strategies in Hollywood Fiction* (Berkeley: University of California Press, 1993).

37. *Wife of General Ling*.

38. Dai Ailian, *Wo de yishu*, 12.

39. Joan Erdman, "Performance as Translation: Uday Shankar in the West," *Drama Review: TDR* 31, no. 1 (Spring 1987): 64–88; Prarthana Purkayastha, "Dancing Otherness: Nationalism, Transnationalism, and the Work of Uday Shankar," *Dance Research Journal* 44, no. 1 (Summer 2012): 68–92; "The Alhambra," *Times*, October 3, 1934; "Arts Theatre Club," *Times*, November 13, 1934; "The Sitter Out," *Dancing Times*, February 1939, 599; "Sai Shōki," *Dancing Times*, January 1939, 511; "The Sensation of Paris," *Picture Post*, February 25, 1939, 60.

40. "The Spirit of China," *South China Morning Post*, October 16, 1940. Uday Shankar's Almora center, founded in 1938 in India, was supported financially by Dorothy and Leonard Elmhirst, the owners of Dartington Hall. Prarthana Purkayastha, *Indian Modern Dance, Feminism and Transnationalism* (Houndmills, UK: Palgrave Macmillan, 2014), 59–70. The Indonesian group's 1939 performance in London was part of a fund-raiser for a hospital in China, and Dai states that seeing these dancers perform gave her ideas for her own choreography. Dai Ailian, *Wo de yishu*, 73.

41. Richard Glasstone, *Story of Dai Ailian*, 19.

42. "Miss Tai Ai-lien: Famous Dancer in the Colony," *South China Morning Post*, April 1, 1940; Dai Ailian, *Wo de yishu*, 76.

43. Suzanne Walther, *The Dance of Death: Kurt Jooss and the Weimar Years* (Chur, Switzerland: Harwood Academic Publishers, 1994).

44. "The Green Table" program notes by Kurt Jooss, T Arts Dance 1A, Folder G, Jooss Leeder School/Dance Performance Programmes, Dartington Hall Trust Archives.

45. Walther, *Dance of Death*, 58–73; *Kurt Jooss: A Commitment to Dance*, directed by Annette von Wangenheim (New York: Insight Media, 2001).

46. Peter Alexander, "Ballet Jooss and Ballet Russe," *Dancing Times*, July 1938, 396–98, 396.

47. Dai Ailian, *Wo de yishu*, 46.

48. According to advertisements, the summer school was scheduled for August 3–30, 1939. "School of the Ballets Jooss," *Dancing Times*, April 1939, 68.

49. On the CCC, see Robert Bickers, *Britain in China: Community Culture and Colonialism, 1900–1949* (Manchester: Manchester University Press, 1999), 233; Arthur Clegg, *Aid China, 1937–1949: A Memoir of a Forgotten Campaign* (Beijing: New World Press, 1989); Tom Buchanan, *East Wind: China and the British Left, 1925–1976* (Oxford: Oxford University Press, 2012). Dai's connection with the CCC was likely mediated by Jack Chen (Chen Yifan, 1908–1995), son of Eugene Chen and sister of Sylvia Chen, who traveled extensively between China, the Soviet Union, and England during the 1930s. In 1936 Jack Chen presented an exhibition of Chinese art with the Artists International Association, which had ties to the CCC. Paul Bevan, *A Modern Miscellany: Shanghai Cartoon Artists, Shao Xunmei's Circle and the Travels of Jack Chen* (Leiden: Brill, 2016). Dai mentions that Jack gave her advice while she was in England. Dai Ailian, *Wo de yishu*, 109–10.

50. "Chinese Dances Featured at London Benefit Party," *China Press*, July 4, 1938; W. A. Darlington, "Play Wright's Club," *Daily Telegraph*, November 28, 1938; "Variety Show—Held in London in Aid of Chinese," *South China Morning Post*, November 29, 1938. See also Dai Ailian, *Wo de yishu*, 75–76; Clegg, *Aid China*, 61.

51. Dai Ailian, *Wo de yishu*, 74–75.

52. "Miss Tai Ai-lien: Famous Dancer."

53. Dai Ailian, *Wo de yishu*, 73.

54. Ibid., 37, 70–72.

55. Ibid., 70–72.

56. "Chinese Dances Featured."

57. Dai Ailian, *Wo de yishu*, 77–78.

58. "Miss Tai Ai-lien: Famous Dancer."

59. Shi Yongqing, "Ye Qianyu xin furen, yiwei Faguo wudaojia," *Zhongguo yitan ribao*, no. 21, (March 26, 1941): 1.

60. Dai Ailian, *Wo de yishu*, 40–57, 80–81.

61. Song and Chen were part of a left-leaning group within the Nationalist Party that had opposed Chiang Kai-shek in the late 1920s and, after being defeated, fled to Moscow.

62. Dai Ailian, *Wo de yishu*, 72, 80–84, 87.

63. "Dance Recital for War Orphans," *South China Morning Post*, September 21, 1940; "Brevities," *South China Morning Post*, October 16, 1940; "Aid for War Orphans," *South China Morning Post*, October 26, 1940; "Benefit Performance to Be Given on Wednesday," *South China Morning Post*, January 20, 1941; H. W. C. M., "Chinese Artistes: Fine Entertainment at King's Theatre to Aid Defense League," *South China Morning Post*, January 23, 1941.

64. Shi Yongqing, "Ye Qianyu xin furen"; Ye Mingming, "Fuqin Ye Qianyu he wo de san ge mama," *Renmin zhoukan*, no. 20 (2016): 84–85.

65. On Ye's work as a cartoon artist in 1930s Shanghai, see Paul Bevan, *A Modern Miscellany.*

66. Hu Cheng, "Dai Ailian relian Wang xiansheng," *Hong Meigui* 1, no. 1 (1946): 3; Jing Pu, "Ye Qianyu Dai Ailian jijiang lai Hu: Zhitongdaohe yijianqingxin," *Xiang-Hai huabao*, no. 5 (1946): 8; Ma Lai, "Guan Dai Ailian zhi wu," *Shanghai tan*, no. 14 (1946): 9; Dai Ailian, *Wo de yishu*, 111–12.

67. The ballet excerpts Dai performed were the Prelude and Waltz from *Les Sylphides*, which she had learned in London from Lydia Sokolova, a former member of Diaghilev's Ballets Russes. An example of Dai's original choreography on a non-Chinese theme was "Ruth the Gleaner," based on the biblical story. "Miss Ai-lien Tai: Assists War Orphans in Hongkong Debut Interpretive Dancing," *South China Morning Post*, October 19, 1940. See also Glasstone, *Story of Dai Ailian*, 8, 33; Dai Ailian, *Wo de yishu*, 85.

68. "Alarm," undated sketch by Ye Qianyu, reprinted in Glasstone, *Story of Dai Ailian*, 37.

69. Dai Ailian, *Wo de yishu*, 73.

70. Ibid., 73.

71. Ibid., 72.

72. "The Spirit of China," *South China Morning Post*, October 16, 1940.

73. "Miss Ai-lien Tai: Assists War Orphans"; H. W. C. M., "Chinese Artistes."

74. Diana Lary, *The Chinese People at War: Human Suffering and Social Transformation, 1937–1945* (New York: Cambridge University Press, 2010); Rana Mitter, *China's War with Japan, 1937–1945: Struggle for Survival* (London: Penguin Books, 2013).

75. Edward M. Gunn, *Unwelcome Muse: Chinese Literature in Shanghai and Peking, 1937–1945* (New York: Columbia University Press, 1980); David Holm, *Art and Ideology in Revolutionary China* (Oxford: Clarendon Press, 1991); Poshek Fu, *Passivity, Resistance, and Collaboration: Intellectual Choices in Occupied Shanghai, 1937–1945* (Stanford, CA: Stanford University Press, 1993); Chang-tai Hung, *War and Popular Culture: Resistance in Modern China, 1937–1945* (Berkeley: University of California Press, 1994).

76. Carolyn FitzGerald, *Fragmenting Modernisms: Chinese Wartime Literature, Art, and Film, 1937–49* (Leiden: Brill, 2013).

77. For more comprehensive accounts of Republican-era dance history, see Liu Qingyi, *Zhongguo wudao tongshi: Zhonghua minguo juan* (Shanghai: Shanghai yinyue chubanshe, 2010); Tong Yan, *Minguo shiqi wudao yanjiu 1912–1949* (Beijing: Zhongyang minzu daxue chubanshe, 2013).

78. On ballroom culture, see Leo Ou-fan Lee, *Shanghai Modern: The Flowering of a New Urban Culture in China, 1930–1945* (Cambridge, MA: Harvard University Press, 1999); Andrew David Field, *Shanghai's Dancing World: Cabaret Culture and Urban Politics, 1919–1954* (Hong Kong: Chinese University Press, 2010). On Li Jinhui, see Andrew F. Jones, *Yellow Music: Media Culture and Colonial Modernity in the Chinese Jazz Age* (Durham, NC: Duke University Press, 2001).

79. For more on ballet in China, see chapter 4.

80. Rebecca Karl, *Mao Zedong and China in the Twentieth-Century World: A Concise History* (Durham, NC: Duke University Press, 2010).

81. Holm, *Art and Ideology in Revolutionary China*; Florence Graezer Bideau, *La danse du yangge: Culture et politique dans la Chine du XXe siècle* (Paris: Éditions La Découverte, 2012).

82. There was no stable orthography for the term *yangge* in China prior to the 1940s. David Holm, "Folk Art as Propaganda: The *Yangge* Movement in Yan'an," in *Popular Chinese Literature and Performing Arts in the People's Republic of China, 1949–1979*, ed. Bonnie McDougall (Berkeley: University of California Press, 1984), 3–35.

83. Holm, "Folk Art as Propaganda."

84. Ellen Judd, "Prelude to the 'Yan'an Talks': Problems in Transforming a Literary Intelligentsia," *Modern China* 11, no. 3 (1985): 377–403; Brian DeMare, *Mao's Cultural Army: Drama Troupes in China's Rural Revolution* (Cambridge: Cambridge University Press, 2015).

85. Wang Hui, "Local Forms, Vernacular Dialects, and the War of Resistance against Japan: The 'National Forms' Debate," trans. Chris Berry, in Wang Hui and Theodore Huters, *The Politics of Imagining Asia* (Cambridge, MA: Harvard University Press, 2011), 95–135, 98. See also Holm, *Art and Ideology in Revolutionary China*.

86. Wang Hui, "Local Forms," 97.

87. Ibid., 106.

88. Mao Zedong, "On New Democracy," in *Selected Works of Mao Zedong*, vol. 2, January 1940, accessed January 28, 2017, https://www.marxists.org.

89. Mao Zedong, "Talks at the Yan'an Forum on Literature and Art," in *Selected Works of Mao Zedong*, vol. 3, May 1942, accessed January 28, 2017, https://www.marxists.org.

90. DeMare, *Mao's Cultural Army*, 155.

91. Judd, "Prelude to the 'Yan'an Talks'"; Liu Xiaozhen, *Zou xiang juchang de xiangtu shenying: cong yige yangge kan dangdai Zhongguo minjian wudao* (Shanghai: Shanghai yinyue chubanshe, 2012).

92. Wu Xiaobang, *Wo de wudao yishu shengya* (Beijing: Zhongguo xiju chubanshe, 1982), 1–10.

93. Wu's interest in dance was piqued by a student performance at Waseda University, which led him to enroll in dance courses at the Dance Research Institute led by Takada Seiko (formerly Hara Seiko, 1895–1977) in Nakano, a suburb in eastern Tokyo. Nan Ma, "Transmediating Kinesthesia: Wu Xiaobang and Modern Dance in China, 1929–1939," *Modern Chinese Literature and Culture* 28, no. 1 (2016): 129–73.

94. Wu Xiaobang, *Wo de wudao*, 10.

95. Ibid., 16–17.

96. Wan Shi, "Wudao yishu: Wu Xiaobang jun chuyan Xiyang wudao di zitai," *Shidai* 8, no. 6 (1935): 12.

97. In October 1935, Wu returned to Tokyo to continue his studies with Takada Seiko. That summer he participated in a life-changing three-week seminar taught by Eguchi Takaya (1900–1977), a disciple of German modern dancer Mary Wigman. Ma, "Transmediating Kinesthesia."

98. Wu Xiaobang, "Wu Xiaobang tan xinxing wuyong," *Diansheng zhoukan* 6, no. 29 (1937): 1264. On the term *buyō/wuyong/muyong* and its different meanings in East Asia, see Judy Van Zile, *Perspectives on Korean Dance* (Middletown, CT: Wesleyan University Press, 2001), 32–45. On Wu's adoption of this term, see Ma, "Dancing into Modernity," 106–8.

99. Wu Xiaobang, "Wu Xiaobang tan."

100. Wu Xiaobang, "Kangzhan sinian lai zhi xin wenyi yundong teji: zai kangzhan zhong shengzhang qilai de wuyong yishu," *Zhong Su wenhua zazhi* 9, no. 1 (1941): 96–98.

101. "Baogao yidian: Wu Xiaobang zai Gang jinkuang," *Zhongguo yitan huabao*, no. 87 (1939): 1.

102. Wu Xiaobang, "Kangzhan sinian lai," 96.

103. Sheng Jie, *Yi wang shi* (Beijing: Zhongguo wenlian chubanshe, 2010), 21–24.

104. "Xinxing wuyongju 'Yingsu hua' de yanchu shi ren shifen xingfen," *Shenbao*, February 23, 1939; Wu Xiaobang and Chen Gexin, "'Yingsu hua' shuoming," *Yiyou* 2–4, no. 5 (1939): 17; Wu Xiaobang, "Shanghai xiju jinkuang: guanyu *Yingsu hua* de yanchu," *Wenxian* 2, no. 6 (1938): D125–28. The date of this source contradicts other contemporary periodicals that date the performance to 1939.

105. *Yingsu hua*, performance photographs, University of Michigan Pioneers of Chinese Dance Digital Archive, https://quod.lib.umich.edu/d/dance11c.

106. Andrew Jones, *Yellow Music*.

107. Wan Shi, "Wudao yishu."

108. Wu Xiaobang, "Wuyong mantan," *Xiju zazhi* 2, no. 4 (1939): 152–54, 154.

109. Wu Xiaobang, "Zhongguo wuyong," *Gengyun*, no. 2 (1940): 30–31, 30.

110. Ibid., 31. *Jianghu* refers to a world outside mainstream society, traditionally associated with itinerant entertainers and knights errant.

111. Wu Xiaobang, "Zhongguo wuyong," 30.

112. Wu Xiaobang, "Kangzhan sinian lai," 97.

113. Ibid., 96.

114. Wu Xiaobang, "Gongzuo shenghuo xuexi: juxi wuyong de jiben xiuyang—jiezou *Tempo*," *Lianhe zhoubao*, no. 16 (1944): 2. On "natural law" and its role in Wu's method, see Ma, "Transmediating Kinesthesia," 138–41.

115. Hung, *War and Popular Culture*, 284.

116. Joshua Goldstein, *Drama Kings: Players and Publics in the Re-creation of Peking Opera, 1870–1937* (Berkeley: University of California Press, 2007).

117. Wu Xiaobang, "Yijiusanjiu nian de gewu jie," *Duhui* 1 (1939): 7; Wu Xiaobang, "Wuyong mantan." For more on Chinese discourses surrounding jazz, see Jones, *Yellow Music*.

118. Wu Xiaobang, "Yijiusanjiu nian."

119. Wu Xiaobang, "Wo weishenme dao Yiyoushe," *Yiyou* 2, no. 4–5 (1939): 18.

120. Dai Ailian, *Wo de yishu*, 87.

121. Pingchao Zhu, *Wartime Culture in Guilin, 1938–1944: A City at War* (Lanham, MD: Lexington Books, 2015), 148–54.

122. The version Dai saw was directed by Hong Shen, a leading practitioner of Western spoken drama. Dai Ailian, *Wo de wudao*, 87.

123. The wedding took place on April 14, 1941. Sheng Jie, *Yi wang shi*, 34.

124. "Wu Xiaobang Sheng Jie zai Yu jiehun," *Dianying xinwen*, no. 121 (1941): 481; Sheng Jie, *Yi wang shi*, 35.

125. "Dai Ailian yu Zhongguo de xin wuyong yundong," *Yiwen huabao* 2, no. 5 (1947): 5–6.

126. Sheng Jie, *Yi wang shi*.

127. This was the basis for Ye's sketch series *Escape from Hong Kong* (1942). FitzGerald, *Fragmenting Modernisms*, 101–6.

128. FitzGerald, *Fragmenting Modernisms*, 107; Dai Ailian, *Wo de wudao*, 127, 134.

129. "Dai Ailian yu Zhongguo."

130. Wu Niang, "Dai Ailian de tufengwu," *Dongnan feng*, no. 20 (1946): 4; Ren Feng, "Dai Ailian he ta de wudao," *Minjian*, no. 5 (1946): 10.

131. "Dai Ailian yu Zhongguo."

132. Peng Song, "Cai wu ji: yi 1945 nian Chuankang zhi xing," *Xinmin bao* (1947), reprinted in Peng Song, *Wudao xuezhe Peng Song quanji* (Beijing: Zhongguo minzu daxue chubanshe, 2011), 3–5.

133. Dai Ailian, *Wo de yishu*, 135.

134. Peng Song, "Cai wu ji."

135. For complete descriptions of the production, see Chen Zhiliang, "Lüetan minjian yuewu: 'Bianjiang yinyue wudao dahui' guanhou gan," *Keguan*, no. 18 (1946): 10; Jing Pu, "Wudao kui bianqing, lianqing ru liehuo," *Xiang-Hai huabao*, no. 2 (1946): 1–2. For photographs, see "Bianjiang gewu zhaodai Zhongwei ji xianzhengyuan, jinwan zai qingnianguan juxing," *Zhongyang ribao*, March 6, 1946; "Dai Ailian lingdao biaoyan bianjiang wudao," *Zhongyang ribao*, April 10, 1946; "Zhongguo wudao di yi bu," *Qingming*, no. 2 (1946): 9–12; "Bianjiang yinyue wudao dahui," *Zhong-Mei zhoubao*, no. 266 (1947): 26–28. Additional reports appeared in *Dongnan feng, Haifeng, Haijing, Kuaihuo lin, Xinxing, Xiang-Hai huabao*, and *Zhonghua quanguo tiyu xiejinhui tiyu tongxun*.

136. Chen Zhiliang, "Lüetan minjian yuewu."

137. Jing Pu, "Wudao kui bianqing."

138. *Zhongguo* literally means "the Middle Kingdom" and is one of the most common premodern and modern equivalents to the English word *China*. However, the meanings of *Zhongguo* have changed over time.

139. James Leibold, *Reconfiguring Chinese Nationalism: How the Qing Frontier and Its Indigenes Became Chinese* (New York: Palgrave Macmillan, 2007), 11.

140. Xiaoyuan Liu, *Recast All under Heaven: Revolution, War, Diplomacy, and Frontier China in the 20th Century* (New York: Continuum, 2010). See also Xiaoyuan Liu, *Frontier Passages: Ethnopolitics and the Rise of Chinese Communism, 1921–1945* (Washington, DC: Woodrow Wilson Center Press, 2004).

141. On the concept of Han identity, see Thomas Mullaney, James Leibold, Stéphane Gros, and Eric Vanden Bussche, eds., *Critical Han Studies: The History, Representation, and Identity of China's Majority* (Berkeley: University of California Press, 2012); Agnieszka Joniak-Lüthi, *The Han: China's Diverse Majority* (Seattle: University of Washington Press, 2015).

142. The Chinese term *minzu* was also a product of this historical moment. According to James Leibold, "The term is thought to be the Chinese equivalent of the Japanese neologism *minzoku*, which itself was coined to translate the German term *Volk*." Leibold, *Reconfiguring Chinese Nationalism*, 8. Over time, the term *minzu* also absorbed ideas from British and Soviet ethnology and nationalities policy. For more on these translingual cultural processes and their shaping of Chinese nationalism in the early twentieth century, see Lydia He Liu, *Translingual Practice: Literature, National Culture, and Translated Modernity—China, 1900–1937* (Stanford, CA: Stanford University Press, 1995).

143. Xiaoyuan Liu, *Recast All under Heaven*, 124–25.

144. Chen Zhiliang, "Lüetan minjian yuewu." Contemporary reports also suggest that the Chongqing mayor, Zhang Dulun, was a major supporter of the show. Jing Pu, "Wudao kui bianqing"; Mozi, "Ye Qianyu furen: Dai Ailian, *Haijing*, no. 5 (1946): 1. On Nationalist frontier work in this region, see Andres Rodriguez, "Building the Nation, Serving the Frontier: Mobilizing and Reconstructing China's Borderlands during the War of Resistance (1937–1945)," *Modern Asian Studies* 45, no. 2 (March 2011): 345–76.

145. On the 1936 Nanjing event, see Chen Zhiliang, "Ji Xibei wenwuzhan zhanlanhui, *Zhongyang ribao*, June 18, 1936; "Xibei wenwuzhan zhanlanhui, biaoyan bianjiang gewu dianying," *Zhongyang ribao*, June 18, 1936; "Kaifa Xibei sheng, Xibei wenzhanhui ying bianjiang gewu dianying," *Zhongyang ribao*, June 19, 1936; "Zai bianjiang gewuhui zhong jingling duo zhong yuewu yihou," *Zhongyang ribao*, June 23, 1936. On the 1945 Chengdu event, see "Jinnü Da Yan Da zhaodai Qiangmin guanguang tuan, bianjiang gewu ji shou huanying," *Yanjing xinwen*, April 11, 1945. On the 1945 Guiyang event, see Zhong Yangbao, "Pochu zhongzu guannian, guli Miao-Han hezuo: Yang Sen jüban 'Miao bao wuyong hui,'" *Daguanyuan zhoubao*, no. 20 (1946): 1.

146. "Bianjiang gewu xinshanghui," *Zhongyang ribao*, January 5, 1947; Qi Wei, "Ji Bianjiang gewu xinshang hui," *Han haichao* 1, no. 1 (1947): 33.

147. Chen, "Dancing Chinese Nationalism and Anticommunism."

148. Inner Mongolia Song and Dance Ensemble, *Jiantuan sishi zhounian jiniance* (Hohhot, China: Neimenggu gewutuan yishu dang'an ziliaoshi, 1986).

149. Zhou Ge, "Neimenggu xin wudao yishu de cuishengzhe: Wu Xiaobang," in *Wu Xiaobang yu Neimenggu xin wudao yishu*, ed. Hua Ying (Beijing: Wudao zazhi she, 2001), 1–4.

150. Wu's work at the Troupe ended in 1947, and accounts by Mongol dancers suggest that he remained aloof from local culture. Renowned Mongol dancer Baoyinbatu (b. 1929) recalls that Wu found the smell of mutton, a common component of Mongol cuisine, "unbearable." Baoyinbatu, "Neimenggu xin wudao yishu de qimengzhe: ji Wu Xiaobang zai Neimeng de rizi li," in Hua Ying, *Wu Xiaobang yu Neimenggu xin wudao yishu*, 22–24, 23.

151. Dai Ailian, *Wo de yishu*, 76.

152. Ibid., 109–12.

153. Ibid., 121.

154. Peng Song, "Wudao de yaolan: Dai Ailian jianli de Yucai wudao zu," *Yucai jianjie tongxun* (December 1947), reprinted in Peng Song, *Wudao xuezhe Peng Song quanji* (Beijing: Minzu daxue chubanshe, 2011), 6–8.

155. Dai Ailian, "Fazhan Zhongguo wudao di yi bu."

156. Ibid.

157. See, for example, Yu Wenzhou, "Dai Ailian de wudao," *Xiao Shanghairen* 1, no. 1 (1946): 10–12; Jing Pu, "Fayang Zhongguo guyou de yishu," *Xiang-Hai huabao*, no. 3 (1946): 1.

158. On the possible connection between Dai's choreography and the artist Qemberxanim, see "Xinjiang gewutuan nüzhujiao dui Dai Ailian you biaoshi," *Xi shijie*, no. 343 (1947): 2.

159. For Chinese-language accounts of Qemberxanim's life, see Qemberxanim, organized by He Jian'an, "Wo de wudao yishu shengya," *Wenshi ziliao xuanji*, ed. Wenshi ziliao yanjiu weiyuanhui (Beijing: Wenshi ziliao chubanshe, 1985), 205–41; Amina, *Qemberxanim de yishu shengya* (Ürümqi: Xinjiang renmin chubanshe, 1988). For a Uyghur-language account, see Tursunay Yunus, *Ussul Péshwasi Qemberxanim* (Ürümqi: Xinjiang People's Publishing House, 2004). I consulted the latter in a commissioned, unpublished English translation by Akram Hélil.

160. On Tamara Khanum, see Langston Hughes, "Tamara Khanum: Soviet Asia's Greatest Dancer," in *The Collected Works of Langston Hughes: Essays on Art, Race, Politics, and World Affairs*, ed. Christopher C. De Santis (1934; repr., Columbia: University of Missouri Press, 2002), 122–27; Mary Masayo Doi, *Gesture, Gender, Nation: Dance and Social Change in Uzbekistan* (Westport, CT: Bergin & Garvey, 2002), 44–45.

161. "Bianjiang gewu: Xinjiang qingnian gewu fangwentuan yuedui," *Jianguo*, no. 21/22 (1947): 3; "Xinjiang gewu fangwentuan zai Shanghai," *Zhong-Mei zhoubao*, no. 270 (1948): 23–28; "Guan Qemberxanim wu" and "Shiqinghuayi de gewu," *Xibei tongxun*, no. 9 (1947): 16; Gao Zi, "Yishu wudao rensheng: wei Xinjiang qingnian gewutuan zuo," *Nanjing zhongyang ribao zhoukan* 2, no. 5 (1947): 4–5, 16; Liu Longguang, "Xinjiang qingnian gewu fangwentuan," *Yiwen huabao* 2, no. 5 (1947): 2–4. See also Justin Jacobs, "How Chinese Turkestan Became Chinese: Visualizing Zhang Zhizhong's Tianshan Pictorial and Xinjiang Youth Song and Dance Troupe," *Journal of Asian Studies* 67, no. 2 (2008): 545–91.

162. "Huanying Xinjiang gewutuan," *Shenbao*, December 3, 1947.

163. Liang Lun, *Wo de yishu shengya* (Guangzhou: Lingnan meishu chubanshe, 2011); Liang Lun, *Wu meng lu* (Beijing: Zhongguo wudao chubanshe, 1990).

164. Chen Yunyi and Liang Lun, with illustrations by Situ Weiping, "Wuyong Chunniu wufa shuoming," *Yinyue, xiju, shige yuekan*, no. 2 (1947): 13–14; Guangdong Province Dancers Association, *Guangdong wudao yi dai zongshi Liang Lun wudao zuopin (zhaopian) ji* (Guangzhou: Yisheng yinshua youxian gongsi, 2011).

165. "Yi bao wuyong ji jiang yanchu," *Xuesheng bao*, no. 16 (1946): 3; Weng Siyang, "Ji Yi bao yinyue wuyong hui," *Xingye youcheng*, no. 134 (1947): 12–13.

166. Among the event's supporters were poet Wen Yiduo and anthropologist Fei Xiaotong.

167. "Wumi xin yanfu: jieshao 'Bianjiang Miao Yi gewu dahui,'" *Zhongguo dianying*, no. 1 (1946): 16.

168. China Music, Dance, and Drama Society, "Ben she jianshi," Malaya tour special issue, *Zhong yi* (1947): 3; Hu Yuzhi, "Renmin yishu yu minzu yishu," Malaya tour special issue, *Zhong yi* (1947): 3.

169. Liang Lun, "Wudao de Zhongguohua wenti," Malaya tour special issue, *Zhong yi* (1947): 13.

170. Peng Song, "Xin Zhongguo huhuan ni: xin wudao yishu cong zheli tengfei," in *Xin Zhongguo wudao de dianjishi*, ed. Dong Xijiu and Long Yinpei (Hong Kong: Tianma chubanshe, 2008), 5–18, 9; Peng Song, "Tan min wu," *Xin yiyuan*, no. 2 (1948): 4–5.

171. "Dai Ailian jinming biaoyan bianjiangwu," *Shenbao*, August 26, 1946; "Dai Ailian biaoqing shenke bianjiangwu xiaokou changkai," *Shenbao*, August 27, 1946; Shang Guanyao, "Shanghai de bayue feng: kan Dai Ailian da tiao bianjiang wu," *Haichao zhoukan*, no. 20 (1946): 8; Yu Si, "Bianjiang wu mai tongtian, Dai Ailian jiang zhengzhuangchuguo," *Haichao zhoubao*, no. 20 (1946): 1; Zi Hong, "Ye Qianyu, Dai Ailian chuguo zuo danbang," *Haiyan*, no. 2 (1946): 9; Zhou Xiagong, "Dai Ailian zhi wu," *Shanghai texie*, no. 14 (1946): 1.

172. The program, in order, consisted of the following: a ballet segment from *Les Sylphides;* two modern dance works, "Ruth the Gleaner" and "Nostalgia"; and seven Frontier Dance works, "Ba'an *xianzi*," "Spring Outing," "Yao Drum," "Jiarong Drinking Party," "The Mute Carries the Cripple," "Kanba'erhan," and "Dance Song of Youth." "Dai Ailian biaoqing shenke"; Qin Sheng, "Dai Ailian zhi wu," *Jia*, no. 8 (November 1946): 19.

173. Peng Song, "Wudao de yaolan."

174. "Ye Qianyu Dai Ailian mingri you Meiguo di Hu," *Shenbao*, October 26, 1947; "Dai Ailian yu Zhongguo"; "Yansu de wuyongjia," *Funü wenhua* 2, no. 9–10 (1947): 30.

175. Other dancers comparable to Dai in media coverage were Wu Xiaobang and Wang Yuan, a female dancer specializing in exotic and burlesque styles. Wu and Wang were no

longer performing regularly in Shanghai when Dai arrived, and critics suggested that Dai had overtaken both in popularity by the end of her tour. Ah Zhen, "Wu Xiaobang lai Hu kai wudao hui," *Dongnan feng*, no. 21 (1946): 1; Shang Guanyao, "Shanghai de bayue feng"; Zhong Ye, "Dai Ailian de wudao jiemu."

176. Yu Wenzhou, "Dai Ailian de wudao."

177. Xiao Kun, "Dai Ailian zhi wu," *Wencui*, no. 45 (1946): 22.

178. Zhong Ye, "Dai Ailian de wudao jiemu," *Haifeng*, no. 17 (1946): 6.

179. Qin Sheng, "Dai Ailian zhi wu."

180. Mao Shoufeng, "Zhongguo wuta yishujia Dai Ailian," *Ri yue tan*, no. 22 (1946): 16–17.

181. "Haofang reqing Dai Ailian de wudao tian," *Piao*, no. 5 (1946): 2.

182. Bai Junan, "Dai Ailian xiwu shi nian," *Daguanyuan zhoubao*, no. 21 (1946): 11.

183. Qin Sheng, "Dai Ailian zhi wu."

184. Fei Hua, "Wang Yuan yu Dai Ailian," *Qi ri tan*, no. 22 (1946): 3.

185. "Dai Ailian biaoqing."

186. Yu Wenzhou, "Dai Ailian de wudao."

187. Qin Sheng, "Dai Ailian zhi wu."

188. Jing Pu, "Fayang Zhongguo guyou."

189. "Guanyu wuyong yishu shu sun ru ying," *Shenbao*, September 6, 1946.

190. "Kuming de Zhongguoren: Ye Qianyu, Dai Ailian di Hu zhi qianqianhouhou," *Yi si qi huabao* 16, no. 8 (1947): 13; "Dai Ailian zai Beiping," *Meigui huabao* 1, no. 1 (1948): 17; "Wulian xin jihua, jiang xunhui yanchu: wudao jia Dai Ailian lai Ping," *Yanjing xinwen* 16, no. 8 (1948): 13; "Wenhuajie xiao xinwen," *Shen bao*, July 12, 1948; Dai Ailian, *Wo de yishu*, 147.

191. Peng Song, "Xin Zhongguo huhuan ni," 5–6.

192. Liang returned to Hong Kong in January 1949, after two years in Southeast Asia. Liang Lun, *Wo de yishu*, 89.

193. Wu Xiaobang, *Wo de wudao*, 88.

194. DeMare, *Mao's Cultural Army*, 147.

195. Fang Ming, "Wendai hui yanchu ershijiuri," *Guangming ribao*, July 28, 1949.

196. "Zuihou jingcai jiemu"; Yu Shan, "Liangge wanhui de guangan," *Guangming ribao*, July 28, 1949; Fang Ming, "Wei baiwan renmin fuwu de Neimeng wengongtuan," *Guangming ribao*, July 16, 1949.

197. Other works in the program were "Pasture Horse," "Daur," "Oroqen," "Blessing the Yurt," "Going to Meet Chairman Mao," "Blacksmith Dance," "Farmer Dance," "Woodcutter Dance," "Cooperation between Soldiers and Civilians Dance," and "The Farmer and the Snake."

198. Fang Ming, "Wendaihui yanchu"; "Zuihou jingcai jiemu," *Guangming ribao*, July 15, 1949; *Bianjiang minjian wudao jieshao dahui*, performance program dated July 26, 1949, reprinted in Dong and Long, *Xin Zhongguo wudao*, 587–92; Liang Lun, *Wu meng lu*, 227–29.

199. These included "Dance of Youth," "Tibetan Spring Outing," "Duan Gong Exorcises Ghosts," "Jiarong Drinking Party."

200. Jin Feng, "Chongjian quanguo wenyi zuzhi," *Renmin ribao*, March 25, 1949; "Chuxi Bali-Bulage shijie yonghu heping dahui Zhongguo daibiaotuan baogaoshu," *Renmin ribao*, June 4, 1949.

201. "Quanguo wendai dahui jin kaimu," *Renmin ribao*, July 2, 1949.

202. Bo Sheng, "Wendai dahui di ba ri," *Renmin ribao*, July 11, 1949; Fang Ming, "Wendai dahui di ba ri zhuanti fayan," *Guangming ribao*, July 11, 1949.

203. "Xinhua diantai," *Guangming ribao*, July 16, 1949.

204. Mao Hui, *Xin Zhongguo wudao shidian* (Shanghai: Shanghai yinyue chubanshe, 2005), 9; "Chuxi shijie qingnianjie ji shijie qingnian dahui," *Renmin ribao*, July 16, 1949.

205. Those on the initial roster who would go on to play leading roles in the PRC dance field were Dai Ailian, Wu Xiaobang, Hu Guogang, Liang Lun, Peng Song (a.k.a. Zhao Yun[Bang]ge), Jia Zuoguang, Chen Jinqing, Sheng Jie, Hu Sha, Zhao Dexian, Long Weiqiu, Tian Yu, and Ye Ning. "Quanguo yinxie wuxie xiangji xuangao chengli," *Guangming ribao*, July 24, 1949.

206. "Quanguo wenxie yingxie deng tuanti chuxi ji changwei jun yi xuanchu," *Guangming ribao*, August 2, 1949.

207. Wu Xiaobang, *Wo de wudao*, 89.

208. Ibid., 91.

209. Liu Min, ed., *Zhongguo renmin jiefang jun wudao shi* (Beijing: Jiefang jun wenyi chubanshe, 2011).

210. Fang Ming, "Qingzhu renmin zhengxie huiyi da gewu zhunbei yanchu," *Guangming ribao*, September 23, 1949; "Minzu de gewu tuanjie de zhengxiang," *Guangming ribao*, September 27, 1949; "Hua Da san bu ji gongyan da gewu," *Guangming ribao*, October 12, 1949.

CHAPTER 2. EXPERIMENTS IN FORM

1. Fang Ming, "Qingzhu renmin"; Hu Sha, "Renmin shengli wansui dagewu chuangzuo jingguo," *Renmin ribao*, November 1, 1949. Exact estimates of the number of people vary. Fang gives the number as 180, but Hu estimates that 250 were involved. About 80 of these were dancers.

2. On recruiting of folk performers, see Fang Ming, "Qingzhu renmin"; on Dai's solo, see "Minzu de gewu"; on Wang Yi and the Shaanbei waist drum dancers, see Chang-tai Hung, "Yangge: The Dance of Revolution," in Chang-tai Hung, *Mao's New World: Political Culture in the Early People's Republic*, (Ithaca, NY: Cornell University Press, 2011), 75–91, 82; Wang Kefen and Long Yinpei, eds., *Zhongguo jinxiandai dangdai wudao fazhan shi, 1840–1996* (Beijing: Renmin yinyue chubanshe, 1999), 179.

3. Hu Sha, "Renmin shengli wansui."

4. Tian Han, "Renmin gewu wansui! Ping 'Renmin shengli wansui' da gewu," *Renmin ribao*, November 7, 1949.

5. Hu Sha, "Renmin shengli wansui."

6. Tian Han, "Renmin gewu wansui!"

7. Dai Ailian, "Fazhan Zhongguo wudao di yi bu."

8. Dai Ailian, to Sylvia (Si-Lan) Chen, May 2, 1950, Jay and Si-Lan Chen Leyda Papers and Photographs, 1913–1987, TAM.083, Box 28, Folder 7, Tamiment Library and Robert F. Wagner Labor Archive, New York.

9. Leyda, *Footnote to History*, 299–310.

10. Dong Xijiu and Long Yinpei, *Xin Zhongguo wudao de dianjishi*.

11. Central Academy of Drama News Group, "Zhongyang xiju xueyuan san ge wengongtuan," *Guangming ribao*, May 23, 1950.

12. Ibid.

13. Ming, "Huanan zuojiamen xie Hainan zhandou yingxiong," *Guangming ribao*, August 12, 1950.

14. Liang Lun, *Wo de yishu shengya*, 103.

15. Central Academy of Drama News Group, "'Heping ge' wuju zuowan zai Jing kaishi shangyan," *Renmin ribao*, October 11, 1950; Ouyang Yuqian, "Jiti de liliang wancheng jiti de yishu," *Renmin ribao*, October 13, 1950.

16. Central Academy of Drama News Group, "'Heping ge.'"

17. "Huanan wenyi jinxun: Guangzhou yanchu 'Chengfengpolang jiefang Hainan,'" *Guangming ribao*, August 25, 1950; South China Cultural Work Troupe, "Chengfengpolang jiefang Hainan," *Renmin huabao* 1, no. 6 (December 1950): 38; Guangdong Province Dancers Association, *Guangdong wudao*, 89–95.

18. Shi Mingxin and Ming Zhi, "Lüetan 'Chengfengpolang jiefang Hainan' de yinyue chuangzuo," *Renmin yinyue*, no. 2 (1951): 26–27, 27.

19. Liang Lun, "Guanyu 'Chengfengpolang jiefang Hainan' de chuangzuo," *Wudao tongxun*, no. 1 *(Huiyan zhuanhao)* (July 1951): 8–10.

20. Shi Mingxin and Ming Zhi, "Lüetan 'Chengfengpolang.'"

21. A popular form of rhythmic storytelling accompanied by wooden clappers, often used in folk performance.

22. Liang Lun, "Guanyu 'Chengfengpolang," 8.

23. Wilcox, "Dancers Doing Fieldwork."

24. Liang Lun, "Guanyu 'Chengfengpolang,'" 8.

25. Guangdong Province Dancers Association, *Guangdong wudao*, 89–95.

26. Shi Mingxin and Ming Zhi, "Lüetan 'Chengfengpolang,'" 26.

27. Ibid., 26.

28. Ibid., 27.

29. Ibid., 27.

30. This account of the percussion instruments is based on Bell Yung, "Model Opera as Model: From *Shajiabang* to *Sagabong*," in McDougall, *Popular Chinese Literature*, 144–64, 150.

31. South China Cultural Work Troupe, "Chengfengpolang," 38; Guangdong Province Dancers Association, *Guangdong wudao*, 89–95.

32. "Geju 'Wang Gui yu Li Xiangxiang' yu wuju 'Heping ge' zuotan," *Renmin yinyue*, no. 1 (1951): 9–16, 13.

33. *Heping ge*, performance program, September 1950, Beijing Dance Academy Archives. See also *Heping ge*, performance program, stage photographs, and director's notes, September 1950, in Dong Xijiu and Long Yinpei, *Xin Zhongguo wudao*, 630–43.

34. Ming, "Baowei shijie heping daxing wuju 'Heping ge' zhengzai paiyan zhong," *Guangming ribao*, August 30, 1950.

35. Ouyang Yuqian, "Jiti de liliang."

36. The dockworker scene was originally set in Japan, but this setting was changed at the last minute due to "inconsistencies with policy." The word *Japan* was inked out in the programs. "Geju 'Wang Gui,'" 13; *Heping ge*.

37. "Geju 'Wang Gui.'"

38. Zhong Dianfei, "Lun 'Heping ge,'" *Wenyi bao*, no. 2 (1950): 27–30.

39. Chen Jinqing, "Canjia paiyan 'Heping ge' de ganxiang," *Renmin xiju*, no. 6 (1950): 27.

40. Wu Yinbo and Xia Yuqing, "Heping ge," *Renmin huabao* 1, no. 6 (December 1950): 38.

41. Ibid.

42. According to the orchestra cast list, the instruments included violins and violas, cellos, contrabass, flutes/piccolos, oboes, clarinets, a bassoon, trumpets, trombones, tubas, timpani, French horns, and pianos. *Heping ge* program in Dong Xijiu and Long Yinpei, *Xin Zhongguo wudao*, 636.

43. "Geju 'Wang Gui,'" 15.

44. Wu Yinbo and Xia Yuqing, "Heping ge"; *Heping ge*, stage photographs in Dong Xijiu and Long Yinpei, *Xin Zhongguo wudao*, 40–42.

45. Guang Weiran, "Zhengshi ziji de cuowu," *Renmin ribao*, January 22, 1952.

46. Sun Jingchen, "Wudao jie weishenme meiyou dongjing," *Renmin ribao*, March 18, 1955; Cheng Yun, "Du 'Yinyue wudao chuangzuo de minzu xingshi wenti,'" *Renmin ribao*, August 18, 1956.

47. "Huanan wenyi jinxun."

48. Wu Yinbo and Xia Yuqing, "Heping ge."

49. South China Cultural Work Troupe, "Chengfengpolang"; Liang Lun, "Guanyu 'Chengfengpolang,'" 10. For comparison, one discount ticket to see *Peace Dove* cost 4,000 yuan at this time. Central Academy of Drama News, "Heping ge xuyan liang tian," *Renmin ribao*, November 18, 1950.

50. Shi Mingxin and Ming Zhi, "Lüetan 'Chengfengpolang,'" 26.

51. Liang Lun, "*Wo de yishu*," 105; Fan Ming, "Kan wudao guanmo huiyan de ji dian ganxiang," *Guangming ribao*, May 24, 1951.

52. Wu Xiaobang, "Yi jiu wu yi nian," *Wudao tongxun*, no. 1 *(Huiyan zhuanhao)* (July 1951): 3.

53. Ibid., 3.

54. Fan Ming, "Kan wudao guanmo."

55. Hu Sha, "Lun xiang minzu chuantong de wudao yishu xuexi," *Wudao tongxun*, no. 1 *(Huiyan zhuanhao)* (July 1951): 5–7, 6.

56. Peng Song, "Xin Zhongguo huhuan ni," in Dong Xijiu and Long Yinpei, *Xin Zhongguo*, 15.

57. Ibid., 16.

58. Guang Weiran, "Zhengshi ziji de." On the importance of this event in Chinese dance drama history, see Yu Ping, *Zhongguo xiandangdai wuju fazhanshi* (Beijing: Renmin yinyue chubanshe, 2004), 70–71.

59. During the early PRC, universities recruited students from nontraditional backgrounds, especially peasants, workers, and soldiers who otherwise would have had little access to higher education. On cultural clashes resulting from such programs, see Douglas A. Stiffler, "Creating 'New China's First New-Style Regular University,' 1949–50," in *Dilemmas of Victory: The Early Years of the People's Republic of China*, ed. Jeremy Brown and Paul Pickowicz (Cambridge, MA: Harvard University Press, 2007), 288–308.

60. The original phrase was "*datui man tai pao, gongnongbing shoubuliao*." Zhong Dianfei, "Lun 'Heping ge,'" 29.

61. Peng Song, "Xin Zhongguo huhuan ni," 17.

62. Yu Ping, *Zhongguo xiandangdai*, 70–71.

63. Guang Weiran, "Tan wuju 'Heping ge' de yanchu," *Renmin ribao*, October 17, 1950.

64. Zhong Dianfei, "Lun 'Heping ge,'" 27–28.

65. Ibid., 28.

66. Ibid., 29.

67. "Geju 'Wang Gui,'" 15.

68. Hu Sha, "Lun xiang minzu," 5.

69. "Renmin shengli wansui," performance programs and photographs in Dong and Long, *Xin Zhongguo*.

70. Tian Han, "Renmin gewu wansui!"

71. Chang-tai Hung, "Yangge," 85–87.

72. For more on this tour, see Emily Wilcox, "Beyond Internal Orientalism: Dance and Nationality Discourse in the Early People's Republic of China, 1949–1954," *Journal of Asian Studies* 75, no. 2 (May 2016): 363–86. For more on the minority tour system as a whole, see Uradyn Bulag, "Seeing Like a Minority: Political Tourism and the Struggle for Recognition in China," *Journal of Current Chinese Affairs* 41, no. 4 (April 2012): 133–58.

73. The Southwest included parts of today's Yunnan, Guizhou, Sichuan, and Tibet.

74. "Zhou zongli huanyan ge minzu daibiao," *Renmin ribao*, September 29, 1950; "Lai Jing canjia guoqing shengdian de gezu daibiao," *Renmin ribao*, October 4, 1950.

75. "Xiannongtan de shenghui," *Guangming ribao*, October 23, 1950.

76. Xiao Feng, "Genzhe ni, Mao zhuxi!" (parts 1–3), *Guangming ribao*, October 11–14, 1950.

77. Chen Zhengqing et al., "Zhonghua renmin gongheguo ge minzu tuanjie qilai," *Renmin huabao* 1, no. 5 (November 1950): 36–38; "Shoudu qingzhu guoqingjie," *Guangming ribao*, October 15, 1950; Ming, "Wei chuangzuo xin de wudao nuli," *Guangming ribao*, October 21, 1950; additional *Guangming ribao* reports on October 17, 23, 26, 29, and 30.

78. *Songs of Tengri Tagh (Tianshan zhi ge)* (Northwest Film Corporation and Central Film Studio, 1948). On the making of this film, see "Xuanweihui yu wenxie zhaodai wenhuajie fangying 'Tianshan zhi ge,'" *Xinjiang ribao*, June 30, 1948; Luo Shaowen, "Lishi de qianying he zuyi: Tianshan gewutuan fangwen zuguo dongnan zhuiji," *Xinjiang yishu*, no. 2 (1997): 34–41.

79. Qemberxanim's "Plate Dance," in *Songs of Tengri Tagh*.

80. Chen Jinqing, "Guanyu xin wudao yishu," *Wenyi bao*, no. 2 (1950): 20–23.

81. Hung, "Yangge," 88–90.

82. Zhong Dianfei, "Lun 'Heping ge,'" 29.

83. Ibid., 29.

84. Wu Xiaobang, "Tuijian Neimeng wengongtuan de 'Ma dao wu,'" *Renmin ribao*, October 15, 1950.

85. Ji Gang, "Kan le 'Yan wu' yihou," *Guangming ribao*, October 18, 1950.

86. Qemberxanim, "Wo de wudao," 237.

87. Ji Lanwei and Qiu Jiurong, *Zhongguo shaoshu minzu wudao shi* (Beijing: Zhongyang minzu daxue chubanshe, 1998), 434.

88. Ibid., 442. Shen Qiru, "Shaoshu minzu yishu de huapu," *Guangming ribao*, October 3, 1951.

89. Qemberxanim, "Wudao jiaoxue jingyan jianshu," in *Wudao xuexi ziliao*, ed. China Dance Art Research Association Preparatory Committee, no. 1 (April 1954): 32–35, 32, Beijing Dance Academy Archives.

90. Ibid., 33.

91. Qemberxanim helped train teachers for the Beijing Dance School. Bai Yu, "Beijing wudao xuexiao kaishi zhaosheng," *Renmin ribao*, July 14, 1954.

92. Qemberxanim, "Wudao jiaoxue"; Qemberxanim, "Wo de wudao," 237.

93. Qemberxanim, "Wo de wudao," 237.

94. The CAD group became known as the Central Song and Dance Ensemble (Zhongyang gewutuan), and the CAN group became known as Central Nationalities Song and Dance Ensemble (Zhongyang minzu gewutuan). "Zhongyang minzu gewutuan qingzhu jiantuan shi zhounian," *Wudao*, no. 5 (1962): 38.

95. On the political significance and relationship of these ensembles, see Zhang Yuling, "Xin Zhongguo 'shiqi nian' zhongzhi yuantuan wudao tuandui zhengzhi gongneng fenxi," *Changjiang daxue xuebao* 35, no. 2 (2012): 115–17.

96. "Zhongyang minzu gewutuan qingzhu jiantuan shi zhounian," 38.

97. "Zhongyang minzu xueyuan minzu wengongtuan xinan gongzuodui luguo Xi'an zhuanfu Chongqing," *Guangming ribao*, September 25, 1952.

98. Ao Enhong, "Gesong meili de shenghuo," *Renmin huabao* 3, no. 1 (1952): 9–10.

99. Elizabeth Wichmann, *Listening to Theatre: The Aural Dimension of Beijing Opera* (Honolulu: University of Hawai'i Press, 1991); Ruru Li, *The Soul of Beijing Opera: Theatrical Creativity and Continuity in the Changing World* (Hong Kong: Hong Kong University Press, 2010).

100. Duhyun Lee et al., *Korean Performing Arts: Drama, Dance & Music Theater* (Seoul: Jipmoondang Publishing, 1997); Judy Van Zile, *Perspectives on Korean Dance* (Middletown, CT: Wesleyan University Press, 2001); Sang Mi Park, "The Making of a Cultural Icon for the Japanese Empire: Choe Seung-hui's U.S. Dance Tours and 'New Asian Culture' in the 1930s and 1940s," *positions* 14, no. 3 (2004): 597–632; Young-Hoon Kim, "Border Crossing: Choe Seung-hui's Life and the Modern Experience," *Korea Journal* 46, no. 1 (Spring 2006): 170–97; E. Taylor Atkins, *Primitive Selves: Koreana in the Japanese Colonial Gaze, 1910–1945* (Berkeley: University of California Press, 2010); Judy Van Zile, "Performing Modernity in Korea: The Dance of Ch'oe Sung-hui," *Korean Studies* 37 (2013): 124–49; Faye Yuan Kleeman, *In Transit: The Formation of the Colonial East Asian Cultural Sphere* (Honolulu: University of Hawai'i Press, 2014); Alfredo Romero Castilla, "Choi Seunghee (Sai Shoki): The Dancing Princess from the Peninsula in Mexico," *Journal of Society for Dance Documentation and History* 44 (March 2017): 81–96.

101. Emily Wilcox, "Locating Performance: Choe Seung-hui, East Asian Modernisms, and the Case for Area Knowledge in Dance Studies," in *The Futures of Dance Studies*, ed. Susan Manning, Janice Ross, and Rebecca Schneider (Madison: University of Wisconsin Press, 2019); Suzy Kim, "Choe Seung-hui between Ballet and Folk: Aesthetics of National Form and Socialist Content in North Korea" (paper presented at the Dancing East Asia conference, University of Michigan, Ann Arbor, MI, April 7, 2017).

102. Li Zhengyi et al., *Zhongguo gudianwu jiaoxue tixi chuangjian fazhan shi* (Shanghai: Shanghai yinyue chubanshe, 2004); Su Ya, *Qiusuo xinzhi: Zhongguo gudianwu xuexi biji* (Beijing: Zhongguo xiju chubanshe, 2004); Li Aishun, "Cui Chengxi yu Zhongguo wudao,"

Beijing wudao xueyuan xuebao, no. 4 (2005): 16–22; Tian Jing and Li Baicheng, eds., *Xin Zhongguo wudao yishujia de yaolan* (Beijing: Zhongguo wenlian chubanshe, 2005).

103. For visual documentation of these changes, see Takashima Yusaburo and Chong Pyong-ho, *Seiki no bijin buyoka Sai Shoki* (Tokyo: MT Publishing Company, 1994); *Choi Seunghee: The Story of a Dancer*, directed by Won Jongsun (Arirang TV, 2008).

104. Kleeman, "Dancers of the Empire," 191–92.

105. Tara Rodman, "Altered Belonging: The Transnational Modern Dance of Ito Michio" (PhD diss., Northwestern University, 2017), 65–70. For another account with conflicting dates, see Toshiharu Omuka, "Dancing and Performing: Japanese Artists in the Early 1920s at the Dawn of Modern Dance," *Experiment* 10 (2004), 157–70.

106. Park, "The Making of a Cultural Icon," 601–13; Taylor Atkins, *Primitive Selves*, 170–75.

107. Kim, "Border Crossing"; Atkins, *Primitive Selves*.

108. Won, *Choi Seunghee*; "Chongyi zhe meili de wuji Cui Chengxi," *Taipingyang zhoubao* 1, no. 84 (1943): 1853.

109. Choe performed for both Japanese soldiers and general audiences. James R. Brandon, *Kabuki's Forgotten War: 1931–1945*, University of Hawai'i Press, 2008), 201; "Zhongguo de Kunjue daodi buru renjia," *San liu jiu huabao* 24, no. 14 (1943): 21; Liu Junsheng, "Lun Cui Chengxi de wudao," *Zazhi* 12, no. 2 (1943): 26–30.

110. Li Aishun, "Cui Chengxi yu Zhongguo wudao," 17.

111. Kleeman, "Dancers of the Empire," 205.

112. Ao Jianqing, "Cui Chengxi, Mei Lanfang huijian ji," *Taipingyang zhoubao* 1, no. 93 (1944): 2102–3; "Cui Chengxi wudao zuotanhui," *Zazhi* 12, no. 2 (1943): 41–46.

113. Su Ya, *Qiusuo xinzhi*, 11.

114. Kleeman, "Dancers of the Empire," 203–4.

115. Ibid., 207.

116. Ibid., 207–8.

117. A. Jituoweiqi and B. Bu'ersuofu, "Zhuming de wudaojia: Cui Chengxi," trans. Wang Jinling, *Renmin ribao*, December 9, 1949; Won, *Choi Seunghee*; Kim, "Choe Seung-hui between Ballet and Folk."

118. "Wenhua bu, quanguo wenlian juxing wanhui 'Cui Chengxi biaoyan chaoxian wuyong,'" *Guangming ribao*, December 13, 1949.

119. For more contextualization of this shift, see Wilcox, "Locating Performance."

120. Bai Sheng, "Zhong Chao renmin zhandou de youyi: fang Chaoxian renmin yishujia Cui Chengxi," *Renmin ribao*, December 11, 1950.

121. Zhu Ying, "Jingshi funü jie kang Mei yuan Chao baojiaweiguo weiyuanhui yaoqing Han Xueya Cui Chengxi jiangyan," *Renmin ribao*, November 27, 1950.

122. "Guonei wenyi dongtai," *Renmin ribao*, February 11, 1951.

123. Bai Sheng, "Zhong Chao renmin zhandou de youyi."

124. Jiang Zuhui (b. 1934) also studied with Choi in 1949–50. Dong Xijiu and Long Yinpei, *Xin Zhongguo*, 528, 731.

125. Chen Jinqing, "Guanyu xin wudao."

126. Ibid., 22.

127. Tian Jing and Li Baicheng, eds., *Xin Zhongguo wudao yishujia de yaolan* (Beijing: Zhongguo wenlian chubanshe, 2005), 284.

128. "Zhengli Zhongguo wudao yishu peizhi zhuanye wudao ganbu," *Guangming ribao*, February 14, 1951.

129. Choe Seung-hui, "Zhongguo wudao yishu de jianglai," *Renmin ribao*, February 18, 1951.

130. Choe Seung-hui, "Zhongguo wudao."

131. For documentation of this program, including courses taught, photographs, and names and biographies of students enrolled, see Tian Jing and Li Baicheng, *Xin Zhongguo*, 271–556.

132. The original quota was for 55 Chinese and 55 North Korean students. On opening day, only 30 North Korean students were enrolled. A retrospective account cites 120 students: 85 Chinese and 35 Korean. Fang Ming, "Peiyang Zhong Chao wudao gongzuo ganbu Cui Chengxi wudao yanjiuban chengli," *Guangming ribao*, March 20, 1951; Gu Yewen, ed., *Chaoxian wudaojia Cui Chengxi* (Shanghai: Wenlian chubanshe, 1951), 53–57; Tian Jing and Li Baicheng, *Xin Zhongguo*, 279–80.

133. Many students in this course went on to become prominent performers, teachers, and choreographers of Chinese dance. Examples include Baoyinbatu, Cui Meishan, Gao Jinrong, Jiang Zuhui, Lan Hang, Li Zhengyi, Shu Qiao, Siqintariha, Wang Shiqi, and Zhang Minxin.

134. Tian Jing and Li Baicheng, *Xin Zhongguo*, 471.

135. Ibid., 475.

136. Ibid., 409.

137. Fang Ming, "Peiyang Zhong Chao."

138. Also known as Eastern dance *(Dongfang wu)*. It was Choi's own creation, based largely on Indian and Thai material.

139. A short documentary film was produced on this program in July 1951. "'Bei Ying' zuijin wancheng liu bu zuixin julupian," *Guangming ribao*, July 12, 1951.

140. "Zhengli Zhongguo wudao," *Guangming ribao*, February 14, 1951; Gu Yewen, ed., *Chaoxian wudaojia Cui Chengxi*, 58–62.

141. Fang Ming, "Peiyang Zhong Chao."

142. Writers used Choe's research to defend the artistic value of xiqu, and a new Center for Xiqu Research was established with Choe's and Dai's support. "Zhongguo xiqu yanjiuyuan chengli," *Renmin ribao*, April 5, 1951; Shi Nan, "Dui xiqu gaige de yixie yijian," *Guangming ribao*, October 12, 1951.

143. Hu Sha, "Lun xiang minzu."

144. "Hongchou wu" performance recording in *Caidie fenfei* (Beijing: Beijing Film Studio, 1963).

145. Xi Zhi, "Chouwu de xuexi guocheng," *Wudao tongxun*, no. 1 *(Huiyan zhuanhao)* (July 1951): 7.

146. Wang Kewei, *Hongchou wu* (Shanghai: Shanghai Lukaiji Bookstore, 1953).

147. Wang Kewei, *Hongchou wu*, 8–23.

148. Tian Jing and Li Baicheng, *Xin Zhongguo*, 286.

149. Dai Ailian, "Qingzhu Cui Chengxi de wudao chuangzuo gongyanhui," *Shijie zhishi*, no. 20 (1951): 16.

150. Dong Xijiu and Long Yinpei, eds., *Xin Zhongguo wudao de dianjishi*, 573.

151. "Beijing wudao xuexiao kaixue," *Guangming ribao*, September 8, 1954.

152. Beijing Dance School started as a six-year program, but there were plans to extend it to seven, or even nine, years. Beijing Dance Academy Annals Editing Committee, *Beijing wudao xueyuan zhi* (Beijing: Beijing gaodeng xuexiao xiaozhi congshu, 1993), 2.

153. Bai Yu, "Beijing wudao xuexiao."

154. Ibid.; Beijing Dance Academy, *Beijing wudao xueyuan zhi*, 1.

155. Beijing Dance Academy, *Beijing wudao xueyuan zhi*.

156. Ibid., 73, 245.

157. The full title was Oriental Music and Dance Course (Dongfang yinyue wudao ban). On its history, see Emily Wilcox, "Performing Bandung: China's Dance Diplomacy with India, Indonesia, and Burma, 1953–1962," *Inter-Asia Cultural Studies* 18, no. 4 (2017): 518–39.

158. Beijing Dance Academy, *Beijing wudao xueyuan zhi*, 249.

159. Bai Yu, "Beijing wudao xuexiao."

160. Beijing Dance Academy, *Beijing wudao xueyuan zhi*, 11. See also "Beijing wudao." Some accounts also include Bai Yunsheng and Liu Yufang. Li Zhengyi, *Zhongguo gudianwu jiaoxue tixi*, 9.

161. Zhao Tiechen, "Xueke lishi huigu," in *Zhongguo wudao gaodeng jiaoyu 30 nian xueshu wenji: Zhongguo minzu minjian wu yanjiu*, ed. Zhao Tiechun (Beijing: Gaodeng jiaoyu chubanshe, 2009), 1–12, 1; Bai Yu, "Beijing wudao xuexiao."

162. "Beijing wudao"; Beijing Dance Academy, *Beijing wudao xueyuan zhi*, 1. Ol'ga Il'ina remained at BDS until November 1956. Beijing Dance Academy, *Beijing wudao xueyuan zhi*, 291. Il'ina was the first of six Soviet instructors who taught in the ballet and choreography programs between 1954 and 1960. Viktor Ivanovich Tsaplin taught choreography between September 1955 and July 1958; Nikolai Nikolaevich Serebrennikov taught partnering between September 1957 and August 1959; Tamara Leshevich taught character dance and European folk dance from September 1955 to July 1958; Valentina Rumiantseva taught ballet between December 1957 and June 1960; and Petr Gusev taught the second dance drama choreography program and helped direct ballet productions between December 1957 and June 1960. Christina Ezrahi helped confirm the identities of these individuals.

163. Beijing Dance Academy, *Beijing wudao xueyuan zhi*, 72. All had worked with Dai and Wu in the 1940s and had been leaders in the Beijing dance scene since 1949.

164. Ibid., 72. Yuan studied ballet with Russian teachers in pre-1949 Shanghai, and Lu danced in the CAD Dance Ensemble.

165. Ibid., 11.

166. Two teachers who initially taught Chinese classical dance at the school were graduates of Choe's CAD course: Li Zhengyi (b. 1929) and Yang Zongguang (1935–1968); Li Zhengyi, *Zhongguo gudianwu*, 12–13; Su Ya, *Qiusuo xinzhi*.

167. Ministry of Culture Beijing Dance School, *Shixi yanchu*, artistic director Ol'ga Il'ina, performance program dated May 1955, Beijing, author's collection. Of twenty-one pieces included in the show, ten were new works of Chinese dance, in styles of Han folk dance, minority dance, and xiqu-style classical dance. The remaining eleven works were ballet or European folk dance. The latter included one solo (a Tajik "Knife Dance" from Igor Moiseyev's Russian folk dance ensemble), three duets (a waltz, a comedic ice skating dance, and a Chinese character dance), a jump-rope dance, a "Little Chicken" dance, and several segments from acts 2 and 3 of *Swan Lake*, including the Mazurka, Hungarian dance, Spanish dance, and the "four swans" dance.

168. Ministry of Culture Beijing Dance School, *Shixi yanchu*. The choreographers listed for this work are Peng Song (Zhao Yunge), Zhu Pin, and Wang Zenan. This piece was also included in the school's contribution to the opening ceremonies of the Beijing summer music and dance season. "Beijing xiaji yinyue wudao wanhui kaimu," *Guangming ribao*, May 31, 1955.

169. Stage photographs dated 1955, Beijing Dance Academy Archives.

170. The Korean dance was adapted by Chen Chunlu and Piao Guangshu. The Uyghur dance was choreographed by Luo Xiongyan and Li Zhengkang, the Tibetan dance by Li Chengxiang, and the Mongol dance by Jia Zuoguang. Ministry of Culture Beijing Dance School, *Shixi yanchu*.

171. Stage photographs dated 1955, Beijing Dance Academy Archives.

172. The tenth work of Chinese dance was not given a stylistic label. It was described as a "children's dance drama based on a folk legend" and was choreographed by Chinese classical dance instructor Tang Mancheng. Ministry of Culture Beijing Dance School, *Shixi yanchu*.

173. Jiang Zuhui performed "Picking Flowers," and Li Zhengyi and Yang Zongguang performed "Interrupted Dream." Ministry of Culture Beijing Dance School, *Shixi yanchu*. Stage photographs dated 1955, Beijing Dance Academy Archives.

174. Ministry of Culture Beijing Dance School, *Shixi yanchu*.

175. Beijing Dance Academy, *Beijing wudao xueyuan zhi*, 251.

176. "Wudaojia de yaolan," *Guangming ribao*, July 7, 1956.

177. Beijing Dance School, *Zhongguo gudianwu jiaoxue fa* (Beijing: Beijing wudao xuexiao ziliaoshi, 1960).

178. "Quanguo yinyue wudao huiyan bimu," *Guangming ribao*, January 24, 1957.

179. Beijing Dance Academy, *Beijing wudao xueyuan zhi*, 249.

180. See Beijing Dance Academy, *Beijing wudao xueyuan zhi*, 15, 249.

181. Wilcox, "Performing Bandung."

CHAPTER 3. PERFORMING A SOCIALIST NATION

1. Wu Xinlu, Qi Guanshan, and Zheng Guanghua, "Qingzhu di liu jie gouqing jie," *Renmin huabao*, no. 10 (1955): 1–3.

2. Dai Ailian, "Yi 'Hehua,'" in *Wudao wuju chuangzuo jingyan wenji*, ed. Zhongguo yishu yanjiuyuan wudao yanjiusuo (Beijing: Renmin yinyue chubanshe, 1985), 20–25; Jia Anlin, ed., *Zhongwai wudao zuopin shangxi: Zhongguo minzu minjian wu zuopin shangxi* (Shanghai: Shanghai yinyue chubanshe, 2004), 221–23.

3. "Lotus Dance" stage photographs, China Opera and Dance Drama Theater Archives; "Zhongguo qingnian yanchu de 'Hehua wu,'" *Renmin ribao*, June 26, 1954; "Lotus Dance" performance recording, in *Zhongguo dangdai wudao jingcui*, directed by Wu Yunming (Beijing: China Academy of Arts Dance Research Institute, 1993).

4. Jia Anlin, *Zhongwai wudao zuopin shangxi*, 221–22.

5. Dai Ailian, "Yi 'Hehua,'" 20–21.

6. Ibid., 20.

7. Xu Jie, "Women de 'Hehua wu,'" *Guangming ribao*, July 31, 1954. According to Dai, the lotus theme was requested by Zhou Enlai to ingratiate China to an Indian delegation

visiting Beijing for the Asia and Pacific Rim Peace Conference in October 1952. Dai Ailian, "Yi 'Hehua,'" 20.

8. Xu Jie, "Women de 'Hehua wu'"; Nicolai Volland, "Translating the Socialist State: Cultural Exchange, National Identity, and the Socialist World in the Early PRC," *Twentieth-Century China* 33, no. 2 (2007): 51–72.

9. "True Folk Art," *Festival: Journal of the International Festival Committee*, no. 24 (August 9, 1953): n.p., World Festival of Youth and Students Collection ARCH01667, Binder 9, Folder 4, International Institute of Social History, Amsterdam; "Festival Cultural Teams Rehearse," *Festival: Journal of the International Festival Committee*, no. 16 (August 1, 1953): 7, World Festival of Youth and Students Collection ARCH01667, Binder 9, Folder 4, International Institute of Social History, Amsterdam.

10. Sheng Jie, "Zai guoji wenhua jiaoliu huodong zhong de Zhongguo wudao," *Wudao*, no. 10 (1959): 6–8, 8; "Un Merveilleux Programme Artistique Chinois," *Festival: Organe du Comité International du Festival*, no. 10 (August 15, 1951): n.p., World Festival of Youth and Students Collection ARCH01667, Binder 9, Folder 4, International Institute of Social History, Amsterdam.

11. "Woguo qingnian yishutuan dejiang mingdan," *Guangming ribao*, August 17, 1953.

12. Chinese Dance Art Research Association, *Zhongguo minjian wudao xuanji* (Beijing: Yishu chubanshe, 1954).

13. "Record Crowd at Chinese Show," *Times of India*, December 20, 1954; "Picking Tea and Catching Butterflies" stage photograph in University of Michigan Pioneers of Chinese Dance Digital Archive, https://quod.lib.umich.edu/d/dance11c; *Zhongguo yishu tuan*, performance program from 1955 tour to Italy, in Sophia Delza Papers, (S)*MGZMD 155, Box 69, Folder 15, Jerome Robbins Dance Division, New York Public Library for the Performing Arts. On the 1954 India tour, see Wilcox, "Performing Bandung."

14. *Zhongguo wudao tupian mulu*, gift album dated September 4, 1955, in KOLO Serbia State Folk Dance Ensemble Archives, Belgrade.

15. "Zhou zongli jiejian Nan minjian gewutuan fuzeren," *Renmin ribao*, August 30, 1955.

16. WFYS festival poster, dated 1957, in World Festival of Youth and Students Collection ARCH01667, Binder 9, Folder 1, International Institute of Social History, Amsterdam.

17. See articles naming the dance in *Guangming ribao*.

18. *Zhongguo yishu tuan*, performance program from 1960 tour to Canada, in Sophia Delza Papers, (S)*MGZMD 155, Box 69, Folder 15, Jerome Robbins Dance Division, New York Public Library for the Performing Arts; *Zhongguo yishu tuan*, performance program from 1960 tour to Colombia, Cuba, and Venezuela, University of Michigan Asia Library Chinese Dance Collection.

19. Cover photo, *Renmin huabao*, no. 19 (1960).

20. Wu Yinxian and Wu Yinbo, "Geming wenyi yundong de fangxiang," *Renmin huabao*, no. 7 (1962): 2–3, 3.

21. *Caidie fenfei* (Beijing Film Studio, 1963).

22. "Zhongzhu Zhonghua renmin gongheguo chengli shiwu zhounian," *Renmin ribao*, October 10, 1964; "Zhong-A youxie dianying zhaodaihui qingzhu Alian guoqing," *Renmin ribao*, July 23, 1964.

23. For a discussion of this assertion and its historical validity, see Yu Ping, *Zhongguo xiandangdai wuju fazhanshi*, 48–49.

24. Song Tianyi, *Zhongwai biaoyan yishu jiaoliu shilüe, 1949–1992* (Beijing: Wenhua yishu chubanshe, 1994), 226–37; Emily Wilcox, "The Postcolonial Blind Spot: Chinese Dance in the Era of Third World-ism, 1949–1965," *positions: asia critique* 26, no. 4 (2018): forthcoming; Wilcox, "Performing Bandung."

25. Sheng Jie, "Zai guoji wenhua jiaoliu huodong zhong de Zhongguo wudao"; Tian Yu, "Shijie qingnian lianhuanjie sanji," *Wudao*, no. 5 (1962): 44–46. Although the PRC was not yet established when the 1949 delegation attended, it was received as a representative of socialist China. "Bashiwu guo qingnian daibiao tongsheng huanhu," *Renmin ribao*, August 20, 1949.

26. Song Tianyi, *Zhongwai biaoyan*, 182–90. These dates are for the first visits of performance delegations specifically featuring dance. In some cases, ensembles that specialized in drama, music, or acrobatics visited earlier.

27. Emily Wilcox, "When Place Matters: Provincializing the 'Global,'" in *Rethinking Dance History: Issues and Methodologies*, 2nd ed., ed. Larraine Nicholas and Geraldine Morris (Abingdon, UK, and New York: Routledge, 2018), 160–72.

28. Chinese and other Asian contributions to international dance developments, though present, were often not acknowledged at this time. Yutian Wong, *Choreographing Asian America* (Middletown, CT: Wesleyan University Press, 2010); Priya Srinivasan, *Sweating Saris: Indian Dance as Transnational Labor* (Philadelphia: Temple University Press, 2012).

29. The *People's Daily* published over thirty articles on this tour, which contain descriptions of local reception and political intrigues surrounding the enlisting of Soviet help to transport the ensemble from Cuba to Canada. I will focus only on the dance program it presented. "Woguo yishutuan zai Weineiruila shouci yanchu," *Renmin ribao*, April 29, 1960; Song Tianyi, *Zhongwai biaoyan*, 186. Song also includes Switzerland on the list of countries visited, but I have not been able to verify this in contemporary sources.

30. On a similarly structured tour sent to the United States in 1978, see Emily Wilcox, "Foreword: A Manifesto for Demarginalization," in *Chinese Dance: In the Vast Land and Beyond*, ed. Shih-Ming Li Chang and Lynn Frederiksen (Middletown, CT: Wesleyan University Press, 2016), ix–xxiii.

31. A program from the Canada portion of the tour is housed in the Sophia Delza collection at the New York Public Library for the Performing Arts; a program from the Latin America portion of the tour is housed in the University of Michigan Chinese Dance Collection (see n. 18). On film footage, see nn. 36–38.

32. Sheng Jie, "Zai guoji wenhua jiaoliu huodong zhong de Zhongguo wudao," 7–8. I am not including segments of Chinese opera that won awards as dance items.

33. The list of dances is the same in the two programs.

34. Thomas S. Mullaney, *Coming to Terms with the Nation: Ethnic Classification in Modern China* (Berkeley: University of California Press, 2011).

35. "Parasol Dance" is described in the program as representing Yunnan Province. However, in Chinese sources, it is consistently associated with Henan. On the regional associations of this dance and "In the Rain," see Wang Kefen et al., *Zhongguo wudao da cidian* (Beijing: Wenhua yishu chubanshe, 2009), 209, 723; "Minjian wudao de xin huaduo," *Guangming ribao*, May 17, 1959.

36. *Bai feng chaoyang* (Beijing Film Studio, 1959).

37. *Caidie fenfei.*

38. *Bai feng chaoyang.*

39. Catherine Yeh, "Politics, Art and Eroticism: The Female Impersonator as the National Cultural Symbol of Republican China," in *Performing the 'Nation': Gender Politics in Literature, Theatre and the Visual Arts of China and Japan, 1880–1940*, ed. Doris Croissant, Catherine Yeh, and Joshua S. Mostow (Leiden: Brill, 2008), 206–39; Catherine Yeh, "China, A Man in the Guise of an Upright Female," in *History in Images: Pictures and Public Space in Modern China*, ed. Christian Henriot and Wen-hsin Yeh (Berkeley: University of California Press, 2012), 81–110.

40. Zi Huayun, *Wudao he wo: Zi Huayun zizhuan* (Chengdu: Sichuan wenyi chubanshe, 1987); Dong Xijiu and Long Yinpei, *Xin Zhongguo wudao de dianjishi*.

41. Zhang Yunqing, "Woguo qingnian yishujia," *Guangming ribao*, August 9, 1957; Feng Shuangbai, ed., *Zhongguo wudaojia da cidian* (Beijing: Zhongguo wenlian chubanshe, 2006), 65.

42. On Siqintariha, see Wilcox, "Dynamic Inheritance."

43. Zhang Yunqing, "Woguo qingnian yishujia"; Jia Anlin, *Zhongwai wudao zuopin shangxi*, 20–30.

44. Zhang Yunqing, "Woguo qingnian yishujia."

45. I have observed these works used as teaching repertoires in Chinese dance schools and performed for historical events, such as anniversaries and tribute concerts. Biographies of dancers from this generation always highlight WFYS awards, which are seen as the most important international accomplishments from this era. For a complete list of award-winning works, see Song Tianyi, *Zhongwai biaoyan*, 290–92.

46. Naima Prevots, *Dance for Export: Cultural Diplomacy and the Cold War* (Middle-town, CT: Wesleyan University Press, 2001); David Caute, *The Dancer Defects: The Struggle for Cultural Supremacy during the Cold War* (Oxford: Oxford University Press, 2003); Clare Croft, *Dancers as Diplomats: American Choreography in Cultural Exchange* (New York: Oxford University Press, 2015).

47. Pia Koivunen, "The World Youth Festival as an Arena of the 'Cultural Olympics': Meanings of Competition in Soviet Culture in the 1940s and 1950s," in *Competition in Soviet Society*, ed. Katalin Miklóssy and Melanie Ilic (New York: Routledge, 2014), 125–142, 138.

48. On political dimensions of these festivals, see Joni Krekola and Simo Mikkonen, "Backlash of the Free World: The US Presence at the World Youth Festival in Helsinki, 1962," *Scandinavian Journal of History* 36, no. 2 (May 2011): 230–55; Margaret Peacock, "The Perils of Building Cold War Consensus at the 1957 Moscow World Festival of Youth and Students," *Cold War History* 12, no. 3 (2012): 515–35.

49. *World Youth Festivals*, World Festival of Youth and Students Collection ARCH01667, Binder 1, Folder 1, International Institute of Social History, Amsterdam.

50. Nicolai Volland, *Socialist Cosmopolitanism: The Chinese Literary Universe, 1945–1965* (New York: Columbia University Press, 2017); Wilcox, "The Postcolonial Blind Spot"; Wilcox, "Performing Bandung."

51. "Cultural Competition in Honor of the 5th Festival Launched by the Magazine *World Youth*" and "The Student Programme at the Fifth World Festival of Youth and Students Preliminary Outline, 1955," World Festival of Youth and Students Collection ARCH01667, Binder 1, Folder 4, International Institute of Social History, Amsterdam.

52. Marcel Rubin, "Art Competitions," *Festival*, no. 2 (October 1958): n.p., World Festival of Youth and Students Collection ARCH01667, Binder 10, Folder 1, International Institute of Social History, Amsterdam.

53. "Programme of 5th August," *Festival: Journal of the International Festival Committee*, no. 20 (August 5, 1953), World Festival of Youth and Students Collection ARCH01667, Binder 9, Folder 4, International Institute of Social History, Amsterdam.

54. "The Student Programme at the Fifth World Festival of Youth and Students Preliminary Outline, 1955." The rules were the same in 1953. See "Reglement des concours internationaux qui ont lieu pendant le festival," *Festival: Journal du Comité Préparatoire International du Festival*, no. 3 (April 28–May 4, 1953), in World Festival of Youth and Students Collection ARCH01667, Binder 9, Folder 4, International Institute of Social History, Amsterdam.

55. Anthony Shay, *Choreographic Politics: State Folk Dance Companies, Representation, and Power* (Middletown, CT: Wesleyan University Press, 2002); Christina Ezrahi, *Swans of the Kremlin: Ballet and Power in Soviet Russia* (Pittsburgh: University of Pittsburgh Press, 2012).

56. "Reglement des concours internationaux qui ont lieu pendant le festival," *Festival*, no. 3, April 28–May 4, 1953; "The Student Programme at the Fifth World Festival of Youth and Students Preliminary Outline, 1955"; articles in *Festival* include "character dance" within these two categories. "Reglement des concours internationaux qui ont lieu pendant le festival" (1953) and "Voulez-vous Etre Laureat?," *Festival*, April 1–15, 1955, World Festival of Youth and Students Collection ARCH01667, Binder 9, International Institute of Social History, Amsterdam.

57. *The VIth World Festival of Youth and Students for Peace and Friendship, Moscow July 28th–August 11th 1957*, Binder 2, 45, World Festival of Youth and Students Collection ARCH01667, International Institute of Social History, Amsterdam; Marcel Rubin, "Art Competitions"; "The VIII Festival of Youth and Students for Peace and Friendship," binder labeled "Eight Festival, Helsinki, 1962," 4–5, World Festival of Youth and Students Collection ARCH01667, International Institute of Social History, Amsterdam.

58. Central Committee of the Union of Working Youth, ed., *The Fourth World Festival of Youth and Students for Peace and Friendship*, Bucharest, August 2–16, 1953 [published 1954], p. 13, World Festival of Youth and Students Collection ARCH01667, binder labeled "Fourth World Festival," International Institute of Social History, Amsterdam. A photograph of Rahman performing Bharatanatyam accompanied by the headline "Ballet" appears in *Festival: Journal of the International Festival Committee*, no. 24 (August 9, 1953): n.p., World Festival of Youth and Students Collection ARCH01667, Binder 9, Folder 4, International Institute of Social History, Amsterdam.

59. Sheng Jie, "Zai guoji wenhua jiaoliu huodong zhong de Zhongguo wudao," 7–8. Xiqu segments occasionally won awards in a category reported in the Chinese media as "classical song and dance" *(gudian gewu)*, but it is unclear what this corresponded to in the WFYS documents.

60. "Reglement des concours internationaux qui ont lieu pendent le festival."

61. The stipulation of seven minutes and eight dancers appears in "The Student Programme at the Fifth World Festival of Youth and Students Preliminary Outline, 1955." A maximum of six dancers appears in "Reglement des concours internationaux du Ve festival," *Festival*, no. 2 (February 15–23, 1955), World Festival of Youth and Students Collection ARCH01667, Binder 9, International Institute of Social History, Amsterdam. However, in "Voulez-vous Etre Laureat?" (April 1955), it appears again as eight.

62. *The VIth World Festival of Youth and Students for Peace and Friendship, Moscow July 28th–August 11th 1957*, 45.

63. Based on a review of all photographs published in *Festival* issues from 1951, 1953, 1955, 1957, 1959, and 1962 housed in the World Festival of Youth and Students Collection ARCH01667, International Institute of Social History, Amsterdam.

64. Some Chinese dance historians regard other works of the pre-1949 era as important precedents for national dance drama. Yu Ping, *Zhongguo xiandangdai wuju fazhan shi*, 12–27.

65. Yu Ping, "Cong 'Renmin shengli wansui' dao Zhonghua 'Fuxing zhi lu': xin Zhongguo wudao yishu fazhan," *Yishu bai jia* 5, no. 110 (2009): 1–5; Xiaomei Chen, *Staging Chinese Revolution: Theater, Film, and the Afterlives of Propaganda* (New York: Columbia University Press, 2017).

66. Li Xiaoxiang, ed., *Zhongguo geju wujuyuan yuanshi* (Hong Kong: Tianma chuban youxian gongsi, 2010).

67. Li Xiaoxiang, *Zhongguo geju wujuyuan yuanshi*, 156.

68. Ibid.

69. "Shoudu quanguo xiqu guanmo yanchu dahui kaimu," *Guangming ribao*, October 7, 1952.

70. In 1954 a Folk Xiqu Ensemble (Minjian xiqutuan) would be formed within CEOT, out of which, in 1956, would emerge a separate ensemble, the Beijing Kunqu Theater (Beijing Kunqu juyuan). After this, the remaining group would become the Dance Drama Research Group (Wuju yanjiu xiaozu) within CEOT. Li Xiaoxiang, *Zhongguo geju wujuyuan yuanshi*.

71. Jin Ziguang, "Weilai de wudao yanyuan," *Renmin huabao* 4, no. 8 (1953): 36–38, 36.

72. Ibid., 36.

73. Ibid.

74. "Women weida de zuguo," *Renmin ribao*, September 9, 1953.

75. Chen Jinqing, "Guanyu xin wudao yishu."

76. Wilcox, "Performing Bandung"; Wilcox, "The Postcolonial Blind Spot."

77. You Huihai, "Wuju 'Bali shengmuyuan' de yanchu," *Guangming ribao*, November 19, 1955.

78. Gao Di'an, "Xuexi Sulian wuju yishu de jingyan, chuangzao women minzu de wuju," *Guangming ribao*, February 19, 1955.

79. Beijing Dance Academy, *Beijing wudao xueyuan zhi*, 13. For more on the content of this course and its results, see V. I. Tsaplin, "Wuju chuangzuo zhong de jige wenti," *Wudao tongxun*, no. 7 (1956): 8–10; Fang Yanqiu, "Wuju chuangzuo zuotanhui," *Wudao tongxun*, no. 6 (1956): 20; Ding Ning, "Cong xinpai de wuju shuoqi," *Renmin ribao*, July 9, 1957.

80. The other two works staged in early 1957 were *Liu Hai Plays with the Golden Frog* (choreographers Wang Ping and Chuan Zhaoxian) and *Bilian chipan* (choreographers You Huihai and Sun Tianlu). Li Xiaoxiang, *Zhongguo geju wujuyuan yuanshi*, 311–17.

81. Zheng appears to have been labeled a Rightist in 1957 and disappeared from documents thereafter.

82. Zheng Baoyun, "Guanyu xiaoxing wuju 'Dao xiancao' de chuangzuo," *Wudao tongxun*, no. 6 (1956): 17–20; Zhang Chun, "Ping wuju 'Dao xiancao' de yanchu ji qita," *Wudao tongxun*, no. 7 (1956): 11–14. On the White Snake legend, see Wilt Idema, *The White Snake and Her Son: A Translation of the Precious Scroll of Thunder Peak with Related Texts* (Indianapolis: Hackett, 2009).

83. Li Xiaoxiang, *Zhongguo geju wujuyuan yuanshi*, 312.

84. "'Dao xiancao' juzhao," *Wudao tongxun*, no. 6 (1956): inside back cover.

85. "Daxing minzu wuju 'Bao liandeng' jijiang shangyan," *Guangming ribao*, August 3, 1957.

86. On this story, see "The Precious Scroll of Chenxiang," trans. Wilt Idema, in *The Columbia Anthology of Chinese Folk and Popular Literature*, ed. Victor Mair and Mark Bender (New York: Columbia University Press, 2011), 380–405.

87. Li Xiaoxiang, *Zhongguo geju wujuyuan yuanshi*, 316–17.

88. Qiu Fan, "Daxing minzu wuju 'Bao liandeng,'" *Wenyi bao*, no. 19 (1957): 15.

89. *Magic Lotus Lantern* stage photographs, *Wudao*, no. 1 (1958): 14–18.

90. *Bao liandeng* (Shanghai Tianma Film Studio, 1959).

91. Jonathan Stock, *Huju: Traditional Opera in Modern Shanghai* (Oxford: Published for the British Academy by Oxford University Press, 2003); Jin Jiang, *Women Playing Men: Yue Opera and Social Change in Twentieth-Century Shanghai* (Seattle: University of Washington Press, 2009); Liang Luo, *The Avant-garde and the Popular in Modern China: Tian Han and the Intersection of Performance and Politics* (Ann Arbor: University of Michigan Press, 2014).

92. Xiaomei Chen, *The Columbia Anthology of Modern Chinese Drama* (New York: Columbia University Press, 2010).

93. Song Yun, "Bao liandeng (wuju gushi)," *Wudao*, no. 1 (1958): 14–15.

94. Long Yinpei, "Chu kai de wuju zhi hua," *Guangming ribao*, November 9, 1957.

95. Ibid.

96. Mei Qian, "Du zhan yi zhi chun: jianping wuju yingpian 'bao liandeng,'" *Renmin ribao*, December 15, 1959.

97. On folk elements in *Magic Lotus Lantern*, see Huang Boshou, "Huiyi wuju 'Bao liandeng' de chuangzuo guocheng," *Wudao wuju chuangzuo jingyan wenji*, ed. Zhongguo yishu yanjiuyuan wudao yanjiusuo (Beijing: Renmin yinyue chubanshe, 1985), 58–62.

98. This term is used in the film's narrative voice-over. *Bao liandeng*.

99. Shu Wei and Su Yun, *Wu hun—Zhao Qing zhuan* (Changchun: Jilin renmini chubanshe, 1991). For a recording of Zhao's "Long Silk Dance," see *Baifeng chaoyang* (Beijing: Beijing Film Studio, 1959).

100. "Spanish Dance" photographs, Beijing Dance Academy Archives.

101. Zhao Qing, interview with the author, July 24, 2013, Beijing.

102. Ibid.; Yin Ying, "San Shengmu jiaose de chuangzuo," *Wudao*, no. 1 (1958): 18–20.

103. Karl, *Mao Zedong and China*, 100–104.

104. Karl, *Mao Zedong and China*; Frank Dikötter, *Mao's Great Famine: The History of China's Most Devastating Catastrophe, 1958–1962* (New York: Walker, 2010); Felix Wemheuer and Kimberley Ens Manning, eds., *Eating Bitterness: New Perspectives on China's Great Leap Forward and Famine* (Vancouver: UBC Press, 2011); Xun Zhou, *Forgotten Voices of Mao's Great Famine, 1958–1962: An Oral History* (New Haven: Yale University Press, 2013).

105. Chang-tai Hung, *Mao's New World*; Krista Van Fleit Hang, *Literature the People Love: Reading Chinese Texts from the Early Maoist Period (1949–1966)* (New York: Palgrave Macmillan, 2013); Zhuoyi Wang, *Revolutionary Cycles in Chinese Cinema, 1951–1979* (New York: Palgrave Macmillan, 2014).

106. Van Fleit Hang, *Literature the People Love*, 148.

107. These include China Railway Art Theater's *Wang Gui and Li Xiangxiang* (1958), Beijing Dance School's *Rather Die Than Submit* (1958) and *Humans Must Overcome Heaven*

(1958), Hunan Provincial Song and Dance Ensemble's *Liu Hai Chops Firewood* (1958), Shenyang Military Political Office Song and Dance Ensemble's *Butterfly Loves Flower* (1959), South Sea Warship Team Literature and Art Representative Team Dance Group's *Hero Qiu An* (1959), General Political Department Song and Dance Ensemble's *The Immortal Fighter* (1959), South China Song and Dance Ensemble's *Xiang Xiuli* (1959), Tianjin People's Art Theater's *Shi Yi and Wang En/Woodcutter Shi Yi* (1959), Guizhou Provincial Song and Dance Ensemble's *Mother* (1959), Wuhan Military District's *Steel Person* (1959), Guangzhou Military Soldier Song and Dance Ensemble's *Five Red Clouds* (1959), Shanghai Experimental Opera Theater's *Dagger Society* (1959), All-China Federation of Trade Unions Cultural Work Troupe Dance Team's *Snatching the Bride* (1959), China Railroad Cultural Work Ensemble's *Twin Lotus Flowers on One Stalk* (1959), Wuhan Army Cultural Work Ensemble's *Remembering Those Years* (1959), South China Song and Dance Ensemble's *Little Story of Pearl City* (1959), Beijing Dance School's *Fish Beauty* (1959), Guizhou Provincial Song and Dance Ensemble's *Bindweed Flower* (1960), South China Song and Dance Troupe's *Cowherd and the Weaving Girl* (1960), and Central Experimental Opera Theater's *Thunder Peak Tower* (1960). List based on works named in article headlines or photo spreads in *Wudao* between 1958 and 1963. See also Zhai Zixia, *Zhongguo wuju* (Beijing: China World Languages Publishing House, 1996), 47–79; Beijing Dance Academy, *Beijing wudao xueyuan zhi*, 169; Feng Shuangbai, *Xin Zhongguo yishu shi 1949–2000* (Changsha: Hunan meishu chubanshe, 2002), 33; Yu Ping, *Zhongguo xiandangdai*, 25; Mao Hui, *Xin Zhongguo wudao shidian*, 55–59; Dong Xijiu and Long Yinpei, *Xin Zhongguo wudao de dianjishi*, 168.

108. Xiaobing Tang, *Chinese Modern: The Heroic and the Quotidian* (Durham, NC: Duke University Press, 2000), 166; Paul Pickowicz, *China on Film: A Century of Exploration, Confrontation, and Controversy* (Lanham, MD: Rowman & Littlefield, 2012), 214.

109. Names for Shanghai Experimental Opera Theater are inconsistent. This name is most common in sources from 1959.

110. Xu Xuezeng, "Xikan hong yun jiang renjian: wuju 'Wu duo hongyun' jieshao," *Renmin ribao*, June 15, 1959; "Shanghai huajujie zuzhi dahui chuan," *Guangming ribao*, August 12, 1959.

111. Resemblance verified through extant stage photographs, programs, reviews, and interviews with original cast members.

112. *Wu duo hongyun* (August First Film Studio, 1960); "Ba yi paishe zhong de wuju pian 'Wu duo hongyun,'" *Dazhong dianying*, no. 23 (1959): 33–34; Xuan Jiang, "Hongyun daizhe xingfu lai," *Renmin ribao*, January 10, 1960; *Xiaodao hui* (Shanghai: Shanghai Tianma Film Studio, 1961); "Kan yinmu shang de wuju 'Xiaodao hui,'" *Dazhong dianying*, no. 11 (1961): 17.

113. The Guizhou Provincial Song and Dance Ensemble's 1960 dance drama *Bindweed Flower (Manluo hua)* was released as a color film (no longer extant) by the Shanghai Haiyan Film Studio in 1961. Ye Lin, "'Manluo hua' kai zai zai yinmu shang," *Dazhong dianying*, nos. 5–6 (1962): 34–35.

114. "Fangshe zui xin zui mei you duo you liang de wenyi 'weixing' chongfen fanying weida zuguo bianhua," *Renmin ribao*, October 30, 1958.

115. Ibid.

116. *Five Red Clouds* creative team, Zha Lie, scribe, "Chuangzuo 'Wu duo hongyun' de tihui," *Wudao*, no. 8 (1959): 4–6; Zhang Tuo, "'Xiaodao hui' chuangzuo de lishi huigu," in

Wudao wuju chuangzuo jingyan wenji, ed. Zhongguo yishu yanjiuyuan wudao yanjiusuo (Beijing: Renmin yinyue chubanshe, 1985), 67–79.

117. Zhou Weilun, "Mantan wuju zhong xin yingxiong renwu de suzao," *Wudao*, no. 1 (1960): 22–23.

118. Wu Xiaobang, "Baihuazhengyan wu dongfeng," *Wudao*, no. 10 (1959): 4.

119. For key texts on this issue, see Yue Meng, "Female Images and National Myth," in *Gender Politics in Modern China*, ed. Tani E. Barlow (Durham, NC: Duke University Press, 1993), 118–36; Mayfair Mei-hui Yang, "From Gender Erasure to Gender Difference: State Feminism, Consumer Sexuality, and Women's Public Sphere in China," in *A Space of Their Own: Women's Public Sphere in Transnational China*, ed. Mayfair Mei-hui Yang (Minneapolis: University of Minnesota Press, 1999), 35–67; Xiaomei Chen, *Acting the Right Part: Political Theater and Popular Drama in Contemporary China* (Honolulu: University of Hawai'i Press, 2002); Shuqin Cui, *Women through the Lens: Gender and Nation in a Century of Chinese Cinema* (Honolulu: University of Hawai'i Press, 2003); Rosemary A. Roberts, *Maoist Model Theatre: The Semiotics of Gender and Sexuality in the Chinese Cultural Revolution (1966–1976)* (Leiden: Brill, 2010); Louise Edwards, *Women Warriors and Wartime Spies of China* (Cambridge: Cambridge University Press, 2016); Zheng Wang, *Finding Women in the State: A Socialist Feminist Revolution in the People's Republic of China, 1949–1964* (Oakland: University of California Press, 2017).

120. I use the term "intersectional" here in reference to a theoretical framework developed in the field of US critical race studies. The term was coined by Kimberlé Crenshaw in 1991. However, feminist historians have found examples of intersectional analysis in activist movements and in the writing of feminists both in the United States and in China in earlier periods. I am drawing on both Crenshaw's ideas and this broader understanding of intersectional analysis in twentieth-century global feminist, socialist, and Third World movements. Kimberlé Crenshaw, "Mapping the Margins: Intersectionality, Identity Politics, and Violence against Women of Color," *Stanford Law Review* 43 (1991): 1241–99; Patricia Hill Collins and Sirma Bilge, *Intersectionality* (Cambridge: Polity Press, 2016); Lydia He Liu, Rebecca Karl, and Dorothy Ko, eds., *The Birth of Chinese Feminism: Essential Texts in Transnational Theory* (New York: Columbia University Press, 2013); Zheng Wang, *Finding Women in the State.*

121. *Xiaodao hui;* Zha Lie, "Wu duo hongyun (wuju wenxue taiben)," *Wudao*, no. 8 (1959): 14–19.

122. Wang's ethnicity is not listed in her biographical entries, suggesting that she identified as Han. Feng Shuangbai, *Zhongguo wudaojia da cidian*, 22.

123. *Bai feng chaoyang.*

124. Li Jian, "Hainan minzu gewutuan you le xin chuangzuo," *Wudao tongxun*, no. 10 (1956): 38.

125. Long Yinpei, "Hainan wudao zhi hua," *Renmin ribao*, January 14, 1957; Hu Guogang, "Wo dui wudao chuangzuo de yixie yijian," *Renmin ribao*, February 8, 1957.

126. Feng Shuangbai et al., *Zhongguo wudaojia da cidian*, 22. Although not located in the capital, this school also had a prestigious pedigree. It had been established in 1949 with a dance program led by Hu Guogang, Wu Xiaobang, and Zha Lie, leading figures in the wartime New Dance and military dance movements. Dai Ailian and Korean dance instructor Piao Yonghu also taught at the school in 1950. By 1952 students were also being trained

in xiqu dance. Liu Min, *Zhongguo renmin jiefang jun wudao shi*, 576; Feng Shuangbai, *Zhongguo wudajia da cidian*, 355; Hu Guogang, "Zai buduan fazhan zhong de budui wudao yishu," *Wudao xuexi ziliao*, no. 1 (1952; repr., April 1954), 9–22, 17.

127. Liu Min, *Zhongguo renmin jiefangjun wudao shi*, 133–36, 577–78; Zha Lie, ed., *Feng yun ji* (Shanghai: Shanghai wenyi chubanshe, 1998), 5–24. On *Mother Calls*, premiered in 1951, see Zhai Zixia, *Zhongguo wuju*, 38–40.

128. Examples include Miao-themed *Bindweed Flower* (*Manluo hua*, 1960) and Mongol-themed *Wulan Bao* (1962).

129. Xu Xuezeng, "Xikan hong," 6.

130. *Five Red Clouds* creative team, "Chuangzuo 'Wu duo hongyun' de tihui."

131. This was a common theme in PRC ethnic minority films of the period. Paul Clark, *Chinese Cinema: Culture and Politics since 1949* (Cambridge: Cambridge University Press, 1987). On these changes, see *Five Red Clouds* creative team, "Chuangzuo 'Wu duo hongyun' de tihui."

132. *Five Red Clouds* creative team, "Chuangzuo 'Wu duo hongyun' de tihui."

133. Magnus Fiskesjö, "The Animal Other: China's Barbarians and Their Renaming in the Twentieth Century," *Social Text* 29, no. 4 (109) (Winter 2012): 57–79.

134. On the musical score, see Yan Ke, "Guanyu wuju 'Wu duo hongyun' de yinyue chuangzuo," *Wudao*, no. 11 (1959): 29–33.

135. I am in conversation here with a broader debate about women's representation in Chinese socialist cinema and theater, which asks whether sex and gender differences were downplayed in revolutionary narratives featuring female protagonists. Most of the current scholarship on this issue has been about works from the Cultural Revolution, not the Great Leap Forward.

136. *Five Red Clouds* creative team, "Chuangzuo 'Wu duo hongyun' de tihui," 5.

137. Only a few English-language studies have addressed national dance dramas of the Great Leap Forward period, and usually not in detail. Mary Swift, "The Art of Dance in Red China," *Thought* 48 (189) (1973): 275–85; Colin Mackerras, *The Performing Arts in Contemporary China* (London: Routledge & Kegan Paul, 1981), 112–14; Paul Clark, *Chinese Cinema*, 201; James Brandon, *The Cambridge Guide to Asian Theatre* (Cambridge: Cambridge University Press, 1993), 56; Edward Davis, *Encyclopedia of Contemporary Chinese Culture* (London: Routledge, 2005), 926–27; Paul Clark, *The Chinese Cultural Revolution: A History* (Cambridge: Cambridge University Press, 2008), 159; Jingzhi Liu, *A Critical History of New Music in China*, trans. Caroline Mason (Hong Kong: Chinese University Press, 2010), 346–47. An exception is Nan Ma's discussion of *Butterfly Loves Flower* (*Die lian hua*) in Ma, "Dancing into Modernity," 203–47.

138. Shanghai Experimental Opera Theater, *Xiaodao hui*, performance program dated May 1960, Beijing, Beijing Dance Academy Archives; Shanghai Experimental Opera Theater, *Xiaodao hui*, performance program, undated, University of Michigan Asia Library Chinese Dance Collection.

139. This character is identified in the 1960 program as "Shanghai magistrate" (*Shanghai daotai*). In the 1961 film, he is identified as a "Qing official" (*Qing guan*).

140. In the 1960 program, the priest is British, but in the 1961 film, he is American.

141. On the Taiping Tianguo, see Jonathan Spence, *God's Chinese Son: The Taiping Heavenly Kingdom of Hong Xiuquan* (New York: W. W. Norton, 1996); Thomas Reilly, *The Taiping Heavenly Kingdom: Rebellion and the Blasphemy of Empire* (Seattle: University of

Washington Press, 2004); Stephen Platt, *Autumn in the Heavenly Kingdom: China, the West, and the Epic Story of the Taiping Civil War* (New York: Alfred A. Knopf, 2012).

142. In the 1960 program, the leader is the French general. However, in the 1961 film, it is the American spy who doubles as a priest. Zhang Tuo, "'Xiaodao hui,'" 73.

143. SEOT was formally established in 1956, but many of its core members had been dancing together in earlier institutions with different names, similar to the situation with the CEOT. According to Shu Qiao, she and others in the ensemble had been taught by three members of the famous "Chuan" generation of Kunqu performers: Fang Chuanling, Hua Chuanhao, Wang Chuanqian. Shu Qiao, interview with the author, August 13, 2015, Shanghai.

144. Qian Renkang, ed., *Shanghai yinyue zhi*, n.d., 111. For an illustrated teaching manual for this work, see Shanghai Experimental Opera Theater, ed., *Jian wu* (Shanghai: Shanghai wenyi chubanshe, 1959).

145. "Zhongguo yishu huaduo shengkai," *Renmin ribao*, August 9, 1957; Shu Qiao, *Jin sheng ling shi* (Shanghai: Shanghai wenyi chubanshe, 2010), 38; Shanghai Experimental Opera Theater, *Jian wu*; Shu Qiao, interview.

146. *Wudao*, no. 1 (1958): cover.

147. On the xiqu-inspired story devices and folk material, see Wang Shiqi, "Minzu wuju de xin chengjiu," *Guangming ribao*, July 30, 1960. For an alternative account, see Zhang Tuo, "'Xiaodao hui.'"

148. Zhong Er, "Minzu wuju you yi kexi de shouhuo," *Guangming ribao*, July 30, 1960.

149. *Xiaodao hui*.

150. Language used in the opening narration of the 1961 film. *Xiaodao hui*.

151. Zhang Tuo, "'Xiaodao hui,'" 68.

152. Ibid., 69.

153. Ibid., 68–73.

154. Ibid., 69.

155. Zhong Er, "Minzu wuju you yi kexi de shouhuo."

156. "Wudao jicheng fayang woguo geming wenyi zhandou chuantong," August 6, 1960.

157. *Xiaodao hui*.

158. This method was also used in the earlier dance productions *Peace Dove* and *Mother's Call*. On the use of similar practices in theater, see Claire Conceison, *Significant Other: Staging the American in China* (Honolulu: University of Hawai'i Press, 2004); Alexa Huang, *Chinese Shakespeares: Two Centuries of Cultural Exchange* (New York: Columbia University Press, 2009); Siyuan Liu, *Performing Hybridity in Colonial-Modern China* (New York: Palgrave Macmillan, 2013).

159. Leng Ronghong and Xing Zhiwen, "*Xiaodao hui* guan hou," *Wudao*, no. 1 (1960): 13–14.

160. Huang Yufu, "Chinese Women's Status as Seen through Peking Opera," in *Holding Up Half the Sky*, ed. Tao Jie, Zheng Bijun, and Shirley L. Mow (New York: Feminist Press at the City University of New York, 2004), 30–38, 34, as cited in Roberts, *Maoist Model Theatre*, 17.

161. On China's shifting socialist gender politics and representations of sex and gender in cultural texts during this period, see Jin Jiang, *Women Playing Men*; Kimberley Ens Manning, "The Gendered Politics of Woman-Work: Rethinking Radicalism in the Great Leap Forward," in *Eating Bitterness*, 72–106; Van Fleit Hang, *Literature the People Love*; Gail

Hershatter, *The Gender of Memory: Rural Women and China's Collective Past* (Berkeley: University of California Press, 2011); Zheng Wang, *Finding Women in the State.*

162. Shanghai Experimental Opera Theater, 1960; *Dagger Society.* Shu went on to become one of the most celebrated and prolific Chinese national dance drama choreographers of the twentieth century.

163. Zhang Tuo, "'Xiaodao hui,'" 79; "Shijie qingnian lianhuanjie ge xiang huodong quanmian zhankai," *Renmin ribao,* August 1, 1962.

164. Goldstein, *Drama Kings,* 258.

165. Ibid., 259.

166. "Quanguo yinyue wudao huiyan bimu," *Guangming ribao,* January 24, 1957.

167. "'Wudao' chuang kan," *Xiju bao,* no. 1 (1958): 23.

168. "Ge lu wenyi dajun jiang xiang guoqing baihua," *Renmin ribao,* September 18, 1959; *Bao liandeng;* "Huanqing jianguo shi zhounian," *Guangming ribao,* September 18, 1959.

169. "Xiang guoqing xianli de guochanpian fengfuduocai," *Renmin ribao,* September 17, 1959; "A'erjiliya, Yilake, Nibu'er san guo zhengdu daibiaotuan zai Jing canguan," *Renmin ribao,* October 1, 1959; "Wo zhu su dashi juxing wanhui qingzhu shi yue geming jie," *Renmin ribao,* November 6, 1959; "Huang zhen dashi she yan zhaodai jieyun Huaqiao de chuanzhang he chuanyuan," *Renmin ribao,* February 19, 1960; "Wo zhu mo dashi deng zai Kasabulanka juxing zhaodai hui," *Renmin ribao,* May 7, 1960; Huang Boshou, "Huiyi wuju 'Bao liandeng.'"

170. Zhang Xiaohu, "Weida de youyi zhencheng de hezuo: zai Xin Xiboliya geju wujuyuan canjia pailian 'Bao liandeng' wuju zaji," *Renmin yinyue,* no. 4 (1959): 11–12. Previously, foreign companies had staged short Chinese choreographies and their own dance productions on Chinese themes but not full-length national dance dramas by Chinese choreographers.

171. Li Xiaoxiang, *Zhongguo geju wujuyuan yuanshi,* 168.

172. Ibid.

173. "Zai Zhonghua renmin gongheguo chengli shisi zhounian qianxi," *Renmin ribao,* September 30, 1963.

174. He Gengxin, "Zhong Ri wudao jia de yishu jiaoliu," *Guangming ribao,* February 20, 1963. Li Xiaoxiang, *Zhongguo geju wujuyuan yuanshi,* 173.

175. Zhang Tuo, "'Xiaodao hui.'"

CHAPTER 4. A REVOLT FROM WITHIN

1. Shu Qiao, *Jin sheng ling shi* (Shanghai: Shanghai wenyi chubanshe, 2010), 80–83.

2. Shu Qiao, *Jin sheng,* 84.

3. Gucheng (Kwok-sing) Li, *A Glossary of Political Terms of the People's Republic of China,* trans. Mary Lok (Hong Kong: Chinese University Press, 1995), s.v. *da zi bao.*

4. Amina, *Qemberxanim de yishu shengya,* 87–95; Tursunay Yunus, *Ussul Péshwasi Qemberxanim.*

5. Liang Lun, *Wo de yishu shengya,* 267–74, 269.

6. Dai Ailian, *Wo de yishu,* 196–216.

7. Wu Xiaobang, *Wo de wudao.*

8. The literal translation of this term is "revolutionary modern ballet dance drama." However, in English, the term "ballet" can encompass the idea of dance drama.

9. "Balei wuju 'Hongse niangzi jun' yanchu chenggong," *Guangming ribao*, October 5, 1964.

10. "Shanghai yanchu daxing xiandai balei wuju 'Baimao nü,'" *Guangming ribao*, May 16, 1965.

11. *Hongse niangzi jun* (Beijing Film Studio, 1971); *Baimao nü* (Shanghai Film Studio, 1971); *Yimeng song* (August First Film Studio, 1975); *Caoyuan ernü* (August First Film Studio, 1975).

12. Lois Wheeler Snow, *China on Stage* (New York: Random House, 1972); Sophia Delza, "The Dance Arts in the People's Republic of China: The Contemporary Scene," *Asian Music* 5, no. 1 (1973): 28–39; R. G. Davis, "*The White-Haired Girl*, A Modern Revolutionary Ballet," *Film Quarterly* 27, no. 2 (Winter 1973–74): 52–56; Norman J. Wilkinson, "Asian Theatre Traditions: *The White-Haired Girl*: From 'Yangko' to Revolutionary Modern Ballet," *Educational Theatre Journal* 26, no. 2 (May 1974): 164–74; Gloria B. Strauss, "China Ballet Troupe: *Hong Se Niang Zi Jun (The Red Detachment of Women)*," *Dance Research Journal* 7, no. 2 (Spring–Summer 1975): 33–34; Estelle T. Brown, "Toward a Structuralist Approach to Ballet: 'Swan Lake' and 'The White Haired Girl,'" *Western Humanities Review* 32, no. 3 (Summer 1978): 227–40; Luella Sue Christopher, "Pirouettes with Bayonets: Classical Ballet Metamorphosed as Dance-Drama and Its Usage in the People's Republic of China as a Tool of Political Socialization" (PhD diss., American University School of International Services, 1979); Jane Desmond, "Embodying Difference: Issues in Dance and Cultural Studies," in *Meaning in Motion: New Cultural Studies of Dance*, ed. Jane Desmond (Durham and London: Duke University Press, 1997), 29–54; Ban Wang, *The Sublime Figure of History: Aesthetics and Politics in Twentieth-Century China* (Stanford, CA: Stanford University Press, 1997); De-Hai Cheng, "The Creation and Evolvement of Chinese Ballet: Ethnic and Esthetic Concerns in Establishing a Chinese Style of Ballet in Taiwan and Mainland China (1954–1994)" (PhD diss., New York University School of Education, 2000); Xiaomei Chen, *Acting the Right Part: Political Theater and Popular Drama in Contemporary China* (Honolulu: University of Hawai'i Press, 2002); Paul Clark, *The Chinese Cultural Revolution: A History* (Cambridge: Cambridge University Press, 2008); Bai Di, "Feminism in the Revolutionary Model Ballets *The White-Haired Girl* and *The Red Detachment of Women*," in Richard King et al., eds., *Art in Turmoil: The Chinese Cultural Revolution, 1966–76* (Vancouver: University of British Columbia Press, 2010), 188–202; Kristine Harris, "Re-makes/Re-models: *The Red Detachment of Women* between Stage and Screen," *The Opera Quarterly* 26, nos. 2–3 (Spring 2010): 316–42; Rosemary A. Roberts, *Maoist Model Theatre: The Semiotics of Gender and Sexuality in the Chinese Cultural Revolution (1966–1976)* (Leiden: Brill, 2010); Barbara Mittler, *A Continuous Revolution: Making Sense of Cultural Revolution Culture* (Cambridge, MA: Harvard University Asia Center, 2012).

13. See also De-Hai Cheng, "Creation and Evolvement of Chinese Ballet."

14. Jennifer Homans, *Apollo's Angels: A History of Ballet* (New York: Random House, 2010).

15. Marcia Ristaino, "White Russians and Jewish Refugees in Shanghai, 1920–1944, As Recorded in the Shanghai Municipal Police Files, National Archives, Washington, DC," *Republican China* 16, no. 1 (1990): 51–72; Harriet Sergeant, *Shanghai* (London: Jonathan Cape, 1991), 31; Frederic Wakeman, "Licensing Leisure: The Chinese Nationalists' Attempt to Regulate Shanghai, 1927–49," *Journal of Asian Studies* 54, no. 1 (February 1995): 19–42.

16. For a description of a local Shanghai group in the early 1930s that included Russian ballet dancers George (Georgi) Goncharov, Vera Volkova, and George Toropov, see Margot Fonteyn, *Autobiography* (London: W.H. Allen, 1975), 36. Anna Pavlova performed in Shanghai in 1922.

17. On "colonial modernity" and China's performing arts, see Andrew Jones, "Yellow Music."

18. Shu Wei and Su Yun, *Wu hun—Zhao Qing zhuan*, 21–22.

19. Ibid. On the class dimension of European-style arts education in China, see Richard Kraus, *Pianos and Politics in China: Middle-Class Ambitions and the Struggle over Western Music* (New York: Oxford University Press, 1989).

20. Sheng Jie, interview with the author, November 8, 2008, Beijing; Sheng Jie, *Yi wang shi*.

21. Zhao Renhui, interview with the author, August 16, 2015, Yanji. See also Zhao Dexian, *Cho Tŭk-hyŏn Kwa Kŭ Ui Muyong Yesul: Cho Tŭk-hyŏn Sŏnsaeng T'ansin 100-tol ŭl Kinyŏm Hayŏ* (Yanji, China: Yŏnbyŏn Inmin Ch'ulp'ansa, 2013); Hae-kyung Um, "The Dialectics of Politics and Aesthetics in the Chinese Korean Dance Drama, The Spirit of Changbai Mountain," *Asian Ethnicity* 6, no. 3 (October 2005): 203–22.

22. Feng Shuangbai, *Zhongguo wudaojia da cidian*, 459; Yang Jie, *Balei wuju 'Baimao nü' chuangzuo shihua* (Shanghai: Shanghai yinyue chubanshe, 2010).

23. See, for example, Lü Zhiyuan, "Dongfang Xiulan Dengbo'er Hu Rongrong," *Dianying* (Shanghai), no. 6 (1938): 1.

24. "Gexing rencai liaoluo, Gong Qiuxia duba yintan: Hu Rongrong tuixiu jiayuan, xuexi gechang yu wudao," *Dazhong yingxun* 3, no. 8 (1942): 761; "Hu Rongrong zhuanxin xueye, bing xuexi gudian wuyong," *Qingqing dianying*, no. 3 (1944): 85.

25. Lu Shifu and Guang Yi, "Hu Rongrong nüshi zhi wudao," *Huanqiu*, no. 39 (1949): 25–26.

26. "Sokolsky Achieves Success as Leader of Flying Ballet," *China Press*, August 4, 1929; "New Ballet Production to Be Given Here Fri: Russian Group to Open Season with Coppelia on November 13, 14," *China Press*, November 12, 1936; "Ballet Russe Scores Again in Fairy-Tale: 'Sleeping Beauty' Given Warm Reception," *China Press*, February 5, 1938; "Le Ballet Russe to Open Season Nov. 26 with Big Double Bill," *China Press*, November 6, 1937. Sokolsky's company also toured Japan in 1936. Amir Khisamutdinov, "History of the Russian Diaspora in Japan," *Far Eastern Affairs*, no. 2 (2010): 92–100.

27. Lu Shifu and Guang Yi, "Hu Rongrong nüshi zhi wudao."

28. "Hu Rongrong nuli wudao: Hu Rongrong zujian wuzi," *Wanhuatong*, no. 5 (1946): 10; N. Sokolsky's School of Ballet, *Coppelia*, performance program dated July 19 and 20, 1948, Shanghai, in Sophia Delza Papers, (S)*MGZMD 155, Box 69, Folder 6, Jerome Robbins Dance Division, New York Public Library for the Performing Arts. For photographs from the production, see Lu Shifu and Guang Yi, "Hu Rongrong nüshi zhi wudao." Hu Rongrong also performs ballet in the 1948 film *Portrait of Four Beauties (Si mei tu)*, directed by Hu Xinling, consulted in the Hong Kong Film Archive.

29. N. Sokolsky's School of Ballet, *Coppelia*.

30. Biographical accounts state that You studied at Sokolsky's studio around this time. See Feng Shuangbai, *Zhongguo wudaojia da cidian*, 459.

31. Dai Ailian, "Fazhan zhongguo wudao di yi bu."

268 NOTES AND REFERENCES

32. Dai Ailian, "Si nianlai wudao gongzuo de zhuangkuang he jinhou de renwu," *Wudao xuexi ziliao*, no. 1 (Beijing: Zhongguo wudao yishu yanjiuhui chouweihui, 1954), 1–8.

33. I witnessed such processes constantly during my fieldwork at the Beijing Dance Academy in 2008–9. On one strand of this debate, see Emily Wilcox, "Han-Tang *Zhongguo Gudianwu* and the Problem of Chineseness in Contemporary Chinese Dance."

34. Sun Jingchen, "Wudaojie weishenme meiyou dongjing," *Renmin ribao*, April 18, 1955.

35. Chuan Ye, "Cong wudao xuexiao shixi gongyan zhong suo gandao de yi dian wenti," *Wudao tongxun*, no. 10 (June 1956): 8–9; Zeng Zongfan, "Women de yijian," *Wudao tongxun*, no. 10 (June 1956): 10–11.

36. Beijing Dance Academy, *Beijing wudao xueyuan zhi*.

37. There were also programs in Oriental Dance and choreography, as discussed in chapter 2, but these were shorter and operated differently from the two main tracks.

38. "Beijing wudao xuexiao fangwen ji," *Wudao*, no. 1 (1958): 22–24.

39. Zhan Mingxin, "Di yici changshi—ji Beijing wudao xuexiao pailian 'Tian'e hu,'" *Guangming ribao*, June 29, 1958; Wu Huaxue, "Beijing wudao xuexiao pailian de 'Tian'e hu,'" *Renmin ribao*, May 21, 1958; "Beijing gongyan zhuming baleiwuju 'Haixia,'" *Renmin ribao*, April 19, 1959.

40. Wu Huaxue, "Woguo di yi duo baleiwu zhi hua," *Renmin huabao*, no. 1 (1959): 28–30; Dai Ailian, "Hai zia," *Renmin huabao*, no. 11 (1959): 18–19.

41. Beijing Dance Academy, *Beijing wudao xueyuan zhi*.

42. *Wudao*, no. 2 (1959): front cover; *Wudao*, no. 6 (1960): inside front cover.

43. Beijing Dance School and Central Academy of Music, *Yu meiren*, undated performance program, Beijing Dance Academy Archives. Wang Shiqi, "Youyi de changshi: lüetan wuju 'Yu meiren' chaungzuo de diandi tihui," *Wenhui bao*, no. 15 (1959): 3.

44. Chen Ailian, interview with the author, April 1, 2009, Beijing.

45. Li Chengxiang, "Daxing wuju 'Yu meiren,'" *Renmin huabao* 11, no. 1 (January 1960).

46. *Yu meiren*, stage photographs dated 1959, Beijing Dance Academy Archives.

47. For the initial debate, see *Wudao*, no. 1 (1960), *Wudao*, no. 2 (1960), and *Wudao*, no. 3 (1960).

48. Wang Shiqi, "Pipan yang jiaotiao, tansuo minzu wuju de xin guilü," *Wudao*, no. 1 (1964): 16–22, 20.

49. Mao Zedong, cited in Wang Shiqi, "Pipan yang jiaotiao, tansuo minzu wuju de xin guilü," 20. English translation from "Talks at the Yenan Forum on Literature and Art," www.Marxists.org.

50. "Huanhu wo guo di yi ge balei wujutuan dansheng," *Wudao*, no. 2 (1960): 16.

51. Beijing Dance Academy, *Beijing wudao xueyuan zhi*.

52. Song Mingbo et al., *Wuyuanchunqiu: Shanghai wudaojia de yaolan* (Shanghai: Shanghai yinyue chubanshe, 2010).

53. Wang Shiqi, "Tan balei wuju 'Xibanya nü'er,'" *Wudao*, no. 2 (1961): 29–31. The story is based on a Spanish play about a peasant uprising.

54. On the differences between these two types of ballets, see Christina Ezrahi, *Swans of the Kremlin*.

55. For a review that explains changes from the Soviet production, see Jin Zheng, "Xikan baleiwuju 'Lei quan,'" *Wudao*, no. 1 (1963): 18–19.

56. "Jing Hu yitan fenfen paiyan xin jiemu yingjie jiajie," *Renmin ribao*, September 9, 1963.

57. Beijing Dance Academy, *Beijing wudao xueyuan zhi*, 91–92.

58. Ibid., 122.

59. Ibid., 123.

60. Clark, *The Chinese Cultural Revolution*, 159.

61. De-Hai Cheng, "Creation and Evolvement of Chinese Ballet."

62. Ou Jian-ping, "From 'Beasts' to 'Flowers': Modern Dance in China," in *East Meets West in Dance: Voices in the Cross-Cultural Dialogue*, ed. John Solomon and Ruth Solomon (New York: Harwood Academic Publishers, 1995), 29–35.

63. Ou Jianping, "China: Contemporary Theatrical Dance," in *The International Encyclopedia of Dance*, ed. Selma Jean Cohen and Dance Perspectives Foundation (New York: Oxford University Press, 2005), electronic.

64. You Huihai, "Taoranting pan de mingzhu," *Renmin ribao*, July 16, 1956.

65. Ibid.

66. You Huihai, "Mantan shinianlai de wuju yishu," *Xiju bao*, no. 17 (1959): 14–16, 15.

67. Ibid., 16.

68. These changes are typically associated with Mao's late 1963 attacks on China's Ministry of Culture. Merle Goldman and Leo Ou-Fan Lee, eds., *An Intellectual History of Modern China* (Cambridge: Cambridge University Press, 2002).

69. Beijing Dance Academy, *Beijing wudao xueyuan zhi*; "Xi'er tongzhi he Aoke tongzhi canguan Zhongguo wudao xuexiao Beijing balei wudao xuexiao," *Renmin ribao*, April 15, 1964.

70. Li Xiaoxiang, *Zhongguo geju wujuyuan yuanshi*.

71. Ibid. Between 1956 and 1962, for example, the CODDT had performed *Madama Butterfly*, *Onegin*, another Italian opera, a Hungarian opera, a Soviet opera, and an Azerbaijan nationality opera.

72. Ibid.

73. "Mingque fangxiang, tigao sixiang, jiaqiang zhandou," *Wudao*, no. 1 (February 1964): 3–6.

74. Ibid., 3.

75. Ibid., 5.

76. Ibid., 5.

77. Ibid., 6.

78. On the Liu Hulan story and its adaptation history, see Brian DeMare, *Mao's Cultural Army*; Louise Edwards, *Women Warriors and Wartime Spies of China*.

79. Chen Jianmin, "Xiang chuantong biaoyan yishu xuexi," *Wudao*, no. 1 (February 1964): 29–30.

80. Ibid., 30.

81. Li Zhengyi, "Cong Zhongguo gudianwu jiaocai zhong suo gandao de wenti," *Wudao*, no. 1 (February 1964): 23–26, 25.

82. David Caute, *The Dancer Defects*; Clare Croft, *Dancers as Diplomats*; "Dancing the Cold War: An International Symposium," Columbia University Harriman Institute in New York, February 16–18, 2017.

83. Wilcox, "Performing Bandung."

84. Tian Han, "Riben Songshan balei wutuan he tamen de 'Baimao nü,'" *Xiju bao*, no. 6 (1958): 10–15; Chen Jinqing, "Jiechu de balei yishu, zhandou de geming reqing: Guba balei wutuan yanchu guanhou," *Renmin ribao*, February 7, 1961.

85. "Woguo shiyan balei wujutuan dao Yangguang," *Guangming ribao*, January 9, 1962. See also Song Tianyi, *Zhongwai biaoyan*, 187.

86. On the cultural significance of this shift, see Alexander Cook, ed., *Mao's Little Red Book: A Global History* (Cambridge: Cambridge University Press, 2014).

87. On *Red Poppy* in China's ballet history, see Nan Ma, "Is It Just 'a' Play? The Red Detachment of Women in a Cold War Perspective" (paper presented at the Sights and Sounds of the Cold War in the Sinophone World conference, Washington University in St. Louis, St. Louis, MO, March 25–26, 2017). On Matsuyama Ballet's *White-Haired Girl* in the development of revolutionary ballet, see Clark, *The Chinese Cultural Revolution*, 162. For programs from the Matsuyama Ballet performances in China, see *Riben Songshan balei wutuan*, University of Michigan Asia Library Chinese Dance Collection.

88. Such ideas reinforced colonial racial hierarchies that valued ballet as "universal" and "modern" because of its associations with whiteness. See Jose Reynoso, "Choreographing Modern Mexico: Anna Pavlova in Mexico City (1919)," *Modernist Cultures* 9, no. 1 (2014): 80–98.

89. Clark, *Chinese Cultural Revolution*.

90. Glasstone, *Story of Dai Ailian*.

91. Although Dai led ballet institutions, she was also critical of ballet and encouraged her colleagues to be more discriminating in their study of it. Dai Ailian, "Chuangzuo he fazhan women de xin wudao," *Guangming ribao*, March 18, 1964.

92. Yingjin Zhang, *Chinese National Cinema* (New York and London: Routledge, 2004), 217; Judith Zeitlin, "Operatic Ghosts on Screen: The Case of *A Test of Love* (1958)," *Opera Quarterly* 26, nos. 2–3 (Spring–Summer 2010): 220–55.

93. "Shanghai shiyan gejuyuan shangyan xinjin chuangzuo geju wuju jiemu," *Guangming ribao*, March 11, 1962; *Wudao*, no. 4 (1962): back cover; *Renmin huabao* 13, no. 10 (1962): front cover; Xiao Qingzhang, "Meili de shenhua wuju 'hou yi,'" *Wenhui bao*, no. 12 (1962): 2. Shu Qiao, *Jin sheng*, 80, 84.

94. Song Tianyi, *Zhongwai biaoyan*, 292; *Caidie fen fei*.

95. *Caidie fen fei*.

96. "Mingque fangxiang," 5.

97. Zhou Zemin and Cheng Peng, "Xin shidai gewu yishu de fengshou: ji Jiefang jun di san jie wenyi huiyan," *Renmin ribao*, May 10, 1964; Luo Mingyang, "Zhenfenrenxin de zhandou gewu," *Guangming ribao*, April 23, 1964. A series of articles on this event appears in *Wudao*, no. 3 (1964) and *Wudao*, no. 4 (1964). See also Liu Min, *Zhongguo renmin jiefangjun wudao shi*.

98. *Xuri dongsheng* (August First Film Studio, 1964); *Dongfeng wanli* (August First Film Studio, 1964); "Di san jie quanjun wenyi huiyan wudao jiemu shezhi liang bu caise jilupian," *Guangming ribao*, July 27, 1964.

99. *Xuri dongsheng*; Emily Wilcox, "Joking after Rebellion: Performing Tibetan-Han Relations in the Chinese Military Dance 'Laundry Song' (1964)," in *Maoist Laughter*, ed. Jason McGrath, Zhuoyi Wang, and Ping Zhu (Hong Kong: Hong Kong University Press, forthcoming).

100. *Xuri dongsheng;* Zhang Wenming and Fu Zhongshu, "Xiang yingyongbuqu de Meiguo heiren xiongdi zhijing: chuangzuo 'Nuhuo zai ranshao' de xinde," *Wudao,* no. 3 (1965): 8–10.

101. Ouyang Yuqian, "Sulian balei shijie di yi: kan 'Baoshi hua,' 'Leidian de daolu' de ganxiang," *Renmin ribao,* October 13, 1959; Siyuan Liu, *Performing Hybridity;* Christopher Tang, "Homeland in the Heart, Eyes on the World: Domestic Internationalism, Popular Mobilization, and the Making of China's Cultural Revolution, 1962–68" (PhD diss., Cornell University, 2016); Wilcox, "Performing Bandung"; Wilcox, "The Postcolonial Blind Spot."

102. *Dongfeng wanli.*

103. "Daxing xiandai balei wuju 'Hongse jiangzijun' yanchu chenggong" and "Minzu wuju 'ba nü song' zai Jing yanchu," *Renmin huabao* 15, no. 11 (1964): 40.

104. Huang Boshou, "Yong baleiwu wei geming yingxiong suxiang: zan 'Hongse niangzi jun," *Wudao,* no. 6 (1964): 36–37; Pang Zhiyang, "Gaoge jianwu song ying: wuju 'Ba nü song' guanhou," *Wudao,* no. 6 (1964): 38–39.

105. Zhao Qing, interview with the author, July 24, 2013, Beijing.

106. Ye Lin, "Zai minzu wuju zhong wei geming yingxiong suxiang," *Guangming ribao,* October 6, 1964.

107. Pang Zhiyang, "Gaoge jianwu song ying."

108. Li Xiaoxiang, *Zhongguo geju wujuyuan yuanshi,* 75.

109. "Minzu wuju 'Ba nü song.'"

110. Huang Boshou, "Yong baleiwu wei geming yingxiong suxiang."

111. Ibid.; *Hongse niangzi jun.*

112. *Yinyue wudao shishi: Dongfang hong,* performance program dated October 1964, Beijing, University of Michigan Asia Library Chinese Dance Collection.

113. For more on this form of performance, see Xiaomei Chen, *Staging Chinese Revolution.*

114. *Yinyue wudao shishi: Dongfang hong.*

115. "Yinyue wudao shishi 'Dongfang hong' jieshao," *Wudao,* no. 6 (1964): 40–49.

116. "Shoudu juxing shengda wanhui qingzhu weida jieri yanchu daxing yinyue wudao shishi 'Dongfang hong,'" *Guangming ribao,* October 3, 1964; He Shiyao and Qian Hao, "Dongfang hong: yinyue wudao shishi," *Renmin huabao* 15, no. 12 (1964): 22–24.

117. *Dongfang hong* (Beijing Film Studio, August First Film Studio, and Central News Documentary Film Studio, 1965). The film does not contain the last segment of the original production, which depicted Chinese people uniting with revolutionary people of the world. Otherwise, the film matches closely with stage photographs and descriptions of the 1964 version.

118. *Dongfang hong; Yinyue wudao shishi: Dongfang hong.*

119. Ibid.

120. "Shoudu juxing zhiyuan Yuenan fandui Meiguo qinlüe gewu yanchu," *Guangming ribao,* April 27, 1965; He Shiyao and Ao Sihong, "Gewu 'Yelin nuhuo,'" *Renmin huabao,* no. 7 (1965): 36–44.

121. "Daxing gewu 'Feng lei song' zai shoudu gongyan," *Wudao,* no. 4 (1965): 19; Ke Ping, "Zou zai geminghua de dalu shang: shiping daxing gewu 'Women zou zai dalu

shang,'" *Wudao*, no. 4 (1965): 17–19; Yi Shuren, "Shidai de zui qiang yin: jieshao daxing gewu 'Yanzhenyidai,'" *Wudao*, no. 5 (1965): 9–10.

122. "Juexing de feizhou, zhandou de feizhou! Ji liu chang wuju 'Gangguohe zai nuhou' de yanchu," *Guangming ribao*, June 27, 1965; Li Xiaoxiang, *Zhongguo geju wujuyuan yuanshi*.

123. Music and Dance Historical Epic *East Is Red* Choreography Group, "Benteng de jiliu: wuju 'Gangguohe zai nuhou' de chuangzuo chubu tihui," *Wudao*, no. 4 (1965): 3–6.

124. Photos published in *Guangming ribao*, June 27 and July 6, 1965; *Wudao*, no. 4 (1965); Li Xiaoxiang, *Zhongguo geju wujuyuan yuanshi*.

125. "Tongtai yanchu daxing minzu wuju 'Liangshan jubian,'" *Guangming ribao*, April 11, 1965.

126. Akeshelin and Gao Keming, "Baiwan nongnu xin xiang dang: 'Fanshen nongnu xiang taiyang' yanchu gaikuang," *Wudao*, no. 6 (1965): 7–8; *People's Communes Are Good* Literary Creation Group and Choreography Group, "Yi bu shehuizhuyi xin mukamu de dansheng," *Wudao*, no. 6 (1965): 8–10.

127. Pu Zhengguang, "Kuayue shiji de feiyue: 'Liangshan jubian' guanhou," *Wudao*, no. 3 (1965): 28–29.

128. "Tongtai yanchu daxing minzu wuju."

129. Yin Peifang et al., "Women shi zenyang kuachu zhe yi bu de: chuangzuo balei wuju 'Hong sao' de tihui," *Wudao*, no. 5 (1965): 14–16; "Shanghai yanchu daxing xiandai balei wuju 'Baimao nü,'" *Guangming ribao*, May 16, 1965.

130. Trial performances of this revised work began in 1971, although the final version was set in 1974. "Jiang Qing, Zhang Chunqiao, Yao Wenyuan tongzhi peitong . . . guankan geming xiandai wuju 'Yimeng song' shiyan yanchu," *Guangming ribao*, August 4, 1971; "Geming xiandai wuju 'Yimeng song,'" *Renmin huabao*, no. 10 (1975): 18–34; *Yimeng song*.

131. *Baimao nü*; *Yimeng song*.

132. Beijing Dance Academy, *Beijing wudao xueyuan zhi*.

133. Li Xiaoxiang, *Zhongguo geju wujuyuan yuanshi*.

134. Dong Feng, "Da lianhe da pipan, tongda 'Luoshui gou,'" *Guangming ribao*, July 30, 1967.

135. "Beijing balei wudao xuexiao geming shisheng," *Guangming ribao*, July 24, 1967.

136. "Guangming de geming wenyi yangban," *Renmin huabao*, no. 8 (1967): 10–11. The term "model works" started to be used in relation to the two ballets by December 1966; "Shijian Mao zhuxi wenyi luxian de guanghui yangban," *Renmin ribao*, December 9, 1966.

137. Names of the lead characters in *Red Detachment of Women* and *White-Haired Girl*.

138. Wang Kefen and Long Yinpei, *Zhongguo jinxiandai*, 317.

139. Mittler, *A Continuous Revolution*; Paul Clark, Laikwan Pang, and Tsan-Huang Tsai, eds., *Listening to China's Cultural Revolution: Translations between Music and Politics* (New York: Palgrave Macmillan, 2015); Laikwan Pang, *The Art of Cloning: Creative Production during China's Cultural Revolution* (London: Verso, 2017).

140. Wilcox, "Dialectics of Virtuosity."

141. Zhang Ke, *Wuzhe duanxiang* (Beijing: Xinhua chubanshe, 2001); Li Zhengyi, *Zhongguo gudianwu jiaoxue*; Nan Shan, "Zhou Enlai yu Dongfang gewutuan de weiliaoqing," *Yan-Huang chunqiu*, no. 10 (1997): 2–6.

142. Dai Ailian, "Ballet in China," *Britain-China* 33 (Autumn 1986): 10–12, 10.

143. Clark, *Chinese Cultural Revolution*, 168.

144. Li Chengxiang, "Pojiu chaungxin, wei fazhan geming de balei wuju er fendou," *Wudao*, no. 2 (1965): 16–20.

145. Dai Ailian, *Wo de yishu.*

146. Jian Guo, Yongyi Song, and Yuan Zhou, *The A to Z of the Chinese Cultural Revolution* (New York: Rowman and Littlefield, 2006), 160–61; He Libo, "Zhuang Zedong, Liu Qingtang, Qian Haoliang de renshengchenfu," *Tongzhou gongjin*, no. 9 (2013): 53–59.

147. Huang Boshou, "Yong baleiwu wei geming," 36

148. An early use of this phrase appears in "Hong taiyang zhaoliang le balei wutai," *Renmin ribao*, April 26, 1967.

CHAPTER 5. THE RETURN OF CHINESE DANCE

1. Geremie Barmé, *In the Red: On Contemporary Chinese Culture* (New York: Columbia University Press, 1999), xii.

2. See, for example, Dai Ailian, "Wo de qieshen tihui," *Wudao*, no. 1 (1978): 14–15; Jia Zuoguang, "Zasui jingshen jiasuo gan geming," *Guangming ribao*, December 27, 1977; Beijing Dance School, "Shiqi nian wudao jiaoyu shiye de chengji burong mosha," *Guangming ribao*, January 22, 1978.

3. Beijing Railroad Workers Amateur Propaganda Troupe, "'Sirenbang' pohuai qunzhong wenyi huodong," *Wudao*, no. 5 (1976): 12–13.

4. China Dance Drama Ensemble Large Criticism Group, "Boxia 'qishou' de huapi," *Wudao*, no. 5 (1976): 14–16.

5. Mao Hui, *Xin Zhongguo*, 96, 130.

6. The Beijing Dance School, which was founded in 1954 and operated from 1964 to 1966 as two institutions, stopped classes in June 1966 due to the Cultural Revolution. It was temporarily replaced in 1971 with a ballet-focused program inside a consolidated Central May 7th Art School (from 1973, Art University). In December 1977, China's Ministry of Culture eliminated the Central May 7th Art University and restored the seven independent art schools that had existed before 1966, including BDS. In 1978 BDS expanded to become a university-level institution, renamed the Beijing Dance Academy, with the secondary school remaining as an attached institution. Beijing Dance Academy, *Beijing wudao xueyuan zhi.*

7. These ensembles, in order, specialized in Chinese folk dance, Chinese minority dance, national dance drama, dances of the Third World (a.k.a. Oriental Dance), and ballet. Mao, *Xin Zhongguo*; Li Xiaoxiang, *Zhongguo geju wujuyuan yuanshi*; "Dongfang gewutuan zhengshi huifu juxing huibao yanchu," *Guangming ribao*, September 28, 1977; "Wenhua bu jueding huifu suoshu yishu tuanti de jianzhi he mingcheng," *Guangming ribao*, April 13, 1978. As a subordinate of the Minority Affairs Division, rather than the Ministry of Culture, the Central Nationalities Song and Dance Ensemble was not subject to the Ministry of Culture announcement. The ensemble appears to have been restored in 1975, as newspaper citations for the ensemble reappear on October 12, 1975.

8. The national dance ensemble operating during the Cultural Revolution was the Worker Peasant Soldier Ballet Ensemble (Gongnongbing balei wujutuan, renamed in 1969 the China Dance Drama Ensemble [Zhongguo wujutuan]).

9. Beijing Dance Academy, *Beijing wudao xueyuan zhi*; Mao Hui, *Xin Zhongguo*; Li Xiaoxiang, *Zhongguo geju wujuyuan yuanshi.*

10. Liu Min, ed., *Zhongguo renmin jiefangjun*, 584.

11. "Wuxie Guangdong fenhui huifu huodong," *Wudao*, no. 1 (1978): 47.

12. The Shanghai Dance School, established in 1960, was modeled on the Beijing Dance School's dual-track model, with programs in Chinese dance and ballet. Like the Beijing Dance School, the Shanghai Dance School closed during the Cultural Revolution and was replaced by a consolidated ballet-focused program, known as the May 7th Dance Training Class. Once the school reopened, its dual-track structure was restored as well. Song Mingbo, *Wuyuan chunqiu*, 36–37.

13. "Wudao jianxun," *Wudao*, no. 4 (1978): 22–23; "Liaoning, Xinjiang, Shandong, Sichuan wuxie fenhui xiangji huifu huodong," *Wudao*, no. 5 (1978): 13.

14. "Deng Xiaoping fuzongli zhuchi yi Zhou Enlai zongli mingyi juxing de shengda zhaodaihui," *Renmin ribao*, October 1, 1975. Other prominent figures from the dance field in attendance were Li Chengxiang, Bai Shuxiang, and Zhang Jun (1935–2012).

15. "Relie qingzhu Zhonghua renmin gongheguo chengli ershiba zhou nian," *Guangming ribao*, October 1, 1977.

16. "Zhongguo wenlian quanguo weiyuanhui juxing kuoda huiyi," *Guangming ribao*, June 6, 1978.

17. The roster included Feng Guopei, Bai Shuxiang, Chen Jinqing, Wu Xiaobang, Baoyinbatu, Zhao Qing, Zhao Dexian, Hu Rongrong, Liang Lun, Qemberxanim, Sheng Jie, Siqintariha, and Dai Ailian. "Di si ci wendaihui chuxituan mingdan," *Renmin ribao*, October 31, 1979.

18. "Wenlian mingyu zhuxi, zhuxi, fuzhuxi mingdan," *Renmin ribao*, November 17, 1979.

19. "Zhongguo wenlian ge xiehui, yanjiuhui xin xuanchu de zhuxi, fuzhuxi," *Renmin ribao*, November 17, 1979.

20. "Quanguo weiyuanhui xianhou zhaokai xuanchu zhengfuzhuxi he changwei," *Renmin ribao*, August 2, 1949.

21. Beijing Dance Academy, *Beijing wudao xueyuan zhi*, 24.

22. Beijing Dance Academy, *Beijing wudao xueyuan zhi*, 72–77.

23. "Mao zhuxi Zhou zongli qinqie guanhuai de yingpian 'Dongfang hong' chongjian tianri," *Guangming ribao*, December 30, 1976.

24. "'Dong fang hong' (yinyue wudao shishi)," *Wudao*, no. 1 (1977): 10–24.

25. *Dongfang hong*.

26. Jia Zuoguang, "Zasui jingshen." See also Zhang Ke, *Wuzhe duanxiang*, 253–57.

27. "Wuju 'Xiaodao hui' you jiang gongyan," *Renmin ribao*, January 1, 1977; Shanghai Opera Theater, "'Xiaodao hui' de xinsheng," *Guangming ribao*, February 3, 1977; "Zalan 'Sirenbang' wenyi de jiefang: wuju 'Xiaodao hui' huode xinsheng zai Shanghai chongyan," *Wudao*, no. 1 (1977): 33.

28. "Daxing wuju 'Die lian hua' zai shoudu chongxin shangyan," *Guangming ribao*, August 17, 1977.

29. Zhu Youxia, "Youyi de tansuo kegui de jingyan," *Wudao*, no. 6 (1978): 19–20; "Guoqingjie qijian shoudu wenyi wutai," *Guangming ribao*, October 1, 1978.

30. "Guoqingjie qijian shoudu wenyi wutai," *Guangming ribao*, October 1, 1978; Zhao Qing, "Nanwang de guanhuai," *Wudao*, no. 5 (1978): 25–26; Li Xiaoxiang, *Zhongguo geju wujuyuan yuanshi*.

31. Zhang Tuo, "Laolong guanbuzhu geming wenyi de chuntian: kongsu 'Siren bang' dui wuju 'Xiaodao hui' de pohai," *Renmin ribao*, January 30, 1978.

32. Performing Arts Company of the People's Republic of China, performers list. Internal document dated May 1978, personal collection of Thomas B. Gold.

33. The works included "Bow Dance" (Gong wu, 1959); "Cup and Bowl Dance" (Zhong wan wu, 1961); "Hourglass Drum Dance" (Changgu wu, 1950s); "Lotus Dance" (Hehua wu, 1953); "Laundry Song" (Xi yi ge, 1964); "Militiawomen of the Grassland" (Caoyuan nüminbing, 1959); "Peacock Dance" (Kongque wu, 1956); "Picking Grapes" (Zhai putao, 1959); "Red Silk Dance" (Hongchou wu, 1951); and "Spring River and Flowers on a Moonlit Night" (Chun jiang hua yueye, 1957). Performing Arts Company of the People's Republic of China, performance works list, personal collection of Thomas B. Gold. Performance programs also consulted in Sophia Delza Papers, (S)*MGZMD 155, Box 61, Folder 6, Jerome Robbins Dance Division, New York Public Library for the Performing Arts.

34. In 1959 Wu Xiaobang stated that the agreed-upon prime age for dancers was thirty for men and twenty-three for women, after which performers were expected to retire or change professions. "Wei le wudao shiye de fanrong changsheng!," *Renmin ribao*, April 30, 1959.

35. On the US reception of this tour, see Wilcox, "Foreword: A Manifesto for Demarginalization."

36. *Die lian hua* (Changchun Film Studio, 1978).

37. *Caihong* (Inner Mongolia Film Studio, 1979).

38. "Daxing wuju 'Die lian hua'"; Pang Zhiyang, "Wuju 'Die lian hua' chuangzuo tihui," *Wudao*, no. 6 (1978): 13–16. See also Nan Ma, "Dancing into Modernity."

39. Siqintariha, "Zai dang de minzu zhengce de guanghui zhaoyao xia fazhan minzu de wudao shiye," in *Siqintariha Menggu wu wenji*, ed. Siqintariha (1979; Hohhot, China: Neimenggu renmin chubanshe, 2008), 3–14.

40. *Die lian hua*.

41. *Caihong*. On Siqintariha, see Wilcox, "Dynamic Inheritance."

42. Huang Jingming, "Shengkai de caoyuan zhi hua," *Nanfang ribao*, May 7, 1978, reprinted in Inner Mongolia Song and Dance Ensemble, *Jiantuan sishi zhounian jiniance*, 56–58.

43. "Qingzhu Zhonghua renmin gongheguo chengli sanshi zhounian xianli yanchu huodong," *Guangming ribao*, January 5, 1979; Du Qingyuan, "Jianguo sanshi zhounian xianli yanchu shengli jieshu," *Guangming ribao*, February 20, 1980; Su Zuqian, "Pi lu chuang guan xin hua jing yan: wuju chuangzuo xihuo fengshou," *Guangming ribao*, February 22, 1980.

44. Liu Haixiang, "Xishuangbanna feilai de kongque: ji wudao yanyuan Yang Liping," *Renmin ribao*, January 27, 1987.

45. This work went through at least three versions between 1986 and 2003, each with different music and changes to the choreography and lighting. Ting-Ting Chang, "Choreographing the Peacock: Gender, Ethnicity, and National Identity in Chinese Ethnic Dance" (PhD diss., University of California, Riverside, 2008). Here, I am analyzing this version (circa 2003): https://www.youtube.com/watch?v = rgwGSQRboYU. For two alternate versions, see "Que zhi ling" and "Kongque wu," in Zhang Fengsheng, *Yang Liping wudao DVD* (Jilin: Jilin wenhua yinxiang chubanshe, n.d.).

46. Jin Hao, *Xin shiji Zhongguo wudao wenhua de liubian* (Shanghai: Shanghai yinyue chubanshe, 2007); Mu Yu, "Yang Liping minzu gewu de yishu yu ziben luoji: 'Yunnan yingxiang' shi zhounian qishi," *Minzu yishu yanjiu*, no. 2 (2015): 45–53.

47. *Yunnan yingxiang*, live performance, Yunnan Arts University Experimental Theatre, Kunming, China, December 13, 2013; *Kongque*, live performance, Yunnan Arts University Experimental Theatre, Kunming, China, December 22, 2013.

48. Ting-Ting Chang, "Negotiating Chinese National Identity through Ethnic Minority Dance on the Global Stage: From *Spirit of the Peacock* to *Dynamic of Yunnan*" (paper presented at the Association for Asian Studies Annual Meeting, Toronto, Canada, March 15–18, 2012).

49. Wang Wei, "Tan wudao 'Zhaoshutuan yu Nanmuluoluan' de yanchu ji qita," *Bianjiang wenyi*, no. 12 (1956): 74–77; "Quanguo zhuanye tuanti yinyue wudao huiyan wudao jiemu juzhao," *Wudao congkan*, no. 1 (May 1957): n.p., University of Michigan Chinese Dance Collection.

50. Yan Wu, Zhou Changzong, and Duan Wenhui, "Xuxu duo duo 'di yi dai' he 'di yi ge,'" *Guangming ribao*, May 19, 1961; Du Hui, "Jin kongque dao le Beijing," *Guangming ribao*, December 1, 1979; Dao Guo'an and Zhu Lanfang, "Daizu minjian shenhua wuju 'Zhao Shutun yu Nanmunuonuo,'" in *Wudao wuju chuangzuo jingyan wenji*, 345–52. According to one author, the full-length version of the production was suppressed before it could be completed. Wang Yan, "Fei wu ba! Meili de kongque: Daizu minjian wuju *Zhao Shutun* guanhou," *Wudao*, no. 5 (1979): 33–35. A local gazetteer, however, states that the dance drama was performed on January 23, 1963, to celebrate the tenth anniversary of the founding of the Xishuangbanna autonomous state. Dao Jin'an et al., eds., *Xishuangbanna Daizu zizhizhou minzu zongjiao zhi* (Xishuangbanna: Yunnan minzu chubanshe, 2006).

51. Xiao Si, "Jingyan de wuju xin hua: wuju 'Silu hua yu' 'Zhao Shutun yu Nanmunuonuo' zuotanhui jishi," *Wudao*, no. 6 (1979): 20–22; Jin Xiang, "Xishuangbanna de yi ke mingzhu: wuju 'Zhao Shutun yu Nanmuruona' guanhou," *Renmin yinyue*, no. Z1 (1979): 27–29; Wang Xuexin, "Baizu de jin kongque: Yang Liping," *Xin guancha*, no. 10 (1985): 20–26. According to one author, Yang was initially removed from the Beijing tour in favor of a dancer of Dai ethnicity (Yang herself identifies as Bai, not Dai), but at the last minute, she was returned to the role after leaders were unhappy with the replacement. Xiao Gang, "Kongque gongzhu Yang Liping," *Zhe yi dai*, no. 6 (1987): 4–7.

52. The work toured internationally under the name *Peacock Princess*, with the ensemble name Yunnan Song and Dance Ensemble. "Yunnan gewutuan zai Xianggang yanchu shoudao haoping," *Guangming ribao*, October 6, 1980; "Youhao wanglai," *Renmin ribao*, November 11, 1980; "Yunnan gewutuan zai Xinjiapo yanchu 'Kongque gongzhu,'" *Renmin ribao*, January 6, 1981; Xiao Gang, "Kongque gongzhu."

53. Qing Xianyou, "Fang Xishuangbanna minzu gewutuan," *Jin ri Zhongguo*, no. 7 (1982): 47–51.

54. On costumes and props used in early peacock dances in different parts of Yunnan, see Nie Qianxian et al., eds., *Zhonghua wudao zhi Yunnan juan (shang ce)* (Shanghai: Xuelin chubanshe, 2007).

55. "Shuangren kongque," performance photograph in "Zhongyang minzu xueyuan," *Renmin huabao* 5, no. 7 (1954): 20–22.

56. Li Jiajun, "Kongque gongzhuxing minjian gushi de qiyuan he fazhan," *Sixiang zhanxian* 11, no. 2 (1985): 42–50.

57. Toshiharu Yoshikawa, "A Comparative Study of the Thai, Sanskrit, and Chinese Swan Maiden" (paper presented at the International Conference on Thai Studies, Chulalongkorn University, Thailand, August 1984).

58. Terry Miller, "Thailand," in *The Garland Handbook of Southeast Asian Music*, ed. Terry Miller and Sean Williams (New York and London: Routledge, 2008), 121–82.

59. Chen Guipei, "Daizu minjian wenxue de chuanbozhe: 'zanha' he 'aizhang,'" *Guangming ribao*, November 16, 1956. Qu Yongxian, "Cultural Circles and Epic Transmission: The Dai People in China," *Oral Tradition* 28, no. 1 (March 2013): 103–24. According to an undated gazetteer, at least nine different versions of the story existed in Dai areas, both in copied versions of narrative poems and in folk prose legends. Titles of these stories include "Zhao Shutun," "Hunter and the Peacock (Zhao Shutun and Nanmuluoluan)," "Zhao Shutun and Lanwuluona," "Langluo'en," "Nan tui Han," and the like. *Zhongguo minsu tongzhi minjian wenxue zhi xia*, 539–40, n.d.

60. Yan Die and Chen Guipei, trans., "Zhao Shutun (Daizu minjian xushishi)," *Bianjiang wenyi*, no. 12 (1956): 3–29; Li Qiao, ed., based on oral transmission from Diao Faxiang, Kang Langshuai, Ma Hongde, and Li Lan, "Zhao Shutun he Nanmuluoluan (Daizu shenhua)," *Caodi*, no. 12 (1957): 37–40; Dao Jin'an, *Xishuangbanna Daizu*, 20.

61. Cheng Shifa, "Zhao Shutun (Lianhuanhua si fu)," *Meishu zazhi*, no. 10 (1957): 32–33; *Chaoshutun and Nannona* (Beijing: Foreign Languages Press, 1961); "Woguo zui chang de yibu caise mu'ou pian 'Kongque gongzhu,'" *Guangming ribao*, December 12, 1963; Jin Chong, Li Fang, and Guo Sijiu, eds., *Zhongguo xiqu zhi Yunnan juan* (China Xiqu Gazetteer Editing Committee, 1994), 107.

62. Yan Die et al., "Zhao Shutun," 5–6.

63. Ibid., 6.

64. Wang Wei, "Tan wudao," 74–75.

65. Ibid., 75–76.

66. "Quanguo zhuanye tuanti."

67. *Kongque gongzhu* (Shanghai: Shanghai Animation Film Studio, 1963). For more on this film, see Sean Macdonald, *Animation in China: History, Aesthetics, Media* (New York and London: Routledge, 2016), 113–29.

68. This seems to be a reference to the female immortal image in Mei Lanfang's *Goddess Scatters Flowers (Tiannü sanhua)*.

69. Similar skirts appear in both Mao Xiang's *Peacock Duet* and Jin Ming's *Peacock Dance*, but the collars clearly reference the Xishuangbanna ensemble's dance drama designs.

70. *Bai feng chaoyang*.

71. Jin Xiang, "Xishuangbanna de," 29.

72. Yan Die et al., "Zhao Shutun," 15–16.

73. Ibid., 16.

74. Ibid., 16.

75. Because this version was never performed in a national festival and came under attack not long after it was completed, less documentation is available about it in national-level print media. More research would need to be done using local sources to determine its exact form and content. However, the fact that commentators on the 1978 version, including its choreographer Dao Guo'an, all trace its origins to this earlier production suggests that there were likely strong similarities between the two.

76. Wang Yan, "Fei wu ba!," 33.

77. Jia Zuoguang, "Yongyu shijian yongyu chuangxin tan wuju 'Zhao Shutun yu Nanmunuonuo' de yishu chengjiu," *Bianjiang wenyi*, no. 11 (1980): 65–66, 65.

78. "Daizu wuju 'Zhao Shutun' zhong de kongque gongzhu," *Renmin huabao*, May 1979, cover photo. Compare to photographs in Wang Wei, "Tan wudao" and "Quanguo zhuanye tuanti," 1957.

79. Xiao Si, "Jingyan de," 21.

80. Zhao Xiushan, "Lanzhou shangyan wuju 'Silu hua yu,'" *Guangming ribao*, June 27, 1979.

81. Liang Shengming and Du Hui, "'Silu hua yu' wei Zhongguo wuju kaipi le xin lu," *Guangming ribao*, October 30, 1979; "Xianli yanchu ping jiang gongzuo yuanman jieshu," *Renmin ribao*, April 9, 1980.

82. Gansu Provincial Song and Dance Theater, *Silu hua yu*, performance program, Beijing, National Centre for the Performing Arts, August 2009; Zhao Zhixun et al., eds., '*Silu hua yu' ping jie* (Lanzhou: Gansu Provincial Song and Dance Ensemble, 2000).

83. "Meikuang yishutuan fu Meiguo Jianada fangwen yanchu," *Renmin ribao*, October 11, 1982.

84. *Silu hua yu* (Xi'an Film Studio, 1982); "Silu hua yu," *Dianying zhi you* no. 9 (1982): 21–22; "Jianxun," *Guangming ribao*, January 2, 1983.

85. Gansu Provincial Song and Dance Theater, *Silu hua yu*, live performance, National Centre for the Performing Arts, Beijing, August 2009.

86. In addition to the locations listed in chapter 5, the Gansu ensemble performed *Flowers* in Japan, Latvia, Macao, Russia, Spain, Taiwan, Thailand, and Turkey. Gansu Provincial Song and Dance Theater, performance program; Zhao Zhixun, '*Silu hua yu*.'

87. Wu Xiaobang, "Zhongguo wuju zai qianjin: kan 'Silu hua yu' you gan," *Guangming ribao*, October 30, 1979.

88. Ibid.; Xiao Si, "Jingyan de"; Song Shouqin, "Youyi lu shang fei xin hua: shitan wuju 'Silu hua yu,'" *Wudao*, no. 5 (1979): 30–32; Xiao Yunru, "Sheng Tang jing, Dunhuang hua, Silu hua: manhua wuju 'Silu hua yu,'" *Shaanxi xiju*, no. 12 (1981): 3–5.

89. Ning Qiang, *Art, Religion, and Politics in Medieval China: The Dunhuang Cave of the Zhai Family* (Honolulu: University of Hawai'i Press, 2004), 1.

90. Gao Jinrong, *Dunhuang shiku wuyue yishu* (Lanzhou: Gansu renmin chubanshe, 2000).

91. Lanlan Kuang, "Staging the Cosmopolitan Nation: The Re-Creation of the Dunhuang Bihua Yuewu, a Multifaceted Music, Dance, and Theatrical Drama From China" (PhD diss., Indiana University, 2012); Kuang Lanlan, *Dunhuang bihua yuewu: 'Zhongguo jingguan' zai guoji yujing zhong de jiangou, chuanbo yu yiyi* (Beijing: Shehui kexue wenxian chubanshe, 2016).

92. Valerie Hansen, *The Silk Road: A New History* (Oxford: Oxford University Press, 2012), 167.

93. Hansen, *The Silk Road*, 168.

94. Patricia Buckley Ebrey, "A Cosmopolitan Empire: The Tang Dynasty 618–907," in *The Cambridge Illustrated History of China*, 2nd ed. (Cambridge: Cambridge University Press, 2010), 108–135.

95. Ibid., 108.

96. Gansu Song and Dance Ensemble, *Silu hua yu*, PRC Thirtieth Anniversary Festival performance program, October 1979, Beijing, Beijing Dance Academy Archives; Gansu Song and Dance Ensemble, *Silu hua yu*, stage recording, early 1980s, private collection of He Yanyun.

97. Wu Xiaobang, "Zhongguo wuju"; Song Shouqin, "Youyi lushang."

98. Gao Jinrong, *Dunhuang shiku*, 14. Gao gives the total number of caves as 452.

99. Zhao Xian, "Silu hua yu de wudao yuyan," *Wenyi yanjiu*, no. 2 (1980): 98–102.

100. Ibid., 100; Gansu Song and Dance Ensemble, *Silu hua yu*, stage recording; *Silu hua yu*, film.

101. Gansu Song and Dance Ensemble, *Silu hua yu*, stage recording; *Silu hua yu*, film.

102. Liu Shaoxiong, "Tansuo, qiujiao yu qiujing: 'Silu hua yu' chuangzuo tihui," in *Wudao wuju chuangzuo jingyan wenji*, ed. Zhongguo yishu yanjiuyuan wudao yanjiusuo (Beijing: Renmin yinyue chubanshe, 1985), 297–302.

103. Liu Shaoxiong, "Tansuo, qiujiao," 298; Duan Wenjie, "Zhenshi de xugou: tan wuju 'Silu hua yu' de yixie lishi yiju," *Wenyi yanjiu*, no. 2 (1980): 103–8.

104. Liu Shaoxiong, "Tansuo, qiujiao," 299–300.

105. Ibid., 301.

106. Ye Ning, "Nannengkegui de chuangzuo," *Renmin ribao*, November 11, 1979.

107. Michael Sullivan and Franklin D. Murphy, *Art and Artists of Twentieth-Century China* (Berkeley: University of California Press, 1996), 106.

108. Sullivan and Murphy, *Art and Artists*, 106.

109. Gansu Song and Dance Ensemble, performance program.

110. FitzGerald, *Fragmenting Modernisms*, 111–12.

111. Ibid., 113–14.

112. Dai Ailian, *Wo de yishu*, 127. See also Peng Song, "Cai wu ji."

113. Dai Ailian, "Fazhan Zhongguo wudao di yi bu."

114. Gao Jinrong, *Dunhuang shiku*, 83–84.

115. "Feitian wu," in *Zhongguo minjian wudao tupian xuanji*, ed. Zhongguo wudao yishu yanjiuhui (Shanghai: Shanghai renmin meishu chubanshe, 1957); Dai Ailian, "Tan feitian," in *Wudao wuju chuangzuo jingyan wenji*, ed. Zhongguo yishu yanjiuyuan wudao yanjiusuo (Beijing: Renmin yinyue chubanshe, 1985), 34–36.

116. "Du wu, shuangren wu biaoyanhui," *Wudao*, no. 8 (1961); Li Lanying, "Feitian," *Renmin huabao* 14, no. 4 (1963): cover image.

117. "Biaoxian woguo renmin weida yishu chengjiu," *Guangming ribao*, April 12, 1951.

118. "Zhengwuyuan wenjiao weiyuanhui jiajiang Dunhuang wenwu yanjiusuo gongzuo renyuan," *Guangming ribao*, June 11, 1951.

119. "Beijing daxue lishi xi juban 'Dunhuang bihua zhanlanhui,'" *Guangming ribao*, November 23, 1954; "Dunhuang yishu zhanlanhui kaimu," *Guangming ribao*, October 9, 1955; Gao Jinrong, *Dunhuang shiku*, 41–42.

120. "Dunhuang Tangdai bihua zhong de feitian," *Wudao tongxun*, no. 1 *(Huiyan zhuanhao)* (July 1951): cover.

121. Yin Falu, "Cong Dunhuang bihua lun Tangdai de yinyue he wudao," *Wudao xuexi ziliao*, no. 4 (June 1954): 46–57.

122. "Gudai wudao tupian," *Wudao xuexi ziliao*, no. 10 (August 1956): 141–58; "Wuguo de gudai wudao," *Wudao tongxun*, no. 11 (1956): 37–38; Wang Kefen, "Woguo fengfu de gudai wudao ziliao," *Wudao tongxun*, no. 12 (1956): 21; Dong Xijiu, "Nishang yuyi wu," *Wudao tongxun*, no. 12 (1956): 22; Harada Yoshito, "Zhongguo Tangdai nüzi de fushi," trans. from Japanese by Dong Xijiu, *Wudao congkan*, no. 2 (June 1957): 120–30.

123. "Gudai wudao tupian," 155.

124. Yu Weng, "Canlan de guoqu, Guanghui de weilai: canguan Zhongguo wudao yishu yanjiu hui 'Zhongguo wudao shiliao chenlieguan,'" *Wudao*, no. 1 (1958): 51–54.

125. Ouyang Yuqian, "Shitan Tangdai wudao," *Wudao*, 4 (1959): 30–33; Dong Qing, "Tangren shige zhong de yuewu ziliao," *Wudao*, no. 12 (1959): 26; Ouyang Yuqian, "Tangdai wudao xutan," *Wudao*, no. 6 (1960): 27–28.

126. Wu Xiaobang, "Liangnian jian," *Wudao xuexi ziliao*, no. 11 (October 1956): 17–20.

127. Ye Ning, "Tan zhengli yanjiu Zhongguo gudian wudao zhong de jige wenti," *Wudao xuexi ziliao*, no. 11 (October 1956): 68–80.

128. Ibid., 70.

129. "Bao liandeng (wuju gushi)," *Wudao*, no. 1 (1958): 14–15; *Bao liandeng*.

130. Yin Ying, "San Shengmu jiaose de chuangzuo," *Wudao*, no. 1 (1958): 18–20, 18.

131. Feng Shuangbai, *Zhongguo wudaojia da cidian*, 115–16.

132. Li Kaifang, "Yu zhuo jin diao silu hua: jieshao wuju 'Silu hua yu' de jiwei zhuyao yanyuan," *Dangdai xiju*, no. 12 (1981): 6–10, 9.

133. Ibid., 7–8.

134. Zhai Zixia, *Zhongguo wuju*.

135. Lan Hang, "Wuju 'Wencheng gongzhu' zai Jing gongyan," *Guangming ribao*, December 7, 1979.

136. Su Zuqian, "Pi lu chuang."

137. Li Yaozong, "Wuju yishupian de xin tansuo: Zangzu wuju 'Zhuowa sangmu' song wutai dao yinmu," *Renmin ribao*, September 29, 1984.

138. *Zhuowa sangmu* (Emei Film Studio, 1984).

139. Yi Kai and Zhang Shiying, "Guoqing shoudu wenyi wutai qixiang yixin," *Renmin ribao*, September 28, 1985.

140. Wilcox, "Han-Tang *Zhongguo Gudianwu* and the Problem of Chineseness in Contemporary Chinese Dance: Sixty Years of Controversy," *Asian Theatre Journal* 29, no. 1 (2012): 206–32.

141. Inus's appearance can be seen as a product of China's shifting foreign relations and political economy in 1979, when Deng Xiaoping, China's new leader, was aligning with the US capitalist bloc, introducing market reforms, and encouraging foreign trade. Emily Wilcox, "Performing the Post-Mao Economy: Global Capitalism and the Merchant Hero in *Flowers and Rain on the Silk Road*" (paper presented at the Association for Theater in Higher Education Annual Meeting, Chicago, IL, August 11–14, 2016).

142. Both Shang and Wang taught workshops in Beijing in 1980. Wang returned in 1983 with Australian-born Martha Graham dancer Ross Parkes and taught another series of workshops in Beijing, Shanghai, Kunming, Guangxi, and Guangdong. Wang also set up the US-China Dance Exchange Program at the University of Iowa. Xiao Zhao, "Shang Rubi zai Beijing," *Wudao*, no. 3 (1980): 25. Wang Xiaolan, Meiguo xiandaiwu lüetan," *Wudao*, no. 4 (1980): 35–37; "Chinese Coup for Festival," *Canberra Times*, February 2, 2006; Liao Weizhong, "Meiguo wudao jia Wang Xiaolan, Lusi Pakesi zai Guangzhou," *Wudao yanjiu*, no. 3 (1983): 115.

143. For a detailed account of this program, including personal testimonies by the artists involved, see Ruth Solomon and John Solomon, eds., *East Meets West in Dance: Voices in the Cross-Cultural Dialogue* (1995; New York: Routledge, 2011). See also *Routledge Encyclopedia of Modernism*, s.v. "Guangdong Modern Dance Company," by Emily Wilcox, 2016, electronic.

144. Wilcox, "Moonwalking in Beijing."

CHAPTER 6. INHERITING THE SOCIALIST LEGACY

1. Zhang Dongliang, "Weile zhongbing fuqin de xiaorong: Xinjiang meinü yi wu duo-jun," *Qiaoyuan*, no. 9 (2014): 16–17.

2. *Zhongguo hao wudao* (Zhejiang Satellite TV, 2014).

3. Zhang Dongliang, "Weile zhongbing," 17; Wang Yongge, "Dui xin shiji Xinjiang wudao jiaoyu fazhan de sikao," *Xinjiang yishu*, no. 6 (2000): 57–58.

4. Field visit to Xinjiang Art Academy, Ürümqi, August 2015.

5. Dilaram Mahamatimin, interview with the author, August 9, 2015, Ürümqi.

6. Zhang Dongliang, "Weile zhongbing," 16.

7. Maimaitimi Rozi (b. 1932), interview with the author, August 9, 2015, Ürümqi. Qem-berxanim's teacher, Tamara Khanum, was famous for being the first woman in Uzbekistan to dance in public without a veil. According to Mary Masayo Doi, one of Khanum's students was murdered by her own brother because of the perceived humiliation caused by her danc-ing publicly. Mary Masayo Doi, *Gesture, Gender, Nation.*

8. Amina, *Qemberxanim de yishu shengya*, 34.

9. Inspired by historical texts for a type of "disc bell dance" practiced in the Xinjiang region during the Tang dynasty (618–907), Qemberxanim and her sister, also a dancer, cre-ated a dance transliterated into Chinese as "Muxigulati," in which the performer wears four walnuts on one finger and bells of different sizes on her other fingers, wrists, shoulders, and feet. Amina, *Qemberxanim*, 34–35.

10. National Centre for the Performing Arts, "Zhongguo wudao shi'er tian: Gao Du tuijian: Gulimina zuopin 'Gulimina,'" publicity brochure, 2015.

11. Ibid.

12. *Gulmira*, live performance, National Centre for the Performing Arts Multi-functional Theatre, Beijing, August 25, 2015.

13. "Kan shouyu," *Beijing wudao xueyuan xuebao*, no. 4 (2004): 3.

14. Pan Zhitao, ed., *Dadi zhi wu: Zhongguo minzu minjian wudao zuopin shangxin* (Shanghai: Shanghai yinyue chubanshe, 2006).

15. *Dadi zhi wu*, performance recording by the Beijing Dance Academy Department of National Folk Dance (Shanghai: Shanghai yinyue chubanshe, 2006).

16. Jia Anlin, ed., *Zhongwai wudao zuopin shangxi*, 90–93.

17. *Dadi zhi wu*, program notes, cited in Pan Zhitao, *Dadi zhi wu*, 1.

18. From the late 1950s until 2003, the Beijing Dance School (and later the Beijing Dance Academy) followed what was known as the "five nationalities and eight regions" cur-riculum, in which Han, Korean, Tibetan, Mongol, and Uyghur dance were the five required nationality styles in the Chinese national folk dance program. Dai dance was introduced as a required course in 2003, making the *Dances* content reflect the most current curriculum as of 2004. Zhao Tiechen, "Xueke lishi huigu," in *Zhongguo wudao gaodeng jiaoyu 30 nian xueshu wenji: Zhongguo minzu minjian wu yanjiu*, ed. Zhao Tiechun (Beijing: Gaodeng jiaoyu chubanshe, 2009), 1–12.

19. *Dadi zhi wu*, performance recording.

20. "Qunwu: 'Li taiyang zui jin de ren,'" in Pan Zhitao, *Dadi zhi wu*, 20–33, 28.

21. Xu Huan, "Lun Zangzu guwu de yishu meili: yi zuopin 'Li taiyang zuijin de ren' wei anli," *Kexue zixun*, no. 23 (2008): 74.

22. *Dadi zhi wu*, performance recording.

23. "Duwu: 'Feng cai mudan,'" in Pan Zhitao, *Dadi zhi wu*, 58–63.

24. Jin Hao, *Xin shiji Zhongguo wudao wenhua de liubian* (Shanghai: Shanghai yinyue chubanshe, 2007), 43.

25. On the theory and history of Chinese national folk dance, see Xu Rui, *Dangdai Zhongguo minzu minjian wudao chuangzuo de shenmei yu zijue* (Shanghai: Shanghai yinyue chubanshe, 2014).

26. *Dadi zhi wu*, performance recording.

27. "Du qu: 'Shan gu,'" in Pan Zhitao, *Dadi zhi wu*, 34–41.

28. For early examples, see Gao Du, "Dangdai minjian wu jiaoyu pipan," *Wudao*, no. 4 (1996): 45; Yu Ping, "Women yitong gaoge 'Yangyang dage': san lun Zhongguo minjian wu xueke de wenhua jianshe," *Beijing wudao xueyuan xuebao*, no. 3 (1998): 13–17.

29. Ming Wenjun, "'Xueyuan pai' minjian wu cunzai de xueshu yu shehui jiazhi," *Beijing wudao xueyuan xuebao*, no. 4 (1999): 217–20; Zhao Tiechun, "Yu shi jujin, jiwang kailai: Zhongguo minzu minjian wu jiaoxue de lishi chuancheng yu xueke dingwei," *Beijing wudao xueyuan xuebao*, no. 1–2 (2003): 22–30; Pan Zhitao, *Dadi zhi wu*, 6–18.

30. Zhao Tiechun, "Yu shi jujin," 25–26.

31. Pan Zhitao, *Dadi zhi wu*, 16.

32. Zhao Tiechun, "Yu shi jujin," 30.

33. Qing Qing, "Shilun xueyuan pai minzu minjian wu de cunzai yiju: zai tan 'Dadi zhi wu,'" *Beijing wudao xueyuan xuebao*, no. 3 (2005): 39–42; Jin Hao, *Xin shiji*, 41–79.

34. For more on field research practices in Chinese dance, see Wilcox, "The Dialectics of Virtuosity"; Wilcox, "Dancers Doing Fieldwork"; Wilcox, "Dynamic Inheritance."

35. Shao Weiqiu, "Shuixiu jiaoxue zonghengtan," *Beijing wudao xueyuan xuebao*, no. 2 (1999): 20–26.

36. "Shao Weiqiu shuixiu yanjiu keti zhanshi," in Emily Wilcox, field notes, Beijing Dance Academy, Beijing, June 29, 2009.

37. Shao Weiqiu, *Zhongguo gudianwu xiuwu jiaocheng* (Shanghai: Shanghai yinyue chubanshe, 2004).

38. Shao Weiqiu, *Zhongguo xiuwu* (Beijing: Zhongguo luyin luxiang chuban zongshe, 2013).

39. Zhang Jun, "Dui wudao jiaoxue yuanze de renshi he bawo," *Beijing wudao xueyuan xuebao*, no. 1 (1998): 23–29.

40. Zhang Jun, professional résumé, personal communication, 2013.

41. Zhang Jun, *Zhongguo gudianwu jianwu jiaocheng* (Shanghai: Shanghai yinyue chubanshe, 2004); Zhang Jun, *Yan jian xi wu: Zhongguo gudianwu jian wu ji* (Beijing: Tiantian yishu chubanshe, 2012).

42. China National Arts Fund, "2017 niandu wutai yishu chuangzuo zizhu xiangmu shenbao zhinan," China National Arts Fund Official Website, accessed January 26, 2017, www.cnaf.cn.

43. Beihai Song and Dance Drama Theater, *Bihai silu*, performance program, National Centre for the Performing Arts, Beijing, August 3–4, 2013; Liu Kun and Lei Ke, "'Bihai silu' jin Jing jiangshu haishang sichoulu gushi," *Guangming ribao*, October 24, 2012.

44. TAO Dance Theater, *Shuwei xilie 2 & 4 (Number series 2 & 4)*, performance program, National Centre for the Performing Arts, Beijing, August 3–4, 2013. On TAO Dance Theater,

see Emily Wilcox, "Zhongguo de bianyuan, Meiguo de zhongxin: Tao shenti juchang zai Meiguo wudaojie," *Wudao pinglun*, no. 1 (2012): 59–67.

45. A record of NCPA's programming dating to 2010 can be found here: http://en.chncpa.org/whatson/calendar/fullcalendar/.

46. Beihai Song and Dance Drama Theater, performance program, August 2013.

47. Liu Kun and Zhang Weichao, "'Jingchang yan' de cai jiao 'jingpin': ji lishi wuju 'Bihai silu' de shichang tansuo," *Guangming ribao*, August 16, 2013.

48. Ah Cheng and Yi Ping, "Wuju wangzi Liu Fuyang," *Wenhua jiaoliu*, no. 12 (2011): 66–67; Sun Xiaojuan professional profile at http://web.zhongxi.cn/xyjg/jxkyjfbm/wjx/shz/10478.html.

49. *Wulin zhengba* (Shanghai Dragon Television, 2013).

50. Chen Weiya, interview in "Daxing lishi wuju 'Bihai silu' ba yue liangxiang dajuyuan," ed. Cui Yan, *Yule bobao*, 2013, accessed January 26, 2017, www.iqiyi.com/w_19rqvjb85d.html.

51. Liu Kun and Zhang Weichao, "'Jingchang yan.'"

52. Zhaoming Xiong, "The Hepu Han Tombs and the Maritime Silk Road of the Han Dynasty," *Antiquity* 88, no. 342 (December 2014): 1229–43.

53. Liu Kun and Zhang Weichao, "'Jingchang yan'"; Beihai Song and Dance Drama Theater, performance program. On the relationship between government and commerce in regional song and dance ensembles in China, see Wilcox, "The Dialectics of Virtuosity."

54. Ship Technology © Kable 2017, accessed January 26, 2017, www.ship-technology.com.

55. "Di shiyi jie jingshen wenming jianshe 'Wu ge yi gongcheng' (2007–2009) huojiang mingdan," *Guangming ribao*, September 22, 2009.

56. Liu Kun, "*Bihai silu*: heping de xinshi," *Guangming Daily*, October 21, 2011; Ship Technology © Kable 2017, www.ship-technology.com.

57. Hong Yu, "Motivation behind China's 'One Belt, One Road' Initiatives and Establishment of the Asian Infrastructure Investment Bank," *Journal of Contemporary China*, no. 11 (2016): 1–16.

58. Beihai Song and Dance Drama Theater, performance program; Liu Kun and Lei Ke, "*Bihai silu* jin Jing."

59. Liu Kun and Zhang Weichao, "'Jingchang yan.'"

60. Mu Yu, "Zhongguo zhuliu wuju guojixing de wenhua biaoda," *Minzu yishu yanjiu* 29, no. 3 (2016): 48–54.

61. Liu Kun and Lei Ke, "'Bihai silu' jin Jing."

62. Shi Xiaomeng, "Chinese Dance Drama Promotes 'Maritime Silk Road' at UN HQ," *Xinhua News Agency*, February 6, 2015; Tao Yannan, "Dance Drama Navigates Ancient Silk Road," *China Daily: Africa Weekly*, April 24, 2015; "Chinese Dance Drama to Boost Belt and Road Initiative in ASEAN," *Xinhua Economic News*, March 30, 2016.

63. Wilcox, "Performing Bandung."

64. Mu Yu, "Zhongguo zhuliu."

65. Jin Hao, "Wu guo qunshan qi geng xin: ji qingnian wudao biandao Zhang Yunfeng," *Wudao*, no. 3 (2001): 50–51.

66. Li Xin, "Wu zhi xinxing: ji Wu Weifeng," *Wudao*, no. 1 (2002); Jin Hao, "Yingri hehua bieyang hong: cong gudianwu san ge jumu tanqi," *Wudao*, no. 8 (2002): 9–10.

67. Chinese classical dance dramas of the 1980s and 1990s include, for example, *Princess Wencheng* (1980), *Qiu Jin* (1981), *A Dream of Red Mansions* (1980), *Yue Fei* (1982), *To Die*

a Martyr (1982), *Soul of Chu* (1983), *Scent of Mulan* (1984), *Dancers of the Tongque Stage* (1985), *Ode to Confucius* (1987), *Song of Everlasting Regret* (1988), *Tang Xuanzong and Yang Guifei* (1988), *Soul of Humen* (1992), *Sacrifice to Red Plum* (1992), *The White Snake and Xu Xian* (1993), and *Gan Jiang and Mo Ye* (1998). Zhai Zixia, *Zhongguo wuju.*

68. Ballets based on Lu Xun's "The True Story of Ah Q," Cao Yu's *Thunderstorm*, and Ba Jin's *Family* appeared in 1981 and 1983. National dance drama adaptations of Lu Xun's *Sadness* and Cao Yu's *Thunderstorm* were staged in 1981–82 and national dance drama adaptations of Shen Congwen's *Border Town* and Cao Yu's *Thunderstorm* in 1996 and 1999. Zhai Zixia, *Zhongguo wuju*; Jia Anlin, *Zhongguo minzu minjian wu zuopi shangxin.*

69. Jin Hao, "Yingri hehua," 9.

70. "Begonia" was based on a 1941 novel by Qin Shouou, "Chess King" on a 1984 novella by Ah Cheng, and "Rouge" on a 1986 novella by Li Bihua.

71. *Faa yeung nin wa/Hua yang nian hua* (Hong Kong: Jet Tone Films, 2000).

72. *Ruan Lingyu* (Hong Kong: Golden Way Films, 1991).

73. "Yanzhi kou," performance recording, accessed January 26, 2017, https://www.youtube.com/watch?v = 7xIv9jbVsWM.

74. Li Bihua, *Yanzhi kou* (Hong Kong: Cosmos Books, 1986); *Yanzhi kou* (Hong Kong: Golden Way Films, 1987). Chinese dance critics have interpreted the work with reference to both the novella and the film. Jin Hao, "Yingri hehua"; Jin Qiu, ed., *Wudao biandao xue* (Beijing: Gaodeng jiaoyu chubanshe, 2006), 201.

75. Rey Chow, "A Souvenir of Love," in *At Full Speed: Hong Kong Cinema in a Borderless World*, ed. Ester Yao (Minneapolis: University of Minnesota Press, 2001), 209–29, 210.

76. *Yanzhi kou*, 1987.

77. David L. Eng, "Love at Last Site: Waiting for Oedipus in Stanley Kwan's *Rouge*," *Camera Obscura: A Journal of Feminism, Culture, and Media Studies*, no. 32 (1993): 74–101, 97.

78. Chow, "A Souvenir of Love," 220.

79. Jin Qiu, *Wudao biandao xue*, 201.

80. Jin Hao, "Yingri hehua," 10.

81. "Wu yue yi shi," *Duzhe xinshang*, no. 5 (2013): 4; Yu Kailiang and Ye Jin, "Ren shen gongwu, shi hua qi yin pin 'Fei Tang shou Song' zhi sanchong yijing," *Wudao*, no. 7 (2013): 20–21.

82. *Beijing xian wuren gongzuoshi*, publicity brochure (Beijing: Beijing Xianwuren Culture Communication, n.d.).

83. *Xian wuren wudao gongzuoshi*, publicity brochure; *Zhang Yunfeng*, interview with the author, July 10, 2013, Beijing; Zhao Xiaogang, interview with the author, Beijing, July 28, 2013.

84. Liu Min (b. 1958), head of the Dance Department at the PLA Arts Academy, was the chief inspector, and Pan Zhitao and Zuo Qing (b. 1954) served as advisors. Beijing Idle Dancers Studio, *Fei Tang shou Song*, performance program, Beijing Tianqiao Theater, May 18–19, 2013.

85. Zhao Ruheng et al., "Zai manwu zhong xikao: 'wudao juchang "Fei Tang shou Song" chuangzuo yantaohui' fayan jiyao," *Jiefangjun yishu xueyuan xuebao*, no. 3 (2013): 53–72; Mao Yachen, "Qisi qie manwu: 'wudao juchang "Fei Tang shou Song" chuangzuo yantaohui' fayan jiyao," *Wudao*, no. 7 (2013): 16–20.

86. Beijing Idle Dancers Studio, *Fei Tang.*

87. *Fei Tang shou Song*, performance recording, provided by Zhao Xiaogang on behalf of Beijing Idle Dancers Studio.

88. Xu Rui, program notes, in Beijing Idle Dancers Studio, *Fei Tang shou Song*. On the concept of "dance theater" in China, see Mu Yu, "Zhongguo xiandai wuzhe de 'wudao juchang' yishi chutan," *Yishu pinglun*, no. 2 (2012): 56–62.

89. Beijing Idle Dancers Studio, *Fei Tang; shi* and *ci* are types of poems or songs from the Tang and Song periods.

90. Zhang Yunfeng, interview.

91. Wu Weifeng, interview with the author, July 16, 2013, Beijing.

92. Tian Yi, interview with the author, June 24, 2014, Shanghai.

93. Zhao Xiaogang, interview.

94. Zhang Yunfeng, interview with the author, June 24, 2014, Shanghai.

95. Lynn Garafola, *Diaghilev's Ballets Russes* (New York: Oxford University Press, 1989).

96. Lincoln Kirstein, *Movement and Metaphor: Four Centuries of Ballet* (London: Pitman, 1971).

97. Nancy Reynolds and Malcolm McCormick, *No Fixed Points: Dance in the Twentieth Century* (New Haven: Yale University Press, 2003), 56.

98. Beijing Dance Academy Youth Ensemble, *Chun zhi ji*, live performance, Beijing Dance Academy Campus Theater, Beijing, July 7, 2014.

99. Zhang Yunfeng, interview with the author, July 7, 2014, Beijing.

100. Jie Li, "Introduction: Discerning Red Legacies in China," in *Red Legacies in China: Cultural Afterlives of the Communist Revolution*, ed. Jie Li and Enhua Zhang (Cambridge, MA: Harvard University Asia Center, 2016), 1–22, 2.

101. Ibid., 5.

CPSIA information can be obtained
at www.ICGtesting.com
Printed in the USA
LVHW05s0724230918
591081LV00002B/2/P

9 780520 300576